How Congress Works

How Congress Works

Second Edition

Washington, D.C.

Congressional Quarterly Inc.

Congressional Quarterly Inc., an editorial research service and publishing company, serves clients in the fields of news, education, business, and government. It combines Congressional Quarterly's specific coverage of Congress, government, and politics with the more general subject range of an affiliated service, Editorial Research Reports.

Congressional Quarterly publishes the *Congressional Quarterly Weekly Report* and a variety of books, including college political science textbooks under the CQ Press imprint and public affairs paperbacks on developing issues and events. CQ also publishes information directories and reference books on the federal government, national elections, and politics, including the *Guide to the Presidency,* the *Guide to Congress,* the *Guide to the U.S. Supreme Court,* the *Guide to U.S. Elections, Politics in America,* and *Congress A-Z: CQ's Ready Reference Encyclopedia.* The *CQ Almanac,* a compendium of legislation for one session of Congress, is published each year. *Congress and the Nation,* a record. of government for a presidential term, is published every four years.

CQ publishes the *Congressional Monitor,* a daily report on current and future activities of congressional committees, and several newsletters including *Congressional Insight,* a weekly analysis of congressional action, and *Campaign Practices Reports,* a semimonthly update on campaign laws.

An electronic online information system, Washington Alert, provides immediate access to CQ's databases of legislative action, votes, schedules, profiles, and analyses.

Library of Congress Cataloging-in-Publication Data

How Congress Works. -- 2nd ed.
    p.   cm.
    Includes bibliographical references and index.
    ISBN 0-87187-598-5
    1. United States. Congress. I. Congressional Quarterly, inc.
JK1061.H65 1991
  328.73--dc20
                                           91-11116
                                             CIP

Editor: Mary W. Cohn
Production Editor: Nancy Kervin
Contributors: Martha V. Gottron, Patricia Ann O'Connor,
  Nancy Kervin, John L. Moore
Proofreader: Joe Fortier
Index: Julia Petrakis
Cover: Design, Paula Anderson; Photo, Architect of the Capitol

Table of Contents

Introduction

In January 1991 the Congress of the United States met to decide whether the president should be authorized to take the nation into war. In a place where members had been known to wear pig masks to ridicule pork-barrel spending and where each party had booed and hissed the other, discourse was somber, thoughtful, and nonpartisan. Debate on the war resolution reflected an almost idealized image of how Congress should work. The vote, which split largely on party lines, was described as a matter of conscience.

Seven weeks later President George Bush went to Capitol Hill to celebrate victory in the Persian Gulf. Partisan tensions ran high as flag-waving Republicans taunted Democratic opponents of the war resolution. A number of Republicans wore large yellow buttons boasting "I Voted With the President." As the bickering escalated, House Republican Whip Newt Gingrich, Ga., challenged Democrats to concede that they had made a mistake in voting against the war. "Arrogant nonsense," retorted the Democratic Speaker of the House, Thomas S. Foley, Wash. The politics of confrontation had returned to Congress.

Many observers viewed confrontational politics as a natural outgrowth of divided government. For most of the period since 1969 the White House and at least one chamber of Congress had been controlled by opposing parties. This condition, it was said, encouraged policy stalemate, political frustration, and the erosion of public confidence in government.

Others said members were reaping the uncertain harvest of the reform movement that swept Capitol Hill in the 1970s. That heady post-Watergate period brought to Congress a new breed of members, less bound by tradition than their predecessors and less dependent on the political party apparatus for their survival. In earlier years a small group of senior members was able to run Congress because power was concentrated and junior members did not expect to share in its exercise. New rules and procedures adopted in the 1970s made the institution more democratic, diminishing the power of the leaders and the political parties they led.

Effect of Reforms

Post-Watergate reforms weakened committee chairmen, making them more accountable to their colleagues and forcing them to share their power with subcommittee chairmen, whose numbers proliferated. Habits of deference all but evaporated. The seniority system collapsed, as once powerful chairmen were toppled from their posts by vote of party members. New campaign finance laws made members more independent of party appeals by their leaders and more dependent on special interests and movements back home. Political action committees—once hailed as a device to broaden public participation in politics—became the vehicle through which corporations, labor unions, trade associations, ideological organizations, and other groups channeled huge sums of money to favored candidates.

Leaders were left with few tools of discipline to hold their followers in line. "Congress is now crowded with politicians who never knew the era in which backbenchers took care to be seen but not heard," Congressional Quarterly's Janet Hook wrote in 1990. "They owe their seats and careers not to the party apparatus but to their constituents, their consultants, and their political contributors. Gone are the days when their votes were there to be 'delivered'—especially on issues they consider politically dangerous."

Legislative Divisions

The erosion of old structures of legislative leadership was aggravated by a weakening of party identity. Both the Republican and Democratic parties were deeply divided over policy and political strategy in the 1980s. If party leaders had few tools of discipline, they likewise had no clear sense of direction in the political environment facing them in the 1990s. Their problem was compounded by the split of power between a Democratic Congress and a Republican president. Members disagreed on basic legislative strategy: whether their parties' interests were best served by bipartisan efforts to craft legislation or by a confrontational approach that drew clear partisan lines.

Nowhere were the tensions among competing power centers more apparent than in the annual budget exercise, another relic of the Watergate era reforms. The budget process Congress adopted in 1974 was supposed to provide a framework for orderly consideration of the nation's fiscal policy, making it possible to weigh tax and spending choices and to set priorities in a rational way. All too often members bridled at the imperatives of deficit reduction, however, and the process led to stalemate. Then the government might be forced to shut down briefly while Congress rushed to enact huge veto-proof spending packages whose contents were a mystery to most of its members.

The budget process bred resentment among the authorizing and appropriating committees, whose authority diminished as deficit reduction efforts intensified in the 1980s. Reluctant to enact policies that demanded sacrifice, members increasingly left tough legislative decisions to the Budget committees and various task forces and summit groups. But despite their craving for political cover on controversial issues, they resented being left out of the decision making.

A budget summit agreement collapsed in 1990, in an embarrassing defeat for President Bush and top House leaders. Angry members, Democrats and Republicans, vented their frustration at having been left out of the process and their political outrage at unpopular proposals for Medicare cuts, tax increases, and other items. The federal government shut down for three days while House and Senate leaders worked out a new agreement that left many policy details to individual committees, which previously had been excluded from the process.

Failure of Confidence

The budget debacle jarred an electorate whose confidence in Congress had already been shattered by a succession of congressional ethics scandals. Allegations of impropriety had touched the highest levels of Democratic leadership in the House, forcing the resignations in 1989 of Speaker Jim Wright of Texas and Majority Whip Tony Coelho of California. Wright's action was unprecedented; no Speaker before him had been forced from office at midterm.

The 1990 election returns provided compelling evidence of voter dissatisfaction with Congress. While only fifteen House members were defeated for reelection, fifty-three others scored their lowest winning percentage ever, and fifty-seven won with their lowest vote share since they were first elected. Combined, they constituted about one-fourth of the House membership in the 102nd Congress.

Whatever message voters were sending to members of Congress, it was directed at incumbents of both parties in thirty states. A number of House heavyweights were among those members registering their lowest winning percentage. They included Majority Leader Richard A. Gephardt, D-Mo., and the second- and third-ranking members of the Republican leadership in the chamber: Gingrich and Republican Conference Chairman Jerry Lewis of California. Several Democratic committee chairmen also registered personal lows.

Voter dissatisfaction was further reflected in a spate of proposals to limit the number of years a senator or representative might serve in Congress. While the constitutionality of term limitation proposals was widely questioned, the warning to members seemed clear. Voters had lost patience with the state of affairs in Washington. Congress must put its house in order.

Although few members were defeated by the anti-incumbent trend, many returned to Washington looking for some way to respond. When House Democrats met to organize for the 102nd Congress, they ousted two committee chairmen and gave several others a scare. Many Democrats who were backbenchers during the post-Watergate reforms figured prominently in the action.

"There was a mandate, a clear message that the American public felt there should be change and Congress should be more responsible," said Dave McCurdy, D-Okla. "We need strong leadership to address those concerns."

This book charts the procedural and attitudinal changes that have occurred in Congress since the post-Watergate reforms of the 1970s. It describes the role of congressional leaders, the intricacies of the legislative process, the operations of committees and staff, and the variety of divergent pressures that affect the workings of Congress in the 1990s.

Party Leadership in Congress

Organizational structures evolved over 200 years have made today's House and Senate leaders a critical link between the two political parties and the nation's legislative business, between legislators and the president, and between Congress and the voters.

Since the last half of the nineteenth century, when the two-party system became firmly entrenched on Capitol Hill, Congress has been organized on the basis of political party, with each party's congressional leaders seeking to facilitate enactment of the party's legislative program and to enhance the party's national image and electoral fortunes.

In this partisan struggle the majority party has a distinct advantage, since it controls not only the top leadership posts in both the House and Senate, but the legislative committees and subcommittees as well. Through its party leaders and its majorities on the various committees and subcommittees, the majority party is in a position to determine what legislation Congress will consider and when.

The minority party is not powerless, however; depending on its numbers and its unity, the minority can substantially influence both the shape of legislation and the operation of Congress.

The extent to which each party's leadership actually is able to exercise control over its rank and file depends on a multitude of factors, among them the personalities and abilities of the individual leaders, the institutional and party rules and authorities at the leadership's disposal, party unity, party strength, the willingness of the rank and file to be led, the extent of the president's involvement, and the mood in the country. In the past, particularly in the House, a few party leaders have been able to use their personal and institutional authority to dominate the institution they led.

But a series of reforms both inside and outside Congress has changed it markedly from the seniority-driven, hierarchical institution of the 1950s, when House Speaker Sam Rayburn and Senate Majority Leader Lyndon B. Johnson, both Texas Democrats, exercised legendary control over their respective chambers.

Widespread turnover has brought into both chambers younger members, less bound by tradition, who object to being closed out of the process. New rules and procedures have made the institution more democratic. Power that had resided almost exclusively with committee chairmen has been parceled out to subcommittees, and the seniority system has been weakened. At the same time election law reforms, the advent of television campaigning, and the increasing role of political action committees in financing campaigns have made individual members of Congress much less dependent on the political party apparatus for their electoral survival.

Today the job of leading Congress is perhaps more challenging than ever before. The greater independence of members from their political parties and the dispersion of power on Capitol Hill require the leadership to spend more and more time consulting with and responding to the demands of the rank and file.

Leaders must take care to lead in the direction the rank and file wants to go and to involve members in the decision-making process along the way. "In Mr. Rayburn's day," House leader Jim Wright, D-Texas, once commented, "about all a majority leader or Speaker needed to do in order to get his program adopted was to deal effectively with perhaps twelve very senior committee chairmen. They, in turn, could be expected to influence their committees and their subcommittee chairmen whom they, in those days, appointed.... Well, now that situation is quite considerably different. There are, I think, 153 subcommittees [in Congress].... We have relatively fewer rewards that we can bestow or withhold. I think that basically about all the leadership has nowadays is a hunting license to persuade—if we can." [1]

Leadership Positions

Although the strategies of leadership have changed substantially in recent years, the basic leadership structure has remained the same. In the House the leadership consists of the Speaker, who is both the chamber's presiding officer and the majority party's overall leader; the majority and minority floor leaders, who are responsible for handling legislation once it reaches the floor; the assistant floor leaders or whips, who try to convince party members to follow the leadership's program and who serve as the communications nerve center for the parties; and several party committees that develop party strategy, assign party members to the standing committees, assist the leadership in scheduling and keeping track of legislation, and provide campaign assistance to House and Senate candidates.

The Senate has no institutional or party official comparable in power and prestige to the Speaker. The Constitution designates the vice president of the United States as the president, or presiding officer, of the Senate. In his absence the Senate president pro tempore presides. Neither office, however, has been endowed with any commanding legislative or political authority, and neither has ever played much of a leadership role in the Senate. *(Box, p. 29)*

The remainder of the Senate leadership apparatus is similar in structure and function to that of the House.

Of all the party leadership positions in Congress, the only one that has functioned continuously since 1789 is that of Speaker—a post established by the Constitution. Although various members assumed the roles of floor leader and whip from time to time, the positions were not made official in the House until 1899, during a period when parties and partisanship were strong, both in Congress and throughout the country. Formal party leadership positions began to develop in the Senate in the early 1900s, but majority and minority leaders were not officially designated by the party caucuses until the 1920s.

The top leaders of both parties in both chambers are elected by their respective party caucuses, or conferences as three of the four are formally named. (Today only House Democrats refer to their partisan gathering as a caucus.) Factors such as personal style, geographical balance, and length of service traditionally play an important role in the selection of the leadership. In an age of television news and the "thirty-second sound bite," the leaders' ability to serve as effective national spokesmen for their party and legislative program has taken on new importance, as has their ability to use the media adroitly.

Ideologically, leaders tend to represent the center of their party. In this, as well as in their role as mediators, they act in a sense as "middlemen" for the various factions of the party in trying to draft legislative compromises that the party and Congress will accept. "As a member of the leadership," said Senate Majority Whip Robert C. Byrd, D-

W.Va., in 1976, "it is my duty to bring North and South, liberals and conservatives together; to work out compromises. . . . I think it takes a centrist to do that." [2] A conservative when he entered the Senate in 1958, Byrd had moved considerably leftward by the time he was first elected majority leader after the 1976 elections.

Leadership Functions

The powers the leaders may exercise and the ways the leadership functions differ in the House and Senate. In essence House rules allow a determined majority to lead, while Senate rules protect minority rights. Yet House and Senate leaders have the same fundamental job: "to bring," as political scientists Roger H. Davidson and Walter J. Oleszek have written, "coherence and efficiency to a decentralized and individualistic legislative body." [3]

The job has two overlapping, sometimes competing, parts. Leaders, Davidson and Oleszek observe, must constantly balance the needs of Congress as a lawmaking institution against Congress as a representative assembly: "In their 'inside' role, party leaders guide institutional activities and influence policy. Good communications skills, parliamentary expertise, and sensitivity to the mood of the membership and of the electorate are important attributes of an effective leader. . . . In their 'outside' role, party leaders not only help recruit candidates and assist them in their campaigns, but they serve as the party's link to the president, the press, and the public." [4]

In their inside role, leaders organize each chamber and each party within the chamber, setting and reviewing committee jurisdictions and assignments and institutional and party rules. Leaders of each party also work together and with their members, usually through the party caucuses, to

R. Michael Jenkins

Party leaders serve as a link to the president, the press, and the public. Here, leaders meet the press following a 1991 White House meeting on the Persian Gulf crisis. House Speaker Thomas S. Foley, D-Wash., and Senate Majority Leader George J. Mitchell, D-Maine, face the microphones.

develop the party's stand on policy issues. Leaders assign individual bills to the appropriate committee or committees and decide how best to handle each bill as it comes to the floor. Once a bill is on the floor, the leadership is responsible for monitoring the debate and using the rules and procedures in ways that will help the party's chances of legislative success. Throughout, establishing and maintaining party unity is an important goal.

Scheduling business on the floor—deciding what will come to the floor when, under what conditions, and in what order—may be the majority leadership's most important institutional task, and it is a forceful tool in realizing the party's policy agenda. "The power of the Speaker of the House is the power of scheduling," Speaker Thomas P. O'Neill, Jr., D-Mass., declared in 1983. [5]

The leadership often schedules floor action for the convenience of members; little business is scheduled in the House on Mondays and Fridays, for example, so that members can return to their districts for long weekends. The leadership may delay action on a controversial bill until it is sure that it has the winning votes, or it may bring a controversial bill to the floor quickly to prevent opposition from building.

In the Senate, where bills are open to nearly unlimited amendment and debate, the majority leader generally consults with the minority leadership, the floor managers of the bill, and other interested senators to draw up unanimous consent agreements governing floor action on major legislation. These agreements can be quite complicated, stipulating what amendments will be offered—how long they will be debated, and when they will be voted upon. Because a single member can block a unanimous consent agreement, the leaders must take care to ensure an opportunity to speak to all senators who want to be heard on the issue.

The procedure is quite different in the House, where all but the most routine bills typically receive a rule for floor consideration, stipulating how much general debate there will be and what, if any, amendments may be offered—and, sometimes, in what order. Since the mid-1970s, when the Democrats gave their Speaker the authority to appoint the Democratic members of the Rules Committee, its role as an arm of the Democratic leadership has been tightened. The committee has great control over the content of amendments that can be debated and voted upon—to the consternation of House Republicans, who have loudly complained at times that their minority rights have been choked off.

Building winning coalitions is also essential to effective leadership. In the House this leadership function is aided by expanded whip organizations in both parties, which poll party members on specific issues, inform them of upcoming votes, help persuade them to support the party's cause, and ensure that they show up to vote. Ad hoc task forces are also used in both chambers to help build support for specific issues important to the leadership. And for all the partisan rhetoric and real philosophical differences, leaders of both parties try to win support from members of the opposing party on most major legislation and amendments.

In their outside roles, congressional leaders of both parties meet periodically with the president to discuss his legislative agenda, letting him know how their respective memberships are likely to respond to his proposals. The leaders of the same party as the president also generally serve as his spokesmen in the House and Senate, although they remain independent of the president. "I'm the president's friend," Senate Majority Leader Byrd said of President Jimmy Carter. "I'm not the president's man." [6]

Messages through the Media

In both inside and outside roles, skilled use of the media has become a prerequisite for success and even for selection as a leader. Despite his relatively short tenure in the Senate when he ran for majority leader in 1988, George J. Mitchell of Maine won the support of many Democrats who thought he would be a more articulate and appealing public spokesman for Senate Democrats than his opponents.

Leaders in both chambers are routinely available to the news media. The Speaker of the House, sometimes joined by other members of the majority leadership, holds a press conference before each House session begins. Rep. Robert H. Michel, R-Ill., who became minority leader in 1981, holds less frequent press conferences but appears regularly in the Speaker's lobby, where members and the press can meet without interruption from staff or lobbyists. The Senate majority and minority leaders gather with journalists on the Senate floor prior to Senate sessions, to announce the schedule and answer questions. Democratic leaders in both the House and Senate routinely respond to Republican presidential addresses such as the State of the Union message or other speeches calling for legislative action.

Use of the media goes beyond simply articulating party positions. Increasingly the parties are realizing that public opinion is one of the main influences on a legislator's vote and that fights on the House and Senate floor can be won not only by appealing to members of Congress but also by appealing to their constituents. "Being a good legislator means you have to do both," future House Majority Leader Richard A. Gephardt, D-Mo., said in 1985. "If you are going to pass important legislation, you have to both deal with members and put together coalitions in the country." [7] Tactics both parties use to influence public opinion include floor speeches meant to be picked up by the TV news networks and newspaper op-eds written by senior members of key committees.

One of the most adroit congressional manipulators of the media has been House Minority Whip Newt Gingrich of Georgia, a conservative Republican who arrived in the House in 1979, the same year the national cable network C-SPAN began televising House proceedings. Using that medium to attack and confront the Democratic leadership, and on occasion moderate Republicans, Gingrich soon became a visible presence in the national media and a favorite of conservatives throughout the country. "Conflict equals exposure equals power," he once told a *Newsweek* reporter. [8]

The strategy paid off. Gingrich's Conservative Opportunity Society had a significant impact on the shape of the 1984 Republican platform. In 1988 Gingrich filed the formal ethics complaint against Jim Wright that forced the Speaker to resign his seat a year later. Shortly afterwards, Gingrich was elected minority whip over Minority Leader Michel's preferred candidate.

Tools of Persuasion

Although the greater independence of individual members means leaders in both chambers must rely heavily on persuasion and negotiation, they are not without induce-

Party Control of Congress and Presidency . . .

The stalemate and gridlock that so often characterized executive-legislative relations in the 1980s were blamed in large part on divided government. With the Republicans in control of the White House and the Democrats in control of one or both houses of Congress throughout the decade, conflicts between the president and Congress were inevitable.

But control of Congress and the presidency by the same party does not always guarantee cooperation between the two branches. There have been numerous occasions in American history in which determined lawmakers resisted the proposals of their own presidents, and strong-willed presidents disregarded their party leaders in Congress.

Lincoln, Wilson, the Roosevelts

Many of the conflicts between the White House and Congress when both were controlled by the same party have come at times of strong presidential leadership. Lincoln, Wilson, and the two Roosevelts all had difficulties with their party's congressional leaders, although all four men were largely successful in winning enactment of their programs.

The first important clash of this kind arose during the Civil War, when Republican extremists dominated Congress. In 1861 Congress created a Joint Committee on the Conduct of the War, which went so far as to intervene in military operations. In 1864 Congress sought to undermine Lincoln's liberal reconstruction program by transferring responsibility for reconstruction from the president to Congress. Lincoln pocket-vetoed that bill and, so far as possible, ignored the extremists. He used executive orders to maintain the upper hand, but after Lincoln's assassination Congress achieved the supremacy it was seeking and retained it for more than thirty years.

Theodore Roosevelt was the next strong president to experience difficulty with his own party's congressional leadership. Roosevelt clashed sharply with Sen. Nelson W. Aldrich, R-R.I., the unofficial but acknowledged leader of the Senate's Republicans. Aldrich, for example, refused to support the president's bill to regulate railroad rates in exchange for Roosevelt's agreement to drop tariff reform. After relying primarily on Democrats to report the rate bill from the Senate committee, Roosevelt won agreement from William B. Allison of Iowa, the other

most influential Republican in the Senate, on judicial review of rate adjustments. This maneuver split the opposition and led to passage of the bill by an overwhelming vote. Aldrich, however, continued to oppose administration measures and occasionally won important concessions from the president.

Although relations between President Woodrow Wilson and the Democratic congressional leadership generally were good, party leaders sometimes deserted the president on foreign policy issues. On the eve of the opening of the Panama Canal in 1914, both Speaker Champ Clark, Mo., and House Majority Leader Oscar Underwood, Ala., opposed Wilson's request to repeal a provision of a law exempting American vessels traveling between U.S. ports from having to pay canal tolls. The exemption, which Great Britain said violated an Anglo-American treaty, was eventually eliminated despite the opposition of the House leadership.

In 1917 Rep. Claude Kitchin, D-N.C., who had replaced Underwood as majority leader, opposed Wilson when the president asked Congress to declare war on Germany. Later, Speaker Clark opposed Wilson's request for military conscription. Near the end of Wilson's second term, relations between Clark and the president were nearly nonexistent.

Although Franklin Roosevelt's overall relations with Congress were as good as or better than Wilson's, he still had problems with his own congressional leadership. During his third term the Democratic leadership deserted Roosevelt on major domestic issues. In 1944 Senate Majority Leader Alben W. Barkley, Ky., resigned the post when FDR vetoed a revenue bill. The Democrats promptly reelected Barkley, and the bill was passed over the president's veto.

Madison, Johnson, McKinley

Congressional leaders also frequently clashed with less aggressive presidents of their own party. These conflicts usually occurred when Congress attempted to dominate the president by initiating its own legislative program and directives. One of the earliest examples came during the administration of James Madison, when Speaker Henry Clay forced the president into the War of 1812 against Britain. Another was Clay's successful attempt to pressure

ments and a few punishments to help coax their colleagues into line. A legislator who votes with his party might be rewarded with a better committee assignment or a visit by party leaders to his district during his reelection campaign. A pet program might be handled by a sympathetic committee or attached to an important bill heading for the floor. Leaders can see that a loyal member gets benefits for his district or state—a tax break for a key industry, a new flood control project, or an exemption from clean air rules. Campaign appearances and funds are also distributed judiciously to encourage loyalty.

In addition there are many services the leadership can

offer individual members, what Speaker O'Neill called the "little odds and ends": "You know, you ask me what are my powers and my authority around here? The power to recognize on the floor; little odds and ends—like men get pride out of the prestige of handling the Committee of the Whole, being named Speaker for the day. . . . [T]here is a certain aura and respect that goes with the Speaker's office. He does have the power to be able to pick up the telephone and call people. And members oftentimes like to bring their local political leaders or a couple of mayors. And often times they have problems from their area and they need aid and assistance. . . . We're happy to try to open the door

... Is No Guarantee of Legislative Success

James Monroe into a series of unwanted postwar measures, including a revision of the tariffs.

After the Civil War, the Radical Republicans in Congress were able to push through their own reconstruction policy over President Andrew Johnson's opposition. In the process they almost managed to remove the president.

The next major clash came in 1898. Speaker Thomas Brackett Reed, R-Maine, a strong isolationist, sought but failed to block three controversial aspects of President William McKinley's foreign policy: war with Spain, annexation of Hawaii, and acquisition of the Philippine Islands. Reed's failure to stop McKinley, which led to his retirement from Congress, was due largely to the popularity of the president's policies, not to the successful application of pressure on congressional leaders by McKinley.

Modern Presidents: Johnson, Carter

In the mid-1960s President Lyndon B. Johnson demanded congressional support of his military policies in Southeast Asia. Although the Democratic Congress generally went along with Johnson's conduct of the war, his majority leader in the Senate, Mike Mansfield, D-Mont., actively opposed the president's military venture virtually from the beginning.

Congress was overwhelmingly Democratic throughout the four years Democrat Jimmy Carter was president (1977-81). Nevertheless, many of Carter's proposals and the way they were formulated and presented to his party—received less than enthusiastic support from the leadership in Congress. Said Majority Leader Robert C. Byrd, D-W.Va., in 1980: "At the leadership meetings, he [Carter] urges certain action and says he hopes he'll have our support. But he can't force it. The president is expected to make his proposals, and we have a responsibility to him and the country to weigh them and act on them only if, in the judgment of the Senate, we should."

Success through Bipartisanship

Cases in which a party's congressional leadership has cooperated in a substantial way with a president of the other party are less frequent and have dealt mainly with national security and related issues. One example is Republican President Dwight D. Eisenhower, who worked with a Democratic Congress for six of his eight years in office. Yet Democratic congressional leaders cooperated actively and willingly with the White House most of the time. Speaker Sam Rayburn, Texas, who often described himself as a Democrat "without prefix, without suffix, without apology," generally acted as the president's man in the House. During Eisenhower's second term, Rayburn's liberal critics, dismayed over his seeming inattention to traditional Democratic party causes, began referring to him as an "Eisenhowercrat."

As Senate majority leader, Lyndon Johnson was a firm believer in the bipartisan conduct of foreign policy. In 1980 Rep. John J. Rhodes, R-Ariz., recalled Johnson sitting in on foreign aid conference committee meetings: "He was there, not to ensure the Democratic position would win, but to ensure the administration position would win. He was acting as a broker for the Eisenhower administration. . . . It was often said at that time that 'the president proposes while Congress disposes.' The philosophy is not very popular today, but the people running Congress then were pretty much dedicated to that idea, no matter who the president was."

More recently, George Bush won bipartisan support from Congress to use force in the Persian Gulf crisis, but it came over the objections of Democratic leaders in both the House and Senate.

Ronald Reagan's first year in office was marked by a Republican Senate and a Democratic House more conservative than it had been during Carter's presidency. Working closely with Senate and House Republicans and with conservative Democrats in the House, Reagan was able to put together a string of dramatic victories, including the deepest budget cuts and largest tax reductions ever considered by Congress and a controversial arms deal with Saudi Arabia. In 1986 the Republican president and a divided Congress produced a landmark tax reform bill, largely because both parties saw political gain in passing the bill, and neither wanted to advantage the other party by blocking the reform.

Sources: George B. Galloway, *History of the House of Representatives* (New York: Thomas Y. Crowell, 1961), 260; Irwin B. Arieff, "House, Senate Chiefs Attempt to Lead a Changed Congress," *Congressional Quarterly Weekly Report*, Sept. 13, 1980, 2700.

---

for them, having been in the town for so many years and knowing so many people. We do know where a lot of bodies are and we do know how to advise people." [9]

Punishment for disloyal behavior can be subtle. A member's bid for a local dam or his scheme to revamp national education grants could languish in an unresponsive committee. A request to switch committees, add another staff member, or move to a bigger office could be denied. Sometimes the threat of punishment may be enough to induce a member to fall into step. In rare cases legislators are stripped of committee seniority or a committee post for repeatedly betraying the party position. After

Democratic Rep. Phil Gramm, Texas, masterminded enactment of budgets proposed by Republican President Ronald Reagan, Democratic leaders in 1983 stripped him of his seat on the House Budget Committee. Gramm resigned his House seat, won reelection as a Republican, and soon rejoined the committee as a GOP member.

A Time of Change?

One of the constants about Congress has been its ability to adapt itself, sooner or later, to changes occurring both within and outside the institution. By the end of the

101st Congress in 1990, observers were wondering if such an adaptation was at hand.

The immediate source of the speculation was the months-long wrangle over the fiscal 1991 budget. Before the dust finally settled, a rebellious House had humiliated the president and its own leaders by rejecting a budget alternative those leaders had spent weeks negotiating. White House indecision on tax policy had driven a wedge through the Republican party that was unlikely to disappear with the adjournment of Congress. Although the Democrats had won a tactical advantage on the tax issue, their credibility had waned with that of the rest of the government.

Since the government began to run massive budget deficits in the early 1980s, Congress and the president had frequently come to stalemate over the annual federal budget. But in 1990, with Congress seeming to be on the verge of chaos and breakdown at several points in the process, editorial writers, voters, and even some members of Congress began to ask more urgently than ever before what had happened to political leadership.

"Divided government" was often blamed for the years of deadlock over the budget. Since 1955 Republicans had held the White House for twenty-four years. Democrats had controlled Congress for all but six of those years, 1981-87, when Republicans had controlled the Senate.

Certainly, much of the explanation for the deadlock was the gulf between the political parties on how to shape the nation's fiscal policy. It was not clear, however, whether the government would have acted any more decisively if the same party controlled both Capitol Hill and the White House. Democratic President Carter's rocky relations with a Democratic-controlled Congress provided a sobering counterexample.

Nonetheless, divided government did not make the task in 1990 any easier. As the 101st Congress neared its end, the country was approaching recession, and the persistent budget deficit required Congress not to distribute benefits but to allocate sacrifice. "This is probably the kind of exercise our system does least well," said Speaker Thomas S. Foley, D-Wash.[10]

But divided government was not the complete explanation for the difficulties political leaders faced in Congress. Partisan differences were exacerbated by forces within Congress and the country that had been gathering for years. Many were the direct and indirect results of the reforms that Congress had put in place in the 1970s. By 1990 Congress was filled with politicians who had never known the era in which backbenchers took care to be seen but not heard. They owed their seats and careers not to the party apparatus but to their constituents, their campaign consultants, and their political contributors. Gone were the days when their votes were there to be "delivered"—especially on issues they considered dangerous.

The rise of negative campaign tactics and the thirty-second sound bite made this new generation of politicians see more and more votes as perilous. Many members also felt that party leaders no longer offered them political cover. "There is a sense that they are out there all by themselves," said Foley, "that if they are not careful, no one will be careful for them."

That undertow of political vulnerability, combined with the diffusion of power that resulted from the 1970s reforms and the leadership's lack of effective tools to keep the rank and file in line, made it difficult to impose the discipline needed to solve the deficit problem.

Efforts to impose that discipline—particularly the automatic spending cuts mandated by the Gramm-Rudman-Hollings law if Congress did not meet specified budget targets—led to a new concentration of power in the congressional leadership. By the late 1980s four bills—the budget resolution, the continuing appropriations resolution, the supplemental appropriations bill, and the budget reconciliation measure—were often the only possible vehicles for unrelated domestic legislation. These omnibus bills tended to concentrate power in the members of the few key committees that had jurisdiction—mainly the Appropriations committees in both chambers and House Ways and Means and Senate Finance—and in the party leaders, because they negotiated and mediated what would be acceptable to their members on these must-pass bills.

In 1990 the number of players involved in this process dwindled substantially. When members of a larger budget summit failed to reach any agreement on a bipartisan solution to the burgeoning deficit, just five legislators—the Speaker and the House and Senate majority and minority leaders—worked with three administration officials to draft the deficit reduction plan that the House ultimately rejected. (A compromise package was eventually passed.)

Even on complex and controversial nonbudget measures, the traditional legislative process was often bypassed. Senate Majority Leader Mitchell, for example, took charge of drawing up the Senate's version of the clean air bill in 1990 after it became clear that the draft written by the Environment and Public Works Committee would not survive opposition from the administration and powerful lobbying interests. He then worked very hard to prevent passage of any amendments that might have threatened passage of his compromise bill. Other measures that came to the floor without the usual committee scrutiny included a Senate anticrime bill approved in July 1990 and a 1989 pay raise-ethics package that was put together by special panels appointed by the leadership in both chambers.

On politically sensitive issues, such as a congressional pay raise or a decision to raise taxes, committees and individual members may be happy to have the matter—and any blame for making an unpopular decision—taken out of their hands. But at the same time, members resent being closed out of the decision-making process. "Eight men met in secret for several weeks to prepare this budget," Rep. Dan Glickman, D-Kan., said of the 1990 budget agreement that failed in the House. "That is not the democratic way to do business."

As the 102nd Congress convened in January 1991, at least one legislator, Sen. David L. Boren, D-Okla., was testing sentiment in both the House and Senate for a thorough reexamination of Congress's operations, similar to the self-examination that led to the Legislative Reorganization Act of 1946. "It's been about fifty years since Congress took a comprehensive look at itself . . . and I think it's clear we need to do so again. I think the public is demanding it," Boren said.[11]

House Leadership: A Hierarchy of Support

The party leadership structure is particularly important in the House, because of its size and consequent potential for unwieldiness. In his 1963 study of the House, *Forge of*

Democracy, Neil MacNeil described the chamber's leadership organizations as its "priesthood."

> Indeed, over the years, a hierarchy of leaders has been constructed in the House to support the Speaker, and opposing this hierarchy has been another, created by the minority party and led by the 'shadow' Speaker, the leader of the opposition party. With the hierarchy also has been built a vast array of political and party organizations to assist the Speaker and his lieutenants in the complicated task of making the House a viable, responsible legislative body.[12]

The Role of the Speaker

Widely regarded as the most powerful figure in Congress, the Speaker is the presiding officer of the House of Representatives as well as the leader of the majority party in the House. Since 1947 the Speaker has also been second in line, after the vice president, to succeed the president. "No other member of Congress possesses the visibility and authority of the Speaker . . . ," Davidson and Oleszek have written. "As the 'elect of the elected,' the Speaker stands near the president as a national figure." [13]

The speakership has not always been endowed with such prestige. For the first two decades of Congress, the Speaker was largely a figurehead; not until Henry Clay was elected to the office in 1811 did a Speaker exercise any real leadership in the House. After Clay left the House in 1825, the authority of the Speaker ebbed and flowed, but no Speaker wielded as much influence as Clay until 1890, when Republican Thomas Brackett Reed of Maine used his personal and institutional authority to ensure that the minority could no longer frustrate the legislative actions of a unified majority.

"Czar" Reed was soon followed by Joseph G. Cannon, R-Ill., the Speaker from 1903 to 1911, whose autocratic control over the House led to a revolt against him in 1910. Ultimately the Speaker's powers as presiding officer were limited. Changes in the caucus rules of the two political parties also served to lessen the Speaker's authority.

Cannon's tyrannical rule and the rebellion against it had a lasting effect on the office and the men who have held it. Until the mid-1970s power in the House was concentrated in the hands of the chairmen of the legislative committees. The reforms of the 1970s restored many of the Speaker's powers. Yet every Speaker since Cannon who has been an effective House leader has achieved influence chiefly through personal prestige, persuasion, brokerage, and bargaining.

That is not to say that Speakers do not use their authority to achieve their goals. "Tradition and unwritten law require that the Speaker apply the rules of the House consistently, yet in the twilight zone a large area exists where he may exercise great discrimination and where he has many opportunities to apply the rules to his party's advantage," wrote future Senate parliamentarian Floyd M. Riddick in 1949—a statement as true today as it was then.[14]

But in the modern era, a Speaker must take care to ensure that his actions have the continued support of a majority of his own party. Jim Wright, the one modern Speaker to push his leadership close to the limits of its powers, caused resentment by acting without first consulting other party leaders or the rank and file. That exclusion, coupled with his aggressive, sometimes abrasive, style, left him politically vulnerable when a challenge to his personal ethics arose. The crisis eventually forced Wright to resign both the speakership and his House seat.

Framers' Intentions

The framers of the Constitution were silent on the role they intended the Speaker to play in the House. The Constitution's only reference to the office is in Article I, Section 2, clause 5, which states, "The House of Representatives shall chuse their Speaker and other Officers. . . ." There is no evidence that the Founding Fathers debated this provision.

Two respected authorities on the speakership, Mary P. Follett and Hubert Bruce Fuller, have suggested that this absence of any discussion indicated that the framers thought the Speaker would act as both presiding officer and political leader. "Surely," wrote Follett in *The Speaker of the House of Representatives,* the Speaker could not have been thought of "as a non-political moderator, as a mere parliamentary officer whom it was necessary to dissociate from politics. What [was] intended must be inferred from that with which [the framers] were familiar. . . ." Follett's book, published in 1896, is still widely regarded as the authoritative study of the early development of the office.[15]

What the framers knew were the colonial Speakers. In most cases these Speakers were active politicians who not only presided over the legislatures but also used their positions to further their own or their faction's legislative aims. This concept of the office differed sharply from that of the speakership of the House of Commons. The British Speaker was, and still is, a strictly nonpartisan presiding officer. (The term "Speaker" first appeared in the Commons in 1377, when Sir Thomas Hungerford assumed the post. Until the late seventeenth century, the Speaker in England was directly responsible to the Crown. The term was derived from the fact that it was the duty of the presiding officer to interpret the will of the House of Commons to the Crown.)

In any event, because political parties had not yet been formed, the first Speaker, Frederick A. C. Muhlenberg, Pa., was nonpartisan. His duties, as spelled out by the House on April 7, 1789, were to preside at House sessions, preserve decorum and order, announce the results of standing and teller votes, appoint select committees of not more than three members, and vote in cases of a tie, a practice referred to as the Speaker's "casting" vote. By the Second Congress, clearly defined party divisions had begun to develop, and Muhlenberg's successor, Jonathan Trumbull of Connecticut, displayed definite leanings toward President George Washington's legislative program. In 1796 Speaker Jonathan Dayton, a Federalist, twice voted to produce ties that resulted in the defeat of Jeffersonian motions that would have undermined the Federalist-backed Jay Treaty with Britain.

Party affiliation, although weak and more diffuse than in modern times, also became the basis for choosing the Speaker. In 1799 the Federalists elected Theodore Sedgwick of Massachusetts over Nathaniel Macon of North Carolina to the Speaker's post by a vote of 44-38, a margin that reflected that of the Federalists over the Jeffersonians in the Sixth Congress. Sedgwick, according to Follett, "made many enemies by decided and even partisan acts," so many that the Jeffersonians in the Sixth Congress refused to join in the customary vote of thanks to the

Heated Contests for Speakership . . .

It may be one of the few things that congressional reformers have not changed. At the beginning of every two-year term each party caucus nominates a candidate to be Speaker of the House, and the candidate of the majority party—a Democrat since 1955—wins the office on a straight party-line vote on the House floor.

It was not always that way. Before the two-party system became entrenched on Capitol Hill, factions sometimes so splintered the majority party that the election of a Speaker turned into a battle royal.

Regional disputes, mainly over slavery, produced at least eleven hotly contested races for the speakership before the Civil War. The first was in 1809, when none of the Democratic-Republican candidates was able to achieve a majority on the first ballot. The election finally went to Joseph B. Varnum of Massachusetts after the South's candidate, Nathaniel Macon, N.C., withdrew because of poor health.

Other battles occurred in 1820, when an antislavery candidate, John W. Taylor, D-N.Y., won on the 22nd ballot; in 1821, when Philip P. Barbour, D-Va., won on the 12th; in 1825, when Taylor recaptured the post on the second ballot; in 1834, when John Bell, Whig-Tenn., won on the tenth vote; in 1847, when Robert C. Winthrop, Whig-Mass., won on the third; and in 1861, when Galusha A. Grow, R-Pa., won on the second.

In four instances the House became deadlocked for weeks or months over the election of the Speaker.

1839: New Jersey Controversy

The first of these prolonged battles began on December 2, 1839, when election of the Speaker hinged on the outcome of five contested House seats in New Jersey. Excluding the five New Jersey members, the party lineup in the House was 119 Democrats and 118 Whigs. Democrats sought to organize the House (and elect the new Speaker) before the contested elections were decided; the Whigs wanted to wait until the elections were resolved.

After much debate the House December 14 agreed with the Democratic proposal to vote for Speaker before the contested seats were decided. But Democratic leaders were then unable to hold a sufficient number of members in line to name a Speaker. On December 16 Robert M. T. Hunter, D-Va., who had declared himself an independent, was elected Speaker on the 11th ballot.

1849: Free-Soil Dispute

The next major contest for the speakership developed in 1849, when neither the Whigs nor the Democrats could achieve a majority because the so-called Free-Soil

factions in both parties decided to act independently. The resulting deadlock lasted for three weeks and sixty-three ballots.

The Free-Soilers, who opposed expansion of slavery into the territories, wanted to ensure that certain House committees were controlled by antislavery legislators. They thus opposed the election of the leading candidates for Speaker in both parties: Robert C. Winthrop, Whig-Mass., who they felt had been lukewarm on the issue as Speaker from 1847 to 1849, and Howell Cobb, D-Ga., a strong proponent of slavery. Each faction put up its own candidate—at one time there were eleven—preventing either Winthrop or Cobb from winning a majority.

At various points compromise solutions were considered and rejected, including proposals that the Speaker be chosen by lottery and that members receive no salary or mileage reimbursement until a Speaker was elected. Finally, after the 59th vote, the House agreed to elect the Speaker by a plurality, provided that it be a majority of a quorum. On the 60th vote, Cobb led; on the 61st, Winthrop; and on the 62nd, the vote was tied. The issue was decided on the 63rd vote, when Cobb won a plurality of two votes. "The choice of a very pronounced pro-slavery and southern man at this crisis undoubtedly aggravated the struggles of the following decade," Mary P. Follett noted in her authoritative 1896 book on the speakership.

1855: Kansas and Slavery

Six years later another multifaction battle stemming from the slavery issue delayed election of a Speaker. The specific concern was who would be appointed to the committee investigating the admission of Kansas into the Union: Would the Speaker choose committee members who favored its entry as a free state or as a slave state? The dispute required 133 votes before a Speaker was elected.

Although antislavery forces held a majority of House seats, their ranks were so split by factions—mostly the new Republican party and various Free-Soil groups—that they could not unite behind a single candidate. At the outset of the battle on December 3, 1855, twenty-one candidates were nominated. After 129 ballots, the House decided that the candidate receiving the largest number of votes on the 133rd ballot would be declared the winner. On February 2, 1856, Nathaniel P. Banks, American-Mass., was elected with 103 out of the 214 votes cast.

Banks met the expectations of the antislavery forces by giving them a majority on the Kansas investigating committee. The practical effect of that action, Follett observed, "delayed the settlement of the Kansas episode until after 1857, and this gave time for the anti-slavery forces to organize."

Speaker at adjournment. At the beginning of the Seventh Congress, the Jeffersonians, now in commanding control of Congress, elected Macon to the speakership by a wide margin.

But throughout the early years, and particularly during Thomas Jefferson's presidency, it was the executive, and not the Speaker, who was the real political and legislative leader in the House. As Washington's Treasury secretary, Alexander Hamilton dominated the Federalist majority even during the First Congress by operating through

... Lively but Rare in House History

1859: Impending Crisis

The last of the great pre-Civil War contests over the speakership occurred in 1859. The tone was set on the first day of the session, December 5, when slavery advocates proposed a resolution that anyone who endorsed the sentiments of *The Impending Crisis of the South: How to Meet It,* a book hostile to slavery, was not fit to be Speaker.

The resolution and another introduced the next day were directed at John Sherman, R-Ohio, who had endorsed the book. "The ball thus set rolling," Follett wrote, "the discussion of slavery began, bitter and passionate on one side, eager and vehement on the other. The state of the country was reflected in the struggle for Speaker. The House was the scene of a confusion and uproar which the clerk could not control.... Bitter personal invectives nearly led to personal encounters.... It seemed as though the Civil War was to begin in the House of Representatives."

Sherman led in the early voting, falling only six votes short of a majority on the third ballot. By the end of January, however, Republicans saw that Sherman could not be elected and shifted their support to William Pennington, Whig-N.J., a new and unknown member. On February 1, 1860, after forty-four votes and two months into the session, Pennington was elected with 117 votes, the minimum needed to win. Pennington was the only Speaker other than Henry Clay ever elected to the speakership during his first term. But he did not share Clay's skill. Follett reported that Pennington was regarded as an impartial presiding officer but was "notably ignorant of the practice of the House."

1923: Progressive Insurgency

The only deadlock over the speakership since the Civil War occurred in 1923, when twenty Progressive Republicans held the balance of power in the House. They put up their own candidate, Henry A. Cooper, R-Wis., as a protest against House procedures. After eight inconclusive votes, Nicholas Longworth, R-Ohio, the GOP majority leader, made an agreement with the progressives to liberalize the rules. The next day they threw their support to the Republican candidate, Frederick H. Gillett, R-Mass.

Other Leadership Fights

Since 1923 there have been no floor battles for the speakership. One party has always held a clear majority and has been able to elect its choice on the first ballot. But there have been fights in the party caucuses. In 1933 Democratic Majority Leader Henry T. Rainey of Illinois faced four candidates in his bid to win the nomination in the caucus, which was tantamount to election since the Democrats controlled the House. A northerner and a liberal, Rainey was opposed by the southern establishment that controlled the Democratic party at the time. But with three of the other four candidates from southern states, Rainey had room to maneuver. He was nominated Speaker in a deal that ensured the southern establishment would continue to be the effective ruling power in the House.

No significant battles for the speakership have developed on the Democratic side since 1933; each time a Democratic Speaker has left office, the Democratic majority leader has been elevated to the speakership without much ado. In most cases the Democratic Caucus has then elected the party whip to be majority leader.

That pattern was broken in 1976 when deputy whip Jim Wright of Texas offered himself as an alternative to the bitterly antagonistic front-runners, Phillip Burton of California and Richard Bolling of Missouri. Wright had seemed an unlikely winner when he announced he would enter the contest, but he eliminated Bolling by three votes on the second ballot, and Burton by a single vote on the third ballot. (The whip, John McFall of California, was popular with his fellow Democrats but tainted by his association with the "Koreagate" influence-peddling scandal; he was eliminated from the race on the first ballot.)

House Republicans have had many more contests for party leader in recent decades. In 1959 Charles A. Halleck of Indiana, a conservative, deposed the more moderate Joseph W. Martin, Jr., of Massachusetts as minority leader. Martin had served as Speaker of the House in 1947-49 and 1953-55, the only years the Republicans controlled the House since 1931.

Gerald R. Ford of Michigan ousted Halleck as minority leader in 1965. After the 1980 elections Robert H. Michel was elected minority leader over Guy Vander Jagt of Michigan. Members apparently agreed with Michel's claims that his experience as the party's whip and his negotiating skills would serve House Republicans better than Vander Jagt's claim to be the more effective spokesman for the party.

Sources: George B. Galloway, *History of the House of Representatives* (New York: Thomas Y. Crowell, 1961), 43; Mary P. Follett, *The Speaker of the House of Representatives* (New York: Longmans, Green, 1896; reprint, New York: Burt Franklin Reprints, 1974), 56, 59, 61-62, 95.

supporters in Congress who formed what might be considered the first party caucuses. "Instead of being a forum, where every member was a peer and no man led, where great principles of government were evolved through the give and take of unrestricted discussion, Congress as such

had become in effect a mere ratifying body," wrote Ralph V. Harlow in 1917. "The real work of legislation was put in shape, not in the legislature, but in secret session of the majority party." [16]

Jefferson's secretary of the Treasury, Albert Gallatin,

soon became as adept as Hamilton in guiding administration measures through the party caucus and the House. Jefferson, moreover, carried his control over the legislative branch one step further, picking his own floor leader, who was named chairman of the Ways and Means Committee at the same time. One of these leaders, William B. Giles of Virginia, was actually referred to as the "premier" or "prime minister." As Ronald M. Peters notes, there was little room under Jefferson's shadow for a Speaker to carve out an independent leadership role.[17]

Clay and the Shift of Power

Executive domination of the House came to an end under Jefferson's successor, James Madison. Although nominally supported by the Democratic-Republican (Jeffersonian) majorities throughout his two terms, Madison soon lost control of the party to a band of young "war hawks," who, affronted by British interference with American trade and shipping, advocated war with England. Henry Clay of Kentucky, who had served brief stints as a senator in 1806-07 and 1810-11, entered the House in 1811 as spokesman for the war hawks who had swept seventy House seats in the elections of 1810. Although only thirty-four and a newcomer, he was elected Speaker on his first day in the House. He would soon become the first Speaker of national prominence and the first to use the position to achieve his own ends.

Clay's great success as presiding officer lay in his personal magnetism. "All testify," wrote Follett, "to the marvelous charm of his voice and manner, which attracted

Library of Congress

Henry Clay was chosen as Speaker on the day he entered the House in 1811. A formidable presiding officer, he exerted firm control over the House.

attention, awakened sympathy, and compelled obedience. He had a bold and commanding spirit, which imposed its will upon those around him. He carried all before him with his imperious nature to give him complete ascendancy over his party, and the easy leadership of the House." [18]

Employing to the full his power as Speaker to select committee chairmen and appoint members to committees, Clay immediately filled key positions on the Foreign Affairs, Military Affairs, and Naval Affairs committees with fellow war hawks. On November 29, 1811, less than four weeks after Congress had convened, the Foreign Affairs Committee issued a report recommending that the nation begin immediate preparations for war. President Madison, a leader of the Constitutional Convention and a strong secretary of state under Jefferson, proved to be a weak president. Although he sought a peaceful settlement with England, he was subjected to continuous pressure for war from Clay and the war hawks. Finally, on June 1, 1812, Madison sent Congress a war message. The House voted 79-49 for war three days later.

As congressional historian George Rothwell Brown wrote, in this episode, "Clay had lifted the Speakership of the House to a point of new power and responsibility, the Speaker to a place in the state where, backed by party organization ... he could present to the President a program determining national policy and involving a declaration of war ... against the pacifist sentiment of the President and most of the Cabinet." [19]

According to Peters, Clay was not a particularly good parliamentarian. Another Speaker, Robert Winthrop, said of him that "he was no painstaking student of parliamentary law, but more frequently found the rules of his governance in his own instinctive sense of what was practicable and proper than in Hatsell's Precedents or Jefferson's Manual." [20] Yet Clay was widely respected for his ability to maintain order on the House floor and to bring into line some of the chamber's more unruly members.

A notable example of these talents occurred during the debate on the proposed declaration of war, when John Randolph, a Virginia Democrat who for years had intimidated House members with his rhetoric, sought to take the floor to oppose the war policy. Clay ruled that Randolph could not speak unless he submitted a motion to the House. Randolph did so, whereupon Clay ruled that he still could not speak until the House considered the motion. The House refused to consider it, and Randolph was denied the floor. Clay frequently resorted to such tactics on important issues. In his six terms as Speaker, none of his rulings was overturned, though many were sustained only by strict party-line votes.

In addition to establishing new standards of order for the conduct of business on the House floor, Clay also helped to establish the committee system. There were ten standing committees in the House in 1810, the year before Clay entered the chamber. When he left the House in 1825 there were twenty-eight.[21] Historians and political scientists disagree about whether Clay fostered the committee system primarily to solidify and advance his own position or to improve the efficiency of the House.

Unlike previous Speakers, Clay remained a vigorous spokesman for the interests of his congressional district. He was the first Speaker—and one of the few in history—to vote in instances when his vote could make no difference in the result. Clay's voting practices and his participation in debate set the precedent that Speakers forfeit none of their normal privileges as members.

Clay remained Speaker as long as he was in the House. Although he left his seat twice—in 1814, to help negotiate an end to the War of 1812, and in 1820—he was reelected Speaker as soon as he returned to the House in 1815 and again in 1823. He is the only early Speaker members elected repeatedly "irrespective of their partisan or factional allegiances, their geographic loyalties, or their views."[22]

From Clay to Colfax

For the next four decades, as the issue of slavery grew to dominate the national agenda, factional allegiances and geographic loyalties would divide both the country and Congress. In the House the speakership rarely stayed in one man's possession for more than a single term. Of the fourteen Speakers who presided between 1825, when Clay left the House, and 1861, only three—Andrew Stevenson of Virginia, James K. Polk, the future president from Tennessee, and Linn Boyd of Kentucky—served for more than one Congress. Many election contests for the speakership were marked by multiple ballots; it took sixty-three ballots, for example, before Howell Cobb, a proslavery Democrat from Georgia, was elected Speaker in 1849 by a two-vote margin. *(Contested elections, box, p. 10)*

Given the brief periods that most of these Speakers served, it is little wonder that none of them achieved the stature and influence of Clay. Stevenson, who served between 1827 and 1834, may have come the closest. Although he lacked Clay's magnetism, he was an able politician, actively promoting Andrew Jackson's program in the House. "No Speaker," wrote Follett, "except perhaps Macon, has been so distinctly the president's man...."[23]

Two men, both Republicans, presided over the House during the Civil War, Galusha Grow of Pennsylvania (1861-63) and Schuyler Colfax of Indiana (1863-69). But the real leader of the House during this period was Thaddeus Stevens, the leader of the Radical Republicans, who engineered the impeachment of President Andrew Johnson.

Grow was clearly in thrall to Stevens, and Colfax, while personally popular, was not a forceful Speaker and was, like Grow, regarded by many as Stevens's man. "Colfax possessed neither will nor mind of his own," said historian Fuller. "Thaddeus Stevens furnished him with these mental attributes."[24]

Rise of Minority Obstructionism

While the speakership may have been a position of little real authority by the time the Civil War began, the emergence of the modern two-party system and a new partisanship in the House was soon to produce two of the most powerful Speakers in history. The first Speaker after the Civil War to add any new authorities to the post was James G. Blaine, R-Maine, one of the founders of the Republican party and Colfax's successor. As Speaker from 1869 to 1875, Blaine was the first leader since Clay to organize the House in a way that favored his party's program. Blaine successfully manipulated committee assignments to produce majorities favorable to legislation he desired.

As partisan as he was, Blaine nonetheless refused to use the powers of the speakership to stop the variety of obstructionist tactics that the Democrats used to block action on legislation they did not support but could not defeat through the regular procedures. Chief among these tactics were constant demands for roll-call votes and use of the "disappearing" or "silent" quorum, in which members of the minority party refused to answer to their names even though they were present on the floor. Blaine's reluctance to restrict the rights of the minority party may have stemmed in part from his realization that the Republican party would some day find itself in the minority and wish to avail itself of the same tactics.

When the Democrats won control of the House with the elections of 1874, they elected as their Speaker Michael C. Kerr of Indiana, who died in 1876. They then chose Samuel J. Randall of Pennsylvania, who served as Speaker until 1881 when the Republicans regained control of the House. Randall too refused to curb minority (this time Republican) obstructionism, but he did initiate a thorough revision of the House rules designed "to secure accuracy in business, economy in time, order, uniformity and impartiality."[25] Perhaps the most significant of these revisions, which were adopted in 1880, made the Rules Committee a standing, instead of a select, committee. The Speaker retained chairmanship of the committee, a privilege he had enjoyed since 1858.

Republicans controlled Congress for one term (1881-83), and when Democrats regained control of the House in 1883, they passed over Randall (who opposed the party's low-tariff policy) and elected instead John G. Carlisle of Kentucky, who served as Speaker until 1889. Carlisle was a strong Speaker, deriving much of his authority from his willingness to use his power of recognition to forestall motions he opposed. By asking "For what purpose does the gentleman rise," Carlisle could withhold recognition from any member whose purpose opposed his own.

But like Blaine and Randall before him, Carlisle was reluctant to do anything about minority obstructionism, making him what one commentator called "the slave of filibusters." By the end of his speakership, the minority's use of delaying tactics, coupled with a disappointing legislative record, opened the House to public criticism and demands that the rules be modified "to permit the majority to control the business for which it is responsible," to quote one editorial in the *New York Tribune*.[26]

Reed's Rule

Reform was to come in the person of Thomas Brackett Reed, Republican of Maine. Reed—a physically imposing man at six feet, three inches and nearly 300 pounds, dressed always in black—was Speaker from 1889 to 1891 and again from 1895 to 1899. In his rulings from the chair in his first months in office, later formally incorporated into the rules and procedures of the House, Reed expanded the powers of the office more than any other Speaker except Clay, in essence establishing the absolute right of the majority to control the legislative process.

Even as minority leader, Reed had deplored minority obstructionism. "The rules of this House are not for the purpose of protecting the rights of the minority," he had said, "but to promote the orderly conduct of the business of the House."[27] The minority's rights were preserved in their right to debate and to vote, Reed argued. The dilatory tactics the minority used controverted the essential function of the House, which was to legislate. Once elected Speaker, he determined to do something about the situation.

The Speaker's decision was risky—his Republicans commanded only a seven-vote majority in the House, 166 to the Democrats' 159— not only to his role as Speaker but also to his future political ambitions. Like Clay and Blaine before him, Reed aspired to the presidency. According to historian Barbara Tuchman, Reed confided his decision to attack the silent quorum to no one, not even to Cannon, his closest lieutenant, in part because no one else would have thought he had any chance of success, in part because he was not sure his own party, including Cannon, would support him.

On January 21, 1890, Reed took his first major step against obstructionism by refusing to consider a member's demand for a teller vote on a motion to adjourn. A few days later he announced his intention to disregard all motions and appeals, even if procedurally correct, if their purpose was simply to delay House business.

Then, on January 29, Reed made his assault on the silent quorum. When the Republicans called up the first of several contested election cases, Charles F. Crisp of Georgia, the Democratic leader who would succeed Reed as Speaker in the next two Congresses, objected to considering the Republican motion. The yeas and nays were ordered, and the vote came to 161 "yeas," two "nays" and 165 not voting—mainly Democrats who while not voting were nonetheless present. When the vote was announced, the Democrats immediately claimed that it was invalid because a quorum (165) had not voted, whereupon Reed ordered the clerk to enter the names of those present who had refused to vote. He then ruled that a quorum was present and that consideration of the question was in order.

The House erupted into pandemonium when the quorum count began. Republicans applauded the Speaker. Democrats, wrote historian Tuchman, "foamed with rage. A hundred of them 'were on their feet howling for recognition,' wrote a reporter. 'Fighting Joe' Wheeler, the diminutive former Confederate cavalry general, unable to reach the front because of the crowded aisles, came down from the rear 'leaping from desk to desk as an ibex leaps from crag to crag.' As the excitement grew wilder, the only Democrat not on his feet was a huge representative from Texas who sat in his seat significantly whetting a bowie knife on his boot."[28]

An appeal from the ruling was tabled by a majority of those voting (again with a quorum present but not voting). The following day, the Speaker declined to reconsider the ruling and declared that he would refuse to recognize any member rising to make a dilatory motion. The debate, angry and strident, continued for several more days. At one point, it appeared that a group of irate Democrats were preparing to pull the Speaker out of the Chair. At another point, Democrats decided to leave the chamber, in an effort to deny the Republicans a quorum, but Reed ordered the doors locked, forcing Democrats to hide under their desks and behind screens. Reed was called tyrant, despot, dictator—the epithet that stuck was czar. Throughout it all he remained calm and implacable, and on the fifth day the Democrats conceded, unable to muster a majority to overturn the Speaker's decision.

On February 14, 1890, the House formally adopted new rules incorporating Reed's rulings and other new procedures. The new code, reported by the Rules Committee chaired by Reed, provided that all members must vote unless they had a pecuniary interest in the issue at hand, motions to recess or to fix a date of adjournment would not be entertained when a question was under debate, one hundred members would constitute a quorum in the Committee of the Whole, and the Speaker would entertain no dilatory motions. The House adopted the "Reed Rules" after bitter debate. The most controversial of them— counting present but nonvoting members to make a quorum—was upheld by the U.S. Supreme Court in an 1891 test case (*U.S. v. Ballin*, 144 U.S. 1).

The Democrats regained control of the House in 1890 with such a convincing majority that they were able to reject the Reed Rules. But Reed had not had his final word on the subject. Though the Democrats after the 1892 elections reverted to the Reed rule that set a quorum in the Committee of the Whole at one hundred members, Speaker Crisp refused to count those present but not voting. In his capacity as minority leader, Reed in 1893 and early 1894 organized several Republican filibusters in an effort to force Crisp to count the quorum. These efforts were to no avail until February 1894, when Reed attacked a Democratic-supported measure by calling for one roll call after another and then using the silent quorum tactic to delay action. Despite their majorities the Democrats were unable to muster a quorum on their own, and after two months Crisp was forced to concede; the House adopted a rule allowing the Speaker to declare a quorum when a majority of members were actually present, regardless of whether they answered to their names.

Crisp, the Democratic Speaker during these two terms, used the powers of the speakership as fully as Reed had done. Crisp's tenure is notable in the evolution of the speakership for strengthening the Rules Committee as a tool of the Speaker. Historian Fuller noted that this expanded role for the Rules Committee was a "radical depar-

THOMAS BRACKETT REED,
Member of
Congress and Speaker of the House.
Author of
"Reed's Rules"
and Editor of
"Modern Eloquence"
———
This drawing by
Thomas Nast
was presented to the
Authors Club
by
Frederic Rowland Marvin

National Portrait Gallery

Thomas Brackett Reed was one of the most powerful Speakers in House history. Known as "Czar" Reed, he established the "Reed Rules" to curb Democratic obstructionism in the 1890s.

ture from the long-established rules and principles of parliamentary law and practice." He added that the "tyranny of Reed seemed beneficence when Crisp ruled that not even 'the question of consideration could be raised against a report from the Committee on Rules.' " [29]

"Cannonism"

During their reigns as Speaker, Reed and Crisp centralized power in the House. Not only was the Speaker now able to take effective command of the House, his authority to name the members and chairmen of all committees gave him the power to punish or reward his colleagues. As chairman of the Rules Committee, which had the right to immediate access to the floor, he could control the timing and content of bills to be brought before the House. And with unlimited power of recognition, he could determine in large measure what business would be taken up on the floor of the House. Though these authorities ensured that the House would run efficiently, if abused they could allow a Speaker to tyrannize the House. That is what happened when "Uncle Joe" Cannon was elected Speaker in 1903.

Regaining control of Congress in 1895, the Republicans returned Reed to the speakership. Having broken with President William McKinley over the intervention in Cuba and the annexation of Hawaii and the Philippines, Reed resigned from the House in 1899. Cannon, who had already lost races for the speakership in 1881 and 1889, hoped to succeed Reed then, but the Republicans instead chose David B. Henderson, R-Iowa, who served two ineffective terms as Speaker before retiring from the House. When he was finally elected Speaker in 1903, Cannon was the oldest representative (sixty-seven) and had served longer (twenty-eight years) than any member yet to head the House of Representatives.

Cannon's first years in office gave little indication of what would develop. The affable Speaker was one of the most popular men in Congress, and in his first term, "his natural kindliness and sense of humor fostered a spirit of amicability that influenced the mood of the House." [30] Though he would eventually rescind it, Cannon even granted authority to the Democratic leader, John Sharp Williams, D-Miss., to assign Democrats to committees, subject to Cannon's veto.

But Cannon was a devout conservative, unsympathetic to much of the progressive legislation sought by President Theodore Roosevelt and favored by a growing number of liberal Republicans and Democrats in the House. Though he was forced to accept some of these measures— including the Hepburn Act (1905), which strengthened the power of the Interstate Commerce Commission to set railroad rates, the Pure Food and Drug Act of 1906, and the Mann Act of 1910—he also made increasingly arbitrary use of his powers as Speaker to maintain control of the House.

On days set aside for approval by unanimous consent of purely local bills of minor importance, Cannon moved arbitrarily to reward his friends and punish his enemies. "Often on the success of these bills would depend the reelection of many men in Congress," Fuller wrote. The Speaker's "smile and assent made and unmade members, accordingly, as he bestowed or withheld these powerful benefices." [31] Although the seniority system was still not firmly embedded, Cannon's flagrant disregard for it in assigning members to committees further contributed to the chamber's growing irritation with his rule.

But it was Cannon's use, or misuse, of the Rules Com-

Library of Congress

Speaker Joseph G. Cannon dominated the House from 1903 until 1910, when Republicans and Democrats revolted against his arbitrary rule.

mittee that most offended his colleagues. Before any committee could report legislation to the full House, the committee had to obtain clearance from Rules, and clearance usually was granted only for those measures that met with Cannon's favor. The Rules Committee's special terms and guidelines for bills to be considered by the House—those acceptable to Cannon—usually placed sharp limits on debate and foreclosed floor amendments. The latter practice enabled Cannon and his associates to attach legislative "riders" (nongermane amendments) in committee that might have been defeated on the floor if brought to a separate vote. But because these riders were frequently attached to annual appropriations bills, the House usually accepted them rather than kill the entire bill.

Eventually the persistent use of the Speaker's powers to obstruct the legislative will—not of the majority party itself, but of a new majority of members of both parties— sparked a revolt. In March 1909 the House adopted the Calendar Wednesday rule, setting aside time each Wednesday for committee chairmen to call up bills that their committees had reported but that had not been cleared for floor action by Rules.

At the beginning of a special session that opened a few days later, a group of Republican insurgents joined the Democrats, led by James Beauchamp "Champ" Clark, D-Mo., in a move to curb the powers of the Rules Committee. That effort failed when several Democrats joined the Republican majority in opposition to Clark, and instead the House adopted a weak alternative that made only slight inroads into Cannon's power. Chief among these was the establishment of the Consent Calendar, which set aside two days each month on which individual members could call up minor bills of particular interest to them without prior approval from the Speaker.

In March 1910 the insurgent Republicans found another opportunity to challenge Cannon's iron rule. On

March 17, George W. Norris, R-Neb., the leader of the insurgents, took advantage of a parliamentary opening to move for immediate consideration of a reform resolution that would remove the Speaker from the Rules Committee and expand the committee to fifteen members; the members would be chosen by election of the House and would then choose their own chairman. Cannon stalled for two days, while he pondered a point of order that Norris's motion was out of order, until Republican stalwarts who had gone to their districts for St. Patrick's Day returned to the capital. Finally, on March 19, Cannon ruled that Norris's motion was out of order. The returning Republicans were not enough. The House overturned Cannon's decision, 164-182, and then adopted the reform resolution, which Norris had modified, 191-156. The modification set the size of the Rules Committee at ten members, six from the majority and four from the minority.

In what has been described as one of the most dramatic events in the history of the House, Cannon then announced that he would entertain a motion to declare the chair vacant so that the House could elect a new Speaker. But though they were willing to strip him of his powers, most of the Republican insurgents were not willing to unseat him—or to help put a Democrat in the speakership—and Cannon remained Speaker until the term ended in March 1911.

Decline of the Speaker's Power

When the Democrats won control of the House in 1911, they named Champ Clark their new Speaker and chose Oscar W. Underwood, D-Ala., as majority leader and chairman of the Ways and Means Committee. They also agreed that the Democratic members of Ways and Means would serve as their Committee on Committees to draw up committee assignments for all Democrats, a move that further weakened the powers of the Speaker. (The Democrats retained that arrangement until 1974, when the power to make committee assignments was transferred to the Steering and Policy Committee. In 1917 Republicans set up their own Committee on Committees, which still makes GOP committee assignments.)

The Democrats also retained the Calendar Wednesday and Consent Calendar innovations, as well as a discharge rule, adopted in 1910, which allowed a majority of House members to petition to free legislation bottled up in a committee. A special calendar for private bills was also established.

Because Clark left most of the management of party business to Underwood, the floor leader quickly became the acknowledged leader in the House. "The Speaker became a figurehead, the floor leader supreme," wrote a contemporary observer.[32] Underwood made frequent use of the party caucus to develop unity on legislative issues. Democrats in 1909 had adopted rules that bound all party members to support any party position approved by two-thirds of those Democrats present and voting at a caucus meeting, provided the vote represented a majority of the Democrats in the House. A member could vote against the caucus position only if he considered the position unconstitutional or had made "contrary pledges to his constituents prior to his election or received contrary instructions by resolutions or platform from his nominating authority."

Underwood also used the caucus to develop legislative proposals, which then would be referred to the appropriate committees for formal approval; to instruct committees as to which bills they might or might not report; and to instruct the Rules Committee on the terms to be included in its special orders governing floor consideration on major bills and proposed amendments. The power that had been concentrated in the hands of the Speaker was now transferred to "King Caucus" and the man who dominated it. "Whereas Cannon had often exercised control by keeping unwanted legislation off of the floor," observed Peters, "Underwood sought to control legislation by ensuring a majority vote on the floor. The result was despotism under two different guises."[33]

Rule by caucus worked well as long as Democrats were relatively united on the issues; during President Woodrow Wilson's first term, they were able to enact a large body of domestic legislation. But the Democrats soon began to split over foreign policy, and the effectiveness of the binding caucus had disappeared by the time the Republicans took control of the House in 1919. Once again, however, the Speaker was not the true leader of the House.

The leading contender for the speakership in 1919 was James R. Mann, R-Ill., who had been minority leader since 1911. But many Republicans feared that Mann would try to centralize power in the Speaker's office, so they turned to Frederick H. Gillett, R-Mass., who, like his Democratic predecessor, Champ Clark, declined to assert political leadership. Mann refused the position of floor leader, which was then given to Franklin W. Mondell, R-Wyo. Mann, however, retained substantial influence among House Republicans.

To further ensure decentralization, the Republicans set up a five-member Steering Committee, chaired by the majority leader. The Speaker and the chairman of the Rules Committee were barred from sitting on this committee, though Mondell invited both to attend its meetings, which were held almost daily to discuss party positions and map strategy with committee chairmen and other Republican leaders. "For the most part," Randall B. Ripley reported, "the Steering Committee carried out the wishes of the Republican leaders in the House, even when these were not in accord with the Republican administration." As example Ripley cited Steering Committee opposition that killed a bill to raise civil service pensions despite support from the Coolidge administration, the Senate, and every member of the House Civil Service Committee. Leadership under this system was so diffuse that House Republicans accomplished little during the period. House members, Ripley wrote, "including some committee chairmen, used the loose leadership structure to pursue legislative ends other than those officially sanctioned."[34]

As Speaker from 1925 to 1931, Nicholas Longworth, R-Ohio, sought to centralize power once again in the Speaker's office. Longworth held it "to be the duty of the Speaker, standing squarely on the platform of his party, to assist in so far as he properly can the enactment of legislation in accordance with the declared principles and policies of his party and by the same token to resist the enactment of legislation in violation thereof."[35] One of his first actions was to discipline Republican Progressives; those who had opposed his candidacy for the speakership, and who had also opposed a rules change that made it much more difficult to discharge a bill from committee, found themselves stripped of their committee seniority.

Despite these moves, Longworth as Speaker had few of the powers that enabled Cannon to centralize power in the speakership. He nonetheless was considered an effective Speaker, able, as Peters notes, to wield power and authority not so much by manipulating the rules but "by force of his character." Longworth's style was collegial. Though he made little use of the Steering Committee, he established a small group of trusted associates to help him run the House. Though it appeared contradictory given his stand on strong party leadership, Longworth also was willing to deal with the Democrats not only on policy issues but on scheduling business. He and the Democratic leader, John Nance Garner, D-Texas, began the tradition, later made famous by Rayburn, of the "Board of Education"—gatherings in a Capitol hideaway where leaders from both parties met over drinks to work out accommodations on various matters.

The Power of Persuasion: Rayburn

Democrats regained control of the House in 1931, a position they lost only twice in the next sixty years, in 1947-49 and 1953-55. During the first ten years, four different Democrats held the speakership. Garner was elected Speaker in 1931. When he became vice president in 1933, he was replaced by Henry T. Rainey of Illinois, who died in 1934. Rainey was followed in 1935 by Joseph W. Byrns of Tennessee, who died in 1936. Byrns's successor, William B. Bankhead of Alabama, served as Speaker until his death in 1940. Though some of these men were successful Speakers, none of them left a lasting mark on the office. That was to change with the election in 1940 of Majority Leader Rayburn, who, except for the two Republican Congresses, served as Speaker until his death in 1961.

Rayburn was a strong Speaker—indeed, his reputation reached near mythic proportions in the decades following his death. But the reasons for Rayburn's strength and the style with which he led the House were in sharp contrast to those in play during the Reed and Cannon speakerships.

Rayburn entered the House in 1913, just three years after the revolt against Cannon and at a time when the powers and the stature of the Speaker were at low ebb. By 1940 little real change had been made in the Speaker's powers. The seniority system was well entrenched, which meant that committee chairmen and ranking members could act with a great deal more independence than they could at the turn of the century. In 1940 and for the next two decades most of the chairmen of the major committees were southern Democrats.

At the same time most southern Democrats began to vote with the Republicans on New Deal, and eventually on civil rights, issues, forming a conservative coalition against liberal northern Democrats. Even when the conservative coalition did not form on a particular issue, the thin Democratic majorities could make it difficult for the Democratic leadership to achieve its program. As Rayburn himself put it in 1950, "The old day of pounding on the desk and giving people hell is gone.... A man's got to lead by persuasion and kindness and the best reason—that's the only way he can lead people." [36]

A man of great integrity who venerated the House of Representatives, Rayburn dealt with the individual rather than the party. He sought to bind individual members to him through friendship and favors; he did not force Democrats to vote against their conscience or constituency; he played down partisanship, shunning the use of the caucus and other party mechanisms that he thought divisive and working with minority leaders, even doing the occasional favor for a rank-and-file member of the minority; he cultivated younger members, advising them "to get along, go along."

Rayburn's preferences were controlling when it came to Democratic committee assignments. In 1948 he obtained the removal from the Un-American Activities Committee of three Democrats who had supported Dixiecrat Strom Thurmond in the 1948 presidential campaign. He saw to it that Democrats named to vacancies on Ways and Means were sympathetic to reciprocal trade bills and opposed to reductions in oil depletion allowances. And he turned the Education and Labor Committee from a predominantly conservative body into a more liberal one.

Despite the active presence of the conservative coalition, Rayburn was able to win House passage of an impressive amount of legislation dealing with both foreign and domestic matters, including two far-reaching civil rights bills. He accomplished his goals by working with the other power centers in the House. Rayburn, writes Peters,

> was a man carved for the role he played, yet he was also a shrewd politician who was able to create a political labyrinth in which his own skills would prove most effective. His success lay less in his ability to swing large numbers of votes than in avoiding situations in which that would be necessary. When he wanted legislation stopped, he let others stop it; when he wanted legislation passed, he worked with the committee chairman to get bills that could command a floor majority.... [Rayburn's] emphasis upon the virtue of honesty and his reputation for fairness in dealing with members contributed to the creation of an atmosphere of comity in the House that facilitated his leadership.... He did not win votes by staring people down; instead, he established a set of expectations about behavior that enabled him to deal for votes when necessary. [37]

Transitional Speakers: McCormack, Albert

Rayburn's speakership marked the end of an era. In his later years, younger and more liberal Democrats began to demand changes that would lead to the greatest internal reforms in the history of the House. Indeed, Rayburn's last major victory, in 1961, came in a battle to make the Rules Committee, dominated by conservative southerners, more responsive to the will of the Democratic majority. (Rules Committee, p. 80)

Rayburn's two immediate successors, John W. McCormack, D-Mass., who served as Speaker from 1962 to 1971, and Carl Albert, D-Okla., who was Speaker from 1971 to 1977, had the ill luck to lead the House during a time both of great social and political upheaval within the nation and of great institutional change that neither man was well equipped to manage. McCormack was popular with his colleagues, and like Rayburn, based his leadership on his personal ties to members. But he lacked the persuasive skills of his predecessor and placed considerable reliance on Albert, his majority leader, and on the majority whip, Hale Boggs, D-La.

McCormack's weakness as a leader, coupled with his opposition to reform proposals in the House and his support of President Johnson's escalation of the Vietnam War, frustrated many of the younger, more liberal House Democrats. In 1968 Morris K. Udall, D-Ariz., challenged him for Speaker in the party caucus. McCormack easily won reelection, but soon announced his decision to retire at the end of the Congress.

Albert, too, was generally considered by his colleagues to be a weak leader. His low-key style did not seem suited to the requirements of the times, although any Speaker would have been hard put to guide the House smoothly and firmly through an unparalleled period of internal reform, against the backdrop of U.S. withdrawal from the Vietnam War and the Watergate crisis, which resulted in President Richard Nixon's resignation.

Relations between the Republican president and the Democratic Congress were tense throughout the Nixon presidency. Intent on expanding his own power, Nixon acted with minimal consultation with and concern for Congress. His administration was committed to conservative political and economic programs opposed by the great majority of the Democrats. Their first priority was to halt administration plans to revamp or terminate many of the Great Society programs. The prolonged congressional-executive stalemate that resulted gave rise to frustration in Democratic ranks that found expression, especially in the House, in criticism of the leadership.

Albert also drew criticism from younger and more activist House members for not supporting internal House reforms more vigorously. By the early 1970s a sharp increase in retirements and reelection defeats of much of the "Old Guard" had resulted in a significant infusion of new blood in the House. The average age of House members had crept steadily downward, and most of the new generation were liberal Democrats. With the dramatic turnover in membership—particularly the election of seventy-five new members in 1974—came pressure for changes in House rules and practices. Reforms adopted by the Democratic Caucus in the early 1970s, particularly in 1971, 1973, and 1974, were to have a substantial effect on the way the House and its leaders would conduct their business.

One set of reforms broke the grip senior members held on the House by subjecting committee chairmen to election by secret ballot. In 1975 the caucus deposed three chairmen. Committee chairmen also were forced to share their powers with quasi-independent subcommittees, some of which were led by junior members, even first- and second-termers. Other changes limited House Democrats to one subcommittee chairmanship, gave the subcommittees their own staffs and budgets, and guaranteed each party member an assignment on a major committee.

A second set of reforms granted new powers to the Speaker, making that office potentially stronger than at any time since the reigns of Reed and Cannon. The Speaker was given the right to nominate the chairman and all the Democratic members of the Rules Committee, subject to caucus approval, and that panel once again became an arm of the leadership, not the independent power center it had been in the previous three decades. The Democratic Steering and Policy Committee was set up in 1973 to give coherence and strategy to the party's legislative program and was placed firmly under the Speaker's control. At the end of 1974 the committee was given the authority, formerly held by Ways and Means Democrats, to appoint the Democratic members to House committees, subject to caucus approval, and to refer bills to more than one committee. Although most of these new powers became available during Albert's tenure as Speaker, he made little use of them, leaving them to his successors to exploit.

The Modern Speakership: O'Neill

In many respects Thomas P. "Tip" O'Neill was an unlikely candidate to modernize the speakership. A New Deal liberal, he was to the political left of most of his colleagues. Intensely partisan, he was forced to work with a popular Republican president and a Republican Senate. A consummate practitioner of inside politics, O'Neill faced demands from rank-and-file Democrats for greater participation in the decision-making process. A less-than-commanding public speaker who reserved his public appearances for his Massachusetts constituents, the new Speaker was called upon to be the national spokesman for his party. O'Neill once told a reporter than he was one old dog ready to learn new tricks—and he did learn some, giving many more members, especially junior members, leadership responsibilities and becoming a nationally recognized media celebrity. But his reluctance to temper both his liberal beliefs and his partisanship made coalition-building, even within his own party, difficult at times.

Genial and enormously popular, O'Neill based his leadership on friendships, doing favors for loyal colleagues, taking care of what he called the "little odds and ends." But O'Neill also took some innovative steps to expand participation of the party rank and file in House affairs, enlarging the whip organization and setting up special task forces to help the leadership develop support and strategy on major legislation. One of O'Neill's most successful ploys was the creation of an ad hoc committee in 1977 to draw up comprehensive energy legislation, a top priority of the Carter administration. Although the tactic worked well in that case, policy differences and objections from the standing committees prevented the Speaker from ever using it again.

O'Neill also made use of several powers the House reforms had bestowed upon the Speaker, including the authority to name the Democratic members of the House Rules Committee. Although O'Neill did not demand unstinting loyalty from the Democrats on Rules, he did expect them to support him on key issues. In response to the Republican minority's penchant for offering floor amendments designed to put Democrats on the spot, O'Neill also came to rely heavily on restrictive rules, those specifying which amendments could be offered on the floor and in what order, as a potent tool to maintain control of debate on the House floor. *(Details, p. 51)*

Another tool O'Neill used to help the leadership control the flow of legislation was the authority to refer bills to more than one committee either at the same time or sequentially. If a bill is referred to committees sequentially, the Speaker may also set time limits for committee action. This authority keeps alive bills that otherwise might die in an unfriendly committee.

O'Neill also gave the speakership unprecedented visibility. He was aided by the decision to allow House floor proceedings to be televised to the public, beginning in 1979, and spurred on by criticisms from his colleagues that he was not effectively articulating Democratic alternatives to President Reagan's legislative agenda. Soon the Speaker's office was issuing a steady stream of press releases trying to mobilize support for Democratic party positions. Though previous Speakers had met with reporters before every House session, they usually only answered specific questions. Now O'Neill used them to volunteer information about the goals and achievements of House Democrats and to spar with Reagan on the issues.

O'Neill's attempts at public relations won mixed reviews. His sometimes garbled syntax, his physical bulk, shaggy-dog appearance, and ever-present cigar were reminiscent of the stereotypical backroom pol, an image that some younger members had hoped the Democratic party could shed. Nonetheless, O'Neill affected public attitudes on a variety of questions, some more successfully than others. Nothing the Speaker said or did could have headed off support in the nation or in the House for the 1981 Reagan economic program. But on several foreign policy issues, where there was substantial doubt about Reagan's approach, O'Neill helped solidify Democratic opposition and made it credible to the public. By coming out strongly against the MX missile and U.S. aid to the Nicaraguan contras, for example, the Speaker focused media attention on the anti-Reagan position and almost certainly locked in some Democratic votes on those closely fought issues.

Yet O'Neill's speakership was not an unqualified success. His first year in the post seemed to bear out early predictions that he could be the strongest Speaker since Rayburn. But Carter's weak presidency and new militancy on the part of House Republicans combined with O'Neill's own unyielding partisanship to his disadvantage. Unable to keep his Democrats united, he lost several key votes in his first four years.

Ronald Reagan's election and the loss of several House seats only worsened his situation in 1981-82. Not until House Democrats won thirty-four seats in the 1982 elections was O'Neill able to unite his party in opposition to Reagan's policies. The stalemate that often resulted and the heightened partisan rhetoric that it engendered led to accusations that O'Neill was a heavy-handed partisan and that the Democratic party had no focus and could not govern. When O'Neill did try to exercise policy leadership on an issue, he was often deserted by one wing or another of his party, as he was in 1983, when a number of Democrats—including Majority Leader Wright and Whip Thomas S. Foley, Wash.—voted against O'Neill to support funding for the MX missile.

Despite these setbacks, O'Neill's speakership was never in any jeopardy. But criticisms of his leadership and the clear frustrations among many House Democrats about the image the party was projecting may have weighed in his decision to retire at the end of 1986.

The Limits of Power: Wright

As Speaker, Jim Wright was determined to give House Democrats the policy leadership many of them had found lacking in O'Neill. "I think there's a creative role for the legislative branch and a leadership role for the Speaker ...," Wright once said. "The Congress should not simply react, passively, to recommendations from the president but should come forward with initiatives of its own." [38]

But in pursuing his ambitious agenda for the House, Wright overstepped the limits of the modern speakership's powers. By his second year in the office, Republicans considered him to be the match for Cannon in his treatment of the minority. Democrats were alienated by his failure to practice the politics of inclusion that had become de rigueur. As allegations of financial misconduct, lodged against the Speaker by Republican Rep. Gingrich, developed into a full-blown investigation, Wright found that Democrats willing to support him when he—and they— were winning were not as ready to back him on a question of personal ethics. On May 31, 1989, Wright announced that he would give up the speakership effective June 6, becoming the first Speaker to be forced from office at midterm. A month later he resigned his House seat. *(Speakers and scandals, box, p. 20)*

The first Speaker since McCormack to skip the lowest rung on the leadership ladder, Wright was deputy whip when he ran for majority leader in 1976, winning by a single vote. Unlike his two rivals, Wright had few enemies. He

Associated Press

Ethics charges forced the resignation of Speaker Jim Wright in 1989. Wright, shown here offering his resignation as Speaker of the House, was the first Speaker in history to be forced from office at midterm.

had always compromised personal differences when possible, or disagreed gently if he had to. He also had another advantage: as a member of the Public Works Committee, he had done countless small favors, making sure a dam was put up here or a federal building there. And throughout his ten years as majority leader, Wright continued to do the little favors, devoting months of precious time to public appearances and fund-raising missions in districts throughout the country.

Favors notwithstanding, many members felt a sense of unease, even mistrust, about Wright. Private, competitive, at times aggressively partisan, Wright did not inspire the sort of personal affection that O'Neill had drawn. His reputation for oratorical skills was well deserved, but now and again his speech turned florid, his smile disingenuous. "You watch him and you know when he's going to get partisan," GOP leader Michel said in 1984. "The eyebrows start to rise. The voice begins to stretch out. And the Republicans say, 'Snake oil is at it again.' " [39] Though such descriptions might be dismissed because they came from the opposition, Democrats were nonetheless concerned about the image Wright might convey to the public.

Despite these misgivings, Wright was not challenged when he ran to succeed O'Neill in 1986. His assertions that he would be a strong, policy-oriented Speaker appealed to his Democratic colleagues who not only wanted to demon-

Past Speakers Survived Troubles

Although he was the first House Speaker to be forced out of office at midterm, Jim Wright was not the first to be embroiled in a controversy that attracted national attention and disrupted congressional leadership.

In the closest parallel, the House in 1910 nearly deposed Speaker Joseph G. Cannon, R-Ill., for his heavy-handed use of power.

Wright, a Texas Democrat, stepped down in 1989 following a yearlong inquiry into the ethics of his financial dealings.

Other Speakers have had to weather less intense storms. Wright's predecessor, Thomas P. O'Neill, Jr., D-Mass., was one of dozens of members named in the "Koreagate" influence-peddling scandal of the 1970s, although he was exonerated. James G. Blaine, R-Maine, who was Speaker from 1869 to 1875, had a brush with the Crédit Mobilier bribery scandal. Henry Clay went to the well of the House to defend himself against allegations of impropriety while he was Speaker in 1825.

Cannon: Stripped of Power

The revolt against Cannon exploded in response to his spectacular use of the Speaker's powers to reward friends and punish foes. Cannon freely wielded his authority to control who sat on which committee, which bills went to the floor, and who would be recognized to speak.

Democrats made common cause with insurgent Republicans on March 19, 1910, and defeated Cannon on a procedural question that was, in effect, a referendum on his leadership.

The insurgents went on to ram through rules changes that stripped the Speaker of his right to make committee assignments and of his control of the Rules Committee.

Cannon refused to resign as Speaker, but invited a vote on deposing him. Pandemonium broke loose on the House floor, judging from the notation in the *Congressional Record:* "Great confusion in the Hall."

A resolution declaring the Speaker's office vacant was put to a vote—the only time such a vote has been taken—but Cannon survived, 155-192. It suited the political purposes of some to keep Cannon in office: That made it easier to run against "Cannonism" in the 1910 elections. He lost the speakership after Democrats won a majority of House seats for the first time since 1895.

Nineteenth Century Speakers

In the early nineteenth century Speaker Nathaniel Macon also came close to being deposed. Macon was one of Thomas Jefferson's most devoted loyalists, and was rewarded for his fealty with Jefferson's support during his election as Speaker in 1801.

But Macon later allied himself with a bitter foe of the president's, John Randolph, who broke with Jefferson over a plan to acquire Florida. Jefferson retaliated against Macon by opposing his reelection as Speaker in 1805. Jefferson's effort failed, but it was a close enough decision that Macon chose not to seek another term as Speaker.

John White, one of the more obscure Speakers (1841-43), came under fire for one of the last speeches he gave before leaving the House in 1845 to take a judgeship in Kentucky. After it was disclosed that a particularly eloquent speech he gave had been plagiarized from Aaron Burr, White committed suicide.

While Blaine was Speaker, he was cleared of wrongdoing by a special committee appointed to look into the Crédit Mobilier scandal, in which promoters of the Union Pacific Railroad used stock to bribe members of Congress to support federal subsidies for the railroad.

But other allegations of graft surfaced in 1876, after Blaine left the Speaker's office due to a change of party control in the House.

Blaine took to the House floor to read from letters that supposedly exonerated him. That quelled efforts to censure him, but the scandal didn't help his unsuccessful quest for his party's presidential nomination at the GOP convention just months later.

Blaine was finally nominated in 1884, but he lost the election to Grover Cleveland.

It was a newspaper clipping that drove Henry Clay to defend himself on the floor in 1825. In a published letter, another member accused Clay of cutting a secret deal to support John Quincy Adams for president in exchange for an appointment as secretary of state. The scandal died quickly. Clay asked the House to name a special committee to look into the charges, but the member who had made the allegation refused to appear.

McCormack, O'Neill

More recently, Speaker John McCormack, D-Mass., retired in 1971 after one of his top aides, Martin Sweig, was accused of using the Speaker's office and name for fraudulent purposes, without McCormack's knowledge. McCormack, in his seventies and under pressure from a restive younger generation of lawmakers, had other reasons for leaving the House when he did.

When O'Neill became Speaker in 1977, he immediately faced questions raised in connection with the Korean bribery scandal.

The House Committee on Standards of Official Conduct in January 1977 began an investigation into allegations that as many as 115 members—Republicans and Democrats—had taken illegal gifts from South Korean agents.

Some people suggested that O'Neill, during a 1974 trip to Korea, had asked Korean rice dealer Tongsun Park to make contributions to House members and their wives.

But other members were the principal target, and in July 1978 the committee issued a statement exonerating O'Neill. The panel said the only thing of "questionable propriety" the Speaker had done was to let Park pay for two parties in his honor.

strate that the Democats could govern but also wanted a record to see them through the 1988 presidential campaign.

In his acceptance speech Wright laid out an ambitious agenda for the 100th Congress, calling for renewal of the clean water act and a new highway bill and suggesting that the tax rate for the wealthy be frozen at 1987 levels instead of dropping as scheduled, a proposal that some said put him beyond the majority of the Democrats. By the end of the 100th Congress, not only had the clean water and highway bills become law, but Congress had overhauled the welfare system, approved the biggest expansion of Medicare since its creation, and rewritten U.S. trade law. Most of this legislation had passed the House with bipartisan support.

Although Wright's Democratic colleagues took pride in these legislative achievements, many resented being excluded from the process of achieving them. The "Lone Ranger," as Wright was sometimes dubbed, had a record of springing major decisions without consulting key colleagues. His very public involvement in trying to negotiate a peace plan between the Nicaragua government and the contra rebels not only angered the administration and Republicans in the House but unsettled Democrats who feared that they might be held accountable at the polls if the peace process failed.

Wright was also criticized for his aggressive tactics in getting legislation passed. Rules to guide floor debate grew more restrictive; no amendments, for example, were allowed on the clean water and highway bills or on a moratorium on aid to the Nicaraguan contras. Republicans complained that under Wright, many bills were never given hearings and came to the floor of the House without being reported by committee, that substantive legislation was being enacted through self-executing rules (which provide for the automatic adoption of an amendment or other matter upon adoption of the rule), and that the minority was more often denied its right to try to recommit bills.

Wright's support among his own Democrats was substantially weakened early in 1989 over a proposed pay raise that would have increased congressional salaries by 50 percent. The raise was to take effect if the House and Senate did not veto it by February 9. The initial strategy was to let the pay raise take effect and then to vote on legislation to curb honoraria. But public outrage at the size of the raise—and the fact that it might take effect without a vote in Congress—was overwhelming. After the Senate yielded to the pressure and voted no on the pay raise, Wright scheduled a vote for February 7. When the raise, not surprisingly, was defeated, many Democrats angrily blamed Wright for changing the strategy at the last minute.

Barely a month later, the ethics committee announced that it "had reason to believe" that Wright had violated House rules on financial conduct. In the next few weeks, new allegations of misconduct surfaced, further damaging the Speaker, as did a *Washington Post* story revealing that a top aide to Wright had a criminal record for brutally beating a woman sixteen years earlier. After Wright's attorneys failed to persuade the Ethics Committee to dismiss the charges on technical grounds, the Speaker decided to resign to spare the House the embarrassment of a public investigation of its Speaker. Only days before, Democratic Whip Tony Coelho, D-Calif., had resigned his House seat in the face of allegations of irregularities in his purchase of a $100,000 junk bond.

Political scientist Ronald Peters observes that "if Wright had not been vulnerable to the ethics charges brought against him, it is unlikely that his Republican opponents could have undermined his support in the Democratic Caucus. However, if Wright had led the House differently, neither Republicans nor Democrats would have had a sufficient motive to seek to unseat him." [40] Whether a Speaker who worked more closely with his own leadership and his rank and file and who was less openly partisan would have survived the same ethics charges Wright faced is, of course, conjecture. But the Wright episode clearly shows the potential weakness of a Speaker who fails to develop an atmosphere in which consensus building and shared decision making can flourish. Wright himself seemed to recognize this. "Have I been too partisan? Too insistent? Too abrasive? Too determined to have my way?" he asked in his resignation speech. "Perhaps. Maybe so." [41]

Consensus and Involvement: Foley

On June 6, 1989, the Democratic Caucus nominated Majority Leader Thomas S. Foley of Washington by acclamation to succeed Wright as Speaker. Better known for bringing together warring factions than for drawing up battle plans, Foley seemed well equipped to help the Democrats—and the House—put the Wright episode behind them; in his first speech as Speaker he called for debate "with reason and without rancor."

A thoughtful and articulate man, Foley was perhaps the first Speaker his Democratic colleagues felt comfortable putting in front of a television camera. With a knack for telling stories and a near-photographic memory that helped him to master the substance of most issues that came before him, Foley was a superb negotiator who was on good terms with most Democrats and a good number of Republicans. "Foley has a talent for listening and knowing what other people want," a veteran leadership aide said.[42] He chaired the task force that drew up the Democratic alternative to the 1985 Gramm-Rudman deficit reduction act. He also chaired the 1989 budget negotiations and was the lead negotiator on a comprehensive aid package for the Nicaraguan contras.

Endowed with a sense of detachment rare among politicians, Foley was a cautious, careful political navigator. He did not like to commit himself early on controversial issues, and he could be as skillful at making the case for the opposing side as for his own. "I think I am a little cursed," he said in 1984, "with seeing the other point of view and trying to understand it." Indeed, he was criticized by some for not being partisan enough.

Time would tell whether Foley could be as partisan as his rank and file might want him to be. But it became clear early on that he would practice the strategy of inclusion first adopted by O'Neill. "The reality," he said a few weeks before becoming Speaker, "is that in a modern, participatory Congress . . . the responsibility of leadership and the necessity of leadership is to constantly involve members in the process of decision and consensus." [43]

The Majority Leader

In the modern House, the second in command is the majority leader, whose primary responsibility is to manage the legislative affairs of the chamber. To that end, he helps formulate, promote, negotiate, and defend the party's program, particularly on the House floor. A majority leader was not officially designated in the House until 1899, when

Sereno E. Payne, R-N.Y., was named to the post. But from the earliest days, the Speaker has appointed someone to help him guide his party's legislative program through the House. Occasionally this person was a trusted lieutenant. More often the chairman of the Ways and Means Committee also served as the floor leader, largely because until 1865 the committee handled both revenues and appropriations and thus the bulk of the legislation that came before the House. Payne, for example, was also chairman of the Ways and Means Committee.

After the Appropriations Committee was established, its chairman sometimes served as majority leader. At other times, the Speaker chose his leading rival within the party, presumably either to promote party harmony or to neutralize an opponent. Thus in 1859 William Pennington, R-N.J., the only House member besides Clay to be elected Speaker in his first term, chose as his majority leader his chief rival for the speakership, John Sherman, R-Ohio. And in 1889 Reed named as his majority leader William McKinley, Jr., R-Ohio, who had challenged Reed for the speakership and who, like Reed, had presidential ambitions.

The revolt against Cannon in 1910, which stripped the Speaker of many of his powers, also stripped him of the right to name the majority leader. Since 1911 Democratic majority leaders have been elected by secret ballot in the party caucus. The first two, Underwood and Claude Kitchin, N.C., also chaired the Ways and Means Committee. When the Republicans returned to power in 1919, their Committee on Committees named the majority leader, but since 1923 the Republican Conference, as the caucus is called, has selected the majority leader.

Mondell, the Republican floor leader chosen in 1919, had been chairman of the Ways and Means Committee, but he gave up his committee assignments to help the Speaker manage the House. The first Democratic majority leader to give up his committee assignments was Henry T. Rainey, who resigned his seat on the Ways and Means Committee upon his election as majority leader in 1931. Today the majority leader holds the leadership slot on the House Budget Committee and both the majority and minority leaders are ex officio members of the Permanent Select Intelligence Committee.

Underwood, the first elected majority leader, may also have been the strongest majority leader in the history of the House. Champ Clark, the Democrat who succeeded Cannon as Speaker, gave Underwood a free hand to manage both legislation and the party. "Although I am going to be Speaker . . ., I am going to sacrifice the Speaker's power to change the rules," he declared.[44] As a result of Clark's attitude and the limitations placed upon the Speaker's office, Underwood was able to dominate the House through the Democratic Caucus and his chairmanship of Ways and Means, which assigned members to the standing committees. "The main cogs in the machine were the caucus, the floor leadership, the Rules Committee, the standing committees, and special rules," wrote historian George B. Galloway. "Oscar Underwood became the real leader of the House. He dominated the party caucus, influenced the rules, and as chairman of Ways and Means chose the committees."[45]

But changing circumstances in the years following World War I made it more difficult for Underwood's successors to wield such power. Internal party divisions made the caucus ineffective, while strong Speakers such as Longworth, Garner, and Rayburn elevated the prestige and thus the power of the Speaker. The majority leader eventually came to give up his committee chairmanships, and between 1937 and 1975 the Rules Committee ceased to be an arm of the leadership. The majority leader is now seen as the chief lieutenant to the Speaker, not his rival. The majority leader, Jim Wright wrote in 1976, "must work with the Speaker, in a supportive role, and never against him."[46]

If tradition holds, and the majority leader does not lose his House seat, he is likely to become Speaker eventually. Every Speaker between 1900 and 1990 advanced to that position from either the majority or minority leadership position. Three of the six Democratic Speakers between 1945 and 1990 also served as whip. The exceptions were Rayburn, who was chairman of the Interstate and Foreign Commerce Committee when he was chosen majority leader in 1937; McCormack, who was chairman of the House Democratic Caucus; and Wright, who was a deputy whip and next in line to chair the Public Works Committee when he bid for, and won by a single vote, the floor leader position in 1976.

The duties of the majority and minority leaders are not spelled out in the standing rules of the House, nor is official provision made for them, except through periodic appropriations specifically made for their offices.

In practice, the majority leader's job has been to formulate the party's legislative program in cooperation with the Speaker and other party leaders, to steer the program through the House, to persuade committee chairmen to report bills deemed of importance to the party, and to arrange the House legislative schedule by securing agreement from key members. The majority leader is also the field general for his party on the floor, coordinating with the bill's floor manager and the whip and task force organizations, anticipating and solving problems before they develop.

Like the Speaker, the majority leader is in a position to do many favors for colleagues—scheduling floor action at a convenient time, speaking in behalf of a member's bill (or refraining from opposing it), meeting with a member's important constituents, or campaigning for a member in his home district. While such favors clearly help the leadership build coalitions and maintain party unity, they also seem to be expected by the rank and file.

The Minority Leader

Although individual members occasionally stepped forward to lead the loyal opposition against the majority position on specific bills or issues, the position of House minority leader first became identifiable in the 1880s. Since then the post has always been assumed by the minority party's candidate for the speakership. The titular head of the minority party, or "shadow Speaker" as he is sometimes called, is chosen by the party caucus.

The basic duties of the minority leader were described by Bertrand Snell, R-N.Y., who held the post from 1931 to 1939: "He is spokesman for his party and enunciates its policies. He is required to be alert and vigilant in defense of the minority's rights. It is his function and duty to criticize constructively the policies and program of the majority, and to this end employ parliamentary tactics and give close attention to all proposed legislation."[47] Snell might also have added that if the minority leader's party occupies the White House, he is likely to become the president's chief spokesman in the House.

House Republicans in 1989 chose a strident political activist, Rep. Newt Gingrich of Georgia, left, as minority whip. Gingrich poses here with Minority Leader Robert H. Michel of Illinois, center, and Republican Conference Chairman Jerry Lewis of California.

R. Michael Jenkins

Because the minority's role is to counter the legislative program of the majority, or advance the president's legislative agenda if he is of the same party, it rarely offers its own legislative program. One exception occurred in mid-1980 when the Republicans put together an alternative agenda, largely as a campaign platform for the November elections.

Robert Michel, who became the GOP minority leader in 1981, described his job as twofold: "To keep our people together, and to look for votes on the other side." [48] Michel's greatest success in this regard came in 1981, when Congress, aided by a Republican Senate and a popular president of the same party, passed the Reagan administration's unprecedented budget and tax cut package. Large-scale defections by conservative Democrats in the House made the Republican successes possible.

But such victories are rare for the minority. "One of the minority leader's greatest problems," wrote Ripley, "is the generally demoralizing condition of minority party status." [49] Minority members want the same things majority members do—information, legislative success, patronage, and the like. When they do not get them, the minority leader is often the target of their frustrations. Throughout his term as minority leader Michel was pushed by younger, more conservative, and more aggressive colleagues who urged him to turn the House floor into a theater for all-out partisan warfare. *(Box, p. 24)*

Michel did grow increasingly confrontational during Wright's tenure as Speaker, when he, along with most other House Republicans, believed the Democrats were using the rules to deny them their rights. And he made a Republican takeover of the House in the 1992 elections—the first to be held after the decennial redistricting—a top priority, working with various Republican groups in the House to develop Republican alternatives on issues such as child care, educa-

tion, and health policy. Although some judged him to be one of the most effective House leaders on either side of the aisle since Rayburn, many Republicans felt a need for the strident partisanship offered by Georgian Newt Gingrich and other members of his Conservative Opportunity Society. In 1989 Gingrich defeated Michel's friend and candidate Edward R. Madigan of Illinois, 87-85, to succeed Dick Cheney of Wyoming as minority whip.

"What that says to me," Michel told reporters immediately after Gingrich's election, "is that they want us to be more activated and more visible and more aggressive, and that we can't be content with business as usual." [50]

Party Whips

The term "whip" comes from British fox-hunting lore; the "whipper-in" was responsible for keeping the fox-hounds from leaving the pack. It was first used in the British Parliament in 1769 by Edmund Burke. Though neither party in the House of Representatives designated an official whip until 1897—Rep. James A. Tawney, Republican of Minnesota, was the first—influential members played that role from the outset working to forge consensus on important issues and for particular floor fights.

Unlike the British system, where political parties are well disciplined and a whip's major concern is good party attendance, whips in the U.S. House cajole votes as well as count noses, gather information as well as impart it. "We try to keep our people ... informed of the leadership's position on things—what they'd like, what we're seeking, what we're trying to do," a member of the Democratic whip organization said. "Not only on policy, but also on scheduling and programming.... We pick up static from our people and relay it to the leadership, so that they know what's

Partisan Tensions in the House . . .

Any institution that embraces members with competing ideals and philosophies is likely to break down in partisan bickering from time to time. The U.S. House of Representatives may be the premier example.

Partisanship in the House of Representatives reached new heights—some would say depths—during the 1980s. One factor that accounted for the increased stridency was divided government. Ronald Reagan, judged to be the most conservative president since the 1920s, held the White House from 1981 to 1989; Democrats retained control of the House, but for the first six years of Reagan's presidency, Republicans also controlled the Senate. That made Democratic leaders in the House solely responsible for the success or failure of the party's program in Congress. By the late 1980s Democrats had recaptured control of the Senate. But by then massive budget deficits exacerbated traditional Republican and Democratic arguments about spending priorities.

For their part House Speakers Thomas P. O'Neill, Jr., of Massachusetts, who retired from the House January 3, 1987, and Jim Wright of Texas, who resigned from the House in June 1989, were both highly partisan Democrats who did not feel comfortable working with Republicans on a regular basis. Republicans were outraged in the early 1980s when the Democrats under O'Neill stacked key committees to deny Republicans representation proportional to their numbers in the House. Democrats eventually agreed to increase the number of seats on most major committees. In 1985 a drawn-out fight over a contested election in Indiana's Eighth District further embittered Republicans, who walked out of the House chamber *en masse* after the Democratic candidate was seated on a party-line vote.

Republicans were even more incensed at what they considered to be Wright's heavy-handed partisanship. One of the most divisive incidents occurred October 29,

1987, when Wright forced passage of a deficit-cutting bill that called for taxes Republicans opposed. The Speaker held the vote open an extra ten minutes so a Texas ally could change his vote, making the result 206-205. Angry GOP House members booed Wright after the vote and accused him of stealing their victory.

In May 1988 the Republican minority orchestrated a two-hour series of floor speeches to complain to the House—and the public watching the proceedings on C-SPAN, the national public affairs cable network—that the Democrats were denying them a voice both in committee and on the House floor.

The Gingrich Factor

Much of the partisan tension was deliberately fomented by a group of Republicans led by Rep. Newt Gingrich of Georgia. Since he entered the House in 1979, Gingrich had argued that the badly outnumbered Republican House contingent should forget about compromising to improve Democratic legislation and instead use the chamber as a political forum to express opposition and build political support. To advance his strategy Gingrich and his supporters frequently criticized the Democrats during the "special order" period held after the close of regular business. Like regular business, these proceedings were televised to the nation (although the requirement that the camera remain on the speaker meant that viewers could not know the chamber was often nearly empty), and Gingrich was soon attracting regular attention not only from conservative viewers but also the national media.

In 1984 Gingrich endeared himself to the Republican Right when he humiliated Speaker O'Neill on the House floor. Addressing a nearly empty chamber during the special order period after the close of regular business one night in May, Gingrich denounced Majority Leader

---

going on, but we also pick up information from the leadership and convey it back. It's a two-way conduit." [51]

Specifically, whips of both parties help their floor leaders keep track of the whereabouts of party members and lobby them for their votes. Whips also serve as the party's acting floor leaders in the absence of the regular leaders. They handle the mechanics of polling members both on their views on issues and on the stands on specific floor votes, information that the majority leader uses to determine whether and when to bring a bill to the floor. Through weekly whip notices, whips inform members about upcoming floor action, including key amendments.

The whips are also responsible for ensuring that members are present for tight votes. Sometimes, whips and their assistants stand at the door of the House chamber, signaling the leadership's position on a vote by holding their thumbs up—or down. During recorded votes, a computer on the floor prints out how members have voted. If the vote is close, the whips can use that list as a guide to seek possible vote switches before the result of the vote is announced. Occasionally the whip organization goes to ex-

tremes. In 1984, for example, deputy whip Marty Russo, D-Ill., actually carried Daniel K. Akaka, D-Hawaii, onto the House floor in an effort to persuade him to change his vote.

House Republicans have always elected their whip. The Democratic whip was appointed by the majority leader in consultation with the Speaker until the 100th Congress, when the Democratic Caucus elected Tony Coelho of California. The change had been demanded by younger members who wanted a voice in putting one of their colleagues on the leadership ladder. In recent decades the whip position has frequently been a first step toward the speakership. Members also wanted the whip to act as a liaison between the leadership and the rank and file, and not simply as an enforcer and intelligence gatherer.

Democratic Whip Organization. In recent years the politics of inclusion and the need to build coalitions have induced both parties to expand and enhance their whip organizations. The more elaborate of the two, the Democratic organization, in 1990 had a chief deputy whip, fifteen deputy whips, three whip task force chairmen,

... Stridency Increased in the 1980s

Wright and nine other Democrats for writing a conciliatory letter to Nicaraguan leader Daniel Ortega, addressing him as "Dear Commandante" and calling for a settlement between political factions in that country. Gingrich said the letter was undermining U.S. foreign policy. O'Neill retaliated by ordering the television cameras to pan the chamber during special order speeches so that viewers would see that Gingrich and his supporters were addressing an empty chamber. That move all but guaranteed a confrontation.

A few days later, when Gingrich repeated his charges during regular debate, O'Neill took the floor himself to denounce the Georgian's tactics as "the lowest thing that I have seen in my thirty-two years in Congress." That remark, an obvious violation of House rules of decorum, brought a motion from GOP Whip Trent Lott, Miss., that O'Neill's words be "taken down," or stricken from the record. Presiding officer Joe Moakley, a Massachusetts Democrat with close ties to O'Neill, had no choice but to accept Lott's motion—the first time the words of a Speaker had been taken down since February 12, 1797, when Speaker Jonathan Dayton of New Jersey was called to order for using "improper language" during debate on the House floor.

Intraparty Tensions

Many observers of Capitol Hill predicted that George Bush's election to the White House and Wright's resignation from the House in the wake of a personal ethics scandal would reduce the partisan tensions. In his first months in office, Bush stressed repeatedly that he wanted to work with, not against, Congress. And Thomas S. Foley, D-Wash., the House majority leader who succeeded Wright as Speaker, was known to be a skilled negotiator and consensus builder.

But partisan tensions in the House grew even worse in 1990, complicated by intraparty arguments over whether party interests were better served in a divided government by bipartisan efforts to craft legislation or by a confrontational approach that drew clear partisan lines.

The split among Republicans over that question was never more evident than in the October 5 vote on a budget agreement drafted by a bipartisan summit group. Minority Leader Robert H. Michel, Ill., and Jerry Lewis, Calif., chairman of the House Republican Conference, were the only two GOP leaders to support the president and vote for the agreement. Angered by President Bush's decision to abandon his pledge not to raise taxes, Gingrich, who had been elected GOP whip in 1989, and the rest of the GOP leadership refused to support the budget agreement, denying Michel the whip apparatus the party normally uses to round up votes. Republicans voted against the agreement, 71-105.

Liberal Democrats in the House also grew impatient with low-risk, nonconfrontational strategies. "We've had this phony bipartisanship that said, 'Let's not fight because we don't have the votes,'" Rep. David R. Obey, D-Wis., said during the 1990 budget debate. "If you don't have the votes, at least let people know what you stand for." *

For all the heightened partisan rhetoric, it is important to remember that Congress passes most bills with little dissent and that Democrats and Republicans usually cooperate or compromise on most controversial measures, knowing that voter patience will erode if legislators appear unable to govern.

* Janet Hook, "Budget Ordeal Poses Question: Why Can't Congress Be Led?" *Congressional Quarterly Weekly Report*, Oct. 20, 1990, 3473.

sixty-three at-large whips, and eighteen assistant whips, each of whom represented and focused on a particular region of the country. Two out of every five Democrats were part of the whip apparatus.

With O'Neill's speakership, the Democrats also inaugurated another tactic, the task force, to elicit support for legislation and to give more members an opportunity to participate in the leadership process—and thus a stake in the leadership's success. Concerned that these groups might come to rival the whip organizations, Foley brought the task forces into his tent after he became whip in 1981.

By the late 1980s virtually every bill of significance was given a task force, made up of committee members and noncommittee members with an interest in the issue, before it emerged from committee. The task force's job was to round up support for the bill. Task force members discussed which arguments would work best with which members of Congress and who was best suited to push those points with individual members. Sometimes task forces reached out to unions, trade associations, and others who were lobbying on the issue. If the votes were not there, the

task force and key committee members, under the aegis of the leadership, might even tinker with the substance of the legislation to try to reach a compromise acceptable to a majority.

The tactic proved successful in getting legislation through the House and in involving more members, especially junior members, in the process. "It's helped the leadership to get to know the new members and the new members to get to know the leadership," one member told political scientist Barbara Sinclair. "And it's certainly helped the new members ... understand the need for leadership and followship. I think the guys who have served on task forces know a lot more about the need for a party structure with some loyalty than those who haven't." [52]

Republican Organization. In 1990 Republican Whip Gingrich divided whip responsibilities between two chief deputy whips. Steve Gunderson, Wis., oversaw strategy; as he put it, his "lead is on everything leading up to the floor, articulating the agenda, and creating momentum." [53] Robert S. Walker, Pa., was responsible for floor action. They were assisted by four deputy whips, two assistant deputies, four regional whips, and five strategy whips.

The Party Caucuses

The use of party caucuses—the organization of all members in each party in the House—has waxed and waned since the beginning of Congress. In the Jeffersonian period, the Democratic-Republicans, in conjunction with the president, used the caucus to formulate their party's legislative strategy. During Clay's term as Speaker, most important legislative decisions were still made in the Democratic-Republican caucus; less than two weeks after being seated in 1813, Federalist Daniel Webster concluded that "the time for us to be put on the stage and moved by the wires has not yet come," since "before anything is attempted to be done here, it must be arranged elsewhere." [54]

The nominees for president and vice president were chosen by congressional caucuses from 1800 to 1824. By the 1830s the importance of the caucuses had diminished, and except to nominate the party's candidate for Speaker at the beginning of each Congress, they met rarely during the next sixty years.

In the 1890s the caucus was revived as a forum for discussing legislative strategy. Speaker Reed used the Republican caucus to a limited extent to discuss policy questions. For the most part, though, the caucus under Reed functioned only to give the party's stamp of approval to decisions Reed had already made. In the early 1900s Speaker Cannon called caucus meetings occasionally but manipulated them much as Reed had. It was not until the revolt against Cannon and the return of control of the House to the Democrats that the caucus was restored to its earlier legislative significance.

The Democratic Caucus

In 1909 the Democrats adopted a party rule that the caucus, by a two-thirds majority, could bind its members on a specific vote. Throughout President Wilson's first term, the Democratic leadership used this rule and the caucus effectively, achieving remarkable party unity on a wide range of domestic legislation. But the party began to split over foreign policy issues, and the caucus fell into disuse in Wilson's second term. The binding caucus rule was used during Franklin D. Roosevelt's first term as well, but subsequently it was invoked only on procedural or party issues, such as voting for Speaker, and the rule was finally abolished in 1974.

In recent decades the Democratic Caucus has been revived. In the late 1960s younger House Democrats with relatively little seniority sought to revitalize the caucus as a means of countering the arbitrary authority exercised by committee chairmen and other senior members. The campaign, led by the House Democratic Study Group, began when Speaker McCormack established regular monthly caucus meetings, and it gained momentum in the early 1970s. The result was a basic transferral of power among House Democrats and eventually throughout the House.

The most important change modified the seniority system by making committee chairmen subject to secret-ballot election by the caucus. This modification was achieved in steps and took its final form—automatic secret votes on all chairmen—in December 1974. Early in 1975 the caucus rejected three chairmen, a clear signal that all chairmen in the future would be held accountable to their colleagues and could not expect to exercise the absolute powers they had held when the seniority system all but guaranteed them tenure as chairmen.

The Democratic Caucus instituted other changes that helped transform the House into a more open and accountable institution. It helped enact a House rule requiring committee bill-drafting sessions to be open to the public; Republicans also played an important role in that change. It limited House Democrats to one subcommittee chairmanship and guaranteed each party member a seat on a major committee. It also created a "bill of rights" for subcommittees that gave them considerable independence from committee chairmen. On purely party matters it transferred the authority to make committee assignments from the Democratic members of the Ways and Means Committee to a revamped Steering and Policy Committee and placed that committee firmly under the control of the leadership.

Although the Democratic Caucus focused primarily on procedural reforms during this period, it also gave some attention to substantive issues. In 1972, for example, it forced a House vote on a nonbinding, end-the-Vietnam-War resolution. In 1975 it went on record as opposing more military aid to Indochina, and it voted to order the Rules Committee to allow a floor vote on an amendment to end the oil depletion allowance.

These forays into substantive legislation plunged the caucus into new controversy, partly because it was seen as usurping the powers of the standing committees and undermining the committee system. At least that was the argument expressed by conservative Democratic opponents of the resolutions, which were drafted and backed mainly by the party's liberal bloc. The conservatives insisted that caucus meetings, which had been closed, be opened to the public. That killed the role the caucus played as a "family council," which greatly diminished its usefulness.

Occasionally the caucus still took a stand on a legislative matter. In 1978, for example, it voted 150-57 to approve a resolution urging Ways and Means to roll back a planned Social Security tax increase. President Carter and House leaders backed the increase, however, and thwarted the rollback attempt.

In the early 1980s, under the chairmanship of Gillis W. Long, D-La., the Democratic Caucus took on a new vitality. Under Long, the caucus held regularly scheduled, closed meetings, which once again made it easier to keep party disputes within the family. In addition, fifty caucus members could petition for a meeting, as occurred in September 1983 when members petitioned the caucus for a meeting to discuss the party position on keeping U.S. Marines in Lebanon for another eighteen months. Long also sent caucus members a questionnaire about budget priorities; more than 180 responses were received, resulting in two meetings to discuss the party's position. When Democrats held together on budget matters in 1983, many credited the caucus.

Long also set up a Committee on Party Effectiveness early in 1981 to reassess the party's direction after its election losses in 1980; members of the committee covered a spectrum of political opinion, including several rising stars such as Richard Gephardt, who succeeded Long as caucus chairman. The result was a new agenda for the party, entitled "Rebuilding the Road to Opportunity." In 1984, the Democratic presidential candidates appeared before the caucus.

The power of the caucus over its leaders was convincingly demonstrated in 1983, when Majority Leader Wright and Majority Whip Foley supported President Reagan's request for funds to deploy the MX missile. The vote left some colleagues asking why their leaders were helping to enact the Reagan defense program. Two months later, at the insistence of a freshman Democrat, the caucus met to discuss the issue. In subsequent votes, neither Wright nor Foley voted for the MX.

That sort of disciplinary action is unusual. More often the caucus is used to promote party unity, to develop a consensus on specific issues, and to give all House Democrats an opportunity to be heard. "The caucus is the place where a great deal of freewheeling debate over an issue takes place and where sometimes a consensus develops ...," a senior House Democrat explained. "Most of the discussions, although they have taken place at leadership meetings and at chairmen's meetings and in whips' meetings, have ended up in the broader forum of the caucus where every member of the Democratic party participates. You don't take a vote, but you try to develop a consensus and make concessions where they're necessary and develop the strongest possible position that can be supported by the maximum number of Democrats." [55]

The Republican Conference

The counterpart of the Democratic Caucus, the Republican Conference, is the umbrella organization for House Republicans. Like its Democratic counterpart, the conference sets party rules, builds party unity through retreats and other meetings of the rank and file, and helps to identify campaign issues. The conference also produces legislative status reports and research information on issues pending before the House.

The Republican Conference has rarely served as a policy-setting body, although in the 1965-69 period it was used occasionally to develop policy positions for consideration by the party's leadership. Although he did not try to make it an active arm of the leadership, Minority Leader Michel used the conference as a sounding board to determine the party's position on substantive matters and to communicate the viewpoint of House Republicans to the Republican administration.

The conference occasionally passes resolutions stating House Republican views on particular issues. In what was widely seen as a slap at Republican President Bush, the conference in 1990 approved a resolution opposing any new taxes; Bush had recently renounced his "no new taxes" campaign pledge in an effort to reach agreement with the Democrats on a budget deficit reduction measure.

Committee on Committees

After the House revolt against Cannon in 1910, the power to appoint members of standing committees was taken from the Speaker and vested in the party caucuses. In 1911 the Democratic Caucus delegated the authority to choose the party's committee members to a special Committee on Committees, which was composed of all Democrats on the Ways and Means Committee.

The reforms of the 1970s also affected the committee assignment process. In 1973 the Democratic Caucus expanded the Committee on Committees to include the Speaker, who served as chairman, the majority leader, and

the caucus chairman. In December 1974 the caucus transferred the assignment power to the Steering and Policy Committee, which is composed of the Democratic leaders and their nominees and regionally elected members. The Steering and Policy Committee's recommendations are subject to ratification by the caucus, as were those of Ways and Means, but ratification, particularly of committee chairmen, is no longer perfunctory.

In 1917 the Republican Conference also established a Committee on Committees, which traditionally is chaired by the GOP House leader. Committee assignments, except for the top-ranking members, are not subject to approval by the conference. And in 1989 Republicans gave their minority leader the authority to appoint the GOP members of the Rules Committee.

Speakers often have exercised great influence on committee assignments, even when they were not on the panel making the choices. In the late 1920s, for example, Speaker Longworth had four uncooperative members of the Rules Committee replaced with his own choices. In the 1940s and 1950s Speaker Rayburn intervened frequently to influence the makeup of the Ways and Means Committee, which he insisted be stacked with members opposed to reductions in the oil and gas depletion allowance. Rayburn was from Texas, one of the largest oil-producing states.

Though the Democrats have given their leadership significant powers to fill Democratic committee slots, the leadership is still guided by a need to ensure that members as much as possible receive the assignments they request and that regions and viewpoints are fairly represented. Party loyalty is also a factor, particularly for appointments to the Ways and Means, Rules, Appropriations, and Budget committees.

Steering and Policy Committees

During the twentieth century both parties established groups called "steering committees" to assist the leadership with legislative scheduling and party strategy. The Republican Steering Committee, established in 1919, dominated the business of the House until 1925, when power again shifted to the Speaker. Speaker Longworth largely ignored the Steering Committee. In 1949 the committee was expanded and renamed the Policy Committee. The Policy Committee was considered the chief advisory board for the minority leader from 1959 to 1965, when it was replaced in the role by the GOP Conference. In its current role, the committee develops information on and helps formulate strategy for legislation once it leaves committee. It also helps develop the legislative agenda for House Republicans.

Since 1965 House Republicans have also had a Research Committee, which provides the leadership and the conference with information and recommendations on specific policy issues likely to come before Congress. All Republicans are members of this committee, which is directed by a twenty-two member executive committee that includes the leadership. The committee is broken down further into more than three dozen task forces on a wide range of issues from arms control and terrorism to child care, education, and health.

Democrats established a Steering Committee in 1933, abandoned it in 1956, and reconstituted it in 1962. Its duties and role in the party structure were vague. In 1973 the Democratic Caucus voted to create a new Steering and

Policy Committee to give coherence and direction to the party's legislative strategy. In 1974 the caucus gave the committee authority to make Democratic assignments.

In 1990 the thirty-one member committee consisted of eleven members from the leadership, including the Speaker, who chaired the committee, eight members appointed by the Speaker, and twelve regional members elected by the caucus. The Steering Committee's staff essentially served the needs of the Speaker, keeping track of bills throughout the legislative process, to alert the leadership to any potential problems.

In addition to making committee assignments, the committee acts as an executive committee for the full Democratic Caucus and serves as a forum for the exchange of information. Committee chairmen brief the Steering Committee on important legislation, which not only informs the leadership, but gives the chairmen an idea of how the membership is likely to react to the pending legislation. The committee has occasionally endorsed legislation. Democrats also have a Personnel Committee that selects, appoints, and supervises Democratic patronage appointments.

Three informal party committees also provide research and legislative support for members. The Democratic Study Group is the primary source of research on legislative issues for the Democrats. On the Republican side, the House Republican Study Committee provides similar support to conservative House Republicans, while the Wednesday Group, a by-invitation-only organization, gives GOP moderates in the House a forum to consider legislative and public policy options.

Leadership in the Senate: "We Know No Masters"

Sen. Daniel Webster in 1830 described the upper chamber as a "Senate of equals, of men of individual honor and personal character, and of absolute independence. We know no masters, we acknowledge no dictators...." [56] At the time and for several decades thereafter, the Senate had no structured leadership apparatus. Not until the early twentieth century did either party formally designate a leader to oversee and guide its interests in the Senate. Now both parties name a leader and an assistant leader and have a number of party committees to help them formulate policy and strategy and win reelection.

But Webster's words still hold true; the Senate is essentially a collection of individuals, each of whom is a leader in his own sphere. The independence of the individual senator is further ensured by Senate rules, which protect the rights of the minority against the will of the majority. As Ripley has observed, Senate floor leaders are not "automatically invested with a specific quota of power; they still must create much of their own." [57] Effective leadership in the Senate, even more than in the House, thus depends on the leaders' personal and negotiating skills.

Evolution of Senate Leadership

As with the House, the Constitution did not offer much direction about Senate leadership. Its two references to leadership posts and responsibilities in the Senate (Article I, section 3) stipulate that the vice president shall be president of the Senate and that the Senate shall choose a president pro tempore to preside in the vice president's absence. Neither of these offices has ever been a very effective leadership position. *(Box, p. 29)*

Thus legislative leadership was left to individual senators. Here, as in the House, Alexander Hamilton acted much like a stage manager, controlling floor action through his many friends in the chamber. Jefferson and his Treasury Secretary Albert Gallatin exercised as much control over the Senate as they did over the House. Jefferson, wrote Thomas Pickering of Massachusetts, tries "to screen himself from all responsibility by calling upon Congress for advice and direction.... Yet with affected modesty and deference he secretly dictates every measure which is seriously proposed." [58]

The first significant move toward party organization did not occur until 1846, when the parties began to nominate members of the standing committees. Until 1823 the Senate had chosen committee members by ballot. That year the Senate turned over the appointment process to the presiding officer. Initially this officer was the president pro tempore, but in 1825-27, Vice President John C. Calhoun assumed the power. Hostile to the administration of John Quincy Adams, he used the power to place supporters of Andrew Jackson in key positions. In 1828 the Senate amended its rules to return the appointment power to the president pro tem, who, of course, was selected by the Senate itself. In 1833 the Senate reverted to selection by ballot.

By this time the seniority system had begun to develop, and chairmanships of Senate committees rotated less than they had in the past. Parties began to control assignments, committees began to divide along ideological lines, and minority reports began to appear. By 1846 the routine was formalized. When the second session of the 29th Congress met in December, the Senate began balloting for committee chairmen. Midway through the process the balloting rule was suspended, and on a single ballot the Senate accepted the list of committee assignments that had already been agreed upon by the majority and minority. For the most part, that routine has been followed since.

Immediately before and during the Civil War, party authority extended to substantive as well as organizational matters. In 1858, for example, the Democratic Caucus removed Stephen A. Douglas as chairman of the Committee on Territories, despite his seniority, because he had refused to go along with President James Buchanan and the southern wing of the party on the question of allowing slavery in the territories.

With the end of the Civil War, however, party influence on substantive matters declined. By the time Ulysses S. Grant entered the White House in 1869, political parties required unity only on organizational matters. Disputes over committee assignments were settled in the party caucuses, and pressing issues were discussed there, but there was no way to enforce caucus decisions against senators who refused to be bound by a vote of the majority of their caucus. "I am a senator of the United States," Charles Sumner, R-Mass., once declared. "My obligations as a senator were above any vote in a caucus." [59]

Beginning in the 1870s, Republicans sought to strengthen party control of the Senate by appointing a caucus chairman, who was considered to be the party's floor leader, and setting up a Committee on Committees to recommend committee assignments to the caucus and then

The Senate's Presiding Officers

The only two Senate leaders mentioned by the Constitution have little effective leadership power. Article I, Section 3 provides that the vice president "shall be President of the Senate, but shall have no vote, unless they be equally divided." It also provides that the "Senate shall choose ... a President pro tempore, in the absence of the Vice President, or when he shall exercise the office of President of the United States."

Duties of the Presiding Officer

As presiding officer, the vice president and the president pro tem may recognize members desiring to speak, introduce bills, or offer amendments and motions to bills being debated; decide points of order, subject to appeal to the full Senate; appoint senators to House-Senate conference committees (although it is customary for the presiding officer to take the recommendations of the floor manager of the bill in question); enforce decorum; administer oaths; and appoint members to special committees. The president pro tem may appoint a substitute to replace him in the chair; the vice president may not. As a senator, the president pro tem may vote on all matters; the vice president may vote only to break a tie, as stipulated by the Constitution. Since World War II, vice presidents have cast only 30 votes.

The Vice President as Presiding Officer

It is little wonder that the Senate has not placed any real power with the vice president, who is not chosen by the Senate and may not be sympathetic with the aims of its majority. Precedent was established by John Adams, who, although in agreement with the majority of the Senate during his term as vice president, perceived his role simply as that of presiding officer and made little effort to guide Senate action. His successor, Thomas Jefferson, could not have steered the Federalist-controlled Senate even if he had wanted to.

A few vice presidents have attempted to use their position as presiding officer to achieve a partisan purpose, with varying degrees of success. John C. Calhoun, vice president to John Quincy Adams, was hostile to the Adams administration. Taking advantage of an 1823 rules change giving the presiding officer the right to appoint committee members, Calhoun placed supporters of Andrew Jackson on key committees. But he refused to use the authority exercised by earlier vice presidents to call senators to order for words used in debate.

Nelson A. Rockefeller, vice president to Gerald R. Ford, once used his authority to refuse to recognize a senator who wanted to mount a filibuster against a Ford administration bill. Senators from both parties were incensed at Rockefeller's action and made it very clear that the president's program would suffer if Rockefeller did not desist immediately.

Most vice presidents preside only upon ceremonial occasions or when a close vote on a bill or amendment of interest to the administration is likely to occur. But as president of the Senate, the vice president has an entry to lobby on behalf of the president's program. Walter F. Mondale, D-Minn., who left his Senate seat to become Jimmy Carter's vice president, proved to be an effective spokesman for the White House on numerous occasions.

The President Pro Tempore

The first president pro tempore, John Langdon of New Hampshire, was elected on April 6, 1789, before John Adams appeared in the Senate to assume his duties as presiding officer. When the first vice president took his seat on April 21, Langdon's service as president pro tem ended.

For the next one hundred years, the Senate acted on the theory that a president pro tempore could be elected only in the vice president's absence and that his term expired when the vice president returned. (Unlike modern practice, the vice president frequently presided over the Senate in the nineteenth century.) By 1890 the Senate had elected presidents pro tempore on 153 occasions. In the 42nd Congress alone (1871-73), ten such elections, all of the same senator, were held.

In 1890 the Senate gave the president pro tem tenure of a sort by adopting a resolution stating that "... it is competent for the Senate to elect a president pro tempore, who shall hold the office during the pleasure of the Senate and until another is elected, and shall execute the duties thereof during all future absences of the vice president" until the Senate otherwise orders. That practice was still in use in 1991.

The president pro tem is third in line, behind the vice president and the Speaker of the House of Representatives, to succeed to the presidency. Like the Speaker, he is a member of the majority party, and election is usually by a straight party-line vote. By custom the most senior member of the majority party in terms of Senate service is elected president pro tem. Only one of those elected since 1945 did not follow this pattern: Arthur H. Vandenberg, R-Mich., was the second-ranking Republican when elected in 1947. (Strom Thurmond, R-S.C., was considered the most senior Republican when he was elected president pro tem in 1981 even though John Tower of Texas had served longer as a Republican. Thurmond began his Senate service in 1954 as a Democrat, becoming a Republican in 1964; the Republican Conference agreed to base his seniority on the date he entered the Senate, not the date he switched parties.)

Before 1945 there were some notable exceptions to the custom. George H. Moses, R-N.H., ranked only 15th in party seniority when he was elected president pro tem in 1925, and Willard Saulsbury, D-Del., was still in his first term when elected to the post in 1916.

Few presidents pro tem in the twentieth century have had much influence on the Senate. One who did was Vandenberg, who was also chairman of the Foreign Relations Committee. Vandenberg "no doubt exerted as much influence in what was done and not done as the Speaker of the House," Floyd M. Riddick wrote in 1949.

Leadership Firsts

From the very first, when Oliver Ellsworth of Connecticut exercised "more practical leadership in the day-to-day activities" of the Senate, the upper chamber has had unofficial leaders. But congressional scholars disagree as to who were the first official Senate floor leaders.

Some scholars, among them Randall B. Ripley, hold that the position of floor leader emerged around 1911. The chairmen of the Democratic Caucus—Thomas S. Martin of Virginia from 1911 to 1913 and John W. Kern of Illinois from 1913 to 1917—were clearly the party's leaders in the Senate, although it is unclear that the term "floor leader" was formally applied to either man.

In a pamphlet on the origins of Senate leadership in 1988, Senate parliamentarian emeritus Floyd M. Riddick wrote that neither party's caucus minutes used the term "leader" until 1920, when the Democratic minutes referred to Oscar W. Underwood, D-Ala., as "minority leader." (Underwood had also served two terms as majority leader in the House before being elected to the Senate.) According to Republican Caucus minutes, the first GOP Senate floor leader was Charles Curtis of Kansas (1924).

Source: Walter J. Oleszek, "John Worth Kern," in *First Among Equals,* ed. Richard A. Baker and Roger H. Davidson (Washington, D.C.: CQ Press, forthcoming).

1870s the Republicans had appointed a Steering Committee to help schedule legislative business. Unlike previous caucus chairmen, Allison assumed the chair of this committee and filled it with his allies. For the first time a party organization arranged the order of business in minute detail and managed proceedings on the Senate floor.

Allison also controlled the Committee on Committees. By this time committee chairmanships were filled through seniority, and Allison and Aldrich made no attempt to overturn this practice (to which they owed their own committee chairmanships, Allison of Appropriations, Aldrich of Finance). But seniority did not apply to filling committee vacancies, and here the two found an opportunity to reward their supporters and punish their opponents. "Realizing the potentialities for control in the chamber," wrote historian David J. Rothman, Allison and Aldrich "entrenched and tightened personal leadership and party discipline. Their example would not always be emulated.... Nevertheless, they institutionalized, once and for all, the prerogatives of power. Would-be successors or Senate rivals would now be forced to capture and effectively utilize the party post." [61]

Like Speaker Cannon, who dominated the House for much of the same period, Allison and Aldrich were largely successful in imposing their own conservative political views upon the chamber. Defeats were rare until President Theodore Roosevelt was able to push a part of his legislative program through Congress. The group retained much of its power even after Allison's death in 1908. Though Allison had held the formal positions of power, Aldrich exercised power through the sheer force of his personality; he was considered by many to be the most powerful man in the Senate. But as the number of Republican insurgents in the Senate increased, the once all-powerful group began to weaken, and it quickly disintegrated after Aldrich retired in 1911.

Emergence of Democratic Leaders

A centralized Democratic organization in the Senate developed in the same period. Under the leadership of Arthur P. Gorman of Maryland, who served as chairman of the Democratic Caucus from 1889 to 1899, the Democratic power structure was very similar to that put together by Allison and Aldrich. Gorman consolidated his power by assuming all of the party's top leadership posts himself, including floor leader and the chairmanship of both the Steering Committee and the Committee on Committees. He further solidified his control by appointing his political allies to positions of influence.

Historian Rothman has concluded that the Democratic party structure under Gorman may have been more conducive than the Republican structure to the emergence of an effective and energetic leadership. Rothman notes that Gorman was elected chairman of the caucus not on the basis of seniority, but because of his standing among his colleagues. And Gorman eventually came to appoint the same group of men to the Steering Committee and the Committee on Committees, concentrating power over the party organization in a relatively small number of Democrats. For all but two of his ten years as caucus chairman, however, Senate Democrats were in the minority, and they were often badly divided on substantive issues. As a result Gorman never attained the same degree of power and authority as the Allison-Aldrich team.

to the full Senate. But the power of the caucus chairman, then Henry Anthony, R-R.I., was overshadowed by a Republican faction led by Roscoe Conkling of New York, that held sway for roughly ten years. Though the faction generally controlled the Committee on Committees, it never controlled the Senate's proceedings. Eventually in the early 1880s, it dissolved as a consequence of a series of unsuccessful feuds with Republican presidents over patronage in New York state.

Emergence of Republican Leaders

The emergence of another Republican faction in the 1890s led to establishment of a permanent leadership organization in the Senate. The leader of this faction was Nelson W. Aldrich of Rhode Island, who worked in close alliance with William B. Allison of Iowa, Orville H. Platt of Connecticut, and John C. Spooner of Wisconsin. Aldrich had, in the words of one historian, "made himself indispensable to the party organization [in the Senate], rising step by step as the elders passed out, until in the end he made himself the dictator of the cabal which for a time was the master of the government." [60] Already an influence in the Senate, this group took complete control after Allison, as the member with the longest period of Senate service, was elected chairman of the Republican Caucus in March 1897.

Previous caucus chairmen had not seen the office as a vehicle for consolidating party authority, an oversight that Allison and Aldrich were quick to correct. Since the mid-

Early Effective Leaders

Few of the Senate leaders in the twentieth century were particularly effective. One of the stronger leaders was Democrat John W. Kern of Indiana, whose election as caucus chairman in 1913, after only two years in the Senate, was engineered by progressive Democrats after they first deposed conservative Thomas S. Martin of Virginia. The Democratic Steering Committee, appointed by Kern and dominated by the progressives, assigned members sympathetic to President Wilson's programs to key committees. The Steering Committee also recommended, and the caucus adopted, rules that permitted a majority of committee members to call meetings, elect subcommittees, and appoint conferees. Thus party authority was augmented, and the power of committee chairmen curbed, in a movement that somewhat paralleled the rise of the caucus in the House.

Kern worked hard to push Wilson's progressive program through the Senate, achieving passage of a steep reduction in import duties and imposition of the first income tax under the Sixteenth Amendment, establishment of the Federal Reserve and the Federal Trade Commission, and enactment of antitrust laws, among others. Kern served as majority leader for only four years (he was defeated for reelection to the Senate in 1916). Yet until the 1950s few other floor leaders of either party attained the effectiveness he had achieved.

Massachusetts Republican Henry Cabot Lodge, who served as majority leader from 1919 to 1924, managed twice (in 1919 and 1920) to mobilize the Senate to oppose the Treaty of Versailles, which embodied the Covenant of the League of Nations and which Wilson strongly backed. But on other matters, Lodge was not a particularly effective leader, nor were the other Republicans who served in the 1920s.

President Franklin D. Roosevelt was fortunate in hav-

ing Joseph T. Robinson of Arkansas as the Senate majority leader from 1933 to 1937. Robinson revived the Democratic Caucus, and won agreement from Senate Democrats to make caucus decisions on administration bills binding by majority vote. There is no evidence that Robinson ever made use of the binding rule, but nonbinding caucuses were frequently held to mobilize support. In his four years as majority leader, Robinson pushed through the Senate most of the president's controversial New Deal legislative program, including measures he personally opposed.

Alben W. Barkley of Kentucky, who was elected majority leader after Robinson died of a heart attack in 1937, was also influential with his colleagues, but, like a growing number of Senate Democrats, he did not always support Roosevelt on domestic issues. In 1944 Barkley resigned his leadership post when FDR vetoed a revenue bill. He was promptly reelected by the Democrats, and the bill was passed over the president's veto.

The Johnson Years

In the decades immediately after World War II two Republicans were widely acclaimed as effective Senate leaders. "Mr. Republican," Robert A. Taft of Ohio was the majority leader for only a few months before he died in 1953, but he had been the de facto Republican power in the Senate since the early 1940s, just as Richard B. Russell, Ga., was the real leader of the Senate Democrats. Everett McKinley Dirksen of Illinois, known as the "wizard of ooze" for his florid style, was one of the more colorful personalities to grace the modern Senate. A conservative, he served as minority leader from 1959 until his death in 1969.

Taft and Dirksen employed two different styles—Taft won unity through his intellectual command of the issues; Dirksen won it through negotiation and compromise. Both

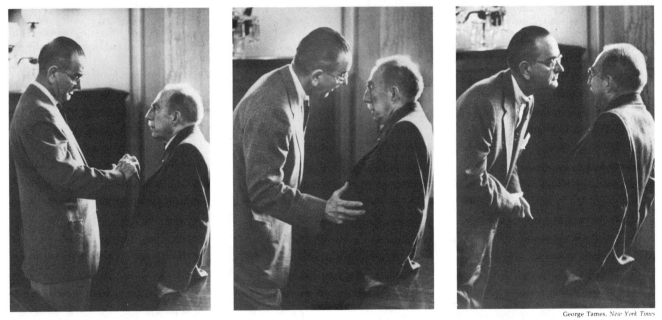

George Tames, *New York Times*

As Senate majority leader, Lyndon B. Johnson had an extraordinary ability to persuade his colleagues in one-on-one encounters. Here he gives "The Treatment" to Sen. Theodore Francis Green of Rhode Island.

men centralized the Republican leadership apparatus, controlling the formulation of Republican policy in the Senate and taking an active part in scheduling and setting floor strategy.

Taft and Dirksen may have had great influence among their Republican colleagues, but their leadership talents were eclipsed by those of Lyndon Baines Johnson. Johnson, wrote political scientist John G. Stewart, "set for himself no less an objective than *running* the Senate, in fact as well as in theory. . . ." [62] Elected minority leader by the Democrats in 1953 after only four years in the Senate, Johnson became majority leader when the Democrats regained control of the Senate after the 1954 elections and served in that position until his resignation to become John F. Kennedy's vice president in 1961.

As a leader Johnson quickly became famous—some would say notorious—for his power of persuasion and his manipulative skills. Johnson was adroit at doing favors for and extending courtesies to his colleagues, their families, and staffs, at maneuvering his supporters onto desired committees and keeping his opponents off. He revitalized the Senate Democratic Policy Committee and modified the seniority system to ensure freshman Democrats at least one major committee assignment, a practice the Republicans also eventually adopted. On the floor he exploited to the fullest the majority leader's right of first recognition by the chair to control what was debated and under what terms. He was the first majority leader to make extensive use of unanimous consent agreements to control debate on legislation. He also used night sessions to wear down senators who might, if fresher, choose to engage in extensive floor debate. Perhaps most important, Johnson kept himself informed about the views and positions of his Senate colleagues through an active intelligence operation headed by Robert G. "Bobby" Baker, secretary to the Senate Democrats.

Johnson, whose entire tenure as both minority and majority leader was spent with Republican President Dwight D. Eisenhower in the White House, was also a master of compromise. He made sure to have allies among conservative southern Democrats and Republicans as well as among northern liberals. Like his mentor, House Speaker Sam Rayburn, Johnson worked to pass those elements of Eisenhower's legislative program that did not challenge basic tenets of Roosevelt's New Deal or Harry S. Truman's Fair Deal. As a result Johnson presided over some of the most productive years in Senate history.

The future president was renowned for what came to be known as the "Johnson Treatment," a tactic he carried with him into the White House. Rowland Evans and Robert Novak gave a vivid description in their book, *Lyndon B. Johnson: The Exercise of Power:*

> The Treatment could last ten minutes or four hours. It came, enveloping its target, at the LBJ Ranch swimming pool, in one of LBJ's offices, in the Senate cloakroom, on the floor of the Senate itself—wherever Johnson might find a fellow senator within his reach. Its tone could be supplication, accusation, cajolery, exuberance, scorn, tears, complaint, the hint of threat. It was all of these together. It ran the gamut of human emotions. Its velocity was breathtaking, and it was all in one direction. Interjections from the target were rare. Johnson anticipated them before they could be spoken. He moved in close, his face a scant millimeter from his target . . . his eyes widening and narrowing, his eyebrows rising and falling. From his pockets poured clippings, memos, statistics. Mimicry, humor, and the genius of analogy made

The Treatment an almost hypnotic experience and rendered the target stunned and helpless.[63]

Johnson's effectiveness lost some of its edge after the 1958 elections added substantially to the Democrats' majority in the Senate. Members began to lose patience with Johnson's intensity; as one observer said, "After eight years of Lyndon Johnson, a lot of senators were just worn out." [64] An influx of liberal Democrats rejected the long-standing notion that junior senators were to be seen and not heard, and they began to chafe under Johnson's centralized leadership. In response Johnson stepped up the number of caucus meetings and named some freshmen to the Policy Committee. But calls from younger liberal members for greater inclusion in party matters continued to build.

By all accounts, Johnson was the most effective leader the Senate had ever seen, if not always the most liked. ("I know he comes off with high marks for getting things done, but he was repugnant to me," one senator recalled. "When I dealt with him I always had the feeling that I was standing on a trap door that was waiting to be sprung." [65]) Like the strong leaders before him, he derived his power primarily from his own force of personality, aided by his skill at finding out what his colleagues needed and wanted. As one observer put it, Johnson "worked at being better informed than anyone else, and that information then made him better equipped than anyone else to broker many agreements." [66]

Although he made innovative use of a number of institutional tools, such as unanimous consent, Johnson left the structure of the Senate itself largely untouched. When he left, Evans and Novak wrote, it was as though the leadership system he had constructed had never existed.

The Age of Collegiality

Meanwhile other factors were changing the Senate substantially. Between the 1950s and the mid-1970s, southern domination and the seniority system gave way to a more decentralized, more democratic institution, in which junior members played a greater role. Party leaders on both sides of the aisle eschewed the arm-twisting tactics that Johnson used so effectively and engaged in a more collegial style of leadership, dependent for its success not on the leader's ability to bend the Senate to his will but on his ability to meet the expectations of his colleagues and to facilitate the conduct of Senate business.

Democrats: Johnson's Successors

Johnson's successor, Mike Mansfield, D-Mont., could not have provided a greater contrast in leadership styles. Known as the "gentle persuader," Mansfield, who served longer than any other majority leader in Senate history (1961-77), was a permissive, at times even passive, leader. "I rarely asked for votes on specific legislation," Mansfield told political scientist Robert L. Peabody in 1972. "I assumed that these people are mature, that they have been sent back here by their constituents to exercise their own judgment. I will say that if on an issue they are doubtful I would hope that they will give the administration, if it's a Democratic administration, the benefit of the doubt. Or if it's a party matter, that they will give the party the benefit of the doubt. But I don't believe in being pressured myself and I don't pressure other senators. I treat them as I would like to be treated myself." [67]

Though Mansfield was criticized for not being sufficiently partisan and for sometimes failing to provide direction, he was working with a larger, more liberal, and less cohesive group of Senate Democrats than Johnson had led. As Davidson noted, "Most senators flourished under Mansfield's regime, for its very looseness gave them the leeway they needed to pursue their increasingly diverse legislative and career goals." [68]

When Mansfield retired from the Senate at the end of 1976, Democrats chose Robert Byrd of West Virginia as his successor. While other senators built their careers on national issues and oratorical flair, Byrd was the quintessential insider, working quietly and diligently to build support through a combination of service to his colleagues and knowledge of Senate rules and procedures, skills he honed to near perfection during his six years as Democratic whip. As majority leader he so disadvantaged his opponents through the artful use of his parliamentary talents that the Republicans hired a parliamentarian Byrd had fired to improve their own procedural strategies.

A more activist leader than Mansfield, Byrd emphasized the need for strong party loyalty and said he wanted to bring about a resurgence of party spirit. He did not see his role as forcing an unpopular measure on his colleagues, who probably would not have accepted such a role in any event, but as trying to find consensus. Byrd tended to go to his colleagues with only the hint of an objective. If a consensus could be found that would attract the necessary number of votes, he would take the bill under his wing. "I talk to senators. I have meetings with senators, I try to stimulate a consensus for a party position on issues where one is necessary," he explained. "By getting a consensus first, senators are more likely to support the leadership."

Byrd had an uneasy relationship with President Carter, who came to the White House in 1977, the year Byrd became majority leader. Byrd seemed to regard Carter as an amateur with little aptitude for the exercise of power. Nonetheless, he repeatedly saved the Democratic administration in difficult legislative situations. Byrd played an indispensable role in the passage of Carter's energy package and in the extension of the deadline for ratification of the Equal Rights Amendment, among other matters. Perhaps his most dramatic rescue operation came in 1978, when he amassed enough votes to ratify the Panama Canal treaties through nonstop negotiation with wavering senators, personal diplomacy with Panamanian officials, and last-minute language changes.

Byrd also took steps to help the Senate conduct its business more smoothly, perfecting the track system that allowed controversial measures to be dealt with while controversial legislation was being debated, and instituting periodic scheduled recesses, known as "nonlegislative work periods." Along the way he found time to write and deliver a series of Senate speeches—later published as a book—chronicling the history of the Senate from 1789 to 1989.

Despite his obvious love and respect for the Senate, Byrd was a private man, withdrawn from his colleagues; a former aide once noted that "Byrd was most comfortable in a room by himself." [69] His inability to develop a personal rapport with fellow senators combined with his emphasis on Senate procedures and prerogatives meant that though he was respected, Byrd was regarded by some as more of a technician than a leader. Rumblings of dissatisfaction grew louder after the 1980 elections, when Republicans took control of the Senate and Byrd was relegated to what for

him was the uncomfortable role of minority leader.

Byrd worked hard to reunite the party, scheduling weekly luncheon meetings of the Democratic Caucus, which had rarely met during the Carter years, and holding a series of weekend retreats in West Virginia where Democratic senators could work through many of their disagreements. He also set up several task forces to propose Democratic alternatives to President Reagan's legislative proposals.

But perceptions lingered that the West Virginian was too stilted and old-fashioned to be the Senate Democrats' national spokesman in the age of television. After the 1984 elections Lawton Chiles, Fla., challenged Byrd unsuccessfully for the leadership post. J. Bennett Johnston, La., spent much of 1986 preparing to challenge Byrd, but when the Democrats regained control of the Senate by a much wider margin than had been expected, he quietly dropped his plans.

In his second tour as majority leader Byrd played the partisan spokesman that his party seemed to want, rallying the Democrats behind an ambitious legislative agenda meant to show that the Democrats could govern. But criticisms of his leadership style and his media image continued, and in the spring of 1988 Byrd announced that he would retire from the leadership post at the end of the year to take up the chairmanship of the Senate Appropriations Committee and to become president pro tempore, where he was expected to be more active than previous holders of that position.

The winner in a three-way race to succeed Byrd was George J. Mitchell of Maine, a former judge. Mitchell was appointed to the Senate to fill a vacancy in 1980 and quickly caught the notice of his colleagues with his keen memory for detail and his command of facts, particularly on environmental issues. He further impressed his fellow senators with his political skills when he came from thirty-six points behind to win election to a full term in 1982 with

R. Michael Jenkins

Congressional leaders meet frequently with the president. President Jimmy Carter hosted this leadership breakfast at the White House in 1978.

61 percent of the vote.

Chosen to chair the Democratic Senatorial Campaign Committee for the critical 1986 elections, Mitchell was instrumental in helping the party regain control of the Senate with a wider-than-expected margin. As a reward he was made deputy president pro tempore, a post created for Hubert H. Humphrey, D-Minn., in 1977 and not occupied since. Appointed in 1986 to the joint committee investigating the Iran-contra scandal, Mitchell proved himself to be an able performer before national television cameras, a factor considered crucial to his election as majority leader over Johnston and Daniel K. Inouye of Hawaii.

In his first year in the position, Mitchell won high marks for his legislative savvy and administration of the Senate. Toward the end of the session, he managed to kill a capital gains tax cut sought by the Bush administration, which had passed the House when nearly a quarter of the Democrats there defected from the party position to support it. Early in 1990 he demonstrated the effectiveness of negotiation and persistence, working out a comprehensive compromise with the White House on a clean air bill when it became clear that the committee version could not overcome a filibuster and then fighting to protect the compromise from major amendment. Mitchell attributed his victory on the floor to direct, personal, face-to-face talks with his colleagues, urging them to stick with the compromise or see the entire bill collapse under the weight of controversial amendments.

Republicans: Changing Styles

Republican leadership styles in the age of collegiality paralleled those of the Democrats. Hugh Scott of Pennsylvania, who was narrowly elected to succeed Dirksen in 1969, was less assertive but perhaps even more flexible than Dirksen. His leadership of compromise and accommodation was very much like Mansfield's, but Scott was considered a rather ineffective leader. His moderate-to-liberal politics sometimes made it difficult for him to serve as a spokesman for the Nixon and Ford administrations, and his support, first of U.S. action in Vietnam long after many of his colleagues and constituents had turned against it, and then of Nixon well into the Watergate crisis, further undermined his standing.

Scott, who retired at the end of 1976, was succeeded by Dirksen's son-in-law, Howard H. Baker, Jr., of Tennessee. Baker had sought the post twice before, running unsuccessfully against Scott in 1969 and 1971. In 1977 his colleagues, apparently convinced that he would be a more articulate spokesman for the party, elected Baker minority leader over minority whip Robert P. Griffin of Michigan by a single vote. When the Republicans took over the Senate in 1980, Baker was made majority leader with no opposition.

A relaxed manner and close friendships with many of his Republican colleagues were Baker's principal assets. He was open and accessible to GOP senators of every ideology and was committed to protecting their rights. As majority leader, Baker was able to hold the disparate group of Republicans together on most issues during Reagan's first year in office. But when the economy faltered in late 1981, old divisions between moderate and conservative Republicans reopened, and unity became more difficult to achieve.

Baker's job was increasingly frustrated by the procedural chaos that gripped the Senate. His penchant for accommodation created a situation in which nearly every senator expected the schedule to conform to his or her personal needs. Floor action was delayed by senators who asked for "holds" on legislation—guarantees that a particular matter would not be taken up until the senator was present to protect his or her interests. Baker eventually announced that he would no longer consider holds sacrosanct, nor would he stack votes for the convenience of members who wanted more time to return to their home states. But there was little Baker could do to prevent individual members from tying up the Senate with filibusters and other delaying tactics.

In January 1983 Baker announced that he would retire from the Senate after the 1984 elections. To succeed him as majority leader, Republicans elected Bob Dole of Kansas over four other candidates. After four years of Baker's easygoing stewardship, Republican senators opted for a leader who they thought would restore some discipline and sense of purpose to a chamber increasingly bogged down in procedural chaos.

In addition to his image as a decisive leader, Dole was known as a superb negotiator with an ability to find compromises where others had failed. "You don't try to cram things down people's throats," he once said. "You try to work it out." Many of his colleagues, especially those up for reelection in 1986, thought he would also be willing to stand up to the Reagan White House when needed to protect their political interests.

With a thin 53-47 Republican majority, Dole produced significant victories, helping to pass tax revision, a new immigration law, a new farm bill, and aid to the Nicaraguan contras. Dole did restore a modicum of discipline to the Senate, but some of his methods—lengthy sessions and complicated parliamentary tactics intended to disarm obstructionists—were not popular with his colleagues and in some instances had only minimal effect. Dole was majority leader for only two years before being relegated to minority leader status in 1987, when the Democrats regained control of the Senate.

Party Whips

The first whips appeared in the Senate about the same time the floor leader positions were being institutionalized. The Democrats designated J. Hamilton Lewis of Illinois their first whip in 1913; in 1915 James W. Wadsworth, Jr., R-N.Y., was named the first GOP whip.

Although the duties of Senate whips are essentially the same as those of their House counterparts, the whip organizations are much less prominent in the Senate than in the House. For one thing, their functions and duties are less institutionalized, and their organizations much less elaborate. In the 101st Congress, Democratic Whip Alan Cranston of California was assisted by a chief deputy whip and eight regional whips, each with an assistant. On the Republican side, Alan K. Simpson of Wyoming had no formal supporting organization. The majority and minority leaders in the Senate generally assume some of the whip's responsibilities.

Senate whips at times have openly defied their own party leaders. Both parties elect their whips in the Senate, and the political maneuvering entailed in running for the office has sometimes led members to back certain senators for reasons that may have little to do with leadership effectiveness.

A serious breach occurred between Majority Leader Mansfield and Russell B. Long, La., the Democratic whip

Campaign Aid: Priority Role for Party Leaders

Helping their members win reelection and wresting seats away from the other party are top priority jobs for party leaders in Congress. Given the ever-mounting cost of House and Senate election campaigns, fund raising is probably the most valuable service the leadership can provide. In addition to attending fund-raising dinners and receptions in members' home districts or states, many leaders in both parties have established their own political action committees (PACs) that solicit money from unions, corporations, and other contributors, which the leaders then channel to candidates.

The major campaign efforts, however, are handled by special party committees set up expressly for the purpose: the Democratic Congressional Campaign Committee (DCCC) and the National Republican Congressional Committee (NRCC) in the House; and the Democratic Senatorial Campaign Committee (DSCC) and the National Republican Senatorial Committee (NRSC) in the Senate. Chaired by members of Congress, these committees help identify candidates to challenge incumbents of the other party or to run for open seats. They brief candidates on the issues and help them with all phases of campaigning, advising—even supplying—campaign managers, finance directors, and press secretaries.

These committees also raise and disburse millions of dollars. For the 1988 elections, the Democratic committees raised and spent nearly $29 million on behalf of their candidates; the Republican committees nearly $97 million.

The party campaign committees are important to candidates not only as sources of money but also because they attract funding from other contributors. Given the high cost of campaigns and the limits on campaign contributions, "$50,000 [from the NRCC] can't make or break a candidate," a spokesman for the House Republican campaign committee said. "What it shows is commitment. . . . Political pros look where the national committees go in." [a]

To help attract that additional funding, the party committees work on selling their candidates to PACs through meetings with the candidates, briefings, even newsletters. Party committees can also play a crucial role by giving a promising challenger money to get his or her campaign off the ground or by channeling funding into a sagging campaign.

Raising campaign funds for one's colleagues is not new. In his book, *The Path to Power*, Robert A. Caro writes that in 1940 Lyndon B. Johnson, then in his third year in the House, tapped into Texas oil money, directing it to Democratic colleagues. [b] His endeavors are credited with saving thirty to forty Democratic seats, which kept the House from going Republican.

In more recent times, House Democratic Whip Tony Coelho of California and Senate Democratic Majority Leader George J. Mitchell of Maine won their leadership positions in part because of their success in directing their respective campaign committees. Indeed, fund raising for colleagues seems to have become a prerequisite for anyone who wants to join the party leadership. Mitchell's two challengers for the post of majority leader both set up their own PACs to direct campaign funds to colleagues. Mitchell did not set up a PAC but indirectly channeled money to colleagues when asked for advice from other PACs and contributors.

Today, campaign aid is one of the services that leaders are expected to provide their rank and file. It is a service that can also benefit the leadership. "I suppose that by making some contributions to colleagues, some colleagues might sense a little closer sense of unity with the leadership program," Majority Leader Jim Wright, D-Texas, commented in 1978. [c]

---

[a] Chuck Alston, "When a Race Is Close, Money Is Competitive," *Congressional Quarterly Weekly Report*, Oct. 29, 1988, 3107.

[b] Robert A. Caro, *The Years of Lyndon Johnson: The Path to Power* (New York: Alfred A. Knopf, 1982), 648-652.

[c] *The New York Times*, Jan. 31, 1978, 13.

---

from 1965 to 1969. The two first clashed in 1966 over Long's proposal for federal subsidies for presidential election campaigns. Long exacerbated the dispute in 1967 by sending a newsletter to constituents in which he listed his disagreements with President Johnson (and Mansfield) on the issue. Mansfield sought to circumvent Long's influence by appointing four assistant whips (although Long eventually won the battle in 1971, when Congress finally approved public financing legislation).

In 1969 Long lost his bid for reelection as whip, perhaps as much because he had been insufficiently attentive to the day-to-day details of the whip's job as because of any lingering ill-feeling between Long and Mansfield. Long was defeated by Edward M. Kennedy, D-Mass., who was neither a particularly active or effective whip, and in 1971 he lost his bid for reelection to Robert Byrd, then secretary of the Democratic Conference.

Cranston, who was elected Democratic whip when

Byrd became majority leader, was particularly effective in that post. A liberal able to build bridges to Senate moderates and conservatives, he demonstrated a remarkable ability to sense shifts in sentiments as legislation moved toward the Senate floor and through the years put together numerous winning coalitions.

Senate whips do not move up the leadership ladder as regularly as House whips do. Although Johnson, Mansfield, and Byrd all did so, Cranston did not even seek the leadership spot when Byrd announced he would vacate it. On the Republican side the only whips to move up to floor leader in recent times have been Dirksen and Scott.

Party Caucuses

The development of party caucuses in the Senate paralleled that of the House. In 1846 the party caucus increased in importance by acquiring the authority to make committee assignments. During the Civil War and Reconstruction era, Republicans used the caucus frequently to discuss and adopt party positions on legislation.

In the 1890s Republican leaders Allison and Aldrich used the caucus extensively and effectively. As Rothman observed, "The Republican caucus was not binding, and yet its decisions commanded obedience, for party leadership was capable of enforcing discipline. Senators could no longer act with impunity unless they were willing to forego favorable committee posts and control of the chamber proceedings." [70]

It is unlikely that any Senate Democrats ever were penalized for not abiding by a binding caucus rule adopted in 1903. But they used the rule to achieve remarkable unity in 1913-14 in support of President Wilson's legislative objectives. Twenty years later, charged with enacting Franklin Roosevelt's New Deal, Democrats readopted the rule. It was not employed, but frequent nonbinding caucuses were held to mobilize support. Since that time neither party has seriously considered using caucus votes to enforce party loyalty on legislative issues.

In recent years both parties have used the caucus, now called "conference," to collect and distribute information to members, to perform legislative research, and to ratify decisions made by the Policy committees. Each caucus meets weekly for Tuesday luncheons to discuss scheduling and strategy. Administration officials frequently attend the GOP lunches.

The Republican Conference also uses its resources to run a sophisticated nationwide public relations effort to bolster the image of Republican senators and to publicize party positions. Begun in 1981 under the leadership of James A. McClure, R-Idaho, the conference provides the news media and public with a steady flow of publicity about the views and accomplishments of Republican senators. To help a member's press secretary better publicize the senator's individual accomplishments, conference staffers provide technical expertise, access to expensive electronic equipment, and backup staff support in the form of ghostwriters, graphic artists, and broadcast assistance. At the same time the conference produces and disseminates its own print and broadcast materials publicizing the accomplishments of Senate Republicans. Senate Democrats leave their partywide public relations activities to their political arm, the Democratic Senatorial Campaign Committee. *(Campaign committees, box, p. 35)*

Other Party Committees

The two Senate parties each have a policy committee, a committee on committees (called the Steering Committee by the Democrats), and a campaign committee. Traditionally the Democratic leader chaired the party conference as well as the Policy and Steering committees, giving him significant potential power to control the party apparatus. Breaking with that custom, George Mitchell gave responsibility for the Steering Committee to Inouye and made Tom Daschle, S.D., cochair, with Mitchell, of the Policy Committee. The Republican Conference and party committees traditionally are chaired by different senators, thus diffusing power among Senate Republicans.

The first of the party committees to be created was the Committee on Committees, which originated during the Civil War era, when Republicans, then in the majority, used a special panel appointed by its party caucus to make both Republican and Democratic committee assignments. Senate Democrats set up a Committee on Committees in 1879. Committee assignments made by each of these committees are subject to ratification by the full chamber. Democratic nominations to committees also must first be

R. Michael Jenkins

The Senate Democratic Conference meets to pick leaders for the 102nd Congress. At the podium is Majority Leader George J. Mitchell, D-Maine.

approved by the party caucus.

What was, in effect, the first Senate Steering Committee was established in 1874, when the GOP Conference appointed a Committee on the Order of Business to prepare a schedule for Senate floor action. That committee was replaced in the mid-1880s by a Steering Committee appointed by the caucus chairman. Democrats established a Steering Committee in 1879 but abandoned it when the Republicans regained control of the Senate and the legislative agenda. They did not set up another Steering Committee until 1893 when the Democrats once again controlled the Senate.

In 1947 both parties created Policy committees that were assigned the scheduling functions of the old Steering committees. At the same time the Democratic Steering Committee, while retaining its name, was reconstituted as the party's committee on committees. The Policy committees—which prepare material on issues and legislation and discuss broad questions of party policy—have been more or less active, depending on the needs of the party leadership and whether the party is in or out of the majority. Under Daschle's leadership, for example, the Democratic Policy Committee stepped up its analysis of the issues and put together an ambitious policy agenda for Senate Democrats.

Notes

1. Christopher J. Deering and Steven S. Smith, "Majority Party Leadership and the New House Subcommittee System," in *Understanding Congressional Leadership*, ed. Frank B. Mackaman (Washington, D.C.: CQ Press, 1981), 288-289.
2. Roger H. Davidson and Walter J. Oleszek, *Congress and Its Members*, 3rd ed. (Washington, D.C.: CQ Press, 1990), 176.
3. Ibid.
4. Ibid., 159.
5. Ibid., 177.
6. Richard E. Cohen, "Byrd of West Virginia: A New Job, A New Image," *National Journal*, Aug. 20, 1977, 1295.
7. Davidson and Oleszek, *Congress and Its Members*, 187.
8. Howard Fineman, "For the Son of C-Span, Exposure Equals Power," *Newsweek*, April 3, 1989, 23.
9. Michael J. Malbin, "House Democrats Are Playing with a Strong Leadership Lineup," *National Journal*, June 18, 1977, 942.
10. Except as otherwise noted, the remainder of this section is drawn from Janet Hook, "Budget Ordeal Poses Question: Why Can't Congress Be Led?" *Congressional Quarterly Weekly Report*, Oct. 20, 1990, 3471-3473.
11. Helen Dewar, "Pressure on Lawmakers for Reforms Is Rising," *The Washington Post*, Jan. 2, 1991, A4.
12. Neil MacNeil, *Forge of Democracy: The House of Representatives* (New York: David McKay, 1963), 87.
13. Davidson and Oleszek, *Congress and Its Members*, 160-161.
14. Floyd M. Riddick, *The United States Congress: Organization and Procedure* (Washington, D.C.: National Capitol Publishers, 1949), 67.
15. Mary P. Follett, *The Speaker of the House of Representatives* (New York: Burt Franklin Reprints, 1974), 25-26 (reprint of 1896 edition).
16. George B. Galloway, *History of the House of Representatives* (New York: Thomas Y. Crowell, 1961), 20.
17. Ronald M. Peters, Jr., *The American Speakership: The Office in Historical Perspective* (Baltimore: Johns Hopkins University Press, 1990), 31.
18. Follett, *The Speaker of the House of Representatives*, 82.
19. George Rothwell Brown, *The Leadership of Congress* (New York: Arno Press, 1974), 37-38 (reprint of 1922 edition).
20. Peters, *The American Speakership*, 35-36.
21. Steven S. Smith and Christopher J. Deering, *Committees in Congress*, 2nd ed. (Washington, D.C.: CQ Press, 1990), 28.
22. Peters, *The American Speakership*, 36.
23. Follett, *The Speaker of the House of Representatives*, 84.
24. Hubert B. Fuller, *The Speaker of the House* (Boston: Little, Brown, 1909), 26.
25. Galloway, *History of the House of Representatives*, 51.
26. Ibid., 132.
27. Ibid., 133.
28. Barbara W. Tuchman, *The Proud Tower: A Portrait of the World before the War: 1890-1914* (New York: Macmillan, 1966), 127.
29. Fuller, *The Speaker of the House*, 244.
30. Peters, *The American Speakership*, 77.
31. Fuller, *The Speaker of the House*, 257.
32. Robert Luce, *Congress: An Explanation* (Cambridge, Mass.: Harvard University Press, 1926), 117.
33. Peters, *The American Speakership*, 94.
34. Randall B. Ripley, *Party Leaders in the House of Representatives* (Washington, D.C.: Brookings Institution, 1967), 101.
35. Galloway, *History of the House of Representatives*, 144.
36. *U.S. News & World Report*, Oct. 13, 1950, 30.
37. Peters, *The American Speakership*, 140-141.
38. John M. Barry, *The Ambition and the Power* (New York: Viking Penguin, 1989), 4.
39. Alan Ehrenhalt, ed., *Politics in America: Members of Congress in Washington and at Home, 1986* (Washington, D.C.: CQ Press, 1985), 1507.
40. Peters, *The American Speakership*, 280.
41. Phil Duncan, ed., *Politics in America, 1990* (Washington, D.C.: CQ Press, 1989), 2.
42. Christopher Madison, "The Heir Presumptive," *National Journal*, April 29, 1989, 1036.
43. Ibid., 1035.
44. Peters, *The American Speakership*, 92.
45. Galloway, *History of the House of Representatives*, 108.
46. Barbara Sinclair, *Majority Leadership in the U.S. House* (Baltimore: Johns Hopkins University Press, 1983), 46.
47. Floyd M. Riddick, *Congressional Procedure* (Boston: Chapman & Grimes, 1941), 345-346.
48. Irwin B. Arieff, "Inside Congress," *Congressional Quarterly Weekly Report*, Feb. 28, 1981, 379.
49. Ripley, *Party Leaders in the House of Representatives*, 29.
50. Duncan, ed., *Politics in America, 1990*, 470.
51. Sinclair, *Majority Leadership in the U.S. House*, 57.
52. Barbara Sinclair, "Majority Party Leadership Strategies for Coping with the New U.S. House," in *Understanding Congressional Leadership*, ed. Frank H. Mackaman (Washington, D.C.: CQ Press, 1981), 202.
53. Ronald D. Elving, "Gingrich Lieutenants Balance Political Style and Tactics," *Congressional Quarterly Weekly Report*, April 8, 1989, 733.
54. Galloway, *History of the House of Representatives*, 130.
55. Sinclair, *Majority Leadership in the U.S. House*, 96-97.
56. George H. Haynes, *The Senate of the United States: Its History and Practices*, vol. 2 (Boston: Houghton Mifflin, 1938), 1003.
57. Randall B. Ripley, *Power in the Senate* (New York: St. Martin's Press, 1969), 24.
58. W. E. Binkley, *The Powers of the President* (New York: Russell & Russell, 1973), 52.
59. David J. Rothman, *Politics and Power: The United States Senate 1869-1901* (Cambridge, Mass.: Harvard University Press, 1966), 19.
60. Charles O. Jones, *The Minority Party in Congress* (Boston: Little, Brown, 1970), 48.
61. Rothman, *Politics and Power*, 44.
62. John G. Stewart, "Two Strategies of Leadership: Johnson and Mansfield," in *Congressional Behavior*, ed. Nelson W. Polsby (New York: Random House, 1971), 61-92.
63. Rowland Evans and Robert Novak, *Lyndon B. Johnson: The Exercise of Power* (New York: New American Library, 1966), 104.
64. Roger H. Davidson, "The Senate: If Everyone Leads, Who

Follows?" in *Congress Reconsidered,* 4th ed., ed. Lawrence C. Dodd and Bruce I. Oppenheimer (Washington, D.C.: CQ Press, 1989), 280.

65. Ross K. Baker, *Friend and Foe in the U.S. Senate* (New York: The Free Press, 1980), 203.

66. Barbara Sinclair, "Congressional Leadership: A Review Essay," in *Leading Congress: New Styles, New Strategies,* ed. John J. Kornacki (Washington, D.C.: CQ Press, 1990), 141.

67. Robert L. Peabody, "Senate Party Leadership: From the 1950s to the 1980s," in *Understanding Congressional Leadership,* ed. Frank B. Mackaman (Washington, D.C.: CQ Press, 1981), 59.

68. Davidson, "The Senate: If Everyone Leads, Who Follows?" 281.

69. Janet Hook, "Mitchell Learns Inside Game; Is Cautious as Party Voice," *Congressional Quarterly Weekly Report,* Sept. 9, 1989, 2294.

70. Rothman, *Politics and Power,* 60.

Selected Readings

Alexander, De Alva Stanwood. *History and Procedure of the House of Representatives.* Boston: Houghton Mifflin, 1916.

Baker, Richard A., and Roger H. Davidson, eds. *First Among Equals: Senate Leaders of the 20th Century.* Washington, D.C.: CQ Press, forthcoming.

Baker, Ross K. *Friend and Foe in the U.S. Senate.* New York: The Free Press, 1980.

———. *House and Senate.* New York: W. W. Norton, 1989.

Baldwin, Louis. *Hon. Politician: Mike Mansfield of Montana.* Missoula, Mont.: Mountain Press Publishing, 1979.

Barry, John M. *The Ambition and the Power.* New York: Viking Penguin, 1989.

Bolles, Blair. *Tyrant from Illinois: Uncle Joe Cannon's Experiment with Personal Power.* New York: W. W. Norton, 1951.

Bolling, Richard W. *House Out of Order.* New York: E. P. Dutton, 1965.

———. *Power in the House: A History of the Leadership of the House of Representatives.* New York: E. P. Dutton, 1968.

Brown, George Rothwell. *The Leadership of Congress.* New York: Arno Press, 1974.

Burns, James MacGregor. *Leadership.* New York: Harper and Row, 1978.

Busby, L. White. *Uncle Joe Cannon.* New York: Henry Holt, 1927.

Byrd, Robert C. *The Senate, 1789-1989: Addresses on the History of the United States Senate.* Washington, D.C.: Government Printing Office, 1988.

Chiu, Chang-Wei. *The Speaker of the House of Representatives since 1896.* New York: Columbia University Press, 1928.

Clancy, Paul, and Shirley Elder. *Tip: A Biography of Thomas P. O'Neill, Speaker of the House.* New York: Macmillan, 1980.

Clark, Joseph S. *The Senate Establishment.* New York: Hill & Wang, 1963.

Davidson, Roger H., and Walter J. Oleszek. *Congress and Its Members.* 3rd ed. Washington, D.C.: CQ Press, 1990.

Dodd, Lawrence C., and Bruce I. Oppenheimer, eds. *Congress Reconsidered.* 4th ed. Washington, D.C.: CQ Press, 1989.

Evans, Rowland, and Robert Novak. *Lyndon B. Johnson: The Exercise of Power.* New York: New American Library, 1966.

Fiorina, Morris P., and David W. Rohde, eds. *Home Style and Washington Work: Studies of Congressional Politics.* Ann Arbor: University of Michigan Press, 1989.

Follett, Mary P. *The Speaker of the House of Representatives.* New York: Longmans, Green, 1896. Reprint. New York: Burt Franklin Reprints, 1974.

Fuller, Hubert Bruce. *The Speakers of the House.* Boston: Little, Brown, 1909.

Galloway, George B. *History of the House of Representatives.* New York: Thomas Y. Crowell, 1961.

Hardeman, D. B., and Donald C. Bacon. *Rayburn.* Austin: Texas Monthly Press, 1987.

Haynes, George H. *The Senate of the United States: Its History and Practice.* 2 vols. Boston: Houghton Mifflin, 1938.

Hinckley, Barbara. *Stability and Change in Congress.* 4th ed. New York: Harper and Row, 1988.

Jones, Charles O. *The Minority Party in Congress.* Boston: Little, Brown, 1970.

Kornacki, John J., ed. *Leading Congress: New Styles, New Strategies.* Washington, D.C.: CQ Press, 1990.

Loomis, Burdett A. *The New American Politician.* New York: Basic Books, 1988.

Mackaman, Frank H., ed. *Understanding Congressional Leadership.* Washington, D.C.: CQ Press, 1981.

MacNeil, Neil. *Dirksen: Portrait of a Public Man.* New York: World Publishing, 1970.

———. *Forge of Democracy: The House of Representatives.* New York: David McKay, 1963.

Mann, Thomas, and Norman J. Ornstein, eds. *The New Congress.* Washington, D.C.: American Enterprise Institute for Public Policy Research, 1981.

O'Neill, Thomas P., Jr., with William Novak. *Man of the House: The Life and Political Memoirs of Speaker Tip O'Neill.* New York: Random House, 1987.

Peabody, Robert L. *Leadership in Congress: Stability, Succession and Change.* Boston: Little, Brown, 1976.

Peters, Ronald M., Jr. *The American Speakership: The Office in Historical Perspective.* Baltimore: Johns Hopkins University Press, 1990.

Ranney, Austin. *Channels of Power.* New York: Basic Books, 1983.

Reedy, George E. *The U.S. Senate.* New York: Crown, 1986.

Riddick, Floyd M. *The United States Congress: Organization and Procedures.* Manassas, Va.: National Capitol Publishers, 1949.

Ripley, Randall B. *Congress: Process and Policy.* 4th ed. New York: W. W. Norton, 1988.

———. *Majority Party Leadership in Congress.* Boston: Little, Brown, 1969.

———. *Party Leaders in the House of Representatives.* Washington, D.C.: Brookings Institution, 1967.

———. *Power in the Senate.* New York: St. Martin's Press, 1969.

Robinson, William A. *Thomas B. Reed: Parliamentarian.* New York: Dodd, Mead, 1930.

Rothman, David J. *Politics and Power: The United States Senate, 1869-1901.* Cambridge, Mass.: Harvard University Press, 1966.

Sinclair, Barbara. *Majority Leadership in the U.S. House.* Baltimore: Johns Hopkins University Press, 1983.

———. *The Transformation of the U.S. Senate.* Baltimore: Johns Hopkins University Press, 1989.

Steinberg, Alfred. *Sam Rayburn.* New York: Hawthorne Books, 1975.

Stewart, John. "The Strategies of Leadership: Johnson and Mansfield." In *Congressional Behavior,* edited by Nelson W. Polsby, 61-92. New York: Random House, 1971.

Tuchman, Barbara W. "End of a Dream." In *The Proud Tower: A Portrait of the World before the War: 1890-1914.* New York: Macmillan, 1966.

U.S. Congress. House. *The History and Operation of the House Majority Whip Organization.* 94th Cong., 1st sess., 1975. H Doc 94-162.

U.S. Congress. Senate. *Majority and Minority Leaders of the Senate: History and Development of the Offices of the Floor Leaders.* Prepared by Floyd M. Riddick. 94th Cong., 1st sess., 1975. S Doc 94-66.

———. *Majority and Minority Whips of the Senate: History and Development of the Party Whip System in the United States Senate.* Prepared by Walter J. Oleszek. 92nd Cong., 2nd sess., 1972. S Doc 92-86.

———. *Policymaking Role of Leadership in the Senate* (papers compiled for the Commission on the Operation of the Senate). "Party Leaders, Party Committees, and Policy Analysis in the United States Senate." Prepared by Randall B. Ripley. 94th Cong., 2nd sess., 1976.

Wilson, Woodrow. *Congressional Government: A Study in American Politics.* Boston: Houghton Mifflin, 1885. Reprint. Cleveland: Meridian Books, 1956.

The Legislative Process

Nowhere are policy and process more intertwined than in the Congress of the United States. Congressional procedures, fashioned to assure orderly consideration of legislative proposals, have substantive impact as well.

Skillful legislators use the rules of procedure to advance their policy goals. Sponsors tinker with the wording of a civil rights bill to keep it from being referred to a hostile Senate committee. The Senate attaches major tax legislation to a minor House revenue measure, thus circumventing a constitutional requirement that all revenue bills must originate in the House. An antiabortion amendment is added to a House appropriations bill; the amendment meets House germaneness requirements because it is framed to restrict federal funding for abortions. A radical overhaul of the congressional budget process is rushed through Congress without benefit of conventional committee consideration or extensive floor debate; the shortcut procedures take their toll, however—within months the Supreme Court rules that one of the pivotal features of the legislation is unconstitutional.

Procedure and policy interact at many stages of the legislative process. To become law proposed legislation must be approved in identical form in both the House and the Senate. Legislative proposals are first considered in subcommittee and committee and then debated, amended, and approved by the full House or Senate. After both chambers have acted, any differences in the two versions of the legislation must be resolved, and the final version sent to the president for his signature, which completes the process. (If the president vetoes the legislation, Congress may enact the measure into law by overriding the veto.)

Both chambers have adopted procedures to expedite consideration of minor and noncontroversial legislation. But for controversial measures negotiating this lawmaking course is complicated and time-consuming. At each step of the way the bill's proponents must put together a majority coalition to move the measure to the next step. That calls for continual bargaining and compromise to build winning support for the measure.

The views of the executive branch, constituents, and special interest groups must all be taken into account. At any point the bill is subject to delay, defeat, or substantial modification. "It is very easy to defeat a bill in Congress," President John F. Kennedy once observed. "It is much more difficult to pass one."[1] *(Pressures on Congress, p. 127)*

Importance of Rules

Reinforced by more than two centuries of tradition and custom, congressional rules and procedures can be used to speed a bill to final passage or kill it, expand the policy alternatives available or narrow them, disadvantage the minority or thwart the will of the majority.

Legislators who know the rules and procedures are in a better position to influence the legislative process than those who are not procedural experts. "If you let me write the procedure," Rep. John D. Dingell, D-Mich., once said, "and I let you write the substance, I'll [beat] you every time."[2]

The rules and procedures of the House and Senate differ significantly, reflecting in part the different purposes assigned to each. Because House actions are intended to mirror the will of a national majority, its procedures are intended to ensure that the majority of the nation's representatives will prevail. Because the Senate was designed to check what Thomas Jefferson called the "irregularities and abuses which often attend large and successful legislative majorities," its procedures are intended to ensure that the voice of the individual will be heard. "Senate rules are tilted toward not doing things," Speaker Jim Wright, a Texas Democrat, said in 1987. "House rules if you know how to use them are tilted toward allowing the majority to get its will done."[3]

The sheer size of the House—with 435 members it is more than four times larger than the Senate—means that the House must operate in a more orderly, predictable, and controlled fashion than the Senate. Thus the House is more hierarchically organized and has more rules, which it follows more closely. Because debate is restricted and the amending process frequently limited, the House is able to dispose of legislation more quickly than the Senate.

By comparison, the Senate's smaller size allows it to be more personal and informal in its operations. Although the Senate has an elaborate network of rules and procedures, it more often operates by unanimous consent. Each member, even the most junior, is accorded a deference rarely seen in the House. The privileges of engaging in unlimited debate—the filibuster—and offering nongermane amendments are highly cherished traditions in the Senate that are not permitted under House rules. Given these conditions, it is not surprising that the Senate may spend days considering a measure that the House has debated and passed in a single afternoon.

Terms and Sessions

The two-year period for which members of the House of Representatives are elected constitutes a Congress. Under the Twentieth Amendment to the Constitution, ratified in 1933, this period begins at noon on January 3 of an odd-numbered year, following the election of representatives the previous November, and ends at noon on January 3 of the next odd-numbered year. Congresses are numbered consecutively, and the Congress that convened in January 1991 was the 102nd in a series that began in 1789.

Under the Constitution, Congress is required to "assemble" at least once each year, and the Twentieth Amendment provides that these annual meetings shall begin on January 3 unless Congress "shall by law appoint a different day," which it frequently does. Each Congress, therefore, has two regular sessions, beginning in January of successive years.

The Legislative Reorganization Act of 1970 stipulates that, unless Congress provides otherwise, the Senate and House "shall adjourn *sine die* not later than July 31 of each year" or, in nonelection years, take a thirty-day recess in August. The provision is not applicable if "a state of war exists pursuant to a declaration of war by the Congress." In practice the annual sessions may run as long as a whole year.

Adjournment *sine die* (literally, without a day) ends a session of Congress. Adjournment of the second session is generally the final action of a Congress. Members, however, frequently authorize their leaders to call them back if a national emergency arises. The president may "on extraordinary occasions" convene one or both houses in special session.

Within a session, Congress may adjourn for holiday observances or other brief periods. That practice is known as adjournment to a day certain; lawmakers set a date for the session to reconvene. By constitutional directive neither house may adjourn for more than three days without the consent of the other.

The third session of the 76th Congress was the longest session in history; it lasted 366 days, from January 3, 1940, to January 3, 1941. The first session of the 77th Congress (January 3, 1941, to January 2, 1942) ran 365 days, as did the second session of the 81st Congress (January 3, 1950, to January 2, 1951). *(Longest sessions, p. 151)*

Evolving Rules

Congressional rules and procedures are not static, but evolve in response to changes within Congress. In the modern era several external developments and internal reforms have led to significant changes in the ways the two chambers conduct their business.

One major change that occurred in the 1970s was a new openness in congressional proceedings. For the first time many committees, including Senate-House conference committees, were required to open their meetings to the public; outsiders could sit in as committee members bar-

gained over provisions and language to be included or deleted from bills and resolutions. A rules change in the House in 1970 made it possible to record how each individual voted on floor amendments. Formerly, the House only recorded the total number voting for or against an amendment. The rules change meant that members could not vote one way but say they voted another. *(Voting in the House and Senate, box, p. 54)*

A second development in the 1960s and 1970s was an increase in the number of amendments offered on the floor of each chamber. Several factors contributed to this development. Constituents and special interest groups pressured individual members to take particular stands on particular issues, and members, with one eye always on reelection, wanted to be responsive in ways that would gain them wide recognition with their constituents.

Within Congress, reductions in the authority exercised by committee chairmen and the rise in importance of subcommittees also contributed to greater amending activity. "Weaker full committee chairmen were less able to mold consensus positions in their committees, making it more likely that disputes among committee members would spill onto the floor," political scientist Steven S. Smith wrote. "Subcommittee chairmen, who assumed more responsibility for managing legislation on the floor, often lacked the experience and political clout" to anticipate and divert floor amendments.[4] This combination of diminished committee authority and more assertive members meant that lawmakers in both chambers began to offer more amendments during floor action.

In response leaders in each chamber began to develop ways to limit amendments. In the House that meant writing more restrictive rules limiting the amendments that could be offered to certain pieces of legislation, raising concerns among the minority party that it was being closed out of the debate. In the Senate it meant developing complicated agreements for each major piece of legislation that would reduce the likelihood the Senate would bog down in filibuster and delay, unable to act on important issues in timely fashion.

The number of amendments brought to the House and Senate floors decreased somewhat in the 1980s, partly as a result of these new strategies for dealing with them and partly because massive budget deficits meant that fewer new programs—and therefore fewer amendments to them —were being initiated.

By the mid-1980s the deficit itself—and the special process Congress had devised for dealing with it—had become by far the single most time-consuming issue before Congress. It had also led to the increased use of omnibus bills—the packaging of many, often unrelated, proposals in a single, long piece of legislation. So-called budget reconciliation measures, for example, revised existing laws touching every aspect of government to bring government programs into conformity with the overall budget plan for the year. In addition it became common practice to package all or most of the year's appropriations bills in a single piece of legislation. The opportunities to debate and amend these bills are often severely limited.

Rank-and-file House members were particularly affected by this narrowing of their opportunities to influence legislation. "What we have now is a technique for returning to a closed system where a few people make all the decisions," said Indiana Democrat Philip R. Sharp.[5]

Responding to such complaints, the Democratic Caucus in 1990 approved a new rule giving standing committees the right to a five-day review period for legislation within their jurisdiction that had been developed by an ad hoc task force. The rule was adopted for the 102nd Congress (1991-93).

Throughout the 1980s the tough choices posed by the need to reduce the deficit, frustration over the reduced opportunities to enact new programs, the new assertiveness of individual lawmakers, and increased partisanship posed procedural challenges in both chambers. House Republicans, in the minority for most of the twentieth century, complained, some with bitterness, that the Democratic leadership was restricting floor debate and amendments in ways that trampled minority rights.

Members in both houses began to complain that it was politically difficult to make tough decisions in open committee meetings. Many committees began to close their doors from time to time, although the vast majority of meetings remained open to the public.

The procedural problems were most acute in the Senate, where individual members could, and often did, bring the chamber to a standstill. Many senators were vocal about their dissatisfaction with Senate procedures that let individual members pursue their own legislative interests at the expense of the Senate's interests. Washington Democrat Daniel J. Evans, a former governor and university president, said frustration with the Senate was a major reason he chose not to seek reelection in 1988. "Somehow we must reach a happy compromise between the tyranny of autocratic chairmen and the chaos of a hundred independent fiefdoms," Evans said.[6] Whether the Senate and the House would be able to find the procedural balance each seemed to be seeking remained to be seen at the end of 1990. But one thing was certain: The rules and procedures that had guided Congress for more than 200 years would continue to evolve.

The Sites of Passage

As President Kennedy said, it is easier to defeat legislation than to pass it. And the route a bill must travel before it wins final approval allows many opportunities for its opponents to defeat or delay it. "Legislation is like a chess game more than anything else," Representative Dingell has said. "It is a seemingly endless series of moves, until ultimately somebody prevails through exhaustion, or brilliance, or because of overwhelming public sentiment for their side."[7]

The first place that a bill might run into trouble is in subcommittee or committee, where the measure is likely to receive its closest scrutiny and greatest modification. That occurs in part because committee members and staff have developed expertise in the subject areas within their areas of jurisdiction and in part because committee consideration gives opponents their first formal opportunity to state how the bill needs to be changed to be acceptable to them.

The second place a bill may be delayed is in scheduling for floor action. When, and sometimes whether, a bill is brought to the floor of either chamber depends on many factors, including what other legislation is awaiting action, how controversial the measure is, and whether the leadership judges its chances for passage to be improved by immediate action. The leadership, for example, might decide to delay taking up a controversial bill until its proponents can gather sufficient support to guarantee its passage.

The next hurdle a bill must cross is amendment and passage on the chamber floor. The amending process is at the heart of floor debate in both chambers. Amendments have many objectives. Members may offer amendments to dramatize their stands on issues, even if there is little chance their proposals will be adopted. Some amendments are introduced at the request of the executive branch, a member's constituents, or special interests. Some become tactical tools for gauging sentiment for or against a bill. Others are used to stall action on a bill. In the House, where debate is strictly limited, amendments are often used to buy time; a member may offer a pro forma amendment, later withdrawn, solely to gain a few additional minutes to speak on an issue.

Still other amendments may be designed to defeat the legislation. One common strategy is to try to load a bill with so many unattractive amendments that it will eventually collapse under its own weight. Another strategy is to offer a "killer" amendment, one that if adopted, would cause members who initially supported the bill to vote against it on final passage. Conversely, amendments known as "sweeteners" may be offered to attract broader support for the underlying measure.

Legislation that fails to win passage at any of these points in either the House or Senate is likely to be abandoned for the remainder of that Congress. Those bills that survive may have one additional obstacle to face—the conference committee, a temporary panel of House and Senate members established solely to work out the differences between the two chambers on a particular bill. Sometimes

R. Michael Jenkins

Speaker Thomas S. Foley, D-Wash., swears in members of the House of Representatives as the 102nd Congress convenes.

known as the third house of Congress, conference committees bargain and compromise until they reach a version of the legislation acceptable to a majority of the conferees of each chamber; sometimes the legislation is substantially rewritten in conference. Occasionally conferees cannot strike a compromise, and the legislation dies.

For a small number of measures the final hurdle is approval by the president. All modern presidents have used the veto threat to persuade Congress to pay attention to the executive viewpoint as it considers specific measures. Because most presidents most of the time can muster the necessary support to defeat override attempts in Congress, lawmakers usually try to compromise with the president. Sometimes, however, such efforts fail, and the bill is vetoed.

All of these steps, repeated in endless variation for dozens of major bills, must be completed within the two-year cycle of a single Congress. Any bill that has not received final approval when a Congress adjourns automatically dies and must be reintroduced in the next Congress to begin the entire procedure over again. When a Congress is drawing to a close the pressure to act can be intense, as lawmakers who often have put off making difficult choices rush to keep their bills from dying. In a sentiment as apt in the 1990s as it was in the 1820s, Davy Crockett, a legendary frontiersman who served four House terms, once said: "We generally lounge or squabble the greater part of the session, and crowd into a few days of the last term three or four times the business done during as many preceding months." [8]

Controversial and far-reaching proposals are seldom enacted in a single Congress. More often they are introduced and reintroduced as national sentiment on the issue coalesces and the necessary compromises are struck. The comprehensive revision of the Clean Air Act finally approved in 1990 had been stalled in Congress since 1977 over such controversial issues as acid rain. A bill setting federal standards governing lawsuits over consumer product liability was still far from enactment at the end of the 101st Congress, although it had been considered in the previous four Congresses.

Preliminary Procedures: House and Senate

The procedures for introducing legislation and seeing it through committee are similar in both the House and Senate.

Legislative proposals originate in a number of different ways. Members of Congress, of course, develop ideas for legislation. Assistance in drafting legislative language is available from each chamber's Office of Legislative Counsel. Special interest groups—business, labor, farm, civil rights, consumer, trade associations, and the like—are another fertile source of legislation. Most of these organizations and their lobbyists in Washington provide detailed technical knowledge in specialized fields and employ experts in the art of drafting bills and amendments. Constituents, either as individuals or groups, also may propose legislation. Frequently, a member of Congress will introduce such a bill "by request," whether or not he supports its purposes.

Today much of the legislation considered by Congress originates in the executive branch (although key members of Congress may participate in the formulation of administration programs). Each year after the president outlines his legislative program, executive departments and agencies transmit to the House and Senate drafts of proposed legislation to carry out the president's program or ideas. These bills usually are introduced by the chairman of the committee or subcommittee having jurisdiction over the subject involved, or by the ranking minority member if the chairman is not of the president's party.

Occasionally committees consider proposals that have not been formally introduced. The committee then drafts its own bill, which is introduced by the chairman. This is the usual practice with appropriations and revenue bills. When legislation is heavily amended in committee, all the changes, deletions, and additions, together with whatever is left of the original bill, may be organized into a new bill. Such measures, referred to as "clean bills," are reintroduced, usually by the chairman of the committee, and given a new bill number.

Introduction of Bills

No matter where a legislative proposal originates, it can be introduced only by a member of Congress. In the House, a member (including the resident commissioner of Puerto Rico and the nonvoting delegates of the District of Columbia, Guam, American Samoa, and the Virgin Islands) may introduce any of several types of bills and resolutions by handing them to the clerk of the House or by placing them in a mahogany box near the clerk's desk called the hopper. The member need not seek recognition for the purpose. Senators introduce bills during the "morning hour."

There is no limit to the number of bills a member may introduce. House and Senate bills may have joint sponsorship and carry several members' names. (Before 1967 House rules barred representatives from cosponsoring legislation. Members favoring a particular measure had to introduce identical bills if they wished to be closely identified with the original proposal.) The Constitution stipulates that "all bills for raising revenue shall originate in the House of Representatives," and this stipulation generally has been interpreted to include spending (appropriations) bills as well. All other bills may originate in either chamber.

Major legislation often is introduced in both houses in the form of companion (identical) bills, primarily to speed up the legislative process by encouraging both chambers to consider the measure simultaneously. Sponsors of companion bills also may hope to dramatize the importance or urgency of the issue and show broad support for the legislation. At the beginning of a Congress, members vie to be the sponsors of the first bills introduced and to retain the same bill number in consecutive Congresses on legislation that has not been enacted. In 1987, for example, House Speaker Wright made sure that his top-priority bills for the session were numbers HR 1 and HR 2.

Thousands of bills are introduced in every Congress, but most never receive any consideration, nor is consideration expected. Every lawmaker introduces measures for a variety of reasons—to stake out a stand on an issue, as a favor to a constituent or a special interest group, to get publicity, or to ward off political attack. As congressional expert Walter J. Oleszek writes, once such a bill has been introduced, the legislator can claim that he or she has taken action "and can blame the committee to which the bill has been referred for its failure to win enactment." [9] Of the 11,824 bills introduced in the Senate and House during the 101st Congress (1989-91), only 1,734 were reported by committees and only 484 were enacted into law.

The modern Congress considers and enacts fewer measures than its predecessors. After enactment of the Congressional Budget and Impoundment Control Act of 1974, Congress tended to package many, often unrelated, proposals in lengthy pieces of legislation known as omnibus bills. Each year the House and Senate adopt an omnibus budget resolution setting an overall plan for government spending and revenues. They follow up with another omnibus measure revising government programs to conform to the overall plan. With the advent of massive budget deficits in the early 1980s Congress also began to provide funding for most or all government departments and agencies in a single omnibus appropriations bill, known as a continuing resolution.

At the same time the number of commemorative bills—those designating commemorative days, weeks, or months, for example, or naming federal office buildings after former members of Congress or other government officials—has increased. According to political scientist Roger H. Davidson, the number of such bills grew from 4 percent of all public laws enacted in 1977 to 59 percent in 1985. In that year 30 percent of the bills passed were substantive, involving some sort of policy determination. Eleven percent were administrative in nature. [10]

Bills not enacted die with the Congress in which they were introduced and must be reintroduced in a new Congress if they are to be eligible for further consideration. Treaties are the only exception to this rule; once introduced, they remain pending from one Congress to another.

Major legislation goes through changes in nomenclature as it works its way through the legislative process. When a measure is introduced and first printed, it is officially referred to and labeled as a bill. When it has been passed by one house and sent to the other body it is reprinted and officially labeled an act. When cleared by Congress and signed by the president, it becomes a law (and also may still be referred to as an act).

Types of Legislation

The types of measures that Congress may consider and act upon (in addition to treaties in the Senate) include bills and three kinds of resolutions. They are:

~ Bills—prefixed with HR when introduced in the House and with S when introduced in the Senate, followed by a number assigned the measure based on the order in which it is introduced. The vast majority of legislative proposals—recommendations dealing with either domestic or foreign issues and programs affecting the United States government or the population generally—are drafted in the form of bills. These include both authorizations, which provide the legal authority and spending limits for federal programs and agencies, and appropriations, which actually provide the money for those programs and agencies. When passed by both chambers in identical form and signed by the president (or repassed by Congress over a presidential veto), they become laws.

~ Joint Resolutions—designated H J Res or S J Res. A joint resolution, like a bill, requires the approval of both houses (in identical form) and the signature of the president; it has the force of law if approved. There is no real

---

House and Senate Rules

Article I, Section 5 of the Constitution stipulates that "Each House may determine the Rules of its Proceedings." In addition to the standing rules adopted under this authority, the House and Senate each have a separate set of informal rules, precedents, and customs that guide their conduct of business.

The standing rules of the House are set forth in the *Constitution, Jefferson's Manual, and Rules of the House of Representatives,* or the House Manual as it is commonly called. In addition to the written rules of the chamber, the document contains the text of the Constitution, portions of the manual on parliamentary procedure that Thomas Jefferson wrote when he was vice president, and the principal rulings and precedents of the House. The formal rules of the Senate are found in the *Senate Manual Containing the Standing Rules, Orders, Laws, and Resolutions Affecting the Business of the United States Senate.* Both manuals are printed every two years.

House precedents, unwritten rules based on past rulings of the chair, are contained in three multivolume series: *Hinds' Precedents of the House of Representatives* covers the years 1789 through 1907; *Cannon's Precedents of the House of Representatives* covers from 1908 through 1935; *Deschler's Precedents of the United States House of Representatives,* which was nine volumes as of 1991, covers 1936 through 1977. In addition all important rulings of the chair since 1959 are summarized in *Procedure in the U.S. House of Representatives.* Rulings by the chair in the Senate are much more likely to be appealed to the full membership than they are in the House. As a result there are fewer Senate precedents. All them are contained in a single volume entitled *Senate Procedures: Precedents and Practices,* which is periodically revised and updated.

In addition to precedents, each chamber has particular traditions and customs that it follows—recognition of the Senate majority leader ahead of other senators seeking recognition from the chair is an example of such a practice. Moreover, each party in each chamber has its own set of party rules that can affect the chamber's proceedings. The House Democratic Caucus, for example, can vote to instruct the Democratic members of the House Rules Committee to vote to allow certain amendments to be offered for consideration on the House floor.

Several public laws also contain provisions that affect House and Senate procedures. Two prominent examples are the Congressional Budget and Impoundment Control Act of 1974 and the Balanced Budget and Emergency Deficit Control Act of 1985, better known as Gramm-Rudman-Hollings, after its sponsors.

---

difference between a bill and a joint resolution. The latter generally is used when dealing with a single item or issue, such as a continuing or emergency appropriations bill. Joint resolutions also are used for proposing amendments to the Constitution. Such resolutions must be approved by two-thirds of both houses. They do not require the president's signature but become a part of the Constitution when ratified by three-fourths of the states.

~ Concurrent Resolutions—designated H Con Res or S Con Res. Used for matters affecting the operations of both houses, concurrent resolutions must be passed in the same form by both houses, but they are not referred to the president for his signature, and they do not have the force of law. Concurrent resolutions are used to fix the time of adjournment of a Congress or to express the "sense of Congress" on an issue. Some concurrent resolutions, such as the annual congressional budget resolutions setting Congress's revenue and spending goals for the upcoming fiscal year, can have a substantial impact on all other legislation that Congress considers.

~ Resolutions—designated H Res or S Res. A simple resolution deals with matters entirely within the prerogative of one house of Congress, such as setting the spending levels for the various legislative committees or revising the standing rules of a single chamber. A simple resolution is not considered by the other chamber and is not sent to the president. Like a concurrent resolution, it does not have the force of law. Simple resolutions are also used occasionally to express the opinion of a single house on a current issue. In the House resolutions also embody the special orders or rules granted by the Rules Committee that set guidelines for floor debate on bills.

Bill Referral

Once a measure has been introduced and given a number, it is read and almost always referred to committee. (Very rarely a member might ask unanimous consent that a bill pass immediately. Such bills are usually either noncontroversial or of great urgency.) The Speaker of the House and the presiding officer in the Senate are responsible for referring bills introduced in their respective chambers to the appropriate committees, but the job is usually left to the House and Senate parliamentarians, respectively.

(House and Senate rules require that all bills be read three times before passage, in accordance with traditional parliamentary usage. In the House the first reading occurs when the bill is introduced and printed by number and title in the *Congressional Record*. The second reading occurs when floor consideration begins; often the bill is read section by section for amendment. The third reading comes just before the vote on final passage. Senate rules require bills and resolutions to be read twice, on different legislative days, before they are referred to committee. The third reading follows floor debate and voting on amendments.)

The jurisdictions of the standing committees are spelled out in House Rule 10 and Senate Rule 25, and referrals are generally routine—tax bills go to House Ways and Means and Senate Finance, banking bills to the Banking committees in both chambers, and so on.

Many issues that come before Congress cut across the jurisdictions of several committees. Three House committees—Foreign Affairs, Energy and Commerce, and Ways and Means—might all lay claim to jurisdiction over a trade measure, for example. Occasionally the authors of a bill try to take advantage of overlapping jurisdictions to have their measure referred to a sympathetic committee. The classic example of this strategy was the 1963 civil rights bill. The

House version was referred to the Judiciary Committee, whose chairman supported the measure. The chairman of the Senate Judiciary Committee, however, opposed it; thus the Senate version was drafted in such a way that it would be referred to the more sympathetic Senate Commerce Committee. (The measure guaranteed minorities access to public accommodations, which fell within the commerce clause of the Constitution.)

The Senate, by unanimous consent, has always had authority to refer bills to more than one committee, but the House did not give the Speaker the authority to refer measures to more than one committee (multiple referral) until 1975. In both chambers bills may be referred to two or more committees concurrently or sequentially, or a bill may be split so that part of it is referred to one committee, part to another.

In the Senate multiple referrals may contain a deadline for action by one or more of the committees. Senate rules allow a majority vote to appeal a referral, but in practice referrals are worked out informally beforehand with all interested senators, and formal appeals rarely occur.

The House does not permit a member to appeal a referral (except in the rare case when the referral is obviously a mistake). In addition to referring bills to more than one committee, the Speaker, with the approval of the House, may set up an ad hoc committee to consider a bill. Speaker Thomas P. O'Neill, Jr., D-Mass., did that in 1977 when he created a temporary committee to consider President Jimmy Carter's energy package. In referring bills, the House Speaker may also set deadlines for committee action. At the beginning of the 1983 session O'Neill announced that in some multiple referrals he would designate one committee the primary committee and might "impose time limits on committees having a secondary interest following the report of the primary committee." Multiple referral has given House leaders greater opportunities to ensure that legislation they favor is treated sympathetically and efficiently, and it involves more members in the decision-making process. But multiple referral also means that the legislation has at least one more obstacle to surmount before it reaches final passage. In the 99th Congress, 14 percent of all bills were referred to more than one committee in the House.

In Committee

Although the House and Senate handle bills in different ways when they reach the floor, the committee system in both chambers is similar. The standing committees of Congress, operating as little legislatures, determine the fate of most proposals. Committee members and staff frequently are experts in the subjects under their jurisdiction, and it is at the committee stage that a bill comes under the sharpest scrutiny. If a measure is going to be substantially revised, that revision usually occurs at the committee or subcommittee level.

A committee may dispose of a bill in one of several ways: it may approve, or "report," the legislation with or without amendments; rewrite the bill entirely; reject it, which essentially kills the bill; report it unfavorably or without recommendation, which allows full House or Senate consideration; or simply refuse to consider the bill at all. Sometimes, committee members opposed to a measure will agree to report it, either favorably or unfavorably, to give the House or Senate an opportunity to make a final judgment.

Subcommittee Action

When a bill reaches a committee, it is placed on the panel's calendar. Most standing committees periodically publish cumulative calendars of legislative business, listing all action on the measures referred to them. The full committee may decide to consider a bill in the first instance, but more often the committee chairman assigns it to a subcommittee for study and hearings.

Assigning bills to a sympathetic or unsympathetic subcommittee is one of the ways a committee chairman can influence its outcome. No longer able to dictate committee activities the way they could prior to 1970s procedural reforms, committee chairmen now negotiate with committee members to work out arrangements that will accommodate as many members as possible. But the chairman still controls the committee's funds and can hire and fire most committee staffers. He therefore is in a position either to promote expeditious action on legislation he favors or to encourage delay and inaction on measures he opposes.

Few bills reach the House or Senate floor without first being the subject of subcommittee hearings. Subcommittees usually invite testimony from government officials, who give their views on how the proposed measure would accord with the president's program and policies, and from outside experts, scholars, and special interest groups. Other interested citizens at their own request may be given an opportunity to testify or submit a statement for the record. Most witnesses offer prepared statements, after which they may be questioned by subcommittee members and, on some committees, by staff members.

Hearings are intended as fact-finding forums to educate both members of Congress and the public about specific problems. They may also be used to assess the degree of support or opposition to a particular bill or to promote support or opposition to a bill both in Congress and among the public. Televised hearings in 1987 helped fuel the controversy over the nomination of Robert H. Bork to a seat on the Supreme Court. A certain guarantee of national press coverage is testimony from popular actors and other celebrities who are active in a particular cause—film stars Robert Redford on environmental issues, for example, or Elizabeth Taylor on the need for greater funding for AIDS research.

Many hearings, however, are brief and perfunctory. Because demands on legislators' time are so great, only a few subcommittee members with a special interest in the subject are likely to participate.

Most hearings today are held in open session, although committees dealing with national security and other sensitive or classified information close their meetings. The Armed Services committees use a combination of open and closed (executive) hearings. Until 1971 the House Appropriations Committee held all its hearings in closed session. *(Sunshine reforms, box, p. 83)*

Once the hearings are concluded, the subcommittee meets to "mark up" the bill, considering the contents of each provision and section of the measure, amending some provisions, discarding others, perhaps rewriting the measure altogether. When the markup is finished, the subcommittee reports its version of the legislation, presuming it has not rejected the measure, to the full committee.

Full Committee Action

The full committee may repeat the subcommittee procedures, including additional hearings, or it may simply ratify the action of the subcommittee. Frequently the full committee will make additional amendments. If the amendments are not extensive, the original bill is "reported with amendments." When the bill comes to the floor, the House or Senate must approve, alter, or reject the committee amendments before the bill itself can be put to a vote.

If the changes are substantial and the legislation is complicated, the committee may introduce a "clean bill," which embodies the proposed amendments. The original bill is then set aside and the clean bill, with a new number, is the version reported. In addition to expediting floor action, the clean bill procedure also can eliminate problems of germaneness. House germaneness rules require only that amendments offered on the floor, including committee amendments, be pertinent to the bill; the rules do not apply to provisions of the bill itself. So any amendments made part of a clean committee bill are protected from points of order on the floor.

In 1973 both chambers adopted new rules to encourage more committees to open their markup meetings to the pub-

Washington Post

Members of the Senate Labor and Human Resources Committee meet in ornate committee room to mark up a bill in the 100th Congress.

lic, and today most committee meetings are open. By 1990, however, there was a discernible trend toward closing some meetings, particularly on controversial bills. It was felt that members would make politically difficult decisions more easily in the absence of lobbyists and interested constituents.

When a committee votes to approve a measure, it is said to "order the bill reported." Occasionally, a committee may order a bill reported unfavorably or without recommendation. The House Judiciary Committee, for example, voted 19-17 in June 1990 to report without recommendation a proposed constitutional amendment barring desecration of the American flag. But because a committee can effectively kill a measure by not acting on it, most committee reports recommend passage. Moreover, those bills that are reported favorably have usually been amended to satisfy a majority of the committee's members.

Committee Reports. House rules and Senate custom require that a written report accompany each bill to the floor. The report, written by the committee staff, describes the purpose and scope of the bill, explains any committee amendments, indicates proposed changes in existing law, estimates the additional costs to the government of the recommended program changes, and often includes the texts of communications from department and agency officials whose views on the legislation have been solicited. Committee members opposed to the bill or specific sections of it often submit a minority report.

Since enactment of the Legislative Reorganization Act of 1970, committees have been required to publish in their reports all votes taken on amendments disposed of during markup as well as the vote to report the bill. Only vote totals are required, not the position of individual members on roll calls, although many committees report the breakdown. (Committees are required to keep a record of all roll calls and make it available to the public upon request.)

Reports are numbered, by Congress and chamber, in the order in which they are filed (S Rept 101-1, H Rept 101-1, etc.) and immediately printed. The reported bill is also printed with any committee amendments indicated by insertions in italics and deletions in stricken-through type. The report number and the date the bill was formally reported are also shown on the bill.

Legislative Intent. In some situations, the language of the report is as important as the bill itself. It has been common practice for committees, including House-Senate conference committees, to write instructions in their reports on how government agencies should interpret and enforce the law. And the courts have relied on these guidelines in establishing what is known as "legislative intent."

Lobbyists are also vitally interested in the report language as one way to promote or protect their clients' interests. Many appropriations bills, for example, set out only the amount of money an agency or department might spend. But the accompanying committee report often contains directives on how Congress expects the money to be spent or warnings to bureaucrats not to take certain actions.

House Floor Action: Structured Efficiency

Two centuries of evolution have given the House thick volumes of rules and procedures to guide its floor action,

but the application of these rules and procedures is far from rigid. House decisions can turn in a matter of minutes on what Speaker Sam Rayburn, D-Texas, called "rolling waves of sentiment."

Because of the sheer number of representatives, the House, especially at the end of a session, can appear disorderly, with members milling about in small groups and streaming in and out of the chamber to answer to roll calls. But underlying this general hubbub is a structure for considering legislation that allows the House to act relatively efficiently and expeditiously.

Scheduling Floor Action

After a bill is reported from a House committee and before it is scheduled for floor action, it is placed on one of four legislative calendars. All bills, including authorization bills, having any effect on the Treasury go on the Union Calendar. Technically it is the Calendar of the Committee of the Whole House on the State of the Union, so called because bills listed on it are first considered in the Committee of the Whole House *(see below)* and reported back to the House for a final vote on passage.

Bills that have no effect on the Treasury are placed on the House Calendar. These bills generally deal with administrative and procedural matters and are usually not considered by the Committee of the Whole but taken up directly by the House. Noncontroversial bills are placed on the Consent Calendar.

Private immigration bills and bills for the relief of individuals with claims against the United States are placed on the Private Calendar. This calendar is called the first Tuesday of each month and may be called the third Tuesday. Most private bills are passed without debate, but if two or more members object to a bill, it may be recommitted to the committee that reported it. The Judiciary Committee handles most private relief bills.

The House also uses a Discharge Calendar, to which are referred motions to discharge committees from further consideration of a bill when a majority of the total membership of the House—218—signs a discharge petition. A seldom-used device, discharge motions may be taken up on the second and fourth Mondays of each month. (Those days are also set aside for consideration of business presented by the Committee on the District of Columbia.) *(Discharge procedure, box, p. 48)*

These five calendars are printed in one document titled *Calendars of the United States House of Representatives and History of Legislation.* This calendar is printed daily when the House is in session. The first issue of the week lists in numerical order all House and most Senate measures that have been reported by committees, with a capsule history of congressional action on each. It also includes a general index and other valuable reference material. Midweek issues deal only with that week's legislative action.

Bills are placed on the calendars in the order in which they are reported. But they do not usually come to the floor in chronological order; in fact, many never come to the floor at all. The Speaker of the House, working with the majority leader, determines which bills will come to the floor and when. How the bill will be handled on the floor depends on whether it is noncontroversial, privileged, or major legislation that requires a special rule from the Rules Committee.

A Typical Day in the House

A typical day in the House of Representatives would go something like this:

~ The chaplain delivers the opening prayer, and a House member leads the chamber in the Pledge of Allegiance.

~ The Speaker approves the Journal, the record of the previous day's proceedings. Often a member demands a roll-call vote on the approval of the Journal.

~ After the House receives messages from the Senate and the president, grants committees permission to file reports, and conducts other similar procedural activities, members are recognized for one-minute speeches on any topic.

~ The House then turns to its legislative business. Virtually every bill of any significance is considered under a rule that sets guidelines for floor action. The rule is usually approved with little opposition, but the vote can be a first test of a bill's popularity. If the rule restricts the amendments that may be offered, those barred from offering amendments often work with opponents of the bill itself to defeat the rule.

~ After the rule is adopted, the House resolves into the Committee of the Whole to consider the bill. The Speaker relinquishes the gavel to a chairman, who presides over the Committee. Debate time is controlled by the managers of the bill, usually the chairman and ranking minority member of the standing committee with jurisdiction over the measure.

After time for general debate has expired, amendments that are permitted under the rule may be offered. Debate on the amendments is conducted under a rule that limits to five minutes the time each side can speak. Members may obtain additional time by offering pro forma amendments to "strike the last word."

Voting is by voice, the usual procedure; division (members stand to be counted); teller (a seldom-used procedure in which members walk past designated tellers); or by electronic device. When members vote electronically, they insert a plastic card into one of many voting stations on the House floor and press a button to record a "yea," a "nay," or a "present." Their vote is immediately recorded on a big screen on the wall above the Speaker's desk and tabulated, giving a running vote total. Most electronic votes last fifteen minutes.

~ After the amending process is complete, the Committee of the Whole "rises," and the chairman reports to the Speaker on the actions taken. Acting once again as the House, the members vote on final passage of the bill, sometimes after voting on a motion by opponents to recommit the bill to its committee of origin.

~ On many noncontroversial bills, the House leadership speeds up action, bypassing the Rules Committee and the Committee of the Whole by waiving or "suspending" the rules. Bills under suspension, sometimes as many as a dozen at a time, are usually brought up early in the week. Suspensions may not be amended, and debate is limited to forty minutes. Members are then asked whether they want to suspend the rules and pass the bill. A single vote accomplishes both steps. A two-thirds vote is needed to suspend the House rules, making it a gamble sometimes to bring up legislation under suspension. Measures that are even less controversial are placed on the Consent Calendar or are passed by unanimous consent.

~ After the House completes its legislative business, members may speak for up to sixty minutes under "special orders." Members must reserve the time in advance but can speak on any topic—often to an almost deserted chamber.

Noncontroversial Legislation

The House has two time-saving procedures for passing noncontroversial bills or bills of minor interest—unanimous consent and suspension of the rules. About 70 percent of all bills brought to the floor are considered under one of these two procedures.

Consent Calendar. Any member of the House may request that a noncontroversial bill already on the Union or House Calendar be placed on the Consent Calendar. Bills on this calendar may be called up on the first and third Mondays of each month. On these days, immediately after the reading of the Journal, the Speaker directs the clerk to call the bills that have been on the Consent Calendar for at least three legislative days in the order that they appear on the calendar. (The Journal is the official account of House proceedings; it reports actions taken but not the accompanying debate.)

The first time a bill is called, the objection of a single member can block its consideration. If objection is made, the bill is carried over to the next day that the Consent Calendar is called. If the bill is called a second time and three objections are heard, the bill is stricken from the Consent Calendar; it still remains on the House or Union Calendar, however. If there are fewer than three objections, the bill is passed without debate. Ordinarily the only amendments considered to legislation on the Consent Calendar are those sponsored by the committee that reported the bill.

Official objectors—three from each party—are appointed by the majority leader and minority leader at the beginning of each Congress to keep an eye on the Consent Calendar. They generally object to consideration of any measure from the Consent Calendar that costs more than $1 million or changes existing federal policy on either domestic or foreign matters. They also object to consideration of bills where there may be substantial opposition or on which a full debate may be thought necessary because of the measure's complexity.

The manager of a bill on the Consent Calendar who anticipates objection to its consideration may postpone action on the measure by asking that it be passed over "without prejudice." In that case no objection is recorded

Prying Loose Legislation Stuck in Committee . . .

The House has two procedures—the discharge petition and Calendar Wednesday—designed to bring to the floor legislation that has been blocked by a legislative committee. Both devices were instituted in the early 1900s during the speakership of Joseph G. Cannon, R-Ill., in an effort to circumvent the near-complete control the dictatorial Speaker held over the legislative agenda. Today these procedures are rarely used and even more rarely successful. *(Cannon speakership, p. 15)*

Discharge Petition

The modern discharge petition, first adopted in 1910 and last modified in 1935, enables a majority of the membership to bring before the House any public bill blocked in a standing committee or any special rule stuck in the House Rules Committee. In addition, the discharge procedure may be used to dislodge a special rule from the Rules Committee on any bill that has been before a standing committee—a combination of the first two procedures.

This is how the procedure works. If a bill has been before a legislative committee for at least thirty days or before the Rules Committee for at least seven days, any member may file a discharge motion, popularly known as a discharge "petition," which members may sign when the House is in session. The names of members who sign the petition are not made public, and members may withdraw their names until 218 members—a majority—have signed.

When a majority is reached, the petition is placed on the Discharge Calendar, where it must remain for seven legislative days before it can be called up. On the second and fourth Mondays of each month, except during the last six days of the session, any member who has signed the petition may be recognized to move that the committee be discharged. Debate on the motion is limited to twenty minutes, divided equally between proponents and opponents. If the motion carries, any member who signed the petition can move for immediate consideration of the bill, which then becomes the business of the House until it is resolved. If the House postpones action on the discharged measure, it is placed on the appropriate calendar, to be called just as other measures are.

Partly because the process is so cumbersome and time-consuming, partly because members are usually reluctant to challenge committees so directly, the discharge petition has seldom been successful. Between 1935 and 1988, 431 discharge petitions were filed, but only twenty-one measures or rules were actually discharged. Of these, only sixteen passed the House and only three were ultimately enacted.*

Discharge petitions nonetheless can serve a purpose by focusing attention on a particular issue and sometimes forcing the recalcitrant committee to take action. In 1985, after 200 members signed a petition filed by Harold L. Volkmer, D-Mo., to discharge a Senate-passed bill weakening federal gun controls from the Judiciary Committee, that committee hastily reported out gun control legislation. Ultimately Volkmer's version of the measure passed the House, in part because his discharge petition, which was eventually signed by 218 members, forced the Rules Committee to make his version in order on the floor.

Constitutional amendments are frequently the subjects of discharge petitions. In 1982 Barber B. Conable, Jr., R-N.Y., successfully discharged a rule from the Rules Committee that brought to the floor a constitutional

---

against the bill, and its status on the Consent Calendar remains unchanged.

Suspension of the Rules. The suspension procedure is most often used to bring to the floor noncontroversial measures that have been reported from committee, but other bills, even those just introduced, may also be taken up under suspension. Because of his authority to recognize members, the Speaker of the House has total control over this means of bringing legislation to the floor. Arrangements to receive recognition to offer a suspension motion are made in advance.

Any member may move to "suspend the rules and pass the bill . . .," although it is generally the committee chairman, with the concurrence of the committee's ranking minority member, who offers these motions. A suspension motion may be debated for forty minutes and may not be amended from the floor, although committee amendments are permitted if stipulated in the motion.

Two-thirds of the members present must vote to suspend the rules; the vote is also a vote to pass the measure involved. If a suspension motion is not approved, the bill may be considered later under regular House procedures. In 1979 the House amended its rules to give the Speaker discretion to delay final votes until all the suspension bills scheduled for the day have been debated. The bills then may be called up at some time within the next two days and voted on in succession, without interruption. The Speaker was also given discretion to shorten the time for each recorded vote from fifteen minutes to five.

Suspension of the rules is in order on Mondays and Tuesdays of every week and during the last six days of the session, when there is usually a great backlog of legislation awaiting action. Members who might have voted against a measure under the suspension procedure earlier in the session because of the bar to floor amendment might in the final days support a suspension motion on the grounds that the unamended measure is better than no measure at all.

Because they require a two-thirds vote to pass, most bills brought up under suspension of the rules are relatively noncontroversial. In the late 1970s, however, the Republicans accused the Democrats of using the shortcut procedure to push through some complex or controversial legislation without adequate debate or the opportunity to offer amendments. By 1978 the procedure had become as much of an issue as the bills themselves. The Democrats were highly embarrassed that year when a controversial education aid bill supported by President Carter failed under

... Discharge, Calendar Wednesday, Extraction

amendment requiring a balanced budget. It was the first time since 1965 that the discharge strategy had been used successfully against the Rules Committee. The amendment died, however, when it fell short of the two-thirds majority vote required to pass a constitutional amendment.

Calendar Wednesday

Calendar Wednesday is a little-used method for bringing to the House floor a bill that has been blocked by the Rules Committee. Under the procedure, each Wednesday committees may be called in alphabetical order for the purpose of bringing up any of their bills, except those that are privileged, on the House or Union Calendar. General debate is limited to two hours, and action must be completed in the same legislative day. Bills called up from the Union Calendar are debated in the Committee of the Whole, with amendments considered under the five-minute rule.

The procedure is dispensed with during the last two weeks of the session and may be dispensed with at other times by a two-thirds vote. In practice it is usually set aside by unanimous consent.

Several limitations make the process cumbersome to use. Because committees are called alphabetically, those near the end of the list may have to wait several weeks before they are reached, and once a committee has brought up one bill under the procedure, it may not bring up another until all other committees have been called. Because the bill must be disposed of in a single day, opponents need only delay to kill the bill.

During the 98th Congress (1983-85), Republicans

regularly objected to dispensing with Calendar Wednesday in an effort to pressure the Democratic leadership to schedule floor action on legislation they supported, such as school prayer measures and a constitutional amendment calling for a balanced budget. On January 25, 1984, a minor agricultural bill was passed under the Calendar Wednesday procedure—the first such passage since May 1960. Finding the process as cumbersome and ineffective as its earlier users had, the Republicans eventually stopped objecting to dispensing with Calendar Wednesday.

Extraction

The Rules Committee may also wrest a bill out of committee by writing a rule for its consideration on the House floor. This authority is rarely used because it is viewed by most committees as a usurpation of their authorities. In 1988 Rules Committee Chairman Claude Pepper, D-Fla., agreed not to offer an amendment providing long-term care for the elderly to a Medicare bill in exchange for a leadership promise to schedule a separate floor vote on his long-term care bill, which had not been reported from the Ways and Means Committee. Ways and Means Chairman Dan Rostenkowski, D-Ill., objected that the bill had been removed from his committee's consideration, and the House by a vote of 169-243 defeated the extracted rule that would have allowed floor debate on the unreported bill.

* Richard S. Beth, "The Discharge Rule in the House of Representatives: Procedure, History, and Statistics," Congressional Research Service, Library of Congress, March 2, 1990.

---

suspension on a vote of 156-218, in part because members were angry about the large numbers of suspension bills.

In 1979 the Democratic Caucus formalized guidelines that prohibited any bill with an estimated cost of more than $100 million in a single year from being taken up under suspension, unless the Democratic Steering and Policy Committee granted a waiver to the Speaker. Major legislation, however, is still passed under suspension, either because there is substantial bipartisan support for it or because an emergency situation warrants.

Privileged Legislation

Certain legislation from six standing committees is considered "privileged" and may be brought directly to the floor without a rule from the Rules Committee. General appropriations bills and continuing appropriations resolutions reported after September 15; budget resolutions reported by the Budget Committee in accordance with the Congressional Budget and Impoundment Control Act of 1974; and revenue bills reported from Ways and Means are all privileged, as are certain matters under the jurisdictions of the House Administration, Rules, and Ethics committees. Most privileged bills must lie over, usually for three days, to

give members an opportunity to read the committee report on the legislation. Special rules from the Rules Committee must lie over only for a single day, while Budget Committee resolutions must lie over for at least ten days. Conference reports, attempts to override a presidential veto, and certain House amendments to Senate bills are also privileged.

Although a rule is not required to bring privileged legislation to the floor, the managers of privileged legislation will often seek a rule both to waive points of order that might be lodged against the bill and to restrict or prevent the offering of floor amendments. Appropriations bills, for example, frequently contain authorizing language, which violates House rules. A waiver protects such language from a point of order, which, if upheld, would return the measure to committee. To prevent floor amendments from unraveling compromises that the committees have negotiated, the Ways and Means and Budget committees often seek rules that permit only specified amendments to be offered on the floor.

Major Legislation and the Rules Committee

Virtually all major legislation, including privileged bills and any measure considered controversial, is routed through the Rules Committee before going to the floor. The purpose is twofold. First, a special rule makes a bill in order for floor consideration even though it is not at the top of whichever calendar it is on. If bills were called in the order in which they appeared on the House calendars, much significant legislation would never reach the House floor. Second, the special rule sets out the guidelines for floor debate and amendment on the legislation.

Because it controls the flow of legislation from the committees to the full House, the power of the Rules Committee is considerable and its role in the legislative process crucial. The Rules Committee chairman has wide discretion in arranging the panel's agenda. Scheduling—or not scheduling—a Rules hearing on a bill usually determines whether it ever comes before the House for debate.

In the past the committee has used that power to kill bills it opposed even though they were supported by the majority leadership and a majority of the House. Since the House reforms of the 1970s, however, the Rules Committee has become an arm of the majority leadership and usually works with the Speaker and majority leader to expedite action on measures the leadership favors and to block or delay unwanted legislation. In this latter capacity the committee is not necessarily being obstructionist but instead is taking the heat for the rest of Congress. The Rules Committee and the leadership also consult often on the terms of debate and amendment that will be allowed for each bill. *(History of Rules Committee, p. 80)*

Rules Committee Hearings. Usually the chairman of the committee or subcommittee that reported the bill requests a rule, technically a House resolution specifying a "special order of business." At Rules Committee hearings the chairman of the legislative committee, supported by the bill's sponsors and other committee members, proposes a rule to the Rules Committee. Members who oppose the bill or who want to offer floor amendments to it may also testify.

Rules Committee hearings also serve as a dress rehearsal for the bill's floor managers. As political scientist Bruce I. Oppenheimer has pointed out, "The Rules Committee dress rehearsal gives them a chance to make errors and recover before going to the floor." [11] The Rules Committee hearing is also the first time a bill has been aired outside the committee and so is the first opportunity for its managers to gauge the reception it is likely to receive from other members.

Drafting the Rule. All rules limit the time for general debate on the House floor. The time permitted varies (it is often one hour equally divided between the two parties), depending largely on how controversial the bill is. Many rules also waive points of order against certain provisions of the bill or against specified amendments that are expected to be offered on the floor. This waiver permits the House to violate its own rules by barring any objections to such violations.

During the 1980s the committee granted an increasing number of "blanket waivers," barring all points of order that might be raised against a particular bill. Most blanket waivers were granted for conference reports and for omnibus bills. The committee justified the increase by pointing to the growing number and complexity of procedural requirements, such as those added by the Gramm-Rudman-Hollings deficit reduction law, which made it difficult to specify exactly which rules needed to be waived. Failure to waive a specific rule would give opponents of the bill an opening to challenge it.

Republicans in the House have expressed their displeasure with the trend toward blanket waivers. They "are indicative of the [majority] leadership's willingness to permit committees to circumvent and violate House rules in order to advance their legislative agenda," GOP Whip Trent Lott, Miss., himself a member of the Rules Committee, said in December 1977.[12] Nonetheless, Republicans have supported such waivers when passage of an essential

R. Michael Jenkins

Speaker Foley testifies before the House Rules Committee on legislation dealing with the Persian Gulf war in 1991.

bill, such as a continuing appropriations resolution, has been at issue.

Rules also govern amending activity on the floor. The committee traditionally grants three kinds of rules affecting amendments. An open rule permits any germane amendment to be offered on the floor at the appropriate time. A rule that bars all but committee amendments is referred to as a closed, or "gag," rule. A modified rule generally permits amendments only to certain provisions or sections of the bill or to specific subjects dealt with in the bill.

Shift toward Restrictive Rules

Until the 1980s the vast majority of rules were open. Closed rules were generally reserved for tax bills and other measures too complicated or technical to be tampered with on the House floor. But in the 1970s a number of developments led the Rules Committee to begin to draft more modified rules that specified which amendments could be offered and often stipulated in what order they would be considered.

For one thing, the decision to allow recorded votes on floor amendments significantly increased the number of amendments offered. Before 1971 only vote totals, not individual votes, were recorded on floor amendments, which made members much more accountable to their colleagues than to their constituents. Once their votes were routinely made public, however, members found it to their advantage to offer and vote for amendments their constituents supported even if those amendments were opposed by the reporting committee. Activist junior Republicans also took advantage of recorded votes to force the Democrats to vote repeatedly on politically sensitive issues such as abortion. *(Recorded votes, p. 148)*

The erosion of seniority and the rise of subcommittees also had its effects. When most bills were managed by the chairman of the committee reporting the bill, or his designee, rank-and-file members tended to accept committee bills on the floor, in part because the chairman, and often others on the committee, had developed expertise in the subject area and in part because members might need cooperation from the chairman in the future. With the increase in the importance of subcommittees in the late 1970s, many bills came to be managed on the House floor by junior members often inexperienced in House procedure and without acknowledged expertise in the subject matter. In these situations, rank-and-file members were less inclined to defer to the subcommittee's judgment and to offer amendments of their own on the House floor.

In short, the number of amendments offered on the floor increased substantially. According to political scientists Stanley Bach and Steven S. Smith, the number of floor amendments more than doubled, from 792 in the 92nd Congress (1971-73) to 1,695 in the 95th Congress (1977-79) before beginning to decline again.[13] And with this explosion of amendments the Democratic leadership and bill managers found it more and more difficult to know what was likely to be offered on the floor, whether it would win, and how long the whole process might take.

This pressure to regain control over the amending process was reinforced by at least two other developments. First, the decision to allow a bill to be referred to more than one committee created a need for mechanisms by which conflicting recommendations could be resolved on the House floor in an orderly fashion. Second, many mem-

bers were eager to open Ways and Means bills to at least some adjustment on the floor. In 1973 the Democratic Caucus began to require committee chairmen to give advance notice in the *Congressional Record* whenever they intended to seek a closed rule. The caucus also can vote to instruct Democrats on Rules to vote to make certain specific amendments in order during floor consideration.

As a result of all these factors, the Rules Committee began to draft more rules controlling the amendment process. In the 95th Congress (1977-79) only 15 percent of the rules reported to the House were closed or restrictive; by the end of the 101st Congress (1989-91), that number had risen to 55 percent.

The kinds of restrictive rules vary considerably. The Rules Committee may simply require that amendments will be in order only if they have been printed in the *Congressional Record* in advance of the debate. This practice may actually increase the number of amendments rather than reduce them. "When you see you are fixin' to be cut off and not be able to have an opportunity to offer an amendment you start conjuring up all possible amendments and you put them in the *Record*," Lott said.[14] But advance notice does help the leadership anticipate floor action and develop strategy to deal with it.

Bills that have been referred to more than one legislative committee can present special problems to the Rules Committee, particularly if the legislative committees report conflicting provisions. To prevent divisiveness, embarrassment, and perhaps defeat on the House floor, Rules will often ask the committees to try to negotiate their differences before a rule is granted. The resulting compromise, rather than the original reported legislation, is then made the basic legislation to be debated and amended on the House floor. If negotiations are unsuccessful, the Rules Committee may write a rule that allows members to vote on the alternatives.

Structured Rules. That option is an example of a structured rule. Such rules specify the amendments that can be offered, by whom, and sometimes, in what order they will be considered. Structured rules may also set time limits on debate for the amendments. Most structured rules are restrictive in that they prevent members from offering some amendments. However, structured rules may also be expansive, by making it in order for the House to consider amendments that are not germane to the bill. Expansive rules may also allow members to offer as floor amendments bills that have not been reported from committee, or even bills that have not been introduced.

While some structured rules are clearly written to give an edge to the legislative proposal preferred by the majority leadership, many of these rules are intended primarily as a way to organize debate on the House floor and to ensure that members are given an opportunity to debate the major amendments and alternatives to a particular bill. In these cases, Bach and Smith have written, "the intent of special rules is to minimize uncertainty about process, not about policy—to control in advance what alternatives will be presented, not what the final shape of the legislation will be." [15]

"King-of-the-Hill" Rules. One of the newer and more creative of the restrictive rules is known as the "king-of-the-hill" or "king-of-the-mountain" rule. It makes in order a series of alternatives to the bill under consideration and provides that even if a majority votes for two or more of the alternatives, only the last one voted upon wins.

This procedure circumvents House rules that prohibit amending any portion of a bill that has already been amended. In cases where the alternative favored by the majority leadership is sure of winning, these rules are a means to satisfy various factions within the House by letting them present, and the members vote upon, their alternatives. In cases where the outcome is uncertain, positioning the preferred alternative last can give it an edge over its competitors.

Self-Executing Rules. Another innovative mechanism that Rules began to use in the 1980s was the self-executing rule, under which adoption of the rule also resulted in adoption of an amendment or amendments. Self-executing rules were devised to expedite consideration of Senate-passed amendments to House bills and to make technical corrections, but they have also been used to enact more substantive and controversial measures.

In 1987, for example, a vote for a rule on a continuing appropriations resolution also had the effect of exempting members of Congress from a controversial pay raise. A vote for a rule on another continuing resolution earlier in the year was also a vote to provide $3.5 billion in humanitarian assistance to Nicaragua "contras" fighting the Sandinista government there. The move, which was supported by the leadership of both parties, avoided a direct vote on the controversial issue of continued aid to the contras. The rule was adopted by voice vote.

House Floor Procedures

It is on the chamber floors that the procedural differences between the House and Senate are most visible. Because of its size the House adheres strictly to detailed procedures for considering legislation. These procedures, which limit debate on bills and amendments, are designed to ensure majority rule and to expedite action. Although the opposition can slow legislation from time to time in the House, it usually cannot impede it altogether. In contrast, the much smaller Senate emphasizes minority rights and virtually unlimited debate.

The House tends to operate on a Monday-to-Thursday schedule, with Mondays reserved primarily for noncontroversial legislation considered under shortcut procedures such as suspension of the rules or unanimous consent. Sessions are occasionally scheduled for Friday, but the day is often left free so that legislators can return to their districts for the weekend.

Daily sessions normally begin at noon, although earlier meetings are common. The day opens with a prayer and the pledge of allegiance, followed by approval of the Journal. Often a member demands a roll-call vote on approval of the Journal. This request may be dilatory in nature, or it may serve to determine which members are present. Once the Journal has been approved, the Speaker recognizes members for one-minute speeches and submission of material to be inserted in the *Congressional Record*. Bills are introduced, reports filed, and messages—mainly from the president and the Senate—received.

Once this preliminary business is concluded, the House turns to the legislative business of the day. If the House is to take up legislation under its shortcut procedures, it remains sitting as the House, with the Speaker presiding. The rules for considering and passing legislation

under these expediting procedures have been set out above. Most major legislation, however, comes to the House floor under a special rule and is subject to a much more elaborate procedure. The process involves three steps: adoption of the rule governing debate on the bill; general debate on the bill itself and consideration of any amendments by the Committee of the Whole; and final passage of the bill by the full House.

Adoption of the Rule

Floor action on a major House bill ordinarily begins when the Speaker recognizes the member of the Rules Committee who has been designated to call up the rule for the bill. The rule may be debated for up to one hour, with half the time allotted to opponents of the rule. A simple majority is sufficient to adopt a rule.

Rules are seldom rejected. In 1987 the House voted 203-217 to reject the rule for consideration of budget reconciliation legislation because it included the text of a major welfare reform bill. The Rules Committee immediately revised the rule by dropping the welfare provisions. However, under normal circumstances, a rule may not be taken up the same day it is reported unless permitted by a two-thirds vote of the House, and in this case it was unlikely that a two-thirds vote could be mustered. In a neat parliamentary maneuver, Speaker Wright adjourned the House, reconvening it one minute—and one legislative day—later. Although Republicans bitterly complained about Wright's tactics, the House adopted the revised rule.

Opponents may also seek to amend a rule by defeating the "previous question." The previous question, a parliamentary device used only in the full House, is a motion that, if adopted, cuts off all further debate and amendments and requires an immediate vote on the matter at hand. Routinely, the Rules Committee member handling the rule will move the previous question to bring the rule to a vote. If that motion is defeated, the rule is then open to amendment.

Action in the Committee of the Whole

Once the rule has been adopted, the House resolves itself into the Committee of the Whole House on the State of the Union to debate and amend the legislation. Not a committee as the word is usually understood, the Committee of the Whole is rather a parliamentary framework to expedite House action. Although all 435 House members are members of the Committee of the Whole, business may be conducted with a quorum of one hundred members rather than the 218 members required in the full House. Amendments are debated under the five-minute rule, which in theory but not in practice limits debate to five minutes for and against the amendment. Twenty-five members, a fourth of a quorum, may demand a recorded vote in the Committee of the Whole; forty-four, a fifth of a quorum, is needed to order a recorded vote in the full House. The Speaker does not preside over the Committee of the Whole but selects another member of the majority party to take the chair.

The Committee of the Whole cannot pass a bill. Instead it reports the measure back to the full House with whatever changes it has made. The House then may pass or reject the bill or recommit it to the legislative committee where it originated. Amendments adopted in the Committee of the Whole may be put to a second vote in the full

In this 1985 picture House Speaker Thomas P. O'Neill, Jr., D-Mass., meets with Democratic floor leaders to discuss budget strategy.

George Tames, *New York Times*

House. The Committee of the Whole itself may not recommit a bill, although it may recommend to the full House that the enacting clause be stricken—a parliamentary motion that, if adopted, kills the measure. Recommittal as well as other motions must be voted on in the House rather than in the Committee of the Whole. Thus, when such a motion is offered during floor debate, the Committee of the Whole must interrupt its work and go through the formal step of rising and returning to the House to dispose of the motion. The House then reconvenes as the Committee of the Whole to continue debate and amendment of the bill.

The Committee of the Whole has no counterpart in the Senate. The concept developed in the British House of Commons when the Speaker was considered to be an agent of the king. During periods of strained relations between the king and the lower house of Parliament, the procedure allowed members of Commons to elect a chairman of their own and to discuss matters, particularly matters pertaining to the king's household expenses, without observing the normal restrictions that applied to a formal session of the House of Commons.

General Debate

After resolving into the Committee of the Whole, the first order of business is general debate on the bill. General debate, as Oleszek noted, serves both practical and symbolic purposes: complicated or controversial provisions of the legislation may be explained, a legislative record developed for the administrative agencies that administer the bill and the courts that interpret it, a public record built for legislators to campaign on. In the process, Oleszek wrote, general debate "assures both legislators and the public that the House makes its decisions in a democratic fashion with due respect for majority and minority opinion." [16]

The rules on most bills allot an hour of general debate, although more time may be granted for particularly controversial measures. The allotted time is divided equally be-

tween and controlled by the floor managers for the bill. Ordinarily the chairman of the committee or subcommittee that reported the measure acts as the floor manager for the bill's supporters, while the ranking minority member or his designee leads the opposition. If the ranking minority member supports the legislation, which often happens, he may allot some of his time to members opposing the bill. A bill that has been referred to more than one committee might have multiple floor managers, each of whom is responsible for the part of the bill that was before his or her committee.

Floor managers are exactly what their name implies—managers of legislation while it is on the floor of the House, marshaling speakers and support for the majority or minority position. Regardless of his personal view on the measure or amendments, the majority floor manager is responsible for presenting the committee's bill in the most favorable light and for fending off undesirable amendments. The mark of a successful majority floor manager is his ability to get a bill passed without substantial change. The minority manager is expected to line up convincing arguments against the legislation and for amendments, if the rule permits, that would make the measure more acceptable to the opposition.

The importance of the managers is evident in their physical location on the House floor; they occupy designated seats at tables on either side of the center aisle, and they are permitted to bring up to five committee staff members onto the floor to assist them. Usually the floor manager opens and closes debate for his or her side and, by yielding time, controls who else will speak on the bill or amendment. Floor managers also are recognized by the chair before other members.

The Amending Process

Amendments, which provide a way to shape bills into a form acceptable to a majority, may change the intent,

Methods of Voting in the House and Senate:

The House and Senate have each developed their own procedures for voting. Guiding them in many cases are voting rules spelled out in the Constitution. Most specific are requirements for roll-call votes, or "yeas and nays." One rule is aimed at preventing secret ballots: "The yeas and nays of the members of either house on any question shall, at the desire of one fifth of those present, be entered on the Journal." For votes to override presidential vetoes, the Constitution requires that "the votes of both houses shall be determined by yeas and nays, and the names of persons voting for and against the bill shall be entered on the Journal."

House

The House regularly uses four types of votes. Occasionally, the House takes several votes on the same proposition, using first simple and then more complex voting methods, before a decision is reached. The vast majority of votes are cast when the House sits as the Committee of the Whole, the session used for amending legislation. *(Details, p. 52)*

A voice vote is the quickest method of voting, and the type usually used when a proposition is first put to the House. The presiding officer calls for the "ayes" and then the "noes," members shout in chorus on one side or the other, and the chair decides the result.

If the result of a voice vote is in doubt or a single member requests a further test, a division, or standing vote, may be demanded. In this case those in favor of the proposal and then those against it stand up while the chair takes a head count. Only vote totals are announced; there is no record of how individual members voted. Few issues are decided by division vote. If an issue was important enough for members to seek a standing vote, then the losing side, hoping to reverse the outcome, usually will ask for a recorded vote. The recorded vote draws many more members to the chamber.

Recorded votes, which record how individual members vote on a bill or amendment, comprise the bulk of members' voting records. Since 1973 the House has used an electronic voting system for recorded votes. Members insert white plastic cards into one of forty voting boxes mounted on the backs of chairs along the aisles of the House chamber. When a member punches a button to indicate his position, a giant electronic board behind the Speaker's desk immediately flashes green for "yes" and red for "no" next to the legislator's name. Members may also vote "present," which shows up as a yellow light on the board. A recorded vote may be ordered upon demand of one-fourth of a quorum (twenty-five) when the House is meeting as the Committee of the Whole. One-fifth of a quorum (forty-four) is required when the House is meeting in regular session. Members have fifteen minutes to record their votes, although this time is sometimes shortened to five minutes if a number of votes have been clustered.

Until 1971 votes in the Committee of the Whole were taken by methods that did not record the stands of individual members. Many questions were decided by teller votes; the chair appointed tellers representing opposite sides on a vote and directed members to pass between them up the center aisle to be counted—first the "ayes" and then the "noes." Only vote totals were announced on teller votes.

In the 1960s moderate and liberal Democrats began to object to the unrecorded votes in the Committee of the Whole because members could not be held accountable for saying one thing to their constituents but voting the opposite way.

"A member can vote for any number of amendments which may cripple a water pollution bill or render ineffective a civil rights bill or fail to provide adequate funding for hospital construction or programs for the elderly, and then he can turn around on final passage and vote for the bill he has just voted to emasculate by amendment," Wisconsin Democrat David R. Obey said of the voting system.

A provision of the Legislative Reorganization Act of 1970 opened the way for "tellers with clerks," or recorded teller votes. This procedure made it possible to record the votes of individual members in the Committee of the Whole. When the change first went into effect, members were required to write their names on red or green cards, which they handed to tellers. After the electronic voting system was installed in 1973, the recorded teller vote process became known simply as a recorded vote.

Until the teller votes changes of the 1970s, yeas and nays were the only votes on which House members were individually recorded. Yeas and nays are ordered upon demand of one-fifth of those present, and they are not taken in the Committee of the Whole. During roll-call votes, members are required to vote "yea" or "nay." Representatives who do not wish to vote may answer "present." The Speaker's name is called only at his request. He is required to vote only if his vote would be deciding.

Use of the electronic system has blurred the distinction between yeas and nays and other recorded votes. Before the electronic voting system was installed, yeas and nays were taken by calling the roll, a time-consuming process in the 435-member House. Each roll call took about half an hour. The Speaker still retains the right to call the roll rather than use the electronic voting system. And the old-fashioned method is used when the electronic system breaks down, as it does from time to time.

Senate

Only two types of votes are in everyday use in the Senate—voice votes and roll-call votes. Standing votes are seldom employed. The Senate does not use the teller vote and has no electronic voting system.

As in the House, the most common method of deciding issues is by voice vote. The presiding officer determines the outcome. One-fifth of the senators present (the Constitution requires a minimum of eleven) must support a demand for a roll call. However, most of the time a

Putting Members' Positions on the Record

Warren K. Leffler, *U.S. News & World Report*

request for a roll call will be granted by unanimous consent. By tradition, the Senate always uses roll calls when voting on treaties.

The Senate usually allows fifteen minutes for a roll-call vote, although unanimous consent requests may shorten the voting time in specific situations. The fifteen-minute period may also be extended to accommodate late-arriving senators.

Pairs

Pairs are "gentlemen's agreements" that House and Senate members use to cancel out the effect of absences on recorded votes. A member who expects to be absent for a vote pairs off with another member, both of them agreeing not to vote. Pairs are not counted in vote totals, but their names are published in the *Congressional Record,* along with their stands, if known. If the vote is one that requires a two-thirds majority, a pair requires two members favoring the action and one opposed to it.

There are three types of pairs. A live pair involves a member who is present for a vote and another who is absent. The member in attendance votes and then with-

draws the vote, announcing that he or she has a live pair with an absent colleague and stating how the two members would have voted, one in favor, the other opposed. A live pair may affect the outcome of a closely contested vote because it subtracts one "yea" or one "nay" from the final tally.

A general pair, widely used in the House, does not entail any arrangement between two members and does not affect the vote. Members who expect to be absent notify the clerk that they wish to make a general pair. Each member is then paired with another desiring a pair, and their names are listed in the *Congressional Record,* but their position on the issue is not identified. A specific pair is similar to a general pair, except that the opposing stands of the two members are identified and printed in the *Record.*

Cannon's Procedure in the House of Representatives notes that pairs are voluntary agreements between members: "The rules do not specifically authorize them and the House does not interpret or construe them or consider complaints arising out of their violation. Such questions must be determined by the interested members themselves individually."

conditions, or requirements of a bill; modify, delete, or introduce provisions; or replace a section or the entire text of a bill with a different version. Amendments that seek to revise or modify parts of bills or other amendments are called perfecting amendments.

Amendments that seek to add extraneous matter to the bill under debate are called riders. Because House rules require amendments to be germane, or relevant, to the bill itself, riders are not as common in the House as they are in the Senate. Any member may raise a point of order on the floor that an amendment is not germane, but if there is general agreement on the need or desirability of a nongermane amendment, the point of order may never be raised. Amendments identical to amendments already disposed of are also not in order.

Substitute amendments aim at replacing pending amendments with alternatives. A variation of the substitute, known as an amendment in the nature of a substitute, seeks to replace the pending bill with an entirely new measure. The bill reported by the committee frequently is an amendment in the nature of a substitute for the original bill; the rule for its debate typically stipulates that it shall be considered the original bill for purposes of amendment.

Debate on Amendments. Once general debate is completed on any bill that has been given an open rule, the measure is read for amendment, which constitutes the second reading of the bill. The special rule usually specifies that each part of a bill must be considered in sequential order. The bill may be read paragraph by paragraph, section by section, or title by title, and amendments are offered to the appropriate part as it is read. Once the reading of that part is completed, amendments to it are no longer in order except by unanimous consent. On occasion the Rules Committee may allow the bill to be considered as read and open to amendment at any part. Alternatively, the floor manager may make a unanimous consent request that the bill be open to amendment. Committee amendments are always considered before amendments offered from the floor.

Debate on any amendment is theoretically limited to five minutes for supporters and five minutes for opponents. Members regularly obtain more time, however, by offering pro forma amendments to "strike the last word" or "strike the requisite number of words." Under the Legislative Reorganization Act of 1970, ten minutes of debate, five minutes on each side, are guaranteed on any amendment that has been published in the *Congressional Record* at least one day before it is offered on the floor (if it is in order under the special rule), even if debate has been closed on the section of the bill to which the amendment is proposed. The change thus assured that opponents could not block even an explanation of an important pending amendment, but it has also been used on a few occasions as a delaying device by members who have had dozens of amendments to a bill printed in the *Record,* all of which may be called up and debated for ten minutes.

Degrees of Amendments. Provided the special rule on the bill has not imposed specific restrictions, four types of amendments may be pending at any one time: an amendment to the text of the bill; an amendment to that amendment, which is called a perfecting amendment; a substitute amendment for the original amendment; and a perfecting amendment to the substitute. An amendment to an amendment to an amendment, known as an amendment in the third degree, is barred under House rules.

Although there is no prescribed order for offering perfecting and substitute amendments, House precedent stipulates the order in which they are disposed of. Amendments to the original amendment are voted on first. Only one perfecting amendment is in order at a time, but once it has been disposed of, another may be offered immediately. When all perfecting amendments to the original amendment have been disposed of, perfecting amendments to the substitute amendment are taken up, one at a time. The perfected substitute is voted on next, followed by a vote on the original amendment as amended. If the substitute has been adopted, this last vote will be on the perfected original amendment as amended by the perfected substitute. A diagram of a so-called amendment tree and the order in which amendments must be voted on are shown below.

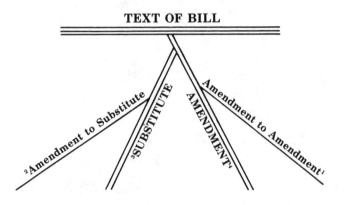

TEXT OF BILL

More than one vote may be taken on any given amendment. The Committee of the Whole may first take a voice vote and then, if members request, move on to standing, teller, or recorded votes before finally deciding the questions. First-degree amendments (original amendments as amended and amendments in the nature of substitutes, as amended) adopted in the Committee of the Whole are subject to roll-call votes after the committee rises and the chamber resumes sitting as the full House. Few separate votes actually are taken, and the full House rarely rejects amendments adopted in the Committee of the Whole. Amendments defeated in the Committee of the Whole cannot be offered again at this stage.

Action by the Full House

When the Committee of the Whole has completed its work, it "rises," according to the House's parliamentary terminology. The Speaker returns to the chair and the erstwhile chairman of the Committee of the Whole formally reports the bill to the House, with any amendments that have been passed.

If the previous question has been ordered by the special rule governing the bill—the usual procedure—the full House then votes immediately on amendments approved by the Committee of the Whole. As already noted, members may demand a roll call on any amendment adopted in the Committee of the Whole. Amendments not considered separately are approved en masse by a pro forma voice vote.

Once the amendments have been disposed of, the question is on engrossment (the preparation of an accurate version of the bill including all amendments) and third reading, by title only, of the bill. At this point, a member opposed to the bill may offer a motion to recommit the measure to the committee that reported it. There are two kinds of recommittal motions: a simple motion to recommit, which kills the bill if it is adopted; and a motion to recommit with instructions. The minority often moves to recommit with instructions directing the committee to report the bill back with amendments forthwith; this tactic offers the minority members one last chance to amend the bill to their satisfaction. If adopted, the instructions become part of the legislation; the bill in this case is not literally recommitted to the committee that reported it.

The motion to recommit is privileged and is guaranteed by House rules. A motion to recommit with instructions may be barred by the special rule governing the bill. The Republican minority, which often uses a recommittal motion with instructions to present its alternative to the legislation at hand, has complained bitterly about what its members refer to as a denial of their basic rights.

A motion to recommit with instructions may be debated for ten minutes, although since 1985 the majority floor manager—but not the minority floor manager—may ask for up to an hour of debate, which is then divided evenly between the two sides. That change was a direct result of a motion by California Republican Dan Lungren in September 1984 to recommit the fiscal 1985 continuing appropriations resolution with instructions to add to it a Senate-passed crime bill, which, among other things, overhauled federal sentencing procedures. The House version of the crime bill had been bottled up in the Judiciary Committee. The motion was debated for ten minutes, and the House, to the majority leadership's embarrassment, adopted it on a vote of 243-166. The continuing resolution was then passed, and the crime package was eventually enacted.

The Lungren motion was unusual because few recommittal motions are ever adopted. But the vote on a motion to recommit is sometimes a better indication of the members' views on a bill than the vote on final passage. Some members, for example, may support the general purposes of a bill but prefer a different approach. In such cases, they may vote to recommit but then turn around and vote for the measure on passage. Or politics may come into play, with a member simply wanting to be recorded on both sides of the bill.

If the motion to recommit is rejected, which it almost always is, the next step is the vote on final passage. If the bill is passed, a pro forma motion to reconsider the final vote is usually offered. A supporter of the bill then offers a counter motion to "lay the motion on the table," or kill reconsideration, thus safeguarding final passage. With that, the bill is considered to be formally passed by the House. At this point, the bill officially becomes an "act," although it generally still is referred to as a bill.

An engrossed copy of the bill, including changes made during floor action, is certified in its final form by the clerk of the House and transmitted to the Senate for its consideration. (An engrossed bill in the Senate must be certified by the secretary of the Senate.)

Senate Floor Action: Flexibility, Informality

House members elected to the Senate are inevitably struck by the difference in the way the two chambers operate.

The Presiding Officer

Members of the House and Senate take turns presiding over floor debate, a job some view as drudgery and others see as an honor requiring finesse and skill. Members may speak on the floor only if the presiding officer permits, or "recognizes," them. The presiding officer also rules on points of order and delivers other pronouncements that regulate floor debate. Members may appeal, or challenge, the presiding officer's decisions, and his ruling can be overturned by majority vote.

In the Senate it once was common for the vice president, its constitutionally designated president, to preside over floor debates. In the modern Senate the vice president seldom is called in unless his vote might be needed to break a tie.

The president pro tempore—usually the senior member of the majority party in the Senate—may preside in the absence of the vice president, but generally the Senate puts a freshman member in the chair. That relieves more senior members of a time-consuming task and gives newcomers firsthand lessons in Senate rules and procedures. Not surprisingly, new senators are heavily dependent on the parliamentarian for advice.

The House puts no premium on giving new members experience in the chair. Its formal presiding officer is the Speaker, but he must appoint other representatives to preside when the House is considering bills for amendment in the Committee of the Whole. When sensitive bills are under consideration, his choice turns to senior members who are skilled parliamentarians—such as William H. Natcher, a Kentucky Democrat who entered the House in 1953.

While senators tend to view presiding as drudge work to be avoided, some House members actively seek the duty. In an institution as large as the House, it is one way for members to increase their visibility.

In both the House and Senate only members of the majority party preside. Until 1977 members of each party took turns presiding in the Senate. The practice was ended following an incident in which the presiding officer, a member of the minority party, broke with Senate custom by denying recognition to the majority leader.

Although the Senate has an elaborate framework of parliamentary machinery to guide its deliberations, in practice its procedures are far more flexible than those of the House. Almost anything can be done by unanimous consent. That very flexibility also means that a single member can delay or threaten to delay action on a bill until his or her wishes are accommodated or a compromise is struck.

From time to time the Senate reviews its procedures in an attempt to pick up the pace and predictability of action in the chamber. But the Senate is rarely receptive to the proposals for change that come forth from these reviews, largely because they almost always entail curbs on the rights of the individual member.

Howard H. Baker, Jr., R-Tenn., expressed the prevailing attitude early in 1982: "The Senate is a great institution. It is the balance wheel which keeps democracy on track. It is the framework on which the Republic is constructed. It is the essence of compromise. It is the only place where there is unfettered expression of individual views. It is the last fortress that can be used to defend against the tyranny of a temporary majority. I would not change a thing about that." [17]

Scheduling in the Senate

In a chamber devoted to preserving individual rights, the challenge of scheduling floor action can sometimes be formidable. Senators can—and do—insist that the legislation in which they are interested be scheduled for floor action at a time convenient to them. At the same time senators faced with ever-increasing political, constituent, and legislative demands on their time have sought greater predictability in the Senate schedule.

Scheduling in the Senate is primarily the responsibility of the majority leader, who works closely with the majority party's policy committee, committee chairmen, and other partisan colleagues to develop a legislative program acceptable to a majority of the party. Because of the need to secure unanimous consent to bring up a bill, the majority leader also works closely with the minority leader and his staff in working out the schedule. This bipartisan cooperation is in sharp contrast to the House, where scheduling is solely a responsibility of the majority party.

A system based largely on unanimous consent also necessitates that the membership be kept informed about the status of pending legislation. The majority leader regularly begins each session with an announcement of the day's anticipated schedule and concludes it with the likely program for the next session. Whip notices, televised floor proceedings, and an automatic telephone connection to each member's office help the leadership keep the membership informed.

To the extent possible the modern leadership tries to accommodate the schedules of individual senators. Most leaders have acknowledged the frustration inherent in the job. "It is extremely difficult to deal with the wishes of 99 other senators, attempting to schedule legislation," Robert Byrd said in 1987, "because in almost every case, at any time it is scheduled, it inconveniences some senator...." [18]

All legislation reported from Senate committees is placed on the Calendar of General Orders, while all treaties and nominations that require the Senate's "advice and consent" are placed on the Executive Calendar. To consider treaties or nominations, the Senate resolves into "executive session" either by motion or unanimous consent. There are no restrictions on when the Senate may enter executive session.

Senate rules require bills and reports to lie over on the calendar for one legislative day before they are brought to the floor. This rule is usually waived by unanimous consent, but another rule that requires that printed committee reports be available to members for two days before the measure is debated is generally observed.

The leadership has evolved several ways to handle the various scheduling problems it regularly confronts. Starting in 1988, for example, the Senate worked for three weeks and then took a week off, giving members a set time to return to their states without running the risk of missing votes in the Senate or other legislative work of importance to them.

In the early 1970s Majority Leader Mike Mansfield, D-Mont., devised a system that allowed several pieces of legislation to be considered simultaneously by designating specific periods each day when the measures would be

C-SPAN/Nan M. Gibson

"Today we catch up with the twentieth century," said Senate Majority Leader Bob Dole, R-Kan., as the Senate began live television coverage of its floor proceedings in 1986. Minority Leader Robert C. Byrd, D-W.Va., looks on from the other side of the aisle.

considered. The track system, still in use in the early 1990s, was especially useful when a bill was being filibustered. The filibustered bill occupied one track, while the Senate could proceed by unanimous consent to other legislation on the second track.

Unanimous Consent Agreements

The leadership has been most innovative with its use of unanimous consent requests, traditionally the mechanism the Senate uses to expedite business by circumventing its own rules. As its name implies, a unanimous consent request may be blocked by a single objection. Once the request is agreed to, however, its terms are binding and can be changed only by another unanimous consent request.

There are two kinds of unanimous consent requests. Simple requests, which can be made by any senator, usually deal with routine business—asking that staff members be allowed on the floor, that committees be allowed to meet while the Senate is in session, that material be inserted in the *Congressional Record,* and the like. Noncontroversial matters, including minor legislation, private bills, and presidential nominations may be considered by unanimous consent; generally these matters are cleared with the leadership beforehand.

Complex unanimous consent requests set out the guidelines under which a piece of major legislation will be considered on the floor. In some respects like a special rule for guiding debate in the House, these unanimous consent requests usually state when the bill will come to the floor and set time limits on debate, including debate on motions, amendments, and final passage. For that reason they are often referred to as time agreements. Frequently the agreements stipulate that any amendments offered must be germane, but, unlike House rules, they rarely limit the number of amendments that may be offered.

Lyndon B. Johnson began to develop complex unanimous consent agreements during his tenure as majority leader in the late 1950s. Such agreements steadily grew more complex and were applied to more legislation. Negotiating a complex unanimous consent agreement can be complicated and time-consuming, involving the majority and minority leaders, the chairman and ranking minority member of the committee and/or subcommittee with jurisdiction for the bill, and any senator who has placed a "hold" *(discussed below)* on or otherwise expressed strong interest in the measure. The leadership tries to negotiate a unanimous consent agreement before the measure comes to the floor, but additional agreements—to limit time spent on a specific amendment, for example—may be fashioned on the floor.

The fundamental objective of a unanimous consent agreement, as Oleszek has observed, "is to limit the time it takes to dispose of controversial issues in an institution noted for unlimited debate."[19] The agreements are also valuable because they bring some predictability to Senate business.

But complex unanimous consent agreements "must not be viewed as rigid restrictions comparable to those found in House special rules," Steven Smith cautions. The need to obtain unanimous consent to ward off a potential filibuster "forces leaders to make concessions before and during floor debate on a scale that would seem quite foreign in the House. As a result, the new use of complex agreements on the floor does not alter the basic principles of Senate floor politics, which remain rampant individualism and the protection of minority rights."[20]

Holds

One scheduling complication the leadership has been unable to do away with is the practice of "holds." A hold is a request by a senator to the party leadership asking that a certain measure not be taken up. The leadership usually respects most holds; to do otherwise would likely be self-defeating since the senator could easily block any unanimous consent request to consider the measure.

Most holds are kept confidential and are requested simply so that the senator will be told when the bill is likely to come up. But some senators have used them extensively as bargaining tools, to ensure that they will be able to offer their amendments or to force the leadership to call up some unrelated piece of legislation that otherwise might not have been scheduled for the floor. Jesse Helms, R-N.C., frequently placed holds on ambassadorial nominations to pressure the State Department into adopting policies more to his liking. Senators have also placed holds on legislation in behalf of the administration or an interest group.

Other Scheduling Methods

Because the Senate allows nongermane amendments on most legislation, it has little need for procedures to wrest bills out of reluctant committees. A member may simply offer the legislation blocked by a committee as an amendment to another measure being considered on the floor. There are, however, three other ways that a senator may bring a bill to the floor, although none of them is used with any frequency.

First, all measures introduced in the Senate, including House-passed bills, must be read twice on successive legislative days before they are referred to committee. If any senator objects to the second reading of a bill, it is placed immediately on the calendar. This tactic was used to avoid sending the House version of the 1964 civil rights legislation to the Senate Judiciary Committee, which opposed it.

The Senate may also vote to suspend the rules and pass a bill, but the procedure is rarely used, in part because members are reluctant to challenge the committee with jurisdiction for the bill and in part because the motion to suspend is subject to filibuster. The vote to suspend also requires two-thirds approval.

Finally, the Senate may discharge a bill from committee. The motion to discharge, which is debatable, must be made during morning hour. If debate is not completed by the time morning hour ends, the motion is placed on the calendar, where it can be subjected to a series of delays. Only fourteen bills had been successfully discharged from committee by 1990.[21]

Senate Floor Procedures

The Senate usually convenes at noon, although the leadership frequently changes the time, by unanimous consent, to accommodate the daily workload. The Senate chaplain gives an opening prayer, and the previous day's Journal is approved. A rules change in 1986 made approval nondebatable, although amendments to correct the Journal may still be offered and filibustered. The majority leader and then the minority leader are recognized for up to ten minutes each; usually they discuss the Senate's schedule for the day.

What happens next depends on whether the Senate is

A Typical Day in the Senate

A typical day in the Senate might go like this:

~ The Senate is called to order by the presiding officer. The constitutional presiding officer, the vice president, is seldom in attendance. Usually the president pro tempore presides over the opening minutes of the Senate session. During the course of the day, other members of the majority party take turns presiding for an hour at a time.

~ The Senate chaplain delivers the opening prayer.

~ The majority and minority leaders are recognized for opening remarks. The majority leader usually announces his plan for the day's business, which is developed in consultation with the minority leadership.

~ Senators who have requested time in advance are recognized for "special orders"; they may speak on any topic for five minutes.

~ After special orders the Senate usually conducts morning business (which need not be in the morning and should not be confused with morning hour). During morning business senators may introduce bills, receive reports from committees and messages from the president, and conduct other routine chores.

~ Once morning business is completed, the Senate may consider legislative or executive matters. To begin work on a piece of legislation the majority leader normally asks for unanimous consent to call up the measure. If any member objects, the leader may make a debatable motion that the Senate take up the bill. The motion gives opponents the opportunity to launch a filibuster, or extended debate, even before the Senate officially begins to consider the bill. A few measures, such as budget resolutions and reports from House-Senate conference committees, are privileged, and a motion to consider them is not debatable.

Floor debate on a bill is generally handled by managers, usually the chairman and ranking minority member of the committee with jurisdiction over the measure. Some measures are considered under a unanimous consent, or time, agreement in which the Senate unanimously agrees to limit debate and to divide the time in some prearranged fashion. In the absence of a time agreement any senator may seek recognition from the chair and, once recognized, may talk for as long as he or she wishes. Unless the Senate has unanimously agreed to limit amendments, senators may offer as many as they wish. In most cases, amendments need not be germane, or directly related, to the bill.

Most bills are passed by voice vote with only a handful of senators present. Any member can request a roll-call vote on an amendment or on final passage of a measure. Senate roll calls are casual affairs. Senators stroll in from the cloakrooms or their offices and congregate in the well (the area at the front of the chamber). When they are ready to vote, senators catch the eye of the clerk and vote, often by indicating thumbs up or thumbs down. Roll-call votes are supposed to last fifteen minutes, but some have dragged on for more than an hour.

~ Often, near the end of the day, the majority leader and the minority leader quickly move through a "wrap-up" period, during which minor bills that have been cleared by all members are passed by unanimous consent.

~ Just before the Senate finishes its work for the day, the majority leader seeks unanimous consent for his agenda for the next session—when the Senate will convene, which senators will be given special orders, and specific time agreements for consideration of legislation.

beginning a new legislative day. If the Senate recessed at the end of its previous session, it may proceed immediately to any unfinished business. If it adjourned, it must begin a new legislative day, which, after the opening preliminaries, requires the Senate to enter a two-hour period called "morning hour." During that period members conduct what is known as morning business—introducing bills, filing committee reports, and receiving messages from the House and the president.

In the second hour, or at the conclusion of morning business, members may move to consider any measure on the calendar; the motion is not debatable. After morning hour, a motion to consider a nonprivileged measure is debatable. In an attempt to avoid certain filibuster on a defense authorization bill in 1987, Majority Leader Byrd sought to call up the bill during morning hour. But before he could do that, the previous day's proceedings had to be approved. Republicans requested a roll call on approval and then used arcane procedural tactics to slow the roll call. By the time the ensuing wrangle over the rules between Byrd and the Republicans had been untangled, the period for morning hour had expired, and the motion to call up the defense bill was once again debatable.

Morning Business

The decision to adjourn or recess at the end of the day is made by unanimous consent or by motion, usually made by the majority leader. The leadership generally prefers to recess from day to day because it can maintain greater control over the daily schedule. Senators seeking to delay action on a measure, however, may push for adjournment because the convening of a new legislative day offers them more opportunities to slow Senate deliberations.

If the Senate has recessed and there is no morning hour when it next reconvenes, it may still conduct morning business by unanimous consent. Within morning hour, morning business may be followed by the call of the Calendar of General Orders. During this procedure, which is almost always set aside by unanimous consent, the chair calls each bill in the order in which it appears on the calendar. If objection is raised to considering the bill, the chair moves on to the next measure. No senator may speak for more than five minutes on any one bill during the call of the calendar.

Morning hour may be followed by a period of "special orders," when members are given permission to speak for up to five minutes on virtually any topic. Before the Senate permitted its floor sessions to be televised, members could speak for fifteen minutes under special orders. *(Television in Congress, box, p. 62)*

The Senate next turns to any unfinished business. If there is none, or if it is set aside by unanimous consent, the Senate may then take up new business. Most major bills are brought up under unanimous consent agreements worked out in advance by the leadership. If a member objects to a unanimous consent request, the leadership may decide to try to renegotiate the consent agreement or it may move that the Senate take up the bill. Because most such motions are debatable, a filibuster could be launched against the bill before it is even technically on the floor. Some measures, such as budget resolutions and House-Senate conference reports, are privileged, and motions to consider them are not debatable.

Floor Debate

Once a bill is brought to the floor for consideration, floor managers take over the task of guiding the legislation through the amendment process and final passage. As in the House, the chairman and ranking minority member of the committee or subcommittee with jurisdiction for the bill act as the majority and minority floor managers. Floor managers play much the same role in the Senate as they do in the House, mapping strategy for passing the bill, deflecting debilitating or undesirable amendments, offering amendments to attract additional support, and seeing that members in favor of the bill turn out to vote for it.

On measures brought to the floor under a unanimous consent agreement, the time allotted for debate is usually divided evenly between the two opposing sides. If there is no time agreement, any senator may seek recognition from the chair. The chair, however, usually gives preferential recognition first to the majority manager and then to the minority manager. Once recognized, a senator may speak as long as he likes and on any subject he chooses, unless he violates the rules of the Senate. A senator may yield temporarily for the consideration of other business or to another senator who wants to ask a question, but he may not parcel out time to other members, as floor managers in the House typically do.

The Senate does not consider bills in the Committee of the Whole, nor does it set aside a period for general debate before the amending process begins. Amendments are in order as soon as the bill is made the pending order of business.

Debate in the modern Senate is a far cry from debate during the Senate's "Golden Age," when great orators like Daniel Webster, John C. Calhoun, and Henry Clay fought an eloquent war of words over slavery and states' rights. While a few issues still engender lively debate on the floor, Senate speeches are seldom spontaneous; most are prepared by staff and read to an often nearly empty chamber or inserted, unread, in the *Congressional Record.* "Floor debate has deteriorated into a never-ending series of points of order, procedural motions, appeals and waiver votes, punctuated by endless hours of time-killing quorum calls," Sen. Nancy Landon Kassebaum, R-Kan., wrote in the *Washington Post.* "Serious policy deliberations are a rarity. 'Great debate' is only a memory, replaced by a preoccupation with procedure that makes it exceedingly difficult to transact even routine business." [22]

"There is dialogue and debate, but most of it does not take place on the floor under public scrutiny," Sen. Paul Simon, D-Ill., said in 1985.[23] Comparatively few limits are placed on the debate that does occur on the Senate floor. Most unanimous consent agreements limit the time to be spent debating amendments and on debatable motions, points of order, and appeals of rulings. Some agreements also limit the overall time that the entire bill, including amendments, may be debated. A few statutes, such as the 1974 budget act, also effectively prohibit unlimited debate. A motion to table, if adopted, also serves to cut off debate. And under Rule 22, sixty senators may vote to invoke cloture and shut off a filibuster. The "previous question" device, which brings debate to a close in the House, is not used in the Senate.

Senate rules bar members from speaking more than twice on the same subject in the same legislative day. This has not been an effective limit on debate, however, because each amendment is considered a different subject. A rule adopted in 1964 requires debate to be germane for the first three hours following the morning hour, but since morning hour occurs only when the Senate begins a new legislative day, this stricture usually does not apply.

As in the House, the Senate presumes that a quorum is present until a member suggests otherwise. During floor debate a senator will often suggest the absence of a quorum. This is a tactical maneuver designed to occupy time while the leadership negotiates a procedural agreement or to give a senator time to reach the floor to offer an amendment. Except in limited circumstances, the presiding officer is not permitted to count the senators on the floor to see whether a quorum really exists, as the House does, but must proceed to a call of the roll. When the reason for requesting the quorum call is resolved—that is, when the negotiation is completed or the senator is in the chamber and ready to offer his amendment—the call may be suspended by unanimous consent.

This sort of quorum call differs from a "live" quorum, where a member insists upon a majority of the members actually appearing on the Senate floor. By refusing to answer the roll call, opponents of a bill or an amendment can delay action or even try to deny the Senate a quorum—in the absence of a quorum no business or debate may take place and the Senate must adjourn or, in certain cases, recess.

A dramatic example of such an attempt occurred in 1988 during debate on a controversial campaign finance bill. To break a Republican filibuster, Majority Leader Byrd sought to keep the Senate in session all night. Republicans countered by calling for repeated live quorums and then refusing to come to the floor. That forced Democrats to keep enough members present to maintain the quorum needed for the Senate to remain in session. When the Democrats came up short around midnight, Byrd resorted to directing the sergeant at arms to arrest absent senators and bring them to the floor. The sergeant at arms arrested Sen. Bob Packwood, R-Ore., after forcing his way into the senator's office, and escorted him to the entrance of the Senate chamber. When Packwood refused to go in under his own steam, two Capitol police lifted the senator and carried him feet first into the Senate chamber. Byrd had established his quorum, but he was ultimately unable to break the filibuster, and the bill died.

The Amending Process

The flexibility that marks the Senate's rules of procedure also characterizes its amending process. When a bill is

Televised Floor Debates Here to Stay

To the television-viewing audience, that mid-March week in 1979 differed little from previous weeks. But buried somewhere in the ratings was a historical footnote. At noon on March 19, the U.S. House of Representatives made its live television debut.

That appearance was the culmination of years of hard work by proponents of the idea. First proposed in 1944 by then-Sen. Claude Pepper, D-Fla., the movement to open the chambers to television cameras took hold only slowly in a body often resistant to change. Indeed, Senate floor action has been televised only since June 1986.

Sen. Al Gore, D-Tenn., led the fight for television in the House, where he served from 1977 to 1985, and in the Senate, which he entered in 1985. "The marriage of this medium and of our open debate have the potential . . . to revitalize representative democracy," Gore said in the first televised speech in 1979, a one-minute address to the House before the regular legislative day began.

Most observers of Congress agree that despite all the attention it has generated, the presence of television cameras in Congress has ushered in few noticeable changes—besides an increase in blue suits and red ties. "The horror stories that were supposed to happen didn't happen," political scientist Larry Sabato said in 1989, ten years after the House began its telecasts.

By 1989 members and political scientists agreed that the cameras were a fixture in the chambers. Past foes were not calling for their removal, finally resigned to their presence.

"I was wrong," conceded Sen. John C. Danforth, R-Mo., a leading foe of television in the Senate. "My predictions have not come true. The abuse has not occurred. The posturing I forsaw has not come into being."

Dawn of a New Age

Until the early 1970s, television was just a dream to its proponents. But the arrival in Congress of reform-minded members in the wake of Watergate led to an atmosphere more amenable to openness.

In 1977 the Democratic leadership directed the House Select Committee on Congressional Operations to conduct a ninety-day experiment using closed-circuit telecasts of House floor proceedings to members' offices. The experiment was labeled a success, and on October 27, 1977, the House tentatively agreed to go ahead, although it took a while to iron out the details.

In June 1978 news organizations began broadcasting House proceedings over radio, and by March 1979 television had arrived. The Cable Satellite Public Affairs Network (C-SPAN), the private, nonprofit cooperative of the cable television industry, was launched in 1979 with the express purpose of televising Congress.

The Senate proceeded more slowly in bringing in the cameras. Majority Leader Howard H. Baker, Jr., R-Tenn., began the effort in earnest in 1981. In February 1986 the Senate passed a resolution to allow television broadcasting.

For a month the Senate permitted closed-circuit transmissions into members' offices, followed by six weeks of public broadcasts. At the conclusion of the six-week test period, the Senate voted to keep the cameras permanently. And on June 2, 1986, the Senate premiered on a second C-SPAN channel.

Senate rules are fairly strict. Cameras are operated by congressional staff and remain fixed on a single speaker. Initially the House rules were similar. Since May 1984, however, House cameras have often slowly panned the room during votes and special orders, a period at the end of a daily session when members may speak on various topics, usually to a mostly empty chamber. That change in procedure was a direct outgrowth of the most controversial incident in congressional television history.

"Camscam"

In early May 1984, during special orders, Rep. Robert S. Walker, R-Pa., and his colleague Newt Gingrich, R-Ga., harshly lambasted Democratic members, by name, for their foreign policy views. On May 10 Speaker Thomas P. O'Neill, Jr., D-Mass., ordered the cameras to pan the barren chamber during a speech Walker was making.

Angered by this attempt to embarrass them, Republicans confronted O'Neill on the House floor. On May 15 Gingrich engaged the Speaker in a dialogue that quickly came to a boil. O'Neill lost his temper and called Gingrich's speech "the lowest thing I have ever seen in my thirty-two years in Congress."

At the Republicans' insistence the parliamentarian ruled the Speaker out of order for making a personal attack. The incident made quite a fuss at the time, and it also led to a change in the rules to permit future panning of the chamber. *(Details, p. 24)*

The Viewing Audience

The public does watch Congress on television. In 1988 21.6 million households reported watching C-SPAN, which commissioned the survey. The public is not C-SPAN's only audience, though. When Congress is in session it is nearly impossible to find a congressional office without its television tuned to C-SPAN.

Time is a precious commodity for members of Congress. Televised proceedings and committee hearings often allow them to gauge their time better during votes and other floor activities. Members follow the proceedings and committee hearings to keep abreast of the latest developments. Since they can use television to keep up with the action, said political scientist Steven S. Smith in 1989, "members are not quite as reliant on a colleague at the door telling them whether to vote up or down."

Source: John Schachter, "Congress Begins Second Decade Under TV's Watchful Glare," *Congressional Quarterly Weekly Report,* March 11, 1989, 507-509.

taken up for consideration on the Senate floor, any part of the measure is open immediately to amendment. Unlike the House, the Senate is not bound by a five-minute rule governing debate on amendments. Unless limited by a unanimous consent agreement or cloture, debate on amendments may continue until no senator seeks recognition.

Moreover, amendments need not be germane, except in the case of general appropriations bills, bills on which cloture has been invoked, concurrent budget resolutions, and measures regulated by unanimous consent agreement. And the number of amendments that may be offered is rarely limited. Unanimous consent requests may disallow nongermane amendments, but they seldom limit the number of germane amendments that may be offered. Once cloture is invoked, the Senate may consider only those germane amendments that were formally before the Senate when cloture was voted.

Tax legislation is particularly susceptible to nongermane amendments for a special reason. The Constitution requires revenue measures to originate in the House, a stipulation that restricts the Senate to amending House-passed tax bills. Despite the constitutional stricture, the Senate, nonetheless, takes the initiative on tax issues from time to time.

A noteworthy example occurred in 1982, when Congress approved a $98 billion tax increase that the House considered for the first time when it took up the conference report on the bill. The tax increase was required by the fiscal 1983 budget resolution. The House Ways and Means Committee took no action, in part because its members were unable to agree on what should go into a revenue-raising package and in part because Democrats wanted to force Republican President Ronald Reagan to share some of the blame for raising taxes in an election year. The Republican-led Senate Finance Committee wrote a bill raising revenue and then attached it to a minor tax bill the House had passed in 1981. After the Senate passed its version, the full House agreed with the Ways and Means Committee's recommendation to go straight to conference on the House-passed bill as amended by the Senate.

The right of senators to offer nongermane amendments is a primary means of ensuring that legislation does not get bottled up in an unsympathetic committee. In 1983, for example, Senate Finance Committee Chairman Bob Dole, R-Kan., vehemently opposed a proposal to repeal a provision of the 1982 tax bill that required tax withholding on interest and dividends. But when proponents of repeal threatened to attach it to important jobs and Social Security legislation, the Senate leadership agreed to allow it to be offered as an amendment to an unrelated trade bill.

When the Senate requires that amendments be germane, the test is stricter than that in the House. An amendment in the Senate is considered germane only if it deletes something from the bill, adjusts a figure up or down, or restricts the scope of the bill. An amendment is considered nongermane if it in some way expands the scope of the bill, no matter how relevant the subject matter of the amendment may be to the underlying legislation. An amendment adding a fourth country to a bill granting most-favored-nation trade status to three countries would be just as nongermane as an amendment revising the criminal code.

A sponsor may modify or withdraw his amendment at any time before a roll-call vote is ordered on it or it becomes the subject of a unanimous consent agreement. It may then be modified or withdrawn only by unanimous consent. (In the House, members may modify or withdraw their amendments only by unanimous consent.) A member may agree to modify his amendment to make it more acceptable to a greater number of senators. If a senator has offered an amendment simply to make a point, he may choose to withdraw it before it comes to a vote. Amended language cannot be changed again unless the change is part of an amendment that also changes other unamended parts of the legislation.

Amendments offered by the reporting committee are taken up before other amendments. Often, the Senate by unanimous consent agrees to the committee amendments en bloc, particularly if the amendments are extensive, and then provides that the bill as amended is to be "considered as an original text for the purpose of further amendment." Or, as is frequently the case with appropriations bills, the Senate might agree en bloc to all but one or two of the committee amendments, which are then considered separately. Such amendments are themselves open to amendment and must be disposed of before other unrelated amendments are proposed.

As in the House, amendments in the Senate may be amended in the first and second degree, which means that a proposed amendment to a bill may itself be amended. The Senate process, however, differs from the House process in an important if somewhat subtle way. If a senator offers a perfecting amendment to an amendment in the first degree, no other amendment is in order until that perfecting amendment is disposed of. A senator thus may offer a perfecting amendment to a bill and then, if he can gain recognition from the chair, offer a perfecting amendment to his original amendment, thus precluding other senators from offering any other amendments until his perfecting amendment has been voted up or down.

However, an amendment offered as a substitute for a pending amendment does not preclude someone else from offering a perfecting amendment to the pending amendment. The perfecting amendment is voted on first, the substitute second. The perfecting amendment applies only to the original amendment. If the substitute prevails, it replaces both the original amendment and any successful perfecting amendments.

In short, this principle of precedence gives perfecting amendments priority over substitute amendments. It also means that as many as eleven amendments may be pending on the Senate floor at the same time.

In voting on amendments, the Senate makes frequent use of a procedural device known as tabling to block or kill amendments. When approved, a motion to "lay on the table" is considered the final disposition of that issue. The motion is not debatable, and adoption requires a simple majority vote. By voting to table, a senator can avoid being recorded directly on a controversial amendment to a politically sensitive issue.

Filibusters and Cloture

In its most extreme form, the Senate's tradition of unlimited debate can turn into a filibuster—the deliberate use of extended debate or procedural delays to block action on a measure supported by a majority of members. Filibusters once provided the Senate's best theater. Practitioners had to be ready for days or weeks of freewheeling debate, and all other business was blocked until one side conceded. In the modern era drama is rare. Disappointment awaits

Dilatory Debate: A Tactic as Old as the Senate

The Senate was just six months old in 1789 when delaying tactics were first used, by opponents of a bill to locate the nation's capital on the Susquehanna River. By 1840 dilatory debate was so common that Henry Clay of Kentucky was demanding "a rule which would place the business of the Senate under the control of a majority."

The first full-fledged filibusters occurred the next year, when Democrats and Whigs squared off first over the appointment of official Senate printers and then over the establishment of a national bank. Slavery, the Civil War, Reconstruction, and blacks' voting rights in turn sparked the increasingly frequent and contentious filibusters of the nineteenth century. Because the Senate repeatedly rejected efforts to restrict debate, the majority's only recourse was to win unanimous consent for a time limit on considering a bill, on a case-by-case basis.

Minor curbs on debate were adopted early in the twentieth century. But they did not hinder Republican filibusterers from killing two of President Woodrow Wilson's proposals to put the nation on a war footing—a 1915 ship-purchase bill and a 1917 bill to arm merchant ships.

As a political scientist in 1882, Wilson had celebrated "the Senate's opportunities for open and unrestricted discussion." After the 1917 defeat, he railed, "The Senate of the United States is the only legislative body in the world which cannot act when the majority is ready for action. A little group of willful men . . . have rendered the great government of the United States helpless and contemptible."

On March 8, 1917, the Senate yielded to public outcry and adopted a cloture rule (Rule 22), which required a vote of two-thirds of those present to end debate. The rule's framers predicted it would be little used, and for years that was the case.

The first successful cloture motion came in 1919, ending debate on the Treaty of Versailles. Nine more motions were voted on through 1927; three succeeded. Over the next thirty-five years, until 1962, only sixteen were voted on and not one was adopted.

In large part that reflected the politics of civil rights. Southern Democrats successfully filibustered legislation against the poll tax, literacy tests, lynching, and employment discrimination by building an anticloture coalition that included westerners and some Republicans. In 1949 this coalition was able to strengthen Rule 22 by requiring a two-thirds vote of the total Senate membership (sixty-seven in a one-hundred member Senate) to invoke cloture.

That change occurred after a coalition of northern Democrats and moderate Republicans sought to make it easier for the majority to invoke cloture. Undaunted by its failure, the coalition sought to ease Rule 22 nearly every time a new Congress convened.

In 1959 the rule was revised to provide for limitation of debate by a vote of two-thirds of the senators present and voting, two days after a cloture petition was submitted by sixteen senators. If cloture was adopted, further debate was limited to one hour for each senator on the bill itself and on all amendments affecting it. No new amendments could be offered except by unanimous consent. Amendments that were not germane to the pending business and dilatory motions were out of order. The rule applied both to regular legislation and to motions to change the Standing Rules of the Senate.

Slowly, the anticloture coalition began to dissolve. In 1964 the Senate for the first time invoked cloture on a civil rights bill, cutting off the longest filibuster in Senate history. A year later cloture was approved for another civil rights measure, the Voting Rights Act, and in 1968 a filibuster on an open housing bill was cut off.

By the 1970s the liberals' victories on civil rights had cooled their ardor for cloture reform. Moreover, they had become the ones doing much of the filibustering—against President Richard Nixon's Vietnam policies, weapons systems, and antibusing proposals.

In 1973, for the first time in years, the new Senate did not fight over the cloture rule. But in 1975 the liberals tried again—and won. Under the new rule, three-fifths of the Senate, or sixty votes, could shut off a filibuster—seven votes less than was needed under the old rule if every senator voted. (A two-thirds vote of those present and voting was still required to cut off debate on proposed rules changes.)

The 1975 revision made it easier for a majority to invoke cloture. But much of the revision's success relied on the willingness of the senators to abide by the spirit as well as the letter of the chamber's rules. When cloture was invoked on a particular measure, senators generally conceded defeat and proceeded to a vote without further delay.

But in 1976 James B. Allen, D-Ala., began violating this unwritten rule of conduct. By capitalizing on a loophole that permitted unlimited postcloture quorum calls, parliamentary motions, and roll-call votes on amendments introduced before cloture was invoked, Allen was able to delay a vote on the issue itself for far longer than the hour allotted to him under the 1959 rules revision.

The Senate closed this loophole in 1979, when it agreed to an absolute limit on postcloture delaying tactics. The rule provided that once cloture was invoked, a final vote had to be taken after no more than one hundred hours of debate. All time spent on quorum calls, roll calls, and other parliamentary procedures was counted against the one-hundred-hour limit. In 1986 the Senate reduced that limitation to thirty hours. The change, enacted as part of the Senate's decision to allow live television coverage of its floor action, was intended to quicken the pace of the proceedings.

visitors to the Senate gallery who expect a real-life version of Jimmy Stewart's climactic oration in the 1939 movie,

"Mr. Smith Goes to Washington." They are likely to look down on an empty floor and hear only the drone of a clerk reading absent senators' names in a mind-numbing succession of quorum calls. Often today's filibusterers do not even have to be on the floor, nor do the bills they are opposing.

Despite the lack of drama, filibusters are still effective weapons. Any controversial legislation that comes to the floor without a prearranged time agreement is vulnerable to filibuster; success is most likely near the end of the session, when a filibuster on one bill may imperil action on other, more urgent legislation. Filibusters may be intended to kill a measure outright, by forcing the leadership to pull the measure off the floor so that it can move on to other business, but they are often mounted to force a compromise on the measure. Time is such a precious commodity in today's Senate that individual members who even threaten to hold a bill hostage to lengthy debate can usually force compromises on the measure, either in committee or on the floor.

Filibusters have always generated intense debate. Supporters view filibusters as a defense against hasty or ill-advised legislation and as a guarantee that minority views will be heard. Detractors contend that filibusters allow a minority to thwart the will of a majority and impede orderly consideration of issues before the Senate.

Silencing a Filibuster. A filibuster can be ended by negotiating a compromise on the disputed matter. Since 1917 the Senate has also been able to vote to invoke cloture to cut off a filibuster. This cumbersome procedure requires sixteen senators to sign a cloture petition and file it with the presiding officer of the Senate. Two days later, and one hour after the Senate convenes, the presiding officer establishes the presence of a quorum and then poses the question: "Is it the sense of the Senate that the debate shall be brought to a close?" If three-fifths of the Senate votes in favor of the motion, cloture is invoked. (A two-thirds majority of those present and voting is needed to invoke cloture on proposals to amend the Senate's standing rules.)

There is no limit on how long a filibuster must go on before a cloture petition can be filed. "Years ago, even Lyndon Johnson wouldn't try to get cloture until after a week," Sen. Strom Thurmond, R-S.C., said in 1987. "But now, after one day, if the leaders see you are really going to fight, they'll apply cloture immediately." [24] In 1990 Thurmond still held the record for the longest filibuster by a single individual—twenty-four hours and eighteen minutes on a 1957 civil rights bill; the bill became law despite Thurmond's efforts.

Nor are there any limitations on the number of times the Senate can try to invoke cloture on the same filibuster. "There used to be an unwritten rule that three [cloture votes] was enough," former Senate Parliamentarian Robert B. Dove said.[25] But in 1975 the Senate took six cloture votes in a futile effort to cut off debate on a dispute over a contested Senate seat in New Hampshire. And in 1987-88, the Senate took eight cloture votes to shut off a Republican filibuster of a campaign spending bill before conceding defeat and shelving the measure.

Increased Use of Filibusters. For most of the Senate's history, the filibuster was used sparingly and for the most part only on legislative battles of historical importance, such as peace treaties and civil rights matters. Since the mid-1970s, the Senate has seen a significant increase in its use. Members, Sen. Thomas F. Eagleton, D-Mo., said in 1985, "are prepared to practice the art of gridlock at the drop of a speech or the drop of an amendment." [26]

Ironically, a change in Senate rules that made it easier to invoke cloture to cut off a filibuster coincided with their increased use. In 1975, after years of trying, Senate liberals succeeded in pushing through a change in the Senate's cloture rule. Instead of two-thirds of those voting (sixty-seven if all senators are present), three-fifths of the membership, or sixty senators, could invoke cloture on a filibuster. Of the 297 votes taken to silence filibusters since the cloture rule was adopted in 1917, 65 percent occurred between the rule change in 1975 and the end of the 101st Congress in October 1990.

Several factors account for the increase. More issues come before the Senate, making time an even scarcer commodity than it already is. More issues are controversial; constituents and special interest groups put more pressure on members; and members are more apt to pursue their own political goals even if it means inconveniencing their colleagues. In 1990 filibusters and threats of filibuster were common weapons of senators hoping to spotlight, change, delay, or kill legislation.

The track system, which allows the Senate to temporarily set aside a filibustered measure while it considers other legislation, also may have contributed to the heightened use of filibusters. "For senators peripheral to the fight on a filibustered measure, separate tracking made filibusters more tolerable, made them less resentful of the filibustering senators, and even may have reduced the incentive to vote for cloture," Steven Smith wrote. "And for the filibustering senators, tracking may have improved the chances of success and reduced the costs of filibustering." [27]

The Rise and Fall of the Postcloture Filibuster. Traditionally, filibusterers bowed to the inevitable in the face of a successful motion to invoke cloture, abandoning any further attempts to delay action on the disputed measure. After the Senate made it easier to invoke cloture in 1975, however, a postcloture filibuster quickly appeared. The tactic took advantage of the fact that the hour allotted each senator did not count time spent on procedural motions and that all germane amendments offered before cloture was invoked were in order. By filing dozens of amendments, demanding roll calls and quorum calls, and engaging in other parliamentary procedures, senators could delay final action for days or weeks.

The postcloture filibuster was developed largely by James B. Allen, a conservative Democrat from Alabama. But two northern liberals, James G. Abourezk, D-S.D., and Howard M. Metzenbaum, D-Ohio, exploited the tactic fully in 1977, tying up the Senate for two weeks after cloture had been invoked on a bill to deregulate natural gas. The postcloture debate was ended only after the presiding officer, Vice President Walter Mondale, in close consultation with Majority Leader Byrd, took the then-extraordinary step of ruling amendments offered by the two senators out of order.

In 1979 the Senate moved to eviscerate the postcloture filibuster by including all time spent on procedural activities as well as on substantive debate against each senator's allotted hour. That put a one-hundred-hour cap on postcloture debate. Senators were also barred from calling up more than two amendments until every other senator had an opportunity to call up two amendments. And the presiding officer was authorized to rule clearly dilatory motions out of order. In 1986 the Senate agreed to cap postcloture debate at thirty hours. Senators could still be

Congressional Record

The *Congressional Record* is the primary source of information about what happens on the floors of the Senate and House of Representatives. Published daily when Congress is in session, the *Record* provides an officially sanctioned account of each chamber's debate and shows how individual members voted on all recorded votes.

By law the *Record* is supposed to provide "substantially a verbatim report of the proceedings." Exchanges among legislators can be quite lively and revealing. But senators and representatives are able to edit their remarks for the *Record*, fixing grammatical errors or even deleting words spoken in the heat of debate. Speeches not given on the floor are often included, although both the House and Senate have tightened rules about "inserting remarks," as the process is known. The full texts of bills and other documents, never read aloud on the floor, are often printed in the *Record*.

The *Record* is not the official account of congressional proceedings. That is provided in each chamber's *Journal,* which reports actions taken but not the accompanying debate. But the *Record* is used to determine what Congress intended when it passed a law.

History. Before 1825 reports of congressional debates were sporadic. In 1789-90 Thomas Lloyd of New York took down congressional debates in shorthand. Four volumes exist of his *Congressional Register.* Between 1790 and 1825 debate in the House was reported haphazardly by some of the better newspapers. Senate debates scarcely were reported at all. In 1834 Gales and Seaton published the first of forty-two volumes of *Annals of Congress,* which brought together material from newspapers, magazines, and other sources on congressional proceedings from the First through the Twelfth Congress (March 3, 1789, to May 27, 1824).

From 1824 through 1837 Gales and Seaton published a *Register of Debate,* which directly reported congressional proceedings. In 1833 Blair and Rives began to publish *The Congressional Globe,* but debates were still not reported systematically until 1865, when the *Globe* took on a form and style that later became standard. When the government contract for publication of the *Globe* expired in 1873, Congress provided that the *Congressional Record* would be produced by the Government Printing Office.

Proceedings. The *Record* contains four sections. Two of them, the proceedings of the Senate and of the House, are edited accounts of floor debate and other action taken in each chamber. A member may request "unanimous consent to extend my remarks at this point in the *Record*" at any time he or she is able to gain recognition on the floor. When the request is granted, and it almost always is, a member may include a statement, newspaper article, or speech, which will appear in the body of the *Record* where the member requested.

Until March 1978 there was no way to tell whether a lawmaker had actually delivered his or her remarks or had them inserted. Since then, inserted remarks are indicated in the House proceedings by a different typeface; in the Senate they are denoted by black dots, or bullets. If a member reads only a few words from a speech or article, it will appear in the *Record* as if the member had delivered it in its entirety.

Members are allowed to revise and edit the speeches and remarks they deliver during floor debate before they are published in the *Record.* Although most legislators edit their remarks to correct grammar, rarely do they excise entire speeches or even sections of them. From time to time, however, there are complaints that this privilege has been abused.

Since 1979 time cues have marked House floor debate to show roughly when a particular discussion occurred. Senate proceedings have no indication of time.

Extensions of Remarks. In addition to inserting material, senators and representatives are given further space to extend their remarks. They may add such extraneous material as speeches given outside Congress, selected editorials, or letters. Senators may add such material to the body of the *Record;* representatives must place it in the Extension of Remarks section.

Daily Digest. The fourth section of the *Record* is the Daily Digest, which summarizes House and Senate floor action for the day as well as Senate, House, and conference committee meetings. It also notes bills reported, conference committee reports filed, and the time and date of the next House and Senate sessions and all committee meetings. The last issue of the Digest in the week lists the program for the coming week, including legislation scheduled for floor action if it has been announced, and all committee meetings.

At the beginning of each month the Digest publishes a statistical summation of congressional activity in the previous month.

An index to the *Record* is published semimonthly.

Costs. About 20,000 copies of each day's issue of the *Record* are printed. In fiscal 1990 the total cost came to $17.9 million. An annual subscription cost $225 in 1991; an individual copy cost $1.50. Until 1970 a subscription cost only $1.50 a month. The *Record* is also available on microfiche.

Each senator is entitled to thirty-seven free copies for constituents, each representative to twenty-five. Additional copies are provided for office use. Twice as many free copies were provided until rules were changed in 1977.

Rules require that any insert of more than two pages include an estimate of printing costs by the Government Printing Office. One of the most expensive inserts appeared in the issue of June 15, 1987, when Rep. Bill Alexander, D-Ark., inserted 403 pages covering three and a half years of congressional debate on an amendment barring military aid to the antigovernment contra guerrillas in Nicaragua. Estimated cost of the insertion: $197,000.

recognized for an hour, but the time was allocated on a first-come, first-served basis.

Final Senate Action

Once debate on all amendments has ended, a final vote is taken. Senate observers are often surprised to discover that most bills pass by voice votes with only a handful of senators present. Any member, however, can request a roll call on final passage.

After the final vote is announced, the Senate must go through the same procedure of moving to reconsider used in the House. A senator who voted for the bill (or who did not vote) moves to reconsider the vote; a second senator who voted for the bill moves to table the motion to reconsider, and the tabling motion is almost always adopted, usually by voice vote.

Final Action: Resolving Differences

Before a bill can be sent to the president for his signature, it must be approved in identical form by both chambers of Congress. Therefore, after a bill has been passed by one house, an engrossed copy—a final version, including all changes made during floor action—is transmitted to the other chamber.

On most noncontroversial legislation the second chamber simply agrees to the version approved by the first chamber. When that occurs, no further legislative action is required, and the bill can be submitted to the president. Measures accepted by the second chamber without change are usually routine and noncontroversial.

On virtually all major legislation, however, the second chamber approves a version that differs, sometimes radically, from the measure adopted by the first chamber. (Often the second chamber already has a similar measure under consideration.) When that happens, the second chamber has two options. It may return the bill to the chamber of origin, which then has the choice of accepting the second chamber's amendments, accepting them with further amendments, or disagreeing to the other version and requesting a House-Senate conference. Or the second house itself may request a conference.

Sometimes one chamber accepts major amendments made by the other to avoid further floor action that might jeopardize the bill. That occurred on the Alaska lands bill in the postelection session of 1980. Democratic sponsors of the House-passed bill, facing the political realities of the Republican election landslide that November, grudgingly accepted the Senate version, which did not contain as many protections for the environment, rather than risk a conference version or perhaps no bill at all.

Occasionally after both chambers have passed different versions of the same measure, members and staff of the House and Senate committees with jurisdiction for the bill informally work out a compromise that one house adopts as an amendment to the other chamber's version. The latter chamber then agrees to the version as amended.

Just as neither chamber may offer amendments beyond the second degree, neither chamber may amend the other's amendments more than twice. Like other rules, however, this one can be waived and sometimes is. The budget reconciliation act of 1985 was shuffled between the two chambers nine times before agreement was finally reached.

It should be noted that many bills pass one chamber of Congress never to be considered in the other. Those measures, as well as any on which the House and Senate are unable to reconcile their differences, die at the end of the Congress.

Conference Action

Sen. Joel Bennett "Champ" Clark, D-Mo., once introduced a resolution providing that "all bills and resolutions shall be read twice and, without debate, referred to conference." He was joking, of course, but his proposal highlights the crucial role of conference committees in drafting the final form of complex and controversial legislation. Everything the bill's sponsors worked for and all the efforts exerted by the executive branch and private interests to help pass or defeat it can be won or lost during these negotiations. Some of the hardest bargaining in the entire legislative process takes place in conference committees, and frequently the conference goes on for days, weeks, even months, before the two sides reconcile their differences.

During floor consideration of a bill members may adopt certain tactics solely to better position themselves for the bargaining and compromise that is the hallmark of all conference negotiations. A senator, for example, may demand a roll call on a particular amendment to demonstrate to the House the Senate's solid support for the amendment—or its solid opposition. A committee may add some provisions to its version that can be traded away in conference. Or it may deliberately keep out a provision it knows the other chamber favors, again to have something to trade in conference. A floor manager may agree to an amendment knowing that it can be dumped in the conference.

Once in conference, conferees generally try to grant concessions only insofar as they remain confident the chamber they represent will accept the compromises. That is not always possible, however. The threat of a Senate filibuster on the conference version, for example, may influence House conferees to agree to a provision that they know the full House might find distasteful. Time also may be a factor, especially at the end of a Congress when delay might cause a bill to die in conference.

Calling a Conference

Either chamber can request a conference once both have considered the same legislation. Generally, the chamber that approved the legislation first will disagree to the amendments made by the second body and request that a conference be convened. Sometimes, however, the second body will ask for a conference immediately after it has passed the legislation, assuming that the other chamber will not accept its amendments.

Both chambers technically must go to conference on a single bill. Thus one chamber often takes up the other's version of the measure, strikes everything after the enacting clause, and substitutes its version for everything but the other chamber's bill number. Both versions can then be considered by the conference committee.

A conference cannot take place until both chambers formally agree that it be held. The Senate usually requests or agrees to a conference by unanimous consent. In the House this action generally is taken by unanimous consent, by motion, or by adoption by majority vote of a rule from the Rules Committee providing for a conference on a particular bill. Before 1965 the House could bypass the Rules Committee only by unanimous consent or by suspension of the rules, which requires a two-thirds majority. Since 1965, however, a bill may be sent to conference by majority vote, without recourse to the Rules Committee, if the committee with jurisdiction over the bill approves.

Selection of Conferees

The two chambers have different rules for selecting conferees, or "managers," as they are formally called, but in practice both follow similar procedures. House rules grant the Speaker the right to appoint conferees, but he usually does so only after consultation with the chairman and ranking minority member of the committee having jurisdiction over the legislation. Senate rules allow the chamber as a whole to elect conferees, but that rarely happens. The common practice is for the presiding officer to appoint conferees on the recommendation of the appropriate committee chairman and ranking minority member.

The chairman of the committee that handled the legislation usually selects himself, the ranking minority member, and other members of the committee. If a subcommittee has exercised major responsibility for a bill, some of its members may be chosen. Seniority once governed the selection of conferees, but it is quite common today for junior members in each chamber to be chosen, especially if they are particularly knowledgeable about or interested in the bill. Occasionally a member from another committee with expertise in the subject matter of the bill may be named to the conference.

The increase in the size of conference committees has led to ways to limit the role of some conferees, particularly those who are not members of the committee of jurisdiction. "Additional" conferees consider and vote only on specific subjects or sections of the legislation. "Exclusive" conferees are the sole negotiators for their chambers on specified subjects or sections. General conferees, who vote on the same issues as additional conferees, may not participate in these areas unless they are also exclusive conferees.

The number of conferees each chamber selects does not have to be the same. A majority in each delegation will be from the majority party in the chamber, however. That requirement means that each chamber must name at least three conferees on each bill, but there is no upper limit. Bills that have been referred to more than one committee usually entail large conferences because conferees are selected from each of the committees of jurisdiction.

Twenty-three committees, for example, sent conferees to the conference committee on the omnibus trade bill enacted in 1988. Budget reconciliation resolutions generally engender some of the largest conferences because they affect the jurisdictions of almost every House and Senate committee. More than 250 conferees from both houses were appointed as conferees on the 1981 budget reconciliation bill, for example. Such large conferences usually divide up into smaller working groups, or subconferences, that deal only with specific parts of the bill.

Precedent in both the House and Senate indicates that conferees are expected to support the legislative positions of the chamber they represent. However, few legislative committees have hard and fast rules guiding the chairman on his selection of conferees, although most chairmen consult with and take the advice of the ranking minority member in choosing conferees from the minority party.

The lack of guidance frequently has led to charges that a chairman has stacked a conference with members favoring his own position rather than the position of the majority. There also is the question whether conferees are likely to uphold the chamber's position on key points in conference deliberations. A member may have voted for final passage but still have opposed key amendments during committee or floor action.

In 1972 the House ultimately killed a bill to raise the

R. Michael Jenkins

A House-Senate conference on clean air legislation in 1990 included more than 140 members representing nine House and Senate committees.

hourly minimum wage because the likely conferees had not supported the House position. Generally regarded as more liberal than the rest of the House, the Education and Labor Committee had approved the minimum wage bill in 1971. When the bill came to the floor in 1972, the House approved a less-generous substitute version offered by John N. Erlenborn, R-Ill.

Subsequently the Senate passed a version of the bill that was even more liberal than the House committee's original version. The committee chairman, Rep. Carl D. Perkins, D-Ky., then requested unanimous consent to send the bill to conference. Asked by Erlenborn who he had recommended to be conferees, Perkins said they would come from the subcommittee that originally considered the bill. Ten of the eleven Democratic members of the subcommittee had voted against the Erlenborn substitute.

Erlenborn objected to the unanimous consent request, saying it was unfair to send to conference a delegation whose majority had voted against the House-passed version of the bill. Perkins then offered a motion that the House disagree with the Senate version and request a conference to resolve the differences. Perkins' motion was defeated, 190-198. Later the House killed the bill by voting 188-196 against another Perkins motion to request a conference.

In an effort to ensure that its conferees would uphold its position, the House in 1974 modified its rules on conferees selection. The revised rule said that "the Speaker shall appoint [as conferees] no less than a majority of members who generally supported the House position as determined by the Speaker." A further revision, in 1975, said that "the Speaker shall name members who are primarily responsible for the legislation and shall, to the fullest extent feasible, include the principal proponents of the major provisions of the bill as it passed the House."

Either chamber may try to enforce its will by instructing its conferees how to vote in conference, but the rules do not obligate the conferees to follow the instructions. Efforts to instruct conferees may nevertheless reflect the degree of support in the chamber for certain provisions or amendments. Votes to instruct may also serve as warnings that conferees had better not stray too far from the language the chamber originally approved.

Authority of Conferees

Theoretically House and Senate conferees are limited to resolving matters in disagreement between the two chambers. They are not authorized to delete provisions or language that both chambers have agreed to or to draft entirely new provisions. When the disagreement involves numbers, such as the level of funding in appropriations bills, conferees are supposed to stay within the amounts proposed by the two houses. (Generally, they split the difference.)

In practice the conferees have wide latitude, except where the matters in disagreement are very specific. If one chamber has substituted an entirely new version of the bill for that approved by the other chamber—which is frequently the case on major bills—the entire subject is technically in disagreement, and the conferees may draft an entirely new bill if they so choose. In such a case, the Legislative Reorganization Act of 1946 stipulates that they may not include in the conference version of the bill "matter not committed to them by either house." But they may include "matter which is a germane modification of subjects in disagreement."

The House has long objected to the inclusion in conference bills of Senate-passed amendments that are not germane. Because conference agreements may not be amended on the floor of either chamber, the House was often put in a "take-it-or-leave-it" situation, forced either to accept a nongermane amendment it may never have debated or to vote down the entire conference report, including provisions it favored. A series of rules changes in the 1970s, including one in 1972 that allows the House to take separate votes on nongermane amendments in conference reports, has given the House some leverage both in conference and on the Senate floor. Senate floor managers often try to turn away nongermane floor amendments by arguing that they might prevent the entire bill from winning approval in the House.

If the conferees find they are unable to reach agreement, they may return to their respective chambers for instructions. Or they may simply report their failure to reach agreement to the parent chamber and allow the full House or Senate to act as it wishes.

The rules allow House conferees to be instructed or discharged and replaced by new conferees if they fail to reach agreement within twenty calendar days (or within thirty-six hours of their appointment during the last six days of a session). This rule is rarely invoked.

Adoption of the Conference Report

When a majority of the conferees from each chamber have reached agreement on a bill, conference committee staff—generally the staff of the committees with original jurisdiction over the measure—write a conference report indicating changes made in the bill and explaining each side's action. If the two sides have been unable to reach a compromise on particular House or Senate amendments, those amendments are "reported in disagreement" and are acted upon separately after the conference report itself has been agreed to.

The conference report must be signed by a majority of conferees from each chamber and submitted in document form to each house for approval. Minority reports are not permitted. Until the 1970 Legislative Reorganization Act required House and Senate conferees to prepare a joint explanatory statement, the conference report was printed only in the House, together with an explanation by the House conferees. Although the conference report is supposed to be printed in the Senate, that requirement is frequently waived by unanimous consent. The report is always published in the *Congressional Record*. House rules also require that conference reports lie over three days before the House takes them up.

In both chambers debate on conference reports is highly privileged and can interrupt most other business. The House may first send the report to the Rules Committee before the legislation goes to the floor for a final vote on a rule waiving any points of order that might be lodged against the bill.

The house that agreed to the other chamber's request to go to conference on a bill acts first on the conference version. This procedure, followed by custom rather than by rule, is sometimes ignored; the Senate, for example, asked for the conference on the 1981 tax cut, and it acted first on the conference report.

Which chamber acts first or last can occasionally influence the outcome. The chamber to act first has three options: it can agree to the conference report, reject it, or

President Lyndon B. Johnson signs legislation in 1965 establishing the Medicare program, as former President Harry S. Truman looks on. Standing at rear are Lady Bird Johnson, Vice President Hubert H. Humphrey, and Bess Truman.

AP/Wide World Photos

recommit it to the conference committee for further deliberation. Once the first chamber has acted, however, the conference committee is dissolved, and recommittal is no longer an option. The second chamber must vote the conference report up or down.

The pressure on reluctant members to support a report that the other chamber has already approved can be intense. Rep. Jack Brooks, D-Texas, counted on that intense lobbying when he maneuvered in 1979 to have the House take up the conference report creating the Department of Education after the Senate had already agreed to it. Brooks's strategy worked; the House, which had originally approved creation of the department by a four-vote margin, agreed to the conference report with fourteen votes to spare.

The conference version of the bill must be approved or rejected in its entirety by both bodies. Exceptions are made for nongermane Senate amendments and for certain other amendments that are reported in disagreement. Unless a special rule has waived all points of order, any member of the House may make the point of order that a particular section of a conference report contains nongermane material and move to reject the offending language. Forty minutes of debate, equally divided between opposing sides, is allotted for such motions. If the motion carries, the nongermane material is deleted, and the House may go on to approve the conference report minus the deletion. The conference report must then go back to the Senate, which must either accept the report as amended by the House or reject it altogether.

If conferees have been unable to agree on any of the amendments in disagreement, separate votes are taken in both houses to resolve the differences. One chamber may insist on its amendment, or it may move to "recede and concur" in the other chamber's position. Occasionally the amendment in disagreement will be returned to conference for further compromise efforts. In the House certain amendments are reported from conference in "technical disagreement" because they do not conform to House rules.

Such disagreements are resolved on the floor with motions to recede and concur either in the amendment as the Senate passed it or as modified by the conference committee.

Conference reports are seldom rejected, in part because legislators have little desire to begin the entire legislative process all over again and in part because members tend to defer to the expertise of the conferees, just as they tend to defer to the recommendations of the legislative committees. If a bill dies once it has reached conference, it is more likely that conferees have been unable to reach a compromise before the end of the Congress. That is what happened to the 1990 campaign finance bill.

Final Legislative Action

After both houses have given final approval to a bill, a final copy of the bill, known as the enrolled bill, is prepared by the enrolling clerk of the chamber in which the bill originated, printed on parchment-type paper, and certified as correct by the secretary of the Senate or the clerk of the House, depending on which chamber originated the measure. No matter where the bill originated, it is signed first by the Speaker of the House and then by the president pro tempore of the Senate, and sent to the White House.

The president has ten days (not counting Sundays) from the day he receives the bill to act upon it. If he approves the measure he signs it, dates it, and usually writes the word "approved" on the document. The Constitution requires only the president's signature.

A bill may become law without the president's signature in one of two ways. If the president does not sign a bill within ten days (Sundays excepted) from the time he receives it, the bill becomes law provided Congress is in session. A bill may also become law without the president's signature if Congress overrides a veto.

The Veto Power

If the president does not want a bill to become law, he may veto it by returning it to the chamber in which it originated without his signature and with a message stating his objections. If no further action is taken, the bill dies.

The Constitution provides that Congress may attempt to enact the bill into law "the objections of the president to the contrary notwithstanding." A two-thirds vote of those present and voting in both chambers is required to override a veto. There must be a quorum present for the vote, which must be by roll call. Debate may precede the vote, with motions permitted to lay the veto on the table, to postpone action on it, or to refer it to committee.

If the first house to act fails to override the veto, the matter ends there. If the vote to override succeeds, the measure is sent to the second house. If the veto is overridden there, the bill becomes law without the president's signature; otherwise, the veto stands and the bill is dead. The attempt to override can occur at any time remaining in the Congress in which the veto is received.

The Pocket Veto

The Constitution also provides that a bill shall not become law if "Congress by their adjournment prevent its return." The president can then "pocket veto" the bill since he does not have an opportunity to return it to Congress for further consideration.

The president clearly may pocket veto any bills that are still awaiting his approval when Congress adjourns *sine die*. But at the end of 1990 it was still unclear whether it was proper for the president to pocket veto bills between sessions of the same Congress or during congressional recesses. Federal courts had ruled such pocket vetoes by Presidents Richard Nixon and Ronald Reagan to be unconstitutional, but the Supreme Court had not made a definitive ruling on the issue. President George Bush raised the issue again in 1989, when he pocket vetoed a bill during the August recess and another after the 1989 session ended but before the 1990 session began.

Notes

1. Walter J. Oleszek, *Congressional Procedures and the Policy Process*, 3rd ed. (Washington, D.C.: CQ Press, 1989), 17.
2. *National Review*, Feb. 27, 1987, 24.
3. Janet Hook, "Speaker Jim Wright Takes Charge in the House," *Congressional Quarterly Weekly Report*, July 11, 1987, 1486.
4. Steven S. Smith, *Call to Order: Floor Politics in the House and Senate* (Washington, D.C.: Brookings Institution, 1989), 9.
5. *Congress A to Z: CQ's Ready Reference Encyclopedia* (Washington, D.C.: Congressional Quarterly, 1988), 357.
6. Ibid.
7. *The Washington Post*, June 26, 1983, A14.
8. *Congress A to Z*, 186-187.
9. Oleszek, *Congressional Procedures*, 83.
10. Roger H. Davidson and Walter J. Oleszek, *Congress and Its Members*, 3rd ed. (Washington, D.C.: CQ Press, 1990), 315.
11. Bruce I. Oppenheimer, "The Changing Relationship between House Leadership and the Committee on Rules," in *Understanding Congressional Leadership*, ed. Frank H. Mackaman (Washington, D.C.: CQ Press, 1981), 217.
12. Oleszek, *Congressional Procedures*, 127.
13. Stanley Bach and Steven S. Smith, *Managing Uncertainty in the House of Representatives: Adaptation and Innovation in Special Rules* (Washington, D.C.: Brookings Institution, 1988), 28.
14. Janet Hook, "GOP Chafes Under Restrictive House Rules," *Congressional Quarterly Weekly Report*, Oct. 10, 1987, 2452.
15. Bach and Smith, *Managing Uncertainty in the House of Representatives*, 73.
16. Oleszek, *Congressional Procedures*, 149.
17. Smith, *Call to Order*, 243.
18. Jacqueline Calmes, "Byrd Struggles to Lead Deeply Divided Senate," *Congressional Quarterly Weekly Report*, July 4, 1987, 1422.
19. Oleszek, *Congressional Procedures*, 186.
20. Smith, *Call to Order*, 128.
21. Oleszek, *Congressional Procedures*, 234.
22. Nancy Landon Kassebaum, "The Senate Is Not in Order," *The Washington Post*, Jan. 27, 1988, A19.
23. Oleszek, *Congressional Procedures*, 206.
24. Jacqueline Calmes, " 'Trivialized' Filibuster Is Still a Potent Tool," *Congressional Quarterly Weekly Report*, Sept. 5, 1987, 2120.
25. Ibid.
26. Smith, *Call to Order*, 97.
27. Ibid., 96.

Selected Readings

Bacchus, William I. *Inside the Legislative Process.* Boulder, Colo.: Westview Press, 1983.

Bach, Stanley, and Steven S. Smith. *Managing Uncertainty in the House of Representatives: Adaptation and Innovation of Special Rules.* Washington, D.C.: Brookings Institution, 1988.

Berman, Daniel M. *How a Bill Becomes a Law: Congress Enacts Civil Rights Legislation.* New York: Macmillan, 1966.

Bibby, John F. *Congress Off the Record: The Candid Analysis of Seven Members.* Washington, D.C.: American Enterprise Institute for Public Policy Research, 1983.

Birnbaum, Jeffrey H., and Alan S. Murray. *Showdown at Gucci Gulch.* New York: Random House, 1987.

Brown, W. Holmes. *Constitution, Jefferson's Manual, and Rules of the House of Representatives.* 101st Cong., 1st sess., 1989.

Cannon, Clarence, ed. *Cannon's Precedents of the House of Representatives.* 6 vols. Washington, D.C.: Government Printing Office, 1936.

———. *Cannon's Procedure in the House of Representatives.* Washington, D.C.: Government Printing Office, 1963.

Congress A to Z: CQ's Ready Reference Encyclopedia. Washington, D.C.: Congressional Quarterly, 1988.

Cooper, Joseph, and G. Calvin Mackenzie. *The House at Work.* Austin: University of Texas Press, 1981.

Davidson, Roger H., and Walter J. Oleszek. *Congress and Its Members.* 3rd ed. Washington, D.C.: CQ Press, 1990.

———. *Governing: Readings and Cases in American Politics.* Washington, D.C.: CQ Press, 1987.

Deschler, Lewis. *Precedents of the House of Representatives.* 9 vols. Washington, D.C.: Government Printing Office, 1977.

Deschler, Lewis, and W. Holmes Brown. *Procedure in the House of Representatives.* Washington, D.C.: Government Printing Office, 1982; 1987 supplement.

Dodd, Lawrence C., and Bruce I. Oppenheimer, eds. *Congress Reconsidered.* 4th ed. Washington, D.C.: CQ Press, 1989.

Eidenberg, Eugene, and Roy D. Morey. *An Act of Congress: The Legislative Process and the Making of Education Policy.* New York: W. W. Norton, 1969.

Fenno, Richard. *Congressmen in Committees.* Boston: Little, Brown, 1973.

Fox, Harrison W., Jr. *Congressional Staffs: The Invisible Force in American Lawmaking.* New York: The Free Press, 1979.

Froman, Lewis A., Jr. *The Congressional Process: Strategies, Rules, and Procedures.* Boston: Little, Brown, 1967.

Galloway, George B. *The Legislative Process in Congress.* New

York: Thomas Y. Crowell, 1953.

Goodwin, George. *The Little Legislatures.* Amherst: University of Massachusetts Press, 1970.

Hinds, Asher C., ed. *Hinds' Precedents of the House of Representatives.* 5 vols. Washington, D.C.: Government Printing Office, 1907.

Jewell, Malcolm E., and Samuel C. Patterson. *The Legislative Process in the United States.* 4th ed. New York: McGraw-Hill, 1985.

Kingdon, John W. *Congressmen's Voting Decisions.* 3rd ed. New York: Harper and Row, 1989.

Kornacki, John J., ed. *Leading Congress: New Styles, New Strategies.* Washington, D.C.: Congressional Quarterly, 1990.

Loomis, Burdett A. *Setting Course: A Congressional Management Guide.* Washington, D.C.: American University, 1984.

Luce, Robert. *Legislative Procedure.* Boston: Houghton Mifflin, 1922. Reprint. New York: DeCapo Press, 1972.

Malbin, Michael J. *Unelected Representatives.* New York: Basic Books, 1980.

Mann, Thomas E., and Norman J. Ornstein. *The New Congress.* Washington, D.C.: American Enterprise Institute for Public Policy Research, 1981.

Manual on Legislative Procedure in the U.S. House of Representatives. 6th ed. Prepared under the auspices of the Minority Leader, U.S. House of Representatives, 1986.

Nickels, Ilona B. *Parliamentary Reference Sources: An Introductory Guide.* Washington, D.C.: Congressional Research Service, 1986.

Oleszek, Walter J. *Congressional Procedures and the Policy Process.* 3rd ed. Washington, D.C.: CQ Press, 1989.

Ornstein, Norman J., ed. *Congress in Change: Evolution and Reform.* New York: Praeger, 1975.

Ornstein, Norman J., Thomas E. Mann, and Michael J. Malbin. *Vital Statistics on Congress, 1989-1990.* Washington, D.C.: Congressional Quarterly, 1989.

Parker, Glenn R., ed. *Studies of Congress.* Washington, D.C.: CQ Press, 1985.

Peabody, Robert L., and others. *To Enact a Law: Congress and Campaign Financing.* New York: Praeger, 1972.

Price, David. *Who Makes the Laws?* Cambridge, Mass.: Schenkman, 1972.

Redman, Eric. *The Dance of Legislation.* New York: Simon and Schuster, 1973.

Reid, T. R. *Congressional Odyssey: The Saga of a Senate Bill.* New York: W. H. Freeman, 1980.

Riddick, Floyd M. *Senate Procedures: Precedents and Practices.* 97th Cong., 1st sess., 1981. Senate Doc. 97-2.

———. *The U.S. Congress: Organization and Procedure.* Manassas, Va.: National Capitol Publishers, 1949.

Rieselbach, Leroy N. *Congressional Reform.* Washington, D.C.: CQ Press, 1986.

Ripley, Randall B. *Congress: Procedure and Policy.* 4th ed. New York: W. W. Norton, 1988.

Sheppard, Burton D. *Rethinking Congressional Reform: The Reform Roots of the Special Interest Congress.* Cambridge, Mass.: Schenkman, 1985.

Siff, Ted, and Alan Weil. *Ruling Congress: How House and Senate Rules Govern the Legislative Process.* New York: Grossman Publishers, 1975.

Smith, Steven S. *Call to Order: Floor Politics in the House and Senate.* Washington, D.C.: Brookings Institution, 1989.

Smith, Steven S., and Christopher J. Deering. *Committees in Congress.* 2nd ed. Washington, D.C.: CQ Press, 1990.

Unekis, Joseph K., and Leroy N. Rieselbach. *Congressional Committee Politics: Continuity and Change.* New York: Praeger, 1984.

U.S. Congress. Senate. Committee on Rules and Administration. *Senate Manual Containing the Standing Rules, Orders, Laws, and Resolutions Affecting the Business of the United States Senate.* 101st Cong., 1st sess., 1989. Senate Doc. 101-1.

Vogler, David J. *The Third House: Conference Committees in the United States Congress.* Evanston, Ill.: Northwestern University Press, 1971.

Whalen, Charles, and Barbara Whalen. *The Longest Debate: A Legislative History of the 1964 Civil Rights Act.* Washington, D.C.: Seven Locks Press, 1985.

The Committee System

Committees are the infrastructure of Congress. They are where the bulk of legislative work is done—where expertise resides, where policies incubate, where most legislative proposals are written or refined, where many necessary compromises are made, where the public can make its views known, where members of Congress build influence and reputations.

Committees have enormous power. They hold hearings, conduct investigations, and oversee government programs. They initiate bills, approve and report legislation to the floor. They can kill measures through inaction or defeat.

A committee that has subjected a bill to expert scrutiny traditionally has expected its decisions to be upheld on the floor. Committees, according to *Cannon's Procedure in the House of Representatives,* "are not infallible, but they have had long familiarity with the subject under discussion, and have made an intimate study of the particular bill before the House and after mature deliberation have made formal recommendations and, other considerations being equal, are entitled to support on the floor." [1]

It is difficult—at times virtually impossible—to circumvent a committee that is determined not to act. A bill that has been approved by a committee may be amended when it reaches the House or Senate floor, but extensive revisions generally are more difficult to achieve at that stage. The actions of the committees more often than not give Congress its record of legislative achievement and failure.

"The rules and precedents of both chambers reinforce committee prerogatives," congressional expert Walter J. Oleszek has written. And, while there are exceptions to these rules, "members of Congress generally are reluctant to see the committee system weakened by frequent recourse to extraordinary procedures." [2]

Yet, as a result of committee reforms in the 1970s, committees and their leaders are no longer as invincible as they once were. Power has been diffused and rival power centers have emerged. Many lawmakers no longer defer to committees on the details of legislation. There are more floor challenges to more committees now that members have gained the expertise and staff needed to make independent judgments.

Once-unchallenged committee leaders are now held accountable for their actions and can be ousted by a vote of their party. Committees now are sharing their once exclusive domains with other committees, particularly in the House, through the growth of bill referrals to more than one committee. The traditional authorizing committees find their power being diluted, if not eclipsed, by the Appropriations and Budget committees as Congress struggles to control immense federal budget deficits. And summits, task forces, and other ad hoc groups are convened on occasion to handle touchy issues in a seeming indictment of Congress's inability to get things done through traditional channels. Congressional leaders orchestrate a changing legislative process.

The mix of historic precedents and contemporary reforms has left committees in a state of flux. "For many members as well as outside observers, the place of committees in congressional decision making is now ambiguous," wrote Steven S. Smith and Christopher J. Deering in 1990. [3] On the one hand, committees are still the central players in the legislative process. Yet, they are much less autonomous than they were just a few decades earlier.

Emergence of Committees

Over the years the committee system has been buffeted and shaped by changing circumstances, reform movements, competing power centers, assaults by outside forces. Power has ebbed and flowed. Changes and accommodations have been made.

In the earliest Congresses, members were few in number and their legislative workload was light. Temporary committees served their needs. But as the nation grew and took on more complex responsibilities and problems, Congress had to develop expertise and the mechanisms to deal with the changing world. And so, from a somewhat haphazard arrangement of ad hoc committees evolved a highly specialized system of permanent committees.

Standing committees were institutionalized and multiplied in the nineteenth century. Efforts in the twentieth century to consolidate the burgeoning committee system, especially the 1946 Legislative Reorganization Act, served to strengthen the streamlined committees and their leaders.

So overriding did the influence of committees in the legislative process become that scholars over the years called them "little legislatures" [4] and their chairmen "petty barons." [5]

The innate power of the committee system often was exercised arbitrarily by committee chairmen. Until a reform movement swept Congress in the 1970s, committees usually were powers unto themselves. Strong party leadership in Congress might influence committee actions, but most committees—and their chairmen—had sufficient independence to operate pretty much as they wished. The chairmen's power was equaled only by a few party leaders who had great influence, such as House Speaker Sam Rayburn, D-Texas, or Senate Majority Leader Lyndon B. Johnson, D-Texas.

A chairman's power resulted from the rigid operation of the seniority system, under which a person rose to a chairmanship simply through longevity in Congress. The unwritten seniority rule conferred a committee chairmanship on the member of the majority party with the longest continuous service on the committee. As long as his party retained control of Congress, he normally kept this position; if control passed to the other party, he changed places with the ranking member of that party. The seniority system, intermittently observed from the mid-1800s, took firm hold in the Senate after the Civil War. It became entrenched in the House within a few decades of the 1910-11 revolt against an all-powerful speakership.

1970s Revolt and Aftermath

Rule by seniority reigned supreme until the early 1970s. Then, changing circumstances caught up with it. The principal change was the election to Congress of dozens of new members—persons who had little patience with the admonition to newcomers, credited to Speaker Rayburn, that "to get along, go along." New members, who did not have much influence in the Senate or House, joined forces with disgruntled incumbents, who had chafed under the often heavy-handed rule of arbitrary chairmen. Thus, in the late 1960s and early 1970s, began the revolt that was

to undermine the seniority system and lead to numerous other procedural changes that redefined the role and power of committees and their chairmen.

Though the dramatic changes did not come until the 1970s, a portent of things to come occurred after the 1966 election defeat of Howard W. Smith, D-Va., the powerful chairman of the House Rules Committee, the gatekeeper to the House floor. For the first time in its history the committee adopted a set of rules governing its procedures. The new regulations denied the chairman the right to set meeting dates, required the consent of a committee majority to table (kill) a bill, and set limits on proxy voting.

The 1970s revolt began in the House as membership turnover accelerated and the proportion of younger, first- and second-term members increased. These lawmakers demanded fundamental changes in the way Congress—and particularly the committees—operated. Major changes in Democratic Caucus rules and, to a lesser extent, in the standing rules of the House and the Senate, diluted the authority enjoyed by committee chairmen and other senior members and redistributed the power among the junior members.

The single most important factor that undermined the chairmen's authority was the decision by Democrats in both chambers to allow chairmen to be elected by their party's caucus. The change came gradually, beginning in 1971. By 1975 Democrats had adopted rules providing for a secret-ballot election of the top Democrats on committees. A secret vote was automatic in the House and held at the request of 20 percent of Senate Democrats. That year three House chairmen were ousted in caucus elections.

The election requirement made chairmen accountable to their colleagues for their conduct. Caucus election of committee chairmen was only one of a number of changes

Ken Heinen

The House Appropriations Committee prepares annual funding bills for government agencies. Although its powers have been curbed since the 1970s, it remains one of the most influential committees in Congress.

that restricted the chairmen's power. Committees were required under the 1970 Legislative Reorganization Act to have written rules. In 1973 House Democrats adopted a "bill of rights" that reinforced subcommittee autonomy.

In subsequent years House Democrats gave members of each committee the power to determine the number of subcommittees their committee would have. Most committees were required to have subcommittees.

Staffing prerogatives were extended to members other than the chairman. This change made members less subservient to the chairman by giving them professional staff help on legislative issues.

Democrats in both chambers also limited the influence of chairmen and other senior members by restricting the number of chairmanships and committee slots that a member could hold.

As the decade of the 1970s closed, the committee structure was still firmly entrenched in Congress, but much of the power and prestige that had been held by the full committees had been transferred to the subcommittees and to a new, larger corps of chairmen, especially in the House. Subcommittees took on the institutional characteristics and vested interests of their parent committees. People began to talk about "subcommittee government" instead of "committee government" on Capitol Hill.

This empowerment of subcommittees led to a decentralization of power and to heavier legislative workloads for members of both houses. Critics noted a slowing down of the legislative process. "On balance, Congress has become more decentralized, more responsive to a multitude of forces inside and outside its halls, and, as a result, more hard pressed to formulate and enact coherent, responsible public policies," wrote Leroy N. Rieselbach.[6]

So great was the proliferation of subcommittees that limits on their number were set in both chambers. Other changes and accommodations were made as well.

Evolution of the System: Growth and Reform

Congressional committees became a major factor in the legislative process by evolution, not by constitutional design. The committee concept was borrowed from the British Parliament and transmitted to the New World by way of the colonial legislatures, most notably those of Pennsylvania and Virginia. But the committee system as it developed in Congress was modified and influenced by characteristics peculiar to American life.

In the early days of the Republic, when the nation's population was small and the duties of the central government were carefully circumscribed, Congress had little need for the division of labor that today's committee system provides. A people who viewed with grave suspicion the need to delegate authority to elected representatives in Washington were served by a Congress that only grudgingly delegated any of its own powers to committees.

In the early Congresses, legislative proposals were considered first in the Senate or House chamber, after which a special or select committee was appointed to work out the details of the legislation. Once the committee submitted its report on the bill, it was dissolved. Approximately 350 such committees were created during the Third Congress alone.[7]

As legislation increased in volume and complexity, permanent (standing) committees gradually replaced select committees, and legislation was referred directly to the committees without first being considered by the parent body. This procedure gave the committees initial authority over legislation, each in its specialized jurisdiction, subject to subsequent review by the full chamber.

The House led the way in the creation of standing committees. The Committee on Elections, created in 1789, was followed by the Claims Committee in 1794 and by Commerce and Manufactures and Revision of the Laws committees in 1795. The number had risen to ten by 1810. The next substantial expansion of committees did not occur until the administration of President James Monroe (1817-25). Between the War of 1812 and the Civil War the standing committee system became the standard vehicle for consideration of legislative business by the House, but it was not yet fully exploited as a source of independent power. The dramatic growth of the House and its workload contributed to the institutionalization of committees. House Speaker Henry Clay of Kentucky also found a responsive committee system helpful to his policy goals and thus encouraged the creation of committees.[8]

The Senate was slower in establishing standing committees. In the first twenty-five years of its existence, only four standing committees were created, and all of them on the whole were more administrative than legislative. Most of the committee work fell to select committees, usually of three members, appointed as the occasion demanded and disbanded when their task was completed. These occasions were so frequent that during the session of 1815-16 between ninety and one hundred select committees were appointed. Frequently, however, related legislation would be referred to special committees already in existence and the same senators often were appointed to committees dealing with similar subjects.

In 1816 the Senate, finding inconvenient the appointment of so many ad hoc committees during each session, added eleven standing committees to the existing four. By 1863 the number had grown to nineteen.[9] But prior to the Civil War committees still played a relatively small role in the Senate.

Committee Membership

Each chamber developed its own method of making appointments to the committees. The rule established by the House in 1789 reserved to the whole House the power to choose the membership of all committees composed of more than three members. That rule gave way in 1790 to a rule delegating this power to the Speaker, with the reservation that the House might direct otherwise in special cases. Eventually, however, the Speaker was given the right to appoint the members as well as the chairmen of all standing committees, a power he retained until 1911.

The principle that the committees were to be bipartisan, but weighted in favor of the majority party and its policies, was established early.

In making committee appointments and promotions, certain principles governed the Speaker's choices. The wishes of the minority leaders in filling vacancies going to members of their party usually were respected. Generally, seniority—length of service on the committee—and factors such as geographical distribution and party loyalty were considered. But the Speaker was not bound by such criteria, and there were cases where none of those factors outweighed the Speaker's wishes. Despite complaints and vari-

Dates Standing Committees Were Established

Only committees in existence in 1991 are listed. Where committees have been consolidated, the date cited is that of the component committee that was established first. Names in parentheses are those of current committees where they differ from the committees' original names.

House

1789—Enrolled Bills (House Administration)
1795—Commerce and Manufactures
    (Energy & Commerce)
1802—Ways & Means
1805—Public Lands (Interior & Insular Affairs)
1808—Post Office and Post Roads (Post Office &
    Civil Service)
1808—District of Columbia
1813—Judiciary
1813—Pensions and Revolutionary Claims
    (Veterans' Affairs)
1816—Expenditures in Executive Departments
    (Government Operations)

1820—Agriculture
1822—Foreign Affairs
1822—Military Affairs (Armed Services)
1822—Naval Affairs (Armed Services)

1837—Public Buildings and Grounds (Public Works
    & Transportation)

1865—Appropriations
1865—Banking & Currency (Banking, Finance &
    Urban Affairs)
1867—Education & Labor

1880—Rules
1887—Merchant Marine & Fisheries

1942—Select Small Business (Small Business)

1958—Science & Astronautics
    (Science, Space & Technology)
1967—Standards of Official Conduct

1975—Budget

1977—Select Intelligence*

Senate

1789—Enrolled Bills (Rules & Administration)

1816—Commerce and Manufactures
    (Commerce, Science & Transportation)
1816—District of Columbia (Governmental Affairs)
1816—Finance
1816—Foreign Relations
1816—Judiciary
1816—Military Affairs (Armed Services)
1816—Naval Affairs (Armed Services)
1816—Post Office and Post Roads (Governmental
    Affairs)
1816—Public Lands (Energy & Natural Resources)

1825—Agriculture (Agriculture, Nutrition &
    Forestry)
1837—Public Buildings and Grounds (Environment &
    Public Works)
1842—Expenditures in Executive Departments
    (Governmental Affairs)

1867—Appropriations
1869—Education & Labor (Labor & Human
    Resources)

1913—Banking & Currency (Banking, Housing &
    Urban Affairs)

1950—Select Small Business (Small Business)
1958—Aeronautical & Space Sciences (Commerce,
    Science & Transportation)

1970—Veterans' Affairs
1975—Budget
1976—Select Intelligence*

* Both the House and Senate Select Intelligence committees are permanent committees but for reasons relating to congressional rules on committee organization they are listed as select committees.

Sources: George Goodwin, Jr., *The Little Legislatures: Committees of Congress* (Amherst: University of Massachusetts Press, 1970), and *Congressional Directory*, various years.

ous attempts to change the rule, the system remained in force until 1911, when the House again exercised the right to select the members of standing committees.

In the Senate assignment to a committee was made by vote of the entire membership until 1823. Members wishing to serve on a particular committee were placed on a ballot, with the choicest committee assignments going to those receiving the most votes. The senator with the largest number of votes served as chairman.

By the 1820s, however, a number of difficulties with the ballot system had become evident. The arrangement proved tedious and time-consuming and provided no guarantee that the party in control of the chamber would hold a majority of seats on the committee or retain control of the committee chairmanships in the event of a vacancy. Several times in the ensuing years the Senate amended its rules to provide for appointment to committees by a designated official, usually the vice president or president pro tempore. However, abuse of the appointment power and a transfer of power between the two parties compelled the Senate to return to use of the ballot.

In 1823 senators rejected a proposal that the chairmen of the five most important committees be chosen by the full Senate, and that the chairmen then have the power to make all other committee assignments. The Senate instead amended the standing rules to give the "presiding officer" authority to make committee assignments, unless otherwise ordered by the Senate. Since Daniel D. Tompkins, vice president during the administration of James Monroe, scarcely ever entered the chamber, committee selection was left to the president pro tempore, who in effect had been chosen by and was responsible to the Senate majority leadership. But when the next vice president, John C. Calhoun, used the assignment power with obvious bias, the Senate quickly and with little dissent returned to the election method to fill committee vacancies.

This time the chairmen were picked by majority vote of the entire Senate; then ballots were taken to select the other members of each committee, with members' rank on the committee determined by the size of their plurality. The Senate in 1828 changed the rules to provide for appointment to committees by the president pro tempore, but in 1833 it reverted to selection by ballot when control of the Senate changed hands. Since 1833 the Senate technically has made its committee assignments by ballot.

To avoid the inconveniences inherent in the ballot system, it became customary between 1833 and 1846 to suspend the rule by unanimous consent and designate an officer (the vice president, the president pro tempore, or the "presiding officer") to assign members to committees.

The method of selecting committee members in use today was—with some modification—developed in 1846. In that year a motion to entrust the vice president with the task was defeated, and the Senate proceeded under the regular rules to make committee assignments by ballot. But after six chairmen had been selected, a debate began on the method of choosing the other members of the committees. At first, several committees were filled by lists—arranged in order of a member's seniority—submitted by the majority leader. After a number of committees had been filled in this manner, the ballot rule was suspended, and the Senate approved a list for the remaining vacancies that had been agreed upon by both the majority and minority leadership.[10]

Since 1846 the choice of committees usually has

amounted to routine acceptance by the Senate of lists drawn up by special committees of the two major parties (today the Committee on Committees for the Republicans and the Steering Committee for the Democrats).

Proliferation of Subcommittees

The standing committee system, firmly established in the first half of the nineteenth century, expanded rapidly in the second half. Several factors influenced the role of committees, Smith and Deering wrote.

> First, dramatic economic, geographic, and population growth placed new and greater demands on Congress, which responded with more legislation and new committees. Second, further development of American political parties and the increasing strength of congressional party leaders, especially in the late nineteenth century, led to an even greater integration of congressional parties and committee systems. Third, members of Congress, first in the Senate and then in the House, came to view service in Congress as a desirable long-term career, which in turn gave more personal significance to congressional organization, particularly the committee systems.[11]

The number of standing committees reached a peak in 1913, when there were sixty-one in the House and seventy-four in the Senate. The Appropriations, Ways and Means, Finance, and Rules committees, in particular, exercised great influence; some others were created and perpetuated chiefly to provide members with offices and clerical staff.

Initial efforts to consolidate the House committee system occurred in 1909, when six minor committees were dropped. Two years later, when the Democrats took control, six superfluous committees were abolished.

In 1921 the Senate reduced the number of its committees from seventy-four to thirty-four. In many respects this rationalization of the committee structure was simply the formal abandonment of long-defunct bodies such as the Committee on Revolutionary Claims. The House in 1927 reduced the number of its committees by merging eleven expenditures committees, those dealing primarily with oversight, into a single Committee on Expenditures in the Executive Departments.

The next major overhaul of the committee structure took place in 1946 with enactment of the Legislative Reorganization Act. By dropping minor committees and merging those with related functions, the act achieved a net reduction of eighteen in the number of Senate committees (from thirty-three at that time to fifteen) and of twenty-nine in the number of House committees (from forty-eight at that time to nineteen). The act also defined in detail the jurisdictions of each committee and attempted to set ground rules for their operations.

For the next three decades, until a partial reorganization of Senate committees in 1977, only minor changes were made in the committee structure in Congress. During that period many of the achievements of the 1946 act were weakened by the creation of additional committees, as well as the proliferation of subcommittees.

The 1946 act, in fact, had spawned an explosion at the subcommittee level. The number of subcommittees grew gradually after passage of the 1946 act, reaching more than one hundred in the House and more than eighty in the Senate by 1964. Smith and Deering found that: "The growth in the number of subcommittees had roots in the practical problems involved in managing larger and more complex workloads, in the desire of larger numbers of senior members for a 'piece of the action,' and in isolated efforts on individual committees to loosen the grip of chairs on committee activity." [12]

But the creation of a larger network of subcommittees in the years following the 1946 act did not mean that power automatically gravitated there. Until the early 1970s, most House committees were run by chairmen who were able to retain much of the authority for themselves and a few trusted senior members, while giving little power to junior members or subcommittees.

The Seniority System

As the committee system grew, so too did a system that awarded power on committees to the member with longest service on the committee.

Seniority—status based on length of service, to which are attached certain rights and privileges—pervades nearly all social institutions. But in no other political group has its sway been stronger than in the United States Congress.

Despite frequent references to a "seniority rule" and a "seniority system," observance of seniority in Congress was never dictated by law or formal ruling. It developed as a tradition. The formal rules simply stated that the House or Senate should determine committee memberships and chairmen.

Seniority on Capitol Hill is based on the length of service in Congress, referred to as congressional seniority, or on the length of consecutive service on a committee, called committee seniority. As the system developed in both houses, it affected the assignment of office space, access to congressional patronage, and deference shown members on the floor. But seniority was most apparent—and important—in the selection of committee chairmen and in filling vacancies on committees, although state and regional considerations, party loyalty, legislative experience, and a mem-

ber's influence with his colleagues always were important factors in making committee assignments.

Seniority had been relatively unimportant in the early years of Congress, when political parties were weak, turn-over of congressional membership was frequent, and congressional careers were brief.

By 1846, however, party control had become so firm that committee assignment lists supplied by the parties were approved routinely. With party domination of assignments, the principle of seniority also appeared. Seniority came to be applied both to committee assignments and to advancement within a committee.

The seniority principle caught hold earlier in the Senate than in the House. As the Civil War neared, southern Democrats, who dominated Senate committee chairmanships, "supported the hardening of seniority to protect their position so that they could defend slavery," Randall B. Ripley wrote.[13] During the Civil War and Reconstruction period, between 1861 and 1875, Democrats virtually disappeared from Congress, and Republican senators disregarded seniority in committee assignments. But when Democrats began to reappear in the Senate, the Republican majority returned to the seniority system to keep peace among party members. Republican leaders found they had to rely on the support of all their party colleagues, Ripley wrote. And one way to gain this support was to agree to an "automatic and impartial rule for committee advancement. The leaders of the party thus helped institute this limit on their own power." [14]

As committees developed into powerful, autonomous institutions, committee chairmen assumed ever greater powers over legislation. So great was their influence that Woodrow Wilson in 1885 could write: "I know not how better to describe our form of government in a single phrase than by calling it a government by the chairmen of the standing committees of Congress." [15]

In the House committee chairmen and the evolving seniority system suffered a temporary setback during the speakership of Joseph G. Cannon, R-Ill., in the early 1900s.

Courtesy of House Rules Committee

AP/Wide World Photos

Many southern Democrats who opposed the national party program held committee chairmanships, thanks to seniority, in the decades following World War II. As chairman of the House Rules Committee from 1955 to 1967, Rep. Howard W. Smith, D- Va., (left) blocked or delayed liberal Democratic programs. Sen. James O. Eastland, D-Miss., (right) who chaired the Senate Judiciary Committee from 1956 to 1979, was notorious for bottling up civil rights bills sought by party leaders.

The period from the Civil War to 1910 had seen the gradual development of an all-powerful Speaker. Through his power to name committee members and chairmen, the Speaker was able to control legislation, grant favors or impose political punishments, and ride roughshod over the minority party. "Czar" became a title the press frequently bestowed on the Speaker.

Finally, in 1910-11, insurgent Republicans in the House, led by Nebraska's George Norris, combined with Democrats to strip Speaker Cannon of much of his power. The Speaker could no longer name committee members, serve on the Rules Committee, or hold unchallenged control over recognizing representatives who wished to bring legislation to the floor. *(History of speakership, p. 10)*

The successful revolt against Cannon returned the right to appoint committee members and chairmen to the party's Committee on Committees, but it was several decades before the seniority system was strictly followed.

The gradual lengthening of congressional careers had much to do with the dominance of seniority, which was solidified by the Legislative Reorganization Act of 1946. The consolidated committees produced by the act had wider jurisdictions than before, and their chairmen gained greater power.

The Democrats' almost unbroken dominance in Congress during the thirty years after World War II meant relatively little turnover in their membership and long tenure for chairmen elected from the Democrats' safest seats—those in the South and in predominantly urban areas. No committee illustrated the power of seniority more vividly than did the House Rules Committee, which theoretically was regarded as a strong arm of the majority party leadership.

From 1949 until 1979, except for a two-year interval when Republicans ran the House, the Rules Committee was chaired by two elderly Democrats from the rural South and three others who came out of big-city machine politics. They were: Adolph Sabath of Chicago (chairman in 1949-53), who died at age eighty-six while still chairman; Howard W. Smith of Virginia (chairman in 1955-67), leader of the southern bloc in the House, who at age eighty-three was upset in his party's 1966 primary; William M. Colmer of Mississippi (chairman in 1967-73), who retired from Congress upon reaching age eighty-two; Ray J. Madden of Gary, Ind. (1973-77), who became chairman at age eighty and was defeated in the Democratic primary four years later; and James J. Delaney of New York City, who succeeded Madden for one Congress.

"Judge" Smith was so antagonistic to liberal Democratic programs and worked so well with Republicans that Speaker Rayburn reluctantly agreed in 1961 to "pack" the Rules Committee with two additional Democrats willing to vote for Kennedy administration programs. *(House Rules Committee, box, p. 80)*

In the Senate, also, men who were out of step with their party's program chaired important committees thanks to seniority, notably James O. Eastland, D-Miss., chairman of the Judiciary Committee from 1956 to 1979. A party loyalist, Sen. Carl Hayden, D-Ariz., became chairman of the Appropriations Committee at age seventy-eight and served until he was ninety-one, setting a record for longest service in Congress, fifty-six years (counting both House and Senate service). The lengthy terms of these men were testaments to the growing careerism in Congress.

With the long tenure of senior members, a generation gap developed. Roger H. Davidson observed:

In 1973 the average House committee chairman was 66 years old and had almost 30 years of congressional service behind him; the average Senate chairman was 64 years old and had 21 years' experience. Not only did such a situation squander talent in the mid-seniority ranks, but it eventually generated frustration and resentment.[16]

The gap between leaders and backbenchers, covering not only age but also region, type of district, and ideology, "lay at the heart of the Democrats' seniority struggles in the 1970s," Davidson wrote.

The regional imbalance in top committee posts was especially irksome to Democratic liberals. In 1973 the six chairmen of the most powerful committees in Congress—those dealing with taxes, appropriations, and the armed services—came from just four states in the south central part of the country: Louisiana, Arkansas, Mississippi, and Texas.

Congress was ready for change.

1970s Reform Movement

Frustration with the existing system led by the late 1960s to concerted demands for reforms. As Smith and Deering noted:

These demands were especially strong among junior members and some long-standing liberal Democrats, who found their efforts to shape public policy stymied by their more conservative senior colleagues. These members, and the outsiders whose causes they supported, were concerned about issues that were not receiving active committee consideration and did not fall easily into existing committee jurisdictions. A nascent environmental movement, opposition to the Vietnam conflict, and a continuing interest in civil rights legislation placed new challenges before congressional committees.[17]

The reform movement took off in the 1970s. And before the decade was over, the committee system had been radically restructured. The era of the autocratic committee chairman who answered to no one was over. Junior and minority party members of Congress now had positions, privileges, and resources earlier members had been denied. Committee operations and votes were opened to the public eye. *(Open committees, box, p. 83)*

The reforms that swept through Congress had been brewing for years. The trauma of the Vietnam War and then the Watergate scandal heightened dissatisfaction with the old order and old ways of doing things. A generation of younger, less reverent members with new agendas was swept into Congress.

The newcomers balked at the traditions of apprenticeship and deference to committee leaders, Leroy Rieselbach pointed out.

Moreover, many of these new members found it electorally advantageous to run for Congress by running against Congress, ... to criticize the legislative establishment and upon arriving in Washington to adopt a critical, reformist view of congressional structure and procedure. Finally, the new electoral circumstances that protected most incumbents from November surprises at the polls—effective personal campaign organizations and the ready availability of funds from the proliferating political action committees ... —gave new members the independence they needed to pursue their own political agendas, agendas that included reform.[18]

On the House side, the newcomers breathed life into a dormant Democratic Caucus and gave would-be reformers the votes they needed to effect change.

House Rules Committee Functions . . .

The Rules Committee is among the most powerful committees in the House. Often described as the gatekeeper to the floor, the committee works in concert with the majority leadership to control the flow of legislation and set the terms of floor debate.

For all major bills the committee writes a "special rule" that, subject to the approval of the House, sets the time limit on general debate and regulates how the bill may be amended. It may forbid all amendments or, in some cases, all amendments except those proposed by the legislative committee that handled the bill. Thus the committee is able to structure the debate and the types of amendments that will be allowed on legislation or, on occasion, even prevent a bill from coming to the floor.

Increasingly, the Rules Committee must play the role of mediating legislative disputes between committees. The extra work has been caused by a combination of the House Appropriations Committee's practice of adding legislative provisions to spending bills and the referral of bills to multiple legislative panels.

All of this translates into immense power. The way an issue is framed often determines whether a coalition will hold on the floor and how an issue will play in the press.

There have been frequent controversies throughout the history of the House over the function of the Rules Committee in the legislative process: whether it should be merely a clearinghouse (or traffic cop) for legislative business, the agent of the majority leadership, or a super-legislative committee editing the work of the other committees.

Defenders of the Rules Committee system of routing bills maintain it is the only feasible way to regulate the legislative flow efficiently in the 435-member House.

Since the mid-1970s the committee has returned to the role it performed until 1911 as an arm of the majority leadership.

Changing Role of the Committee

The Rules Committee was established in 1789. Originally it was a select committee, authorized at the beginning of each Congress, with jurisdiction over House rules. Since the rules of one Congress usually were readopted by the next, this function was not of great importance, and for many years the committee never issued a report.

In 1858 the Speaker was made a member of the committee, and in subsequent years Rules gradually increased its influence over legislation. The panel became a standing committee in 1880, and in 1883 it began the practice of issuing rules—special orders of business—for floor debate on legislation.

Other powers acquired by the committee over the years included the right to sit while the House was in session, to have its resolutions considered immediately (called privileged resolutions), and even to initiate legislation on its own, like any other legislative committee. Before 1910 the Rules Committee worked closely with the leadership in deciding what legislation could come to the floor. But in the Progressive revolt of 1910-11 against the arbitrary reign of Speaker Joseph G. Cannon, R-Ill., the committee was made independent of the leadership. Alternative methods of bringing legislation to the floor—the Discharge Calendar, Consent Calendar, and Calendar Wednesday procedures—were added to the standing rules. And in 1910 a coalition of Democrats and insurgent Republicans succeeded in enlarging the Rules Committee and excluding the Speaker from it. The ban on the Speaker was repealed in 1946, but subsequent Speakers have never sat on the committee.

By the late 1930s the committee had come under the domination of a coalition of conservative Democrats and Republicans. From that time until the 1970s it repeatedly blocked or delayed liberal legislation.

Opposition to the obstructive tactics of the Rules Committee led, in 1949, to adoption of the "twenty-one-day rule." That rule provided that the chairman of a legislative committee that had approved a bill and requested a rule from the Rules Committee permitting the bill to be brought to the floor, could bring up the rule himself if the committee failed to grant a rule within twenty-one calendar days of the committee's request. The twenty-one day rule required the Speaker to recognize the chairman of the committee wishing to call up the bill. Two years later, after the Democrats had lost twenty-nine seats in the midterm elections, the House repealed the twenty-one-day rule. Although it had been used only eight times, the threat of its use was credited with prying other bills out of the Rules Committee.

House Revolt

At the beginning of the 86th Congress in 1959, a group of liberal Democrats dropped plans to seek a change in House rules that would break the conservative grip on the committee. Speaker Sam Rayburn, D-Texas, assured them that bills reported from their committees would reach the House floor. However, the record of the 86th Congress showed that Rayburn often could not deliver on his promise. After the Rules Committee had blocked or delayed several measures that were to become key elements in the new Kennedy administration's legislative program, Democrats decided to act.

Accordingly, in 1961 the House by a narrow margin agreed to enlarge the committee from twelve to fifteen members for the 87th Congress. That gave Rayburn and

Revival of the Democratic Caucus

In the late 1960s the House Democratic Study Group (DSG) started the drive to overhaul the seniority system

and open House procedures. The outlook for the DSG agenda brightened with the revival of the House Democratic Caucus in 1969 and the retirement of John W. McCormack, D-Mass., as Speaker at the end of the 1970

... as Arm of Majority Leadership

the administration a delicate eight-seven majority on most issues coming before the committee. By raising the number of Democrats to ten from eight (Republicans to five from four), it permitted the appointment to the committee of two pro-administration Democrats. This enlargement was made permanent in 1963.

Nevertheless, dissatisfaction with the Rules Committee continued, and following the Democratic sweep in the 1964 elections the twenty-one-day rule was revived. The new version of the rule, adopted by the House at the opening of the 89th Congress in 1965, did not require the Speaker to recognize a committee chairman wishing to call up a twenty-one-day resolution. Under the 1965 rule the Speaker retained discretion to recognize a committee chairman, so that it became highly unlikely for a bill to come up through this procedure without the approval of the House leadership. The new rule, which also was employed successfully only eight times, was abandoned in 1967, following Republican gains in the 1966 midterm elections.

The House retained another rule, adopted in 1965, that curbed the committee's power to block conferences on legislation. Before 1965 most bills could be sent to a conference committee only through unanimous consent or adoption of a special rule issued by the Rules Committee. The 1965 change made it possible to send any bill to conference by majority vote of the House.

Despite repeal of the twenty-one-day rule in 1967, the committee continued generally to pursue a stance more accommodating to the leadership. Several factors contributed to the committee's less conservative posture. First, it had lost its chairman of twelve years, Howard W. Smith, D-Va., who was defeated in a 1966 primary election. Smith was a skilled parliamentarian and the acknowledged leader of the House's conservative coalition—a voting alliance of Republicans and southern Democrats. He was replaced as chairman by William M. Colmer, D-Miss. Although Colmer also was a conservative, he was unable to exert the high degree of control over legislation that Smith had exercised.

In an attempt to strengthen the leadership's control over the Rules Committee, the Democratic Caucus voted in December 1974 to give the Speaker the power to nominate all Democratic members of the panel, subject to caucus approval. Using this power, Speaker Carl Albert of Oklahoma nominated liberals to fill two vacant positions.

In addition, a set of rules was introduced to govern committee procedures. The rules took from the chairman the right to set meeting dates, a power Smith frequently had used to postpone or thwart action on bills he opposed. The consent of a majority was needed to kill a bill, and limits were placed on proxy voting.

Once the Speaker was given the power to appoint Rules Committee members, the panel operated as an arm of the leadership. Its role varied somewhat, depending on whether the speakership was in the hands of the more detached Thomas P. O'Neill, Jr., D-Mass., or Thomas S. Foley, D-Wash., or the comparatively heavy-handed Jim Wright, D-Texas.

Restrictive Rules

No matter who was Speaker, the panel was used increasingly to limit amendments and debate on the House floor. The growth in the number of restrictive rules issued by the committee at times provoked an outcry from Republicans, particularly during Wright's tenure. But Democratic leaders argued that the Rules panel, far from being the gag-rule enforcer portrayed by Republicans, was an essential tool of a well-managed House. Many experts agreed that, particularly since the arrival in the 1970s of a new breed of legislative activists, there were more occasions when restrictions were needed to make floor debate manageable. Such limits, they argued, helped focus debate on central issues, weed out dilatory amendments, and still ensure that major alternatives were considered.

The reduced proportion of bills open to amendments also reflected institutional changes that had little to do with a deliberate strategy of closing off amendments. Complex debate restrictions became unavoidable to some extent after 1974, when House rules were changed to allow more than one committee to handle a bill. The Rules Committee had to set the guidelines for resolving conflicts and eliminating overlap when multiple committees marked up a single bill.

Moreover, faced with huge budget deficits and waning public enthusiasm for big government programs in the 1980s, the House considered fewer authorizing bills—the sort of legislation that usually got an open rule. Increasingly, authorizing legislation was folded into omnibus measures, which usually were not entirely open to amendment.

The chairmanship of the Rules Committee turned over a number of times in the 1970s and 1980s. Chairmen during the transition period of the 1970s were Ray J. Madden, D-Ind., who became chairman in 1973; James J. Delaney, D-N.Y., in 1977; and Richard Bolling, D-Mo., in 1979. Bolling did much to transform both the internal operations of the committee as well as its role in the House. Under Bolling, two standing subcommittees were created, the committee's staff and budget were enlarged substantially, and the committee's own legislative initiatives were expanded.

Claude Pepper, D-Fla., took over the committee in 1983 when Bolling retired and Joe Moakley, D-Mass., became chairman in 1989 after Pepper's death.

session. With McCormack's departure, dominant committee chairmen lost a powerful ally at the top of the House leadership structure.

The caucus revival meant that moderate and liberal Democrats elected to the House in the 1960s, who were frustrated by the operation of a committee system that tended to freeze them out of power, at last had a vehicle to change House procedures. Their actions were directed at undercutting the power of committee chairmen and strengthening the role of the subcommittees, where the opportunity lay for them to gain a greater role and make an impact on the legislative process.

The drive had a sharp generational edge. Many middle-ranking Democrats elected in the late 1950s and 1960s were allied against the senior members and the leadership. Between 1958 and 1970, 293 Democrats entered the House. Between 1970 and 1974, another 150 Democrats were elected. From this group, many of whom tended to be more moderate or liberal than their predecessors, sprang pressure for reform. This influx of Democrats—especially the seventy-five comprising the "Class of 1974," otherwise known as the "Watergate babies"—provided the votes needed to effect change.

Harbingers of Reform

The push for reform in the early 1960s led to the creation in 1965 of a Joint Committee on the Organization of Congress, headed by Sen. A. S. Mike Monroney, D-Okla., and Representative Madden. The following year the panel recommended a wide-ranging set of reforms, which included proposals to curtail the powers of committee chairmen, to limit committee assignments, and to increase committee staff resources.

Five years later some of the committee's procedural recommendations were enacted into law in the Legislative Reorganization Act of 1970. The law encouraged open committee proceedings, required that committees have written rules, required that all committee roll-call votes be made public, allowed radio and television coverage of committee hearings, and safeguarded the rights of minority party members on a committee. The law made only minor revisions in the committee structure itself, and it left the seniority system intact, after the House rejected two proposals to modify the system.

Although the 1970 law had limited effects, it marked a turning point in the reform movement, signaling an end to an era when committee chairmen and senior members could block reforms and the beginning of nearly a decade of change. Since the reform goals of the two chambers were different and the pressure for change was greatest in the House, subsequent attempts at change took the form of intrachamber reform efforts rather than bicameral action.

Loosening the grip of seniority was seen as a crucial step toward changing committee operations. The issue of committee seniority was treated as strictly a party matter. Democratic leaders feared that if seniority changes were proposed through legislation instead of through party rules, a coalition of members of both parties could upset the majority party's control of the legislative program. When changes in seniority were offered as amendments on the floor of the House and Senate, they consistently had been defeated.

House Committee Changes

The first blow to seniority in the House came in 1971 when both parties decided that the selection of committee leaders no longer had to be dictated by seniority.

In January 1971 the House Democratic Caucus voted to adopt modest changes recommended by its Committee on Organization, Study, and Review, which had been created in 1970 to examine the party's organization and the seniority system. It was headed by Julia Butler Hansen, D-

Wash.

The principal changes agreed upon were:

~ The Democratic Committee on Committees, composed of the Democratic members of the Ways and Means Committee, would recommend to the caucus nominees for the chairmanship and membership of each committee, and such recommendations did not have to follow seniority. (The committee's power was transferred in December 1974 to the Steering and Policy Committee.)

~ The Committee on Committees would make recommendations to the caucus, one committee at a time. Upon the demand of ten or more caucus members, nominations could be debated and voted on.

If a nomination was rejected, the Committee on Committees would submit another nomination.

~ In an important breakthrough for mid-career Democrats, the caucus decided that no member could chair more than one legislative subcommittee. That change made it possible to break the hold of the more conservative senior Democrats on key subcommittees, and it gradually made middle-level and even some junior Democrats eligible for subcommittee chairmanships. The rule in its first year gave sixteen Democrats who were elected to the House after 1958 their first subcommittee chairmanships.

House Republicans also in 1971 agreed that the ranking Republican on each committee would be selected by vote of the Republican Conference, comprised of all House Republicans, and not automatically by seniority.

House Democrats in January 1973 altered their chairmanship selection procedures by allowing a secret-ballot vote on any committee chairman when 20 percent of the caucus demanded it. The expectation was that votes would be taken on all candidates. (This cumbersome procedure was replaced in 1975 by an automatic vote.)

Subcommittee Rights. The House Democratic Caucus in January 1973 adopted a "subcommittee bill of rights." The new caucus rules created a party caucus for Democrats on each House committee and forced the chairmen to start sharing authority with other committee Democrats. Each committee caucus was granted the authority to select subcommittee chairmen (with members allowed to run for chairman based on their seniority ranking on the full committee), establish subcommittee jurisdictions, set party ratios on the subcommittees to reflect the party ratio of the full committee, provide a subcommittee budget, and guarantee all members a major subcommittee slot where vacancies made that possible. Each subcommittee was authorized to meet, hold hearings, and act on matters referred to it. Subcommittee chairmen were empowered to set meeting dates.

Under the bill of rights, committee chairmen were required to refer designated types of legislation to subcommittees within two weeks. They no longer could kill measures they opposed simply by pocketing them.

Compromise Hansen Plan. Further procedural changes, along with minor committee jurisdictional shifts, were approved in 1974 in a new package of recommendations put forward by Hansen's study committee. The Hansen plan was a substitute for a much broader bipartisan proposal, drafted by a select committee headed by Rep. Richard Bolling, D-Mo. The Bolling committee's call for wholesale restructuring of the committee system had triggered a flood of protests from chairmen and committee members who would have been adversely affected, as well

"Sunshine" Reforms Dim in the 1980s

In the 1980s Congress began to sidestep one of the key reforms of the 1970s—"sunshine" rules that opened up previously secret committee proceedings. Although most committee hearings and drafting sessions remained open to the public, key panels increasingly voted to close their doors to consider major legislation.

The sunshine reforms were part of an effort to improve Congress's image, which had suffered dramatic reversals after a series of widely publicized scandals. Proponents maintained that open meetings helped protect the public interest and made lawmakers more accountable to the electorate.

Defenders of closed sessions argued that committee members were more open, markups more expeditious, and better laws written away from lobbyists' glare. Remarkably few objections were raised in the 1980s as key panels increasingly voted to close their doors to consider major legislation.

The House Ways and Means Committee, perhaps the most heavily lobbied committee in the House, chose to close its doors to write such key bills as a historic tax-overhaul bill in 1985 and trade and catastrophic illness insurance bills in 1987. Ways and Means Chairman Dan Rostenkowski, D-Ill., summed up an increasingly prevalent view: "It's just difficult to legislate. I'm not ashamed about closed doors. We want to get the product out."

Other panels—notably House Appropriations subcommittees—also met privately to draft legislation.

Sometimes committees' decisions were made by small groups of members behind the scenes, then ratified in open session. Both chambers' defense and intelligence committees regularly met behind closed doors.

Sunshine Rules. The Legislative Reorganization Act of 1970 encouraged more open committee meetings and hearings and required that all House and Senate committee roll-call votes be made public. The House in 1973 voted to require that all committee sessions be open unless a majority of the committee voted in public to close them. The Senate adopted a similar rule in 1975. Both chambers in 1975 voted to open conference committee sessions, unless a majority of the conferees of either chamber voted in public to close a session. The House amended this rule in 1977 to require a vote by the full House to close a conference committee meeting.

Broadcasts. While the Senate had a long tradition of broadcasting hearings, the House did not sanction such broadcasts until passage of the 1970 reorganization act. In 1974 it decided to allow broadcasts of markup meetings as well. The Senate left decisions on broadcast coverage to its committees; the House standing rules set stringent standards for broadcast coverage of hearings or bill-drafting sessions.

Televised broadcasts of floor debate began in the House in 1979 and in the Senate in 1986. *(Box, p. 62)*

---

as from the lobbyists who dealt with those committees. It was decisively rejected in favor of the Hansen substitute, which made some jurisdictional shifts—such as giving the Public Works Committee control over more transportation matters—but mainly retained the existing committee structure dating from 1946.

Under the Hansen plan, each standing committee's permanent staff, beginning in 1975, was increased from six to eighteen professionals and from six to twelve clerks, with the minority party receiving one-third of each category. And in what would prove to be the most controversial provision, the plan gave the minority party control of one-third of a committee's investigative staff funding. The Democratic Caucus in 1975 repealed this provision, but, as part of the compromise, each side received more staffing and subcommittee chairmen and ranking members were allowed to hire one staff person each to work directly for them on their subcommittees. *(Committee staff, p. 112)*

In other changes, which also took effect in 1975, committees with more than fifteen members (increased to more than twenty members by the Democratic Caucus in 1975) were required to establish at least four subcommittees. This change was directed at the Ways and Means Committee, which had operated without subcommittees during most of the sixteen-year chairmanship of Wilbur D. Mills, D-Ark. It also created an important precedent in that it institutionalized subcommittees for the first time. And committees with more than fifteen members (increased to more than twenty in 1975 by the caucus) were

required to set up an oversight subcommittee or to require their legislative subcommittees to carry out oversight functions.

In addition, the Hansen plan gave the Speaker new powers to refer legislation to more than one committee and banned proxy voting in committee. (In 1975 proxy voting was partially restored by the Democratic Caucus: proxies were allowed on a specific issue or on procedural matters, and they had to be in writing and given to a member, among other requirements.)

More Blows to Seniority. Further changes in House committee operations unrelated to the Hansen plan were made in late 1974 and early 1975 by the Democratic Caucus. Meeting in December 1974 to organize for the next Congress (as had been required under the Hansen plan), Democrats decided to require a secret-ballot vote on the election of each committee chairman. The new procedure allowed competitive nominations for chairmen if the original Steering Committee nominee was rejected. Democrats immediately made use of their new rule by deposing three committee chairmen. *(Details, box, p. 84)*

In other changes the Democratic members of the Ways and Means Committee were stripped of their power to select the party's members of House committees; this authority was transferred to a revamped Democratic Steering and Policy Committee, whose members were appointed by the Speaker. At the same time the caucus increased the size of the Ways and Means Committee from twenty-five to

House Democrats Assert Power to Oust Chairmen . . .

Both political parties in the House and Senate in the 1970s decided that seniority—status based on length of service—should no longer be the sole determinant in selecting committee leaders.

The House Democratic Caucus shook the foundations of the House committee structure by ousting three autocratic chairmen in 1975. It was a watershed that redirected the flow of institutional power in the House.

The use of this authority—or even the threatened use—has given rank-and-file members in each chamber a potent weapon. "At the very least, senior committee leaders [in the House] are on notice that the caucus and their committee colleagues can vote to unseat them," wrote Leroy N. Rieselbach. "The threat of sanctions probably has a similar restraining impact in the Senate, although to date the chamber has faithfully adhered to seniority in selecting committee chairpersons." *

House Chairmen Ousted

In 1971 House Democrats and Republicans decided that seniority need not be followed in the selection of committee leaders. In 1973 Democrats permitted one-fifth of their caucus to force a vote on a nominee for committee chairman, and in 1975 that vote became automatic for all nominees.

Subcommittee leaders were also affected by the reforms. In 1973 Democrats allowed their party members on each committee to select their subcommittee chairmen. And in 1975 Democrats decided that all subcommittee chairmen on the Appropriations Committee should be subject to election by the full Democratic Caucus; on the

highly decentralized Appropriations panel most of the important decisions were made at the subcommittee level, and it was argued that those subcommittee chairmen were as powerful as most chairmen of the legislative committees.

Rank-and-file Democrats in January 1975 asserted their new power by unseating three incumbent chairmen: Armed Services Committee Chairman F. Edward Hébert of Louisiana; Agriculture Committee Chairman W. R. Poage of Texas; and Banking, Currency, and Housing Committee Chairman Wright Patman of Texas. Hébert and Poage were both replaced by the next ranking Democrat on their committees, but, in yet another blow to the seniority system, the fourth-ranking Democrat on the Banking Committee, Henry S. Reuss of Wisconsin, was elected to succeed Patman. The autocratic manner in which the three chairmen had run their committees was primarily responsible for their downfall.

The seniority system suffered another reversal in January 1977 when the Democratic Caucus for the first time rejected a sitting subcommittee chairman of the Appropriations Committee. The target was Robert L. F. Sikes of Florida, the longtime chairman of the Military Construction Subcommittee who had been reprimanded by the House the year before for conflicts of interest.

In 1985 the Democratic Caucus voted to remove Melvin Price of Illinois from the chairmanship of the Armed Services Committee and replace him with Les Aspin of Wisconsin, the panel's seventh-ranking Democrat. House Majority Leader Jim Wright of Texas insisted that the action was not a repudiation of the seniority tradition but instead reflected concerns about the failing health of

thirty-seven members, a change designed to give the committee a more liberal outlook and thus make it more likely to support party-backed proposals on tax revision, health insurance, and other issues.

In actions affecting the independence of subcommittees, the caucus directed that the entire Democratic membership of each committee, rather than the chairman alone, was to determine the number and jurisdiction of a committee's subcommittees. And the caucus specified that no Democratic member of a committee could become a member of a second subcommittee of that committee until every member of the full committee had chosen a subcommittee slot. (A grandfather clause allowed sitting members on subcommittees to protect two subcommittee slots, but this protection was eliminated in 1979.)

One group of subcommittees always had been semi-autonomous—the powerful units of the House Appropriations Committee. The subcommittees were organized to parallel the executive departments and agencies, and most of the annual budget review was done at that level. The staggering size and complexity of the federal budget required each subcommittee to develop an expertise and an autonomy respected and rarely challenged by other subcommittees or by the full committee. Because of the panels' special role the caucus decided that, like full committee chairmen, all nominees for chairmen of these subcommittees would have to be approved by the Democratic Caucus. (Nominees for Appropriations subcommittee chairmen were selected by the membership of each subcommittee, with members bidding for a subcommittee chairmanship in the order of their seniority on the subcommittee.)

The Speaker's powers were further buttressed by allowing him to select the Democratic members of the Rules Committee, subject to caucus approval.

In a change that had been adopted by the Democratic Caucus in December 1976, the chairmen of the Ways and Means and Appropriations committees were stripped of their power to nominate the Democratic members of the Budget Committee; that power was transferred to the Democratic Steering and Policy Committee.

In December 1978 the House Democratic Caucus voted to prohibit, as of the next Congress, a committee chairman from serving as chairman of any other standing, select, special, or joint committee. Each House Democrat was limited to five subcommittee seats on House standing committees. (In 1987 waivers to the five-subcommittee rule—which had become routine—were barred in most cases.) In addition, the caucus decided that the bidding for subcommittee chairmanships would be based on a member's

... as Parties Turn Away from Seniority System

Price, who at eighty was considered too frail to lead the important panel. Ironically, Price had replaced Hébert in the 1975 revolt.

Equally ironic was the near ousting of Aspin two years later. House Democrats were distressed at what many considered Aspin's betrayals on several controversial defense issues. Aspin lost his chair in early January 1987 in a yes-or-no vote in the Democratic Caucus on his reelection, with no other name on the ballot. But two weeks later Aspin, pitted against three others, won back the position by a split vote of the Democratic Caucus.

Democrats ousted two committee chairmen in December 1990, as they organized for the 102nd Congress. Public Works Chairman Glenn M. Anderson, D-Calif., and House Administration Chairman Frank Annunzio, D-Ill., were regarded as weak, ineffective leaders and were replaced by younger, more aggressive Democrats: Robert A. Roe of New Jersey, the No. 2 Democrat on Public Works, and Charlie Rose of North Carolina, the No. 3 Democrat on House Administration. Each chairman was buffeted by a different array of forces, but the tumult was nurtured behind the scenes by an ad hoc group of young and middle-level Democrats—many of whom had a hand in the Watergate-era reforms that made possible such a challenge to a chairman's power. "It sends a message to all chairmen that they have to be more responsive," said David R. Obey, D-Wis. "What this demonstrates is that people don't want to have to work around chairmen. They want to be able to work through them."

In addition to these well-publicized challenges, Democratic caucuses on individual committees have ousted subcommittee chairmen.

Senate Adheres to Seniority

The Senate also decided in the 1970s that seniority should not dictate the choice of committee leaders. Senate Republicans adopted the policy in 1973 and the Democrats in 1975. Yet the Senate continued to adhere to the seniority tradition. In contrast to the House, there had been no dramatic revolts against sitting chairmen as of 1991.

A battle in 1987 over the position of ranking minority member on the Foreign Relations Committee was settled primarily on the issue of seniority. The contest was between moderate Republican Richard G. Lugar of Indiana and conservative Republican Jesse Helms of North Carolina. Lugar had been chairman of the Foreign Relations panel for the previous two years while the Republicans controlled the Senate. But when the Senate reverted to the Democrats, Helms, who had joined the panel the same day as Lugar, decided he wanted the position of ranking Republican on the committee and claimed seniority by virtue of his longer service in the Senate. Helms—and the seniority system—won out. Interestingly, Helms had the support of Lowell P. Weicker, Jr., of Connecticut, one of the most liberal Republicans in the Senate, who could foresee a day when he or another liberal equally out of tune with the GOP mainstream might lay claim to a chairmanship by seniority right. Weicker believed the seniority system was the only sure path to higher office for political mavericks, women, and minorities.

* Leroy N. Rieselbach, *Congressional Reform* (Washington, D.C.: CQ Press, 1986), 81.

---

seniority rank on the full committee, with the exception of Appropriations subcommittee chairmen.

Decline of Reform Zeal. Toward the end of the decade the House reform zeal waned. A House Commission on Administrative Review, headed by Rep. David R. Obey, D-Wis., concluded that members had too many committee assignments and that existing committee jurisdictions were too confused. But its recommendations for improving committee operations went down to defeat in October 1977.

The House in March 1979 set up a Select Committee on Committees to recommend once again how to improve the House's internal organization and operations. But when the panel, chaired by Jerry M. Patterson, D-Calif., closed its doors in April 1980, it left behind barely a trace of its thirteen-month-long effort to change the House committee system. Only one of its recommendations—a plan to create a separate standing committee on energy to untangle overlapping committee jurisdictions—went to the House floor, where the proposal was promptly gutted. In place of the select committee's plan, the House merely decided to rename its Commerce Committee the Energy and Commerce Committee and to designate that panel as its lead committee on energy matters.

The Patterson committee's other recommendations had included proposals to limit subcommittee assignments, as well as the number of subcommittees. The committee said the proliferation of subcommittees had decentralized and fragmented the policy process and had limited members' capacity to master their work. The Patterson committee report emphasized that on no other issue concerning committee reform had it found greater agreement than that there were too many subcommittees in the House and that members had too many subcommittee assignments.

House Democrats in January 1981, in a reversal of the 1970s trend, amended their caucus rules to limit the number of subcommittees and similar committee sub-units that could be established by House standing committees. Under the new rule, the Appropriations Committee was allowed to retain all of its thirteen panels, but all other standing committees were restricted to a maximum of either eight (if the standing committee had at least thirty-five members) or six for smaller committees.

House members in the 101st Congress (1989-91) had an average of 6.8 committee and subcommittee assignments, including 1.8 standing committee assignments, 3.9 assignments on subcommittees of standing committees, and 1.1 other committee assignments.[19]

Senate Committee Changes

While most of the attempts to reorganize the committee system in the 1970s were directed at the House, the Senate committee system was altered in 1977 by the first comprehensive committee consolidation in either house since passage of the 1946 reorganization act. Earlier in the decade the Senate had adopted important procedural changes involving committees.

Challenges to Seniority. The Senate had struck the first successful blow to the seniority system in the post-World War II period. As Senate minority leader in 1953, Lyndon Johnson proposed that all Democratic senators be given a seat on one major committee before any Democrat was assigned to a second major committee. The proposal, which became known as the "Johnson Rule," was a stunning blow to seniority. But it had the backing of Senator Russell—the powerful leader of the southern Democratic bloc that dominated the Senate for years—and was approved by the Democratic Steering Committee, which made Democratic committee assignments in the Senate. It was fitting that Johnson had successfully staged the breakthrough because he was a junior senator, chosen as his party's leader while still in his first Senate term. He had served six terms in the House, however, and become a protégé of House Speaker Rayburn.

Later, Senate Republicans adopted the same party rule, first informally in 1959 and then through the Republican Conference in 1965.

In 1971, under renewed pressure to modify the seniority system, Senate Democrats and Republicans agreed to further changes. Majority Leader Mike Mansfield, D-Mont., announced that a meeting of the Democratic Conference would be held at the request of any senator, and any senator would be free to challenge any nomination by the Steering Committee of a committee chairman. Republicans adopted a proposal that a senator could be the ranking minority member of only one standing committee. (After the GOP took control of the Senate in 1981, Republicans applied the same rule to the selection of committee chairmen.)

The Senate rejected a major challenge to the seniority system in 1971 when it blocked, on a 48-26 vote, a resolution that would have permitted the selection of committee chairmen on some basis other than seniority. The resolution had provided that in making committee assignments "neither [party] conference shall be bound by any tradition, custom, or principle of seniority."

But in 1973 Senate Republicans decided to choose their top-ranking committee members without regard to seniority. Republicans adopted a plan to limit the seniority system by having members of each standing committee elect the top-ranking Republican on that committee, subject to approval by a vote of all Senate Republicans.

And in 1975 Senate Democrats also voted to choose committee chairmen without regard to seniority. A secret ballot would be taken whenever one-fifth of their caucus requested it.

Also in 1975, junior senators obtained committee staff assistance for the first time. A new rule authorized them to hire up to three committee staffers—depending on the number and type of committee assignments they had—to work directly for them on their committees. In the past, committee staff members had been controlled by the chairmen and other senior committee members.

1977 Committee Reorganization. The 1977 Senate reorganization consolidated a number of Senate committees, revised jurisdictions of others, set a ceiling on the number of committees and subcommittees on which a senator could serve or chair, gave minority members a larger share of committee staff, and directed that schedules for committee hearings and other business be computerized to avoid conflicts. The organizational and procedural changes were the product of a special panel, chaired by Sen. Adlai E. Stevenson III, D-Ill.

One of the biggest organizational changes was the consolidation of most aspects of energy policy, except taxes, in one committee. Although the final result fell short of the Stevenson committee's goals for consolidating and merging committees, six committees were abolished: District of Columbia, Post Office, Aeronautical and Space Sciences, and the joint committees on Atomic Energy, Congressional Operations, and Defense Production. (The decision to end the joint committees was a unilateral Senate action. The House continued the Congressional Operations panel as a select committee for another two years.) Special interest groups were able to preserve several other committees slated for extinction.

Changes also were made in Senate committee procedures.

Senate reformers, like their House counterparts, were concerned with the proliferation of committees and subcommittees. In 1947 most senators served on two or three subcommittees. By the 94th Congress (1975-77) they held an average of eleven assignments on subcommittees of standing committees.[20] Stevenson's Select Committee to Study the Senate Committee System stated in its report:

> Proliferation of committee panels means proliferation in assignments held by Senators. And the burdens and frustrations of too many assignments, whatever the benefits, produce inefficient division of labor, uneven distribution of responsibility, conflicts in the scheduling of meetings, waste of Senators' and staff time, unsystematic lawmaking and oversight, inadequate anticipation of major problems, and inadequate membership participation in committee decisions.[21]

As part of the 1977 reorganization, the Senate prohibited a senator from serving as chairman of more than one subcommittee on any committee on which he served. This, in effect, placed an indirect cap on subcommittee expansion by limiting the number of subcommittees of any committee to the number of majority party members on the full committee.

With certain exceptions, each senator was limited to membership on two major committees and one minor committee. Each senator was limited to membership on three subcommittees of each major committee on which he served (the Appropriations Committee was exempted from this restriction). And each senator was limited to membership on two subcommittees of the minor committee on which he served.

Though it was not made a requirement, the Senate adopted language, similar to that in the House, stating it to be the sense of the Senate that no member of a committee should receive a second subcommittee assignment until all members of the committee had received their first assignment.

The Senate also prohibited a senator from serving as chairman of more than one committee at the same time; prohibited the chairman of a major committee from serving as chairman of more than one subcommittee on his major committees and as the chairman of more than one subcommittee on his minor committee; prohibited the chairman of a minor committee from chairing a subcommittee on that committee and prohibited him from chairing more than one of each of his major committees' subcommittees.

The Senate in addition banned any committee from establishing a subcommittee without approval of the full Senate, and required the Rules Committee to establish a central computerized scheduling service to keep track of meetings of Senate committees and subcommittees and House-Senate conference committees.

Finally, the Senate required the staff of each committee to reflect the relative size of the majority and minority membership on the committee. On the request of the minority party members of a committee, at least one-third of the staff of the committee was to be placed under the control of the minority party, except that staff deemed by the chairman and ranking minority member to be working for the whole committee would not be subject to the rule.

1980s Reform Attempts. Frustration with Senate procedures ran high in the 1980s but, despite several serious proposals for reform, no major changes were achieved by the end of the decade.

A 1983 report by former Sens. James B. Pearson, R-Kan., and Abraham Ribicoff, D-Conn., urged major changes in the Senate structure and procedures, including restrictions on subcommittees and a reduction in the number of committees. Under their plan, subcommittees would not have been permitted to report legislation nor would the panels have been staffed, a move aimed at eliminating what they saw as time-consuming specialization at the subcommittee level.

The following year the Temporary Select Committee to Study the Senate Committee System, chaired by Dan Quayle, R-Ind., recommended, among other things, strictly limiting the number of committee and subcommittee assignments each senator could have. The panel called for the strict enforcement of the existing rule allowing senators to serve on two major committees and one minor committee. There were slight reductions in the number of major committee assignments in 1985. In the 101st Congress (1989-91), senators had an average of 11.1 committee assignments, including 3.0 standing committee assignments, 7.0 assignments on the subcommittees of standing committees, and 1.1 other committee assignments.[22]

The Senate Rules and Administration Committee in 1988 proposed changes in committee and floor procedures. To reduce the number of competing demands on senators' time, the panel proposed allowing subcommittees to hold only hearings, thus requiring all legislative drafting sessions to be held at the full committee level.

Committees at Work: The Shape of Power

Committees are Congress's workshops, the place where most of the legislative work is done. Within each chamber there is a committee hierarchy dictated by the content and scope of each panel's jurisdiction and its status as legislative or nonlegislative, permanent or temporary.

Winning choice committee seats is a top priority for new lawmakers, especially in the House. New members recognize that their committee placement can set the tone for their first term in Congress and influence their political future.

The Committee Structure

There are three principal classes of committees in Congress: standing committees, those with permanently authorized staff and broad legislative mandates; select or special committees, those that are supposed to be temporary in that they are authorized to operate for a specific period of time or until the project for which they are created has been completed (these committees' role usually is investigative rather than legislative); and joint committees, which have a membership drawn from both houses of Congress and usually are investigative or housekeeping in nature. Conference committees, a special variety of joint committee, serve only on an ad hoc basis to resolve differences in Senate and House versions of the same legislation. (Box, p. 88)

Below the committee level are a plethora of subcommittees, which are functional subdivisions of the committees. Like the full committees, they are composed of members of the majority and minority parties in roughly the same proportion as the party ratios on the full committees.

At the outset of the 101st Congress (1989-91) there were 295 committees (standing, special and select, and joint) and subcommittees:
~ twenty Senate committees with eighty-six subcommittees.
~ twenty-seven House committees with 150 subcommittees (the subcommittee total includes panels and task forces if a committee had no subcommittees).
~ four joint committees with eight subcommittees.

The Senate had seventeen standing committees (including the Senate Select Committee on Intelligence, which functions as a standing committee) and the House, twenty-three (also counting the House Select Intelligence Committee as a standing committee). The Senate had only two more committees and the House only four more than the number in existence in 1947—the first year following enactment of the 1946 Legislative Reorganization Act.

But that comparison is misleading because the standing committees (including the Intelligence committees) in the 101st Congress had 227 subcommittees (eighty-six in the Senate and 141 in the House), compared with 148 in 1947 (fifty-nine Senate and eighty-nine House).

Standing Committees

The standing committees are at the center of the legislative process. Legislation usually must be considered and approved in some form at the committee level before it can be sent to the House or Senate for further action. (Legislative process, p. 39)

The 1946 reorganization act organized the Senate and House committees along roughly parallel lines. One of the act's purposes was to eliminate confusing and overlapping jurisdictions by grouping together related areas. The legislative committees (as distinct from the Appropriations committees) generally were regrouped to follow the major organizational divisions of the executive branch.

R. Michael Jenkins

Conference Committees

The conference committee is an ad hoc joint committee appointed to reconcile differences between Senate and House versions of pending legislation. Before a bill can be sent to the president, it must be passed in identical form by both chambers. Whenever different versions of the same bill are passed, and neither chamber is willing to yield to the other, a conference becomes necessary to determine the final shape of the legislation. It is unusual for the Senate or House to reject the work of a conference committee.

In the past conference committees were composed of the senior members of the committees that handled the bill. Today junior members of the committee often are appointed and occasionally interested members who are not on the committee. They are appointed by the Speaker of the House and the presiding officer of the Senate upon the recommendations of the committee chairmen and ranking minority members. Although the chairmen, by tradition, pick the conferees in the House, under the rules of that chamber the Speaker retains the latent power to make the appointments, subject only to the restriction that he "shall appoint no less than a majority of Members who generally supported the House position as determined by the Speaker."

Largely because of the addition of junior members of committees and others, the size of conference delegations has increased in recent years. In 1981, for example, more than 250 members of Congress participated in a conference on a budget reconciliation bill. The conference split up into fifty-eight subgroups to consider various sections of the legislation.

There need not be an equal number of conferees (or "managers," as they are called) from each house. Each house's delegation has a single vote, which is determined by a majority vote of its conferees. Therefore, a majority of both the Senate and House delegations must agree before a provision emerges from conference as part of the final bill.

Both parties are represented on conference committees, with the majority party having a larger number, and a majority of conferees from each house must sign the conference report. In the past conference committees met on the Senate side of the Capitol, with the most senior senator presiding, but this custom is no longer followed.

Most conference committees met in secret until late 1975, when both chambers amended their rules to require open meetings unless a majority of either chamber's conferees vote in open session to close the meeting for that day. In 1977 the House amended the rule to require open conference meetings unless the full House voted to close them. That rule was never adopted by the Senate, but in practice Senate conferees have always gone along with the representatives on those occasions—which have been limited to defense and intelligence agency bills—when the House has voted to close a conference committee. Despite the "sunshine" rules, committees have found various ways to avoid negotiating in public, including the use of informal sessions, separate meetings of each delegation with staffers as go-betweens, and meeting rooms too small to accommodate all who wish to attend.

After conferees reach agreement and their report is approved by one of the two houses, the conference committee automatically is dissolved. (If the second chamber were to disapprove the conference report, a new conference committee would have to be appointed, although normally the same team of conferees would be selected.)

The conference device, used by Congress since 1789, had developed its modern practice by the middle of the nineteenth century. *(Current conference procedures, p. 67)*

Responsibility for overseeing the federal bureaucracy was divided roughly as follows: Appropriations committees were to review the budget requests of the federal departments; the Expenditures committees (since renamed House Government Operations and Senate Governmental Affairs) were to oversee the general economy and efficiency of government in administering federal policy and programs; and the legislative committees, along with their other responsibilities, were to oversee the administration of federal programs in their respective fields.

Subcommittees

Most standing committees have a number of subcommittees, which provide the ultimate division of labor within the committee system. Although they enable members of Congress to develop expertise in specialized fields, they often are criticized on grounds that they fragment responsibility, increase the difficulty of policy review, and slow down the authorization and appropriation process.

Subcommittees play a much greater role in the House than in the Senate. In the House subcommittees usually are responsible for hearings and the first markup of a bill, before a measure is sent on to the full committee. In the Senate subcommittees may hold hearings, but the full committee generally does the writing of legislation. And, Smith and Deering write, "on nearly all Senate committees the work of subcommittees on important legislation is shown little deference by the full committees."[23]

Subcommittees also vary in importance from committee to committee. Some, especially the Appropriations subcommittees in both chambers, have well-defined jurisdictions and function with great autonomy. Much of their work—both in the House and Senate—is routinely endorsed by the full committee without further review. Their importance was one reason that House Democrats in 1974 voted to make all Appropriations subcommittee chairmen subject to confirmation by the party caucus.

A few committees—such as the House Ways and Means and Senate Finance committees—resisted the creation of subcommittees, although there were logical subdivisions into which their work could be divided. Subcommittees were established by the Finance Committee in 1970 and by Ways and Means only in 1974—after the Democratic Caucus voted to require them. The subcommittee requirement was established in part because of dissatisfaction with the power and performance of Ways and Means Chairman Mills. Ways and Means subcommittee chairmen became subject to caucus election in 1991, after two chairmen defied the leadership on tax legislation in 1989.

The House and Senate Budget committees were among the few panels that had no subcommittees in the 101st Congress (both committees were exempted from the subcommittee requirement). The House panel, however, did have task forces.

Select and Special Committees

Select and special committees are established from time to time in both chambers to study special problems or concerns, such as hunger or narcotics abuse. Major investigations have been conducted by select committees, such as the Senate panel that investigated the Watergate scandal in 1973-74 and the House and Senate panels that jointly investigated the Iran-contra affair in 1987.

The size and life span of select and special panels usually are fixed by the resolutions that create them. Ordinarily they are not permitted to report legislation. Some of these committees, such as the permanent Select Aging Committee in the House and the Special Aging Committee in the Senate, have gone on from year to year. But, in most cases, they remain in existence for only one or two Congresses.

Unlike most select committees, the Intelligence committees in both chambers consider and report legislation. But this is a special case, as the committees are permanent in everything but name. Because the Intelligence panels' subject matter is narrower than that of most standing committees, they were designated as "select" rather than "standing" committees.

A House Appropriations subcommittee meets in 1989 to draft spending legislation for foreign operations programs.

R. Michael Jenkins

Joint Committees

Joint committees are permanent panels created by statute or by resolution, which also fixes their size. Of the four functioning in 1990, none had the authority to report legislation. One, the Joint Economic Committee, was directed to examine national economic problems and review the execution of fiscal and budgetary programs. It was the only joint committee that had subcommittees. Representative Obey used his chairmanship of Joint Economic to leave an unusually potent political mark for one on the nonlegislative panel, when he developed a key piece of the Democrats' critique of the Reagan administration's economic policy in the 1986 elections.

The Joint Committee on Taxation, made up of senior members of both parties from the House Ways and Means and Senate Finance committees, served chiefly to provide a professional staff on tax issues. The other two joint committees dealt with administrative matters: the Joint Committee on Printing oversaw the Government Printing Office and the Joint Committee on the Library oversaw the Library of Congress.

Chairmanships of joint committees generally rotate from one chamber to another at the beginning of each Congress. When a senator serves as chairman, the vice chairman usually is a representative, and vice versa.

The last joint committee to have legislative responsibilities was the Joint Committee on Atomic Energy, which was abolished in 1977.

Committee Sizes, Ratios

The 1946 reorganization act set not only the jurisdiction of congressional standing committees but also their size. Today, however, the size of committees in both chambers is usually settled through negotiations between majority and minority party leaders. The House dropped size specifications from its rules in 1975, while Senate standing rules in 1990 still included committee size, necessitating some change in that chamber's rules at the beginning of a Congress. Each chamber in effect endorses leadership decisions on committee sizes, as well as party ratios, when it adopts resolutions making committee assignments.

Although the number of standing committees increased by only four in the House and two in the Senate in the 1947-89 period, the number of standing committee seats increased substantially—from 482 to 812 in the House and from 201 to 311 in the Senate. Smith and Deering found that recent House Democratic leaders had expanded committees to meet member demand and maintain party harmony. The authors found less pressure for committee expansion in the Senate due to the fact that most senators held two major committee assignments, compared with just one in the House. They also found that senators generally were less concerned with their committee assignments than their House colleagues.[24]

In the 101st Congress, House committees ranged in size from eleven (District of Columbia) to fifty-seven (Appropriations); Senate committees ranged from eleven (Veterans' Affairs) to twenty-nine (Appropriations).

The standing rules of each chamber are silent on the matter of party ratios on committees. The Senate traditionally has more or less followed the practice of filling standing committees according to the strength of each party in the chamber. While the process usually goes smoothly, in 1989 the routine floor vote to approve committee assignments was delayed while some senators from both parties sought to alter party ratios on a half-dozen committees. When it became clear that no deal would be struck, the Senate ratified its committee lineup.

The House, on the other hand, has been less inclined to allocate minority party representation on committees on the basis of the relative strength of the two parties. House Democratic Caucus rules stipulate that committee ratios be established to create firm working majorities on each committee and instruct the Speaker to provide for a minimum of three Democrats for every two Republicans. (An exception to this is the House Committee on Standards of Official Conduct, which is required by House rules to have an equal number of majority and minority party members.)

Democrats in the House have felt little need to accommodate their political opposition, especially on important House committees such as Appropriations, Rules, and Ways and Means. House Republicans in the 1980s complained bitterly of mistreatment by Democrats and argued that the Democrats had been in the majority for so long that they had become arrogant in the use of power. Fourteen Republicans filed a lawsuit in 1981 after the defeat of their attempts on the floor to change the party ratios on four key committees—Appropriations, Budget, Rules, and Ways and Means—to reflect the gains made by their party in the November 1980 congressional elections. Republicans charged the Democrats with unconstitutionally discriminating against GOP members and their constituents when they set the committee ratios. The case was dismissed by the U.S. District Court for the District of Columbia in October 1981 and the Supreme Court refused to review it in February 1983. In response to the angry Republican protests, Democratic leaders in 1985 agreed to give Republicans more seats on most major committees.

The Chairman's Role

Each committee is headed by a chairman, who is a member of the majority party of a chamber. The chairman is usually the most senior member of the committee, but, because of the reforms of the 1970s, this is no longer an iron-clad rule. Chairmen must now stand for election by their party caucus.

The reforms of the 1970s went a long way toward spreading around the once tightly held power and resources of committee chairmen, especially in the House. The days of autocratic chairmen who could run their committees as they wished are over. Yet committee chairmen are still powerful figures on Capitol Hill. The difference today is the way in which they exercise their many powers. They now must answer to their fellow party members.

At the full committee level, the chairman calls meetings and establishes agendas, schedules hearings, chairs markup sessions, acts as floor manager, recommends conferees, controls the committee budget, supervises the hiring and firing of staff, and serves as spokesman for his committee and party in his area of expertise.

The committee's ranking minority member is also an influential figure. He assists in establishing the committee agenda and in managing legislation on the floor, nominates minority conferees, makes minority committee assignments, and controls the minority staff. He serves as spokesman for the committee's minority members.

Chairmen and ranking minority members often sit "ex officio" on all subcommittees of their committee of which they are not regular members.

Paul Conklin

Secretary of State George Shultz testifies before the Senate Foreign Relations Committee in 1988 on an arms control agreement with the Soviet Union. Press photographers clustered on the floor cover his appearance for the news media.

The 1986 tax reform bill illustrated the continued clout of committee chairmen on Capitol Hill. When House Ways and Means Committee markup of the bill bogged down in 1985, committee chairman Dan Rostenkowski, D-Ill., broke the deadlock with tough backroom negotiations. During Senate Finance Committee consideration of tax reform in 1986, that committee's chairman, Bob Packwood, R-Ore., suspended markup of the bill when it appeared he was going to lose committee votes on several of his proposals. Packwood and his staff director came up with a new tax strategy, then met privately with a core group of senators to forge a bill to take back to the full committee. House-Senate conference agreement was reached only after a series of lengthy, closed-door negotiations between just Rostenkowski and Packwood.

Committee Procedures

Neither chamber of Congress operates under a comprehensive code of committee procedure; general guidelines and restrictions are contained in Senate and House rules, which incorporate many of the provisions in the Legislative Reorganization Acts of 1946 and 1970 and other measures. Democratic Caucus rules have had an even greater impact on committee structure.

One of the basic goals of the 1946 act was to standardize committee procedures in regard to holding regular meeting days, keeping committee records and votes, reporting legislation, requiring a majority of committee members to be in attendance as a condition of transacting committee business, and following set procedures during hearings.

The 1946 rules were not uniformly observed by all committees, and continuing dissatisfaction with committee operations led, in the 1970 reorganization act, to further efforts to reform committee procedures, particularly to make them more democratic and accountable to the membership and the public.

Each Senate and House committee is required to establish and publish rules of procedure. These rules have stipulated that each chamber's standing committees must fix regular meeting days, though the rules authorize the chairman to call additional meetings. The rules also must contain procedures under which a committee majority may call a meeting if the chairman fails to do so.

Committees were required by the 1970 act to keep transcripts of their meetings and to make public all roll-call votes.

In the House the rules require that information about committee votes be made available to the public at the committees' offices; the committees are directed to provide a description of each amendment, motion, order, or "other proposition" voted on and the name of each committee member voting for or against the issue and whether the vote was by proxy or in person, as well as the names of those present but not voting. The rules also require that the results of all votes to report legislation be published in the committee reports; the positions of each member do not have to be included.

In the Senate the rules are less specific. They require that a committee's report on a bill include the results of roll-call votes on "any measure or any amendment thereto" unless the results have been announced previously by the committee. Senate rules require that in reporting roll-call votes the position of each voting member is to be disclosed.

The rules stipulate that it is the chairman's "duty" to see to it that legislation approved by his or her committee is reported. And there are procedures by which a committee majority may force a bill out of committee if the chairman fails to do so. The rules prohibit a committee from reporting any measure unless a majority of its members are actually present, and they place certain limits on proxy

Proxy Voting in Committee

Proxy voting in congressional committees permits one committee member to authorize another member to cast votes for him in his absence. Though on first glance it appears to be an innocuous practice, it has been the bane of the minority party in Congress and a target of reformers for years.

Opponents contend that it encourages absenteeism and irresponsibility. Before the power of committee chairmen was diminished in the 1970s, it also was argued that proxy voting contributed to the domination of committees by the chairmen because the chairmen were in an ideal position to wrest proxies from committee members in return for the favors those members could bestow.

And while chairmen no longer wield the power they once did, proxy voting, according to the minority party, particularly Republicans in the House, allows the majority to abuse the committee system.

"Proxy voting tends to augment the power of the active, not preserve the authority of the absent," Richard L. Hall observes. "Members often duck into a markup for a brief moment, leaving their proxy behind them with little knowledge of the way in which it will be used." *

Before 1970 the use of proxies was regulated either by custom or by guidelines established by individual committees; thus the practice differed from committee to committee. In some committees they never were allowed.

Proxy voting is not permitted on the floor of the Senate or House.

House

The Legislative Reorganization Act of 1970 was the first measure to address the criticisms leveled at proxy voting. That act prohibited the practice unless a committee's written rules specifically allowed it, in which case they were limited to a specific issue (a bill or an amendment or for procedural questions, for internal committee business, etc.). Proxies also had to be in writing, designating the person on the committee authorized to use them.

In October 1974 the House voted 196-166 to ban proxy voting entirely. But the ban did not last long, primarily because Democrats, who as the majority party controlled House operations, benefited from the use of proxies.

Republicans, a minority in the House for all but two Congresses since 1931, have argued that the Democrats' use of proxies allows them to extend their control over the committee system by scheduling numerous committee and subcommittee sessions at the same time. Without proxy votes, the argument goes, the Democrats could not retain control of all committee business on all the committees because of scheduling conflicts. Republicans would then have a better chance of pushing through their amendments.

The Democratic Caucus modified the ban at the beginning of the 94th Congress in 1975. The revision, which was added to the standing rules, once again gave committees the authority to decide whether to permit proxy voting. If a committee allowed proxies, they were to be used only on a specific measure or matter and related amendments and motions. General proxies, covering all matters before a committee for either a specific time period or for an indefinite period, were prohibited, except for votes on procedural matters. As before, they had to be in writing, with a member designated to cast the proxies. The proxy vote also had to be dated and could not be used to make a quorum.

Senate

For Senate committees the 1970 act provided little restraint on the use of proxies. The law said proxy votes could not be used to report legislation if committee rules barred their use. If proxies were not forbidden on a motion to report a bill, they nevertheless could be used only upon the formal request of a senator who planned to be absent during a session.

Senate rules leave it up to individual committees to decide whether or not to allow proxies. To prevent the use of general proxies, Senate rules bar the use of a proxy if an absent member "has not been informed of the matter on which he is being recorded and has not affirmatively requested that he be so recorded." Proxies cannot be counted toward the quorum needed for reporting legislation.

In addition to proxy voting, some Senate committees permit polling—holding an informal vote of committee members instead of convening the committee. Such votes usually are taken by sending a voting sheet to committee members' offices or by taking members' votes by telephone.

Because Senate rules require a quorum to be present for a committee to report legislation, polling is supposed to be restricted to issues involving legislation that is still pending before the committee, to matters relating to investigations, and to internal committee business.

If polling is used to report legislation, any senator can challenge the bill by raising a point of order. Such was the case in December 1980 when opponents of a Carter nominee for a federal judgeship charged that the nomination had not been properly reported because the Judiciary Committee had approved it by a written poll of members.

The issue was dropped and the nominee was approved when Judiciary Chairman Edward M. Kennedy, D-Mass., gained Republican support by agreeing not to push other Carter judicial nominations pending in the committee.

* Richard L. Hall, "Committee Decision Making in the Postreform Congress," in *Congress Reconsidered*, 4th ed., ed. Lawrence C. Dodd and Bruce I. Oppenheimer (Washington, D.C.: CQ Press, 1989), 204.

voting. Members are allowed time to file supplemental and minority views for inclusion in committee reports.

Although the regulations often are set aside, committees are supposed to announce hearings at least one week in advance, in most circumstances to hold meetings in open session, and to require witnesses to file written statements in advance. The rules allow minority party members to call witnesses during at least one day of hearings on a subject.

Committee Assignments

The rules of the House and Senate state that the membership of each house shall elect its members to committees. In practice, representatives of the two parties agree on committee assignments and party ratios in advance and then submit the committee rosters to their party caucuses and finally the full chambers. The key decisions are made in each party's committee on committees, with caucus and floor approval basically pro forma.

With some exceptions, the method currently in general use was adopted by the Senate in 1846 and by the House in 1911. The major difference today is that the list of committee nominees is subject to caucus approval.

The committee assignment procedure applies to all members and takes place at the beginning of every Congress. Barring a change in party control, however, the biennial practice usually affects only new members, who receive committee positions for the first time. Committee assignments also must be made from time to time during a session to fill vacancies caused by a member's death, resignation, or voluntary transfer to another committee. Incumbent members are nearly always permitted to retain their existing assignments. Only rarely is a committee seat taken away to punish a member.

The Seniority Factor

Although the procedural reforms of the 1970s established new methods for selecting committee chairmen, seniority still is normally followed in positioning members on committees and in filling vacancies, with new members being ranked at the bottom of their committees. The seniority tradition is most rigidly observed by Senate Republicans, as evidenced by the 1987 battle between Senators Jesse Helms of North Carolina and Richard G. Lugar of Indiana over the position of ranking Republican on the Foreign Relations Committee. Helms and the principle of seniority won out.

Members who stay on the same committee from one Congress to another are given the same seniority ranking they had in the previous Congress, unless a death, resignation, or retirement on the committee allows them to move up a notch. But if members, even senior members, transfer

Senators Bob Dole, R-Kan., and Jesse Helms, R-N.C., go over the tally sheet following Helms's selection as ranking minority member of the Senate Foreign Relations Committee in 1987.

Jose R. Lopez, *New York Times*

House, Senate Rules Governing Composition . . .

The following guidelines regulated the composition of congressional committees and the selection of committee leaders in the 101st Congress (1989-91). House guidelines are determined for the most part by the Democratic Caucus and Republican Conference, although the rules of the House stipulate certain requirements. Senate guidelines are set forth in the standing rules, with some party regulations. *(Assignment procedures, p. 93)*

House Democrats

The Democrats, through their caucus, divide House committees into three categories: exclusive, major, and nonmajor. Exclusive committees are Appropriations; Ways and Means; and Rules. Major committees are Agriculture; Armed Services; Banking, Finance, and Urban Affairs; Education and Labor; Foreign Affairs; Energy and Commerce; Judiciary; and Public Works and Transportation. Nonmajor committees are Budget; District of Columbia; Government Operations; House Administration; Interior and Insular Affairs; Merchant Marine and Fisheries; Post Office and Civil Service; Science, Space, and Technology; Small Business; and Veterans' Affairs. House select and joint committees remain within the purview of the House leadership, with the Speaker appointing the Democratic members and the minority leader the Republicans.

Democrats serving on an exclusive committee may not serve on any other standing committee (unless the caucus grants a waiver), with the exception of the Budget and House Administration committees. Democratic membership of the Budget Committee must include three members of the Appropriations Committee, three members of the Ways and Means Committee, and at least one from the Rules Committee, as well as one leadership member appointed by the Speaker.

The party's caucus rules guarantee all Democrats a seat on one major or exclusive committee. No Democrat may serve on more than one major and one nonmajor, or on more than two nonmajor committees. An exception allows Democrats to be assigned to either the District of Columbia or Judiciary committees regardless of other committee assignments. Democrats are permitted a maximum of five subcommittee assignments.

Democrats are nominated to most committees by the Steering and Policy Committee, subject to caucus approval. Members of the Rules Committee are nominated by the Speaker, again subject to caucus approval. Votes on individual nominees may be requested, but votes are automatic for all Democratic members of the Budget Committee. Votes are also automatic for new members of the Ways and Means and Appropriations committees.

There are few limits on length of service on committees. However, the rules of the House state that Budget Committee members may serve for only six years in a ten-year period. Exceptions to this include the leadership member of the Budget Committee as well as an incumbent chairman who may stay on an extra two years to serve a second term as chairman. Also, no member may serve on the Committee on Standards of Official Conduct—the ethics committee—or the Permanent Select Intelligence Committee for more than three consecutive terms.

Generally, Democrats are limited to one chairmanship—they may not simultaneously chair another full, select, permanent select, special, ad hoc, or joint committee, unless the caucus grants an exemption in the case of an ad hoc committee. The only exceptions are that the Ways and Means Committee chairman may also serve as chairman of the Joint Committee on Taxation, and the House Administration Committee chairman may chair the Joint Printing Committee and the Joint Committee on the Library.

No chairman of an exclusive or major committee may serve on another standing committee, nor may a standing committee chairman serve on the ethics committee. Committee chairmen may chair only one subcommittee of their committee and may not chair any subcommittee of another committee. No Democrat may chair more than one subcommittee of a committee with legislative jurisdiction, though Budget Committee members are exempt from this rule. The House Administration and ethics committees as well as the joint committees are exempt from all caucus provisions regulating subcommittee chairmanships.

Most nominations for committee chairman are made by the Steering and Policy Committee. Exceptions are the Rules Committee chairman, who is nominated by the Speaker, and the Budget Committee chairman, who is selected from nominations made within the caucus. Nominations are to be made without regard to seniority. The caucus votes on all nominations individually by secret ballot.

Subcommittee chairmen of the Appropriations Committee also are voted on by secret ballot in the party caucus. If an Appropriations subcommittee chairman is deposed, his replacement must come from among the members of that subcommittee. The committee caucus may use subcommittee seniority as the criterion in nominating candidates for subcommittee chairmen.

Beginning with the 102nd Congress (1991-93), subcommittee chairmen of the Ways and Means Committee also are elected by the party caucus.

On other committees subcommittee chairmen are elected by the Democrats on their committee. Committee members are entitled to bid for subcommittee chairmanships in the order of their seniority on the full committee.

House Republicans

The House Republican Committee on Committees classifies committees as red, white, and blue. These cate-

... of Committee Membership and Leadership

gories essentially correspond to the Democrats' exclusive, major, and minor categories, with the notable exception of Energy and Commerce, which is considered a red, or exclusive, committee. In other differences, the Republicans put Interior and Insular Affairs and Science, Space, and Technology in the white, or major, category, while the Democrats classify them as nonmajor. The Democrats consider Education and Labor to be a major committee but the Republicans have it in the blue category.

Members assigned to a red committee may be on no other standing committee unless required by House rules. As with the Democrats, the Budget Committee is an exception: two members of the Appropriations Committee and two members of the Ways and Means Committee also serve on the Budget Committee. (Other GOP Budget members include one member appointed by the Republican leader.)

Other Republicans may serve on only one white committee and one blue committee, or on two blue committees. All limitations on committee assignments can be waived by the Republican Conference.

Republican Conference rules limit most members of the party leadership to service on one standing committee and prohibit them from serving as ranking minority member of any committee. This rule can be waived by the conference.

Ranking minority members of full committees are recommended by the Committee on Committees without regard to seniority and voted on by secret ballot of the conference. However, the GOP leader nominates the Republican members and ranking GOP member of the Rules Committee, subject to conference approval.

Selection of ranking subcommittee members is at the discretion of the ranking minority member of a full committee, unless a majority of the GOP members of the full committee disapprove.

Except for certain rules for ranking committee members, the Republicans have no specific limitations on subcommittee assignments. No Republican may serve as the ranking member of more than one standing, select, or ad hoc committee and of more than one subcommittee of any standing, select, or ad hoc committee, without the approval of the conference. No member may serve as ranking Republican member of more than two subcommittees of the standing, select, and ad hoc committees on which he serves, nor can a Republican be the ranking member on two subcommittees of the same committee, unless this rule is waived by the conference.

The Republicans are subject to the same time limits on service on the Budget, Standards of Official Conduct, and Permanent Select Intelligence committees as the Democrats.

Senate Democrats, Republicans

The Senate divides its standing committees into major and minor committees. Major ones are Agricul-

ture, Nutrition, and Forestry; Appropriations; Armed Services; Banking, Housing, and Urban Affairs; Commerce, Science, and Transportation; Energy and Natural Resources; Environment and Public Works; Finance; Foreign Relations; Governmental Affairs; Judiciary; and Labor and Human Resources. Minor committees are Budget; Rules and Administration; Veterans' Affairs; Small Business; Aging; Intelligence; and Joint Economic. Ethics, Indian Affairs, and the Joint Committee on Taxation are also considered minor committees but do not count toward the limits outlined in the paragraph below, nor does membership on any joint committee that is required by law.

Senators, Democrats and Republicans, shall sit on two major committees and may serve on one minor committee. Only one of the two major committees may be a so-called elite committee—Appropriations, Armed Services, Finance, and Foreign Relations. Senators are limited to membership on three subcommittees of each major committee on which they serve (the Appropriations Committee is exempt from the limit) and on two subcommittees of their minor committees. The chairman or ranking minority member of a committee may serve as an ex officio member without a vote on any subcommittee of that committee. There are numerous exceptions to these regulations that protect incumbent senators who would have been in violation of these rules at the time they took effect. By agreement of the majority and minority leaders, the membership of a committee may be temporarily increased above the official limits set by the rules—but by no more than two members—in order to maintain majority party control, and any member serving on a committee for this purpose would be allowed to serve on three major committees.

Both parties guarantee their members one seat on a major committee before any member receives a second top assignment.

The Senate requires that membership on the Select Intelligence Committee be rotated. No senator may serve on the committee for more than eight successive years.

A senator generally may serve as chairman or ranking minority member of only one full committee. A senator may chair only one subcommittee of each committee on which he serves. The chairman of a major committee may serve as chairman of only one subcommittee of his major committees and one subcommittee of his minor committee. The chairman of a minor committee may not serve as chairman of any subcommittee on that committee; he may chair one subcommittee of each of his major committees.

Senate Democratic nominations for chairmen are made by the Steering Committee and circulated to all Senate Democrats. A rule adopted in 1975 provided for a secret ballot vote on an individual nominee if requested by 20 percent of the Senate's Democrats.

The Republican members of each Senate committee elect the ranking minority member of their committee, subject to the approval of the Republican Conference.

from one committee to another, they are ranked at the bottom in seniority on their new committees.

As a rule, members of Congress remain on their major committees throughout their careers, gradually working their way up in seniority. If a member has done reasonably well, and not made a lot of enemies, he or she usually can expect to become a chairman or ranking minority member despite the changes in seniority since the early 1970s.

Many factors are involved in the decisions of the party leadership in assigning new members to committees, but once members are assigned committees, seniority remains the most important single factor in determining their advancement on that committee.

In the Senate the Democratic committee roster is drawn up by the Democratic Steering Committee, whose chairman and members are appointed by the party leader. The Senate Republican committee roster is drawn up by the Republican Committee on Committees, which is appointed by the chairman of the Republican Conference. Republican party leaders are ex officio members.

In the House the Democratic committee roster is drawn up by the party's Steering and Policy Committee, which is composed of regionally elected members and members appointed by the Speaker, as well as top party and committee leaders who are ex officio members. (From 1911 until 1975, Democratic committee assignments were made by the Democratic members of the Ways and Means Committee.) An exception applies to the Democratic members of the Rules Committee. In 1975 the Speaker was given the power to nominate all party members of that panel. Nominations to all committees, including Rules, are subject to ratification by the caucus.

Republican committee nominations in the House are determined by the party's Committee on Committees, which is made up of the floor leader, the whip, one representative from each state having at least five Republicans in its House delegation, one representative from multistate groups formed by states with four or fewer members, and one representative each from the two most recently elected classes. Members' voting strength is proportional to the size of the delegations they represent, except that the minority leader and the whip have twelve votes and six votes, respectively. This procedure was adopted in December 1988 to give the leadership greater clout against a coup such as occurred in 1986, when a group of members representing Texas and several small states joined forces to appoint their chosen members to key committees, instead of heeding the leadership's choices. The Rules Committee again is an exception: GOP members are appointed by the Republican leader.

Once the committee rosters are approved by the two parties in each chamber, they are incorporated in resolutions and put to votes before the full chambers. With approval usually automatic, the votes merely formalize the committee appointments recommended by the two parties and the party ratios previously agreed upon by the leadership.

Plum Assignments

In both chambers, committee assignments are extremely important to members. The Senate, with less-political selection procedures and proportionately more plum seats than the House, tends to see less maneuvering, lobbying, and horse-trading for desired committee slots. There are fewer members competing for influence and looser floor

rules than in the House. Each senator therefore has a greater chance to affect legislation of all stripes.

In the House influence often is closely related to the committee or committees on which a member serves. Moreover, assignment to a powerful committee virtually guarantees large campaign contributions.

Just wanting to be on a committee is not enough. In most cases members have to fight for assignments to the best committees. In each chamber a few committees are considered glamorous and powerful and difficult to get on. But congressional leaders often have to go looking for "volunteers" to serve on lesser panels.

Traditionally, the premier committees sought by representatives have been Appropriations, Rules, and Ways and Means, although Rules has lost some its attraction in recent years. In the 1980s members also sought seats on Budget and Energy and Commerce.

In the Senate the most popular committees traditionally have been Appropriations and Finance. Both the Budget Committee and Armed Services have also been in demand.

Some panels wax and wane, but Appropriations, Finance, and Ways and Means have never been wholly eclipsed because they control the flow of money into and out of federal coffers. In the 1980s these taxing and spending committees were thrust to the center of action more than ever before by Congress's increasing tendency to pile most of its legislative work onto a handful of fiscal measures.

Jurisdictional Conflicts

Most bill referrals to committees are routine matters handled by the parliamentarians of each chamber. Committee jurisdictions outlined in each chamber's rules, as well as precedents and public laws, normally dictate where a bill is sent. But sometimes things are not quite so clear-cut.

Jurisdictional disputes between and among committees have been evident since the inception of the standing committee system. The Legislative Reorganization Act of 1946 attempted to eliminate the problem by defining each committee's jurisdiction in detail. But the 1946 act was not able to eliminate the problem.

As early as 1947 a fight broke out in the Senate over referral of the controversial armed forces unification bill. In the House the measure had been handled by the Committee on Executive Expenditures (now the Government Operations Committee), which had jurisdiction over all proposals for government reorganization. But in a Senate floor vote that chamber's Armed Services Committee successfully challenged the claim of the Expenditures Committee (now the Governmental Affairs Committee) to jurisdiction over the bill.

Such problems have continued to arise because the complexities of modern legislative proposals make it impossible to define jurisdictional boundaries precisely.

In the House the problem has been aggravated by a failure to restructure the committee system to meet new developments and national problems. The problem of conflicting and overlapping jurisdictions became acutely obvious in the 1970s as Congress attempted to formulate a coherent energy policy. When President Jimmy Carter in 1977 submitted his comprehensive national energy program, the impending jurisdictional tangle forced Speaker

Thomas P. O'Neill, Jr., D-Mass, to establish an ad hoc energy committee to review the work of five House committees and to guide energy legislation through the House. (An attempt to consolidate energy responsibilities in one committee, as the Senate had done in 1977, was soundly defeated in the House in 1980.)

Occasionally, when the opportunity arises, a bill is drafted in such a way that it will be referred to a committee favorable to it. Oleszek cites the classic example of the 1963 civil rights bill, which was worded somewhat differently in each chamber so that it would be referred to the Judiciary Committee in the House and the Commerce Committee in the Senate. Both panels were chaired by strong proponents of the legislation, while the chairmen of the House Interstate and Foreign Commerce Committee (now the Energy and Commerce Committee) and the Senate Judiciary Committee were opposed to the legislation. "Careful drafting, therefore, coupled with favorable referral decisions in the House and Senate prevented the bill from being bogged down in hostile committees." [25]

Most bills, however, are subject to strict jurisdictional interpretation and rarely open to the legerdemain given the 1963 civil rights bill or the special handling the Speaker was able to give the 1977 energy bill. Oleszek observes:

> Committees guard their jurisdictional turfs closely, and the parliamentarians know and follow precedents. Only instances of genuine jurisdictional ambiguity provide opportunities for the legislative draftsman and referral options for the Speaker and the presiding officer of the Senate to bypass one committee in favor of another.[26]

Multiple Referral

The most common solution to jurisdictional conflicts is to refer a bill to two or more committees, a practice called multiple referral. There are three types of multiple referrals: joint, when several committees consider a bill at the same time; sequential, when a bill is referred first to one committee, then to another, and so on; and split, when parts of a bill are referred to different committees—this was the approach O'Neill used for the Carter energy bill. The most common is joint referral, while split referral is the least used.

The practice of multiple referral has long been permitted in the Senate, although it is used less frequently there than in the House, which did not permit multiple referral until 1975. In that year the Speaker was permitted to refer a bill to more than one committee. The Speaker was also given the authority, subject to House approval, to create an ad hoc committee to consider legislation when there were overlapping jurisdictions.

In 1977 the Speaker was permitted to impose reporting deadlines on the first committee or committees to which a bill was referred. In 1981 Speaker O'Neill announced that in making multiple referrals he would consider not only the content of the original bill but also amendments proposed by the reporting committee. And in 1983 the Speaker announced that he had the authority to designate a primary committee on jointly referred bills and impose time limits on other committees after the primary committee issued its report.

Since 1975 multiple referrals have grown significantly in the House, and so has the importance of multiply referred bills. "In one form or another, multiple referral is now employed on a multitude of significant legislation and exists as a prominent feature of congressional operations," wrote Melissa P. Collie and Joseph Cooper. The authors cite as examples of multiply referred House bills in the 100th Congress (1987-89) legislation concerning trade reform, drug control, welfare reform, budget reconciliation, Federal Trade Commission reauthorization, aid to the homeless, catastrophic health care, campaign finance reform, South Africa sanctions, banking deregulation, amendments to the Clean Water Act, airport construction and airline safety, nuclear accident liability, amendments to the Clean Air Act, and extension of the GI bill.[27]

Collie and Cooper interpret the arrival of multiple referral in the House "as a signal that committee turf is no longer what it has been cracked up to be." They contend that legislators have surrendered their exclusive autonomy over legislation for access to all legislation to which they have claims.[28]

The growth of multiple referrals in the House has affected key aspects of the legislative process, including the Speaker's prerogatives, the work of the Rules Committee, floor proceedings, and relations with the executive branch and interest groups. It has encouraged members, committees, and staff aides to negotiate with one another rather than acting separately as traditionally done, according to Davidson, Oleszek, and Thomas Kephart. "More importantly, the procedure at the same time has greatly augmented the powers of the Speaker and the Rules Committee, by strengthening their role in centralizing and coordinating the House's workload. That may well be the most profound effect of the multiple-referral procedure." [29]

A good example of this could be seen in House action on the 1988 omnibus trade bill. After eleven House committees worked on the bill, Speaker Jim Wright's office melded their reports to form a new version. The work of Wright's office was packaged by the Rules Committee into a comprehensive substitute amendment to the trade bill that then became the bill for floor debate.

Spending Rivals

The relationships between the Appropriations and legislative committees traditionally have provided striking illustrations of intercommittee rivalries. Legislative committees handle bills authorizing funds, but only the Appropriations committees are permitted to consider the actual spending permitted for federal agencies and programs. This distinction is usually strictly observed by the legislative committees. The Appropriations committees, in turn, theoretically are barred by the standing rules from inserting legislative provisions in their appropriations bills, but they habitually do so and, despite grumbling from the legislative committees, are seldom overruled on the floor.

The creation of the Budget committees in 1974 added yet another dimension to committee rivalries. The new committees were charged with the task of preparing a congressional budget resolution setting out goals for spending and revenues in the next fiscal year. They also were to monitor the revenue and spending actions of the House and Senate.

With the country's increasing preoccupation with budget deficits in the 1980s, the power relationships among these various committees started to shift. The authorizing committees went from proposing various new programs to a fallback position of defending existing ones. "Squeezed between the budget resolution and appropriations stages, there is little time left for debating the recommendations of the authorization committees," Oleszek observes. "As a result, these panels have lost influence to the Appropriations and Budget committees." [30]

The Appropriations committees also benefited in the 1980s from Congress's increasing reliance on omnibus continuing appropriations resolutions when legislators almost routinely failed to pass some or all of the individual appropriations bills. These bills in the 1980s became vehicles for authorizing legislation. As a result, Smith and Deering note:

> Appropriators gained a voice in shaping legislation that they otherwise would not have had, particularly in conference. And the continuing resolutions gave appropriators—as well as other members through appeals to appropriators and through floor amendments—an opportunity to pursue legislative matters without the consent and cooperation of the affected authorizing committee. [31]

Yet the Appropriations committees also lost influence. They had to share power with party and budget leaders in negotiating budget resolutions and then had to operate within the rigid constraints of those resolutions.

Smith and Deering summed up the power shifts:

> As partisan conflict over budget priorities intensified and produced policy stalemates among the House, Senate, and White House, both appropriations and authorizing committees lost autonomy. Party and Budget Committee leaders became central to resolving the conflict. Normal legislative procedures were ignored, set aside temporarily, and in some cases directly altered. All committees learned new legislative tricks to minimize the damage to programs they wanted to protect, but most could not avoid deep encroachments on their traditional autonomy.... Thus, in the quite unsettled power structure of Congress, leaders and budget committees fared well, appropriations committees survived but were injured, and authorizing committees took strong blows to their autonomy. [32]

Budget Summitry

The frequent use in the 1980s of executive-legislative summit conferences to work out budget issues added yet another twist to the power relationships. Authorizing and appropriations committees—already wary of a budget process that had shifted some of their control over tax and spending issues to the Budget committees—viewed the high-level talks, where budget decisions were further centralized, with even greater suspicion.

A 1989 budget-summit deal collapsed in part because chairmen of key committees required to enact the plan were not involved in crucial negotiations. The tax-writing committees were given a revenue-raising target without any agreement on how the figure would be attained.

Attempting to avoid a replay, congressional and White House leaders involved key committee chairmen in a 1990 budget summit from the start. Although the authorizing committee chairmen were still excluded, the congressional negotiating team included the chairmen and ranking members of the tax-writing and Appropriations committees in both the House and Senate, along with the Budget committees and other congressional leaders. But it was to no avail, as the resulting budget debacle proved.

After intermittent talks beginning in May 1990, two dozen congressional and White House negotiators in September went into seclusion at Andrews Air Force Base outside Washington, D.C., for what they hoped would be a final round of budget talks. A budget agreement ultimately was reached by eight congressional and administration officials.

But many members of Congress were not pleased with an agreement reached by a handful of leaders in secrecy away from Capitol Hill—a process that seemed to some observers to cast aside the committee system and political accountability. Many committee chairmen in the House were up in arms about provisions of the agreement that trod on their turf. More than half of the committee chairmen voted against the budget, along with seven of the thirteen Appropriations subcommittee chairmen. The summit agreement went down to humiliating defeat in the House, leading to a three-day shutdown of the government.

The budget crisis finally was resolved and the resulting budget reconciliation package boded further power shifts in the budget process. The new law gave the executive branch closer scrutiny of legislation as it was being crafted, seemingly at the expense of the Budget committees. Limits and restrictions set by the new budget law appeared likely to curtail the discretion of the Budget committees, while expanding that of the Appropriations committees. But whatever the near-term outcome, the rivalries among the spending committees were certain to continue.

In the aftermath of the budget crisis, the House passed a new rule for the 102nd Congress intended to make it harder for the leadership to circumvent the committee system by writing legislation in a task force, summit, or other ad hoc group. The rule guaranteed that standing committees would have five days to review any proposal drafted by ad hoc groups outside the committee system.

Oversight Mandate

In addition to their lawmaking function, committees bear important responsibilities for overseeing implementation of the laws already on the books.

Congress has given the executive branch broad authority over the vast array of agencies and programs it has created. As the range of activities of the federal government has grown, so too has the need for Congress to oversee how the executive branch administers the laws it has passed. Oleszek explains:

> A thoughtful, well-drafted law offers no guarantee that the policy intentions of legislators will be carried out.... The laws passed by Congress are often general guidelines, and sometimes their wording is deliberately vague. The implementation of legislation involves the drafting of administrative regulations by the executive agencies and day-to-day program management by agency officials. Agency regulations and rules are the subject of "legislative oversight"—the continuing review by Congress of how effectively the executive branch is carrying out congressional mandates. [33]

Congress did not officially recognize its responsibility for oversight until enactment of the 1946 Legislative Reorganization Act. That law mandated that the House and Senate standing committees exercise "continuous watchfulness of the execution by the administrative agencies" of any laws under their jurisdiction. The 1946 law divided oversight responsibilities into three areas: the legislative or authorizing committees were to review government programs and agencies, the appropriations committees were to review government spending, and the House Government Operations and Senate Governmental Affairs committees were to probe for inefficiency, waste, and corruption in the federal government. But, as Oleszek points out, "to some degree, all committees perform each type of oversight."[34]

Since enactment of the 1946 law, Congress has passed several measures affecting oversight activities. In the 1970 Legislative Reorganization Act, Congress increased staff assistance to all House and Senate committees, recommended that committees ascertain whether programs within their jurisdiction should be funded annually, and required most committees to issue oversight reports every two years.

Congress acted in 1974 to improve its oversight procedures when it passed the Congressional Budget and Impoundment Control Act. That act strengthened the role of the General Accounting Office (GAO) in acquiring fiscal, budgetary, and program-related information from federal agencies, authorized the GAO to establish an office to develop and recommend methods by which Congress could review and evaluate federal programs and activities, and authorized committees to assess the effectiveness of such programs and to require government agencies to carry out their own evaluations.

Related changes in committee practices adopted by the House in 1974 required committees with more than fifteen members (raised to twenty in 1975) either to set up an oversight subcommittee or to require their legislative committees to carry out oversight functions.

Legislative subcommittees can carry out oversight only within their limited jurisdictions. On the other hand, most subcommittees set up specifically to conduct oversight usually can operate within the full committee's jurisdiction, a much broader mandate.

The House committee changes also gave some committees special oversight responsibilities that permitted them to cross jurisdictional lines in conducting investigations. In another step affecting oversight, the new procedures permitted committees to almost triple the size of their professional staffs.

In the Senate the 1977 committee reorganization granted several committees "comprehensive policy oversight" responsibilities, comparable to the special oversight mandate in the House. Committees were required to include the regulatory impact of each bill or joint resolution in the reports that accompanied the legislation.

Congressional committees have a variety of ways of exercising their oversight responsibilities. The traditional and most obvious way is through normal legislative procedures. Congress can examine agency performances through committee hearings and investigations, ranging from routine reviews to such highly publicized probes as the 1989 investigation of alleged influence peddling and political favoritism at the Department of Housing and Urban Development and the 1989-90 investigation of alleged fraud and racketeering in the savings and loan industry. Consideration of annual or biennial authorization and appropriations measures provides additional opportunities for oversight.

Special reports required from agencies, investigations by agencies' inspectors general, audits by the GAO, and studies by congressional support agencies are other oversight tools. The substantial growth in reports required by Congress—there were more than 3,000 in 1990—has triggered some complaints within both the executive branch and Congress that legislative committees are attempting to "micromanage" administrative details.

The legislative veto has been a popular oversight mechanism since 1932, when Congress began attaching to various statutes provisions giving the two chambers or individual committees authority to veto government actions, regulations, and orders. Although the constitutionality of many of these provisions was called into question by a 1983 Supreme Court decision, Congress has found ways to continue to exercise this veto power.

Congress also has at its disposal nonstatutory controls, such as informal contacts between executive officials and committee members and staff, and statements made in committee and conference reports, as well as statements during hearings and floor debates. Davidson and Oleszek observe: "There is no measure of their usage, but nonstatutory controls may be the most common form of congressional oversight."[35]

Notes

1. Clarence Cannon, *Cannon's Procedure in the House of Representatives* (Washington, D.C.: Government Printing Office, 1963), 221.
2. Walter J. Oleszek, *Congressional Procedures and the Policy Process*, 3rd ed. (Washington, D.C.: CQ Press, 1989), 107.
3. Steven S. Smith and Christopher J. Deering, *Committees in Congress*, 2nd ed. (Washington, D.C.: CQ Press, 1990), 228.
4. George Goodwin, Jr., *The Little Legislatures: Committees of Congress* (Amherst: University of Massachusetts Press, 1970).
5. Woodrow Wilson, *Congressional Government: A Study in American Politics* (Boston: Houghton Mifflin, 1885; Cleveland: Meridian Books, 1956), 59.
6. Leroy N. Rieselbach, *Congressional Reform* (Washington, D.C.: CQ Press, 1986), 110.
7. George B. Galloway, *Congress at the Crossroads* (New York: Thomas Y. Crowell, 1946), 88.
8. Smith and Deering, *Committees in Congress*, 28.
9. Galloway, *Congress at the Crossroads*, 139-144; Goodwin, *The Little Legislatures*, 11-12.
10. George H. Haynes, *The Senate of the United States*, 2 vols. (Boston: Houghton Mifflin, 1938), 1:273-277.
11. Smith and Deering, *Committees in Congress*, 33.
12. Ibid., 42.
13. Randall B. Ripley, *Power in the Senate* (New York: St. Martin's Press, 1969), 23.
14. Ibid., 47.
15. Wilson, *Congressional Government*, 82.
16. Roger H. Davidson, "Subcommittee Government: New Channels for Policy Making," in *The New Congress*, ed. Thomas E. Mann and Norman J. Ornstein (Washington, D.C.: American Enterprise Institute for Public Policy Research, 1981), 105-108.
17. Smith and Deering, *Committees in Congress*, 45-46.
18. Rieselbach, *Congressional Reform*, 45-46.
19. Norman J. Ornstein, Thomas E. Mann, and Michael J. Malbin, *Vital Statistics on Congress: 1989-1990* (Washington, D.C.: Congressional Quarterly, 1990), 120.
20. Ibid.
21. Senate Temporary Select Committee to Study the Senate Committee System, *First Report, with Recommendations; Structure of the Senate Committee System: Jurisdictions, Numbers and Sizes, and Limitations on Memberships and Chairmanships, Referral Procedures, and Scheduling*, 94th Cong., 2nd sess., 1976, 6.
22. Ornstein, Mann, and Malbin, *Vital Statistics on Congress*, 120.
23. Smith and Deering, *Committees in Congress*, 128.
24. Ibid., 63-67.
25. Oleszek, *Congressional Procedures and the Policy Process*, 87.
26. Ibid., 88.
27. Melissa P. Collie and Joseph Cooper, "Multiple Referral and the 'New' Committee System in the House of Representatives," in *Congress Reconsidered*, 4th ed., ed. Lawrence C. Dodd and Bruce I. Oppenheimer (Washington, D.C.: CQ Press,

1989), 248.

28. Ibid., 254.

29. Roger H. Davidson, Walter J. Oleszek, and Thomas Kephart, "One Bill, Many Committees: Multiple Referrals in the U.S. House of Representatives," *Legislative Studies Quarterly*, XIII, 1 (February 1988), 4.

30. Oleszek, *Congressional Procedures and the Policy Process*, 76.

31. Smith and Deering, *Committees in Congress*, 210-211.

32. Ibid., 211.

33. Oleszek, *Congressional Procedures and the Policy Process*, 263.

34. Ibid., 264.

35. Roger H. Davidson and Walter J. Oleszek, *Congress and Its Members*, 3rd ed. (Washington, D.C.: CQ Press, 1990), 271.

Selected Readings

Collie, Melissa P., and Joseph Cooper. "Multiple Referral and the 'New' Committee System in the House of Representatives." In *Congress Reconsidered*, 4th ed., edited by Lawrence C. Dodd and Bruce I. Oppenheimer, 245-272. Washington, D.C.: CQ Press, 1989.

Cooper, Joseph. *The Origin of the Standing Committees and the Development of the Modern House.* Houston: Rice University, 1971.

Davidson, Roger H. "Subcommittee Government: New Channels for Policy Making." In *The New Congress*, edited by Thomas E. Mann and Norman J. Ornstein, 99-133. Washington, D.C.: American Enterprise Institute for Public Policy Research, 1981.

Davidson, Roger H., and Walter J. Oleszek. *Congress and Its Members.* 3rd ed. Washington, D.C.: CQ Press, 1990.

Fenno, Richard F., Jr. *Congressmen in Committees.* Boston: Little, Brown, 1973.

Galloway, George B. *Congress at the Crossroads.* New York: Thomas Y. Crowell, 1946.

Goodwin, George, Jr. *The Little Legislatures: Committees of Congress.* Amherst: University of Massachusetts Press, 1970.

Hall, Richard L. "Committee Decision Making in the Postreform Congress." In *Congress Reconsidered*, 4th ed., edited by Lawrence C. Dodd and Bruce I. Oppenheimer, 197-223. Washington, D.C.: CQ Press, 1989.

Haynes, George H. *The Senate of the United States.* 2 vols. Boston: Houghton Mifflin, 1938.

Hinckley, Barbara. *The Seniority System in Congress.* Bloomington: Indiana University Press, 1971.

Jones, Charles O. *The United States Congress: People, Place, and Policy.* Homewood, Ill.: The Dorsey Press, 1982.

Longley, Lawrence D., and Walter J. Oleszek. *Bicameral Politics: Conference Committees in Congress.* New Haven, Conn.: Yale University Press, 1989.

McConachie, Lauros. *Congressional Committees.* New York: Thomas Y. Crowell, 1898.

McGown, Ada C. *The Congressional Conference Committee.* New York: Columbia University Press, 1927.

Oleszek, Walter J. *Congressional Procedures and the Policy Process.* 3rd ed. Washington, D.C.: CQ Press, 1989.

Ornstein, Norman J., Thomas E. Mann, and Michael J. Malbin. "Committees." Chap. 4 in *Vital Statistics on Congress: 1989-1990.* Washington, D.C.: Congressional Quarterly, 1990.

Price, David E. *Who Makes the Laws?* Cambridge, Mass.: Schenkman, 1972.

Rieselbach, Leroy N. *Congressional Reform.* Washington, D.C.: CQ Press, 1986.

Ripley, Randall B. *Power in the Senate.* New York: St. Martin's Press, 1969.

Robinson, James A. *The House Rules Committee.* Indianapolis: Bobbs-Merrill, 1963.

Shepsle, Kenneth A. "The Changing Textbook Congress." In *Can the Government Govern?*, edited by John E. Chubb and Paul E. Peterson, 238-266. Washington, D.C.: Brookings Institution, 1989.

Smith, Steven S., and Christopher J. Deering. *Committees in Congress.* 2nd ed. Washington, D.C.: CQ Press, 1990.

Unekis, Joseph K., and Leroy N. Rieselbach. *Congressional Committee Politics: Continuity and Change.* New York: Praeger, 1984.

U.S. Congress. House. Committee on Rules. *A History of the Committee on Rules: 1st to 97th Congress, 1789-1981.* 97th Cong., 2nd sess., 1982. Committee Print.

U.S. Congress. House. Select Committee on Committees. *Final Report of Select Committee on Committees.* 96th Cong., 2nd sess., 1980. H Rept 96-866.

U.S. Congress. Senate. Committee on Rules and Administration. *Report on Senate Operations 1988.* 100th Cong., 2nd sess., 1988. Committee Print 129.

U.S. Congress. Senate. Temporary Select Committee to Study the Senate Committee System. *First Report, with Recommendations; Structure of the Senate Committee System: Jurisdictions, Numbers and Sizes, and Limitations on Memberships and Chairmanships, Referral Procedures, and Scheduling.* 94th Cong., 2nd sess., 1976. S Rept 94-1395.

Congressional Staff

Thousands of people work for Congress, and its elected members depend heavily on these employees. Staff members cannot vote, but their imprint is on every other step in getting a bill passed. The influence of congressional staff is vast. Critics complain the staff exercises too much power and costs too much money. But legislators are asked to debate and vote on a wide range of complex issues, and they need staff to provide the expertise that one person alone simply could not master.

Congress has more staff than any other national legislature. There are nearly twenty thousand aides who work directly for Congress and its 540 voting and nonvoting members (including the delegates from American Samoa, the District of Columbia, Guam, and the Virgin Islands, and the resident commissioner from Puerto Rico). By comparison, the Canadian parliament, with slightly more than four hundred senators and members of parliament, employs about thirty-five hundred staff.[1]

Huge increases in the size of congressional staff came in two waves, after Congress reorganized itself in 1946 and 1970. As the size of staff increased, so did the costs of running Congress, which is now well over a billion-dollar enterprise. As recently as the mid-1960s, the cost of operating Congress was less than one-ninth of what it is today. Legislative branch appropriations, which include some nonlegislative activities, are nevertheless the best measure of its cost that Congress has provided over the years. That figure rose from more than $361 million in fiscal 1970 to more than $1.8 billion in fiscal 1990. The largest share goes to pay salaries.

Another ten thousand or so congressional employees are "support staff." They work for the Library of Congress, the General Accounting Office, or the other large agencies of the legislative branch. This chapter deals primarily with the two groups that work most directly with the members—personal staff and committee staff. *(House and Senate support offices, box, p. 104)*

It is not likely that Congress will shrink its bureaucracy. Members rely heavily on staff during all stages of the legislative process. They draft legislation, negotiate with lobbyists, and plot strategy for floor action. This type of staff has been called "entrepreneurial staff," a phrase coined by David Price, a former political scientist and now a member of the House. Entrepreneurial staff are given responsibility for much of the legislative decision making, with members of Congress backstopping their efforts.[2]

The growth of entrepreneurial staff seems to have been encouraged by members, mostly because of an ever-increasing workload. Issues have become more complex, legislation has become more technical, and constituents are demanding more and more from their representatives and senators.

Many members of Congress also view staff—especially large staffs—as a symbol of prestige and importance. To some members, the larger the staff, the more powerful a member appears. Similarly, many staffers feel that the more powerful the committee or member is that they work for, the more powerful they are.

Ironically, for all the power that many staffers possess, congressional aides are not covered by most federal labor, safety, and health laws. Congress voluntarily complies with civil rights statutes, and the House in 1989 extended to its employees coverage under the Fair Labor Standards Act of 1938. But for the most part, congressional aides have little recourse if they feel they are being mistreated or discriminated against, underpaid, or dismissed without good cause.

Early Staffing Practices

Senators and representatives were reluctant during the early years of Congress to admit that they required staff assistance, either in the committees or in their own offices. According to William L. Morrow, in his book *Congressional Committees*, "Legislators were considered more erudite than most citizens and they believed any suggestion for staff assistance might be interpreted as a lack of confidence in their ability to master their jobs."[3]

Congressional staffing began as clerical assistance. In *Congressional Staffs*, Harrison W. Fox, Jr., and Susan Webb Hammond point out that to this day the account for paying personal staffers is still referred to as "clerk-hire."[4] Permanent, paid staffers were authorized first for committees. Until the 1820s and 1830s there were few standing committees, and members of committees handled committee matters without paid assistance. Congress rejected various requests to employ permanent committee clerks until about 1840 when, after pleas by the chairmen, some clerical help was permitted in emergencies on a per diem or hourly basis. Funds for these part-time assistants were made available through special appropriations.

In 1856 the House Ways and Means and Senate Finance committees became the first to obtain regular appropriations for full-time clerks. Appropriations for other committees followed, but their staffing generally was lim-

These five sisters worked as secretaries for members of Congress in
the 1920s. Congressional employees
today are drawn from a mix of backgrounds, but most are young, male,
and well educated.

Library of Congress

ited to persons hired for housekeeping duties, such as ste-
nographers and receptionists. Members or their personal
aides (who were paid out of members' own pockets) usually
handled substantive committee work and bill drafting. But
the number of committee employees increased very gradually. By 1891 committee staff numbered only forty-one in
the Senate and sixty-two in the House.

By the turn of the century, wrote George B. Galloway,
a specialist on Congress with the Library of Congress for
many years, appropriations acts began to carry line items
specifying funds for the standing committees of the House
and Senate. The first comprehensive pay bill authorizing
appropriations for all legislative employees, including committee clerks, was enacted in 1924. That act appropriated
$270,100 for 141 Senate committee clerks and $200,490 for
120 House committee employees.

Senators were first authorized to hire personal aides in
1885, at a pay rate of six dollars a day. The House passed
similar provisions in 1893. Before this time, members who
were not committee chairmen either worked without personal assistance or they paid aides with personal funds.[5]

Committee staffs and personal office staffs were separated by an ill-defined line, both in practice and by statute.
In the late nineteenth century, when chairmen had the
authority to appoint clerks to assist with committee business, these clerks often worked on the chairman's district
business as well. Debate on a clerk-hire bill in 1892 disclosed that some superfluous committees had been kept in
existence under pressure from their chairmen, primarily so
they would have the services of their committee clerks.

Distinctions between the duties of committee employees and members' personal staff remained blurred well into
the twentieth century. Under provisions of the Legislative
Pay Act of 1929, for example, when a senator assumed the
chairmanship of a committee, the three senior clerks of his
office staff became ex officio clerk and assistant clerks of
that committee. Further, the act stipulated that the clerical
staff of a Senate committee also would serve as secretarial
workers for its chairman.

Congress tried in the Legislative Reorganization Act of
1946 to separate the roles of committee and personal staffs.
That law stated that professional committee staff members
"shall not engage in any work other than committee business, and no other duties may be assigned to them." Nonetheless, committee and subcommittee aides often handle
personal and political work for the chairman of the panel to
which they are attached.

Legislation passed in June 1975 further obscured the
difference between the two types of staffers in the Senate.
That measure allowed senators to hire up to three additional staff members to help with committee duties. *(Details, p. 104)*

Staffing Reforms

Personal staffs did not increase much in size between
the turn of the century and World War II. In 1946 representatives were authorized to employ five aides and the
average Senate office had six staffers. Committee staffs
also did not expand greatly; in 1943 there were 190 Senate
committee aides and 114 in the House.[6]

As early as 1941, however, many in Congress realized
that an overhaul of staffing procedures and the committee
structure was necessary. Many members complained that
an ever-increasing congressional workload placed a heavy
burden on staff. As communications and transportation
improved, voters could demand more from their elected
officials. Consequently, casework increased. Furthermore,
issues and legislation had become more complex. And ironically, because members wanted more staff help, more committees were created, which ultimately created more work.

Another problem that drove Congress to change its
staffing practices was the lack of staff with technical expertise and skills. Congress relied on the executive branch and
lobbying groups to provide specialized assistance and help
with drafting bills. Members became concerned about an
"executive branch dictatorship" and felt that Congress was
becoming a second-class institution. This feeling was underscored by a warning issued to Congress in 1942 by
President Franklin D. Roosevelt, who was frustrated with
Congress's delay in enacting key administration proposals:
"In the event that Congress fails to act, and act adequately,
I shall accept the responsibility, and I shall act." [7]

At that time, as the United States was entering World

War II, Congress did not have the monetary resources to beef up its staff.

> [In 1941], of every seven dollars it authorized the federal government to spend, Congress spent only one cent on itself. Its thirty-two-hundred-member staff was predominantly clerical and custodial, with not more than two hundred persons who could be considered legislative professionals. [Members] were often required to use their office clerks as the principal staff of any committee they chaired, thus ignoring professional competence as the foundation for committee staffing.

Members were afraid to increase the appropriation lest the public view them as unable "to carry traditional legislative burdens." [8]

The lack of professional staff, however, may have been self-inflicted. In 1941, when Sen. A. B. "Happy" Chandler, D-Ky., introduced the idea of allowing each senator one "research expert," many senators balked. "Senior members who chaired committees objected to any plan that would add subject specialists to the clerical ranks, fearing that it might establish a cadre of 'political assistants' who would eventually be in a position to compete for their bosses' jobs." [9]

Nevertheless, Congress was becoming increasingly frustrated with the crush of work and with the resulting lack of effectiveness. In 1944 it created the Joint Committee on the Organization of Congress to study the organization, operation, and staffing of the House and Senate; House, Senate, and committee relations; and relations between Congress and the other two branches of government. Almost two years later the committee issued its report. Congress incorporated most of the recommendations into the Legislative Reorganization Act of 1946, which it passed a few months later in July 1946.

The crux of the 1946 act was to reduce the number of standing committees and to authorize Congress to hire professional committee staff. The number of standing committees in the Senate was reduced from thirty-three to fifteen and in the House, from forty-eight to nineteen. Senators were assigned to two committees instead of as many as nine. Representatives served on one committee instead of five. The jurisdiction of each committee was more strictly defined.

Under the structure that exists today, the standing committees, by statute, are authorized a specified number of employees; select and other special committees annually must get congressional approval of a funding resolution to pay staff and meet other expenses.

The House and Senate Appropriations committees and the Joint Committee on Internal Revenue Taxation had begun building nonpartisan professional staffs in the 1920s. According to political scientist Michael J. Malbin, the success of those staffs led Congress to institutionalize the practice in the 1946 Legislative Reorganization Act.[10] The 1946 act allowed each House and Senate standing committee to hire four professional staff members and up to six clerical workers, selected "solely on the basis of fitness to perform the duties of office." The Appropriations committees, however, were permitted to determine their staff needs by majority vote. Thus, the total number of committee aides allowed under the 1946 act was 340, plus the additional staffers hired by the Appropriations committees.

The Joint Committee on the Organization of Congress recommended that each member be allowed to hire an administrative assistant on the member's personal staff.

The House did not agree and this recommendation was dropped from the final act. But the Senate instituted the reform shortly after passage.[11]

The 1946 act also made the majority party members responsible for the hiring and firing of committee staff. Generally, however, the committee delegated that power to the chairman, who often consulted with the senior minority party member. Usually, chairmen were able to obtain most of the funds they wanted from the House Administration and the Senate Rules and Administration committees, which received the requests from the various committees and, after a review, sent their own funding recommendations to their respective chambers for final approval. The committees could go back to the Administration committees with supplemental requests if needed.

Two other important reforms were contained in the 1946 act. It greatly expanded the Legislative Reference Service (now the Congressional Research Service) and created a group of senior specialists who had expertise in subject areas roughly equivalent to those of the standing committees and were paid salaries comparable to their counterparts' in the executive branch. In addition, the act expanded the bill-drafting service available through the Office of the Legislative Counsel. These reforms were essential "for ensuring Congress's independence of executive dictation." [12]

Although most members thought the 1946 act had greatly improved staffing procedures, there still was concern about the quality of staff. By 1948 ninety-three senators had appointed administrative assistants, but some senators complained that unqualified personal secretaries had been promoted. Some members also felt that committees were not always using the staffing authority or hiring well-trained experts. [13]

By 1965 another joint committee was established to look into these concerns. The committee focused on increasing the number of personal and committee staff, the need for staff with scientific and technical expertise, increasing the amount Congress could pay staff to attract more qualified candidates, and providing more staff for the minority.

Five years later Congress passed the Legislative Reorganization Act of 1970. That law:

~ Increased to six, from four, the number of permanent professional staff employees authorized for each standing committee. Two of the six professional staffers, in addition to one of six permanent clerical staffers provided under previous law, were to be reserved for the exclusive use of the committee's minority party members. That provision did not apply to the House and Senate Appropriations committees or to the House Committee on Standards of Official Conduct.

~ Authorized standing committees, with the approval of the Senate Rules and Administration Committee or House Administration Committee, to hire temporary consultants.

~ Authorized standing committees, with the approval of the Senate Rules and Administration Committee or House Administration Committee, to provide staff members with specialized training.

~ Authorized salary levels for Senate committee staff personnel comparable to those of House committee staff personnel.

~ Redesignated the Legislative Reference Service in the Library of Congress as the Congressional Research Service; redefined its duties to better assist congressional committees by providing research and analytical services, records,

House and Senate Support Offices

For its day-to-day operations, Congress is supported by the offices and staffs of the clerk of the House, the secretary of the Senate, the House and Senate sergeants at arms, the House doorkeeper, the House and Senate parliamentarians, and others.

The functions of the clerk of the House and the secretary of the Senate are administrative as well as quasi-judicial. The majority party elects both of the officials, who generally remain in their posts until that party loses control of the chamber (although each house retains the power to remove its officials).

The clerk and secretary perform a wide range of tasks. They process all legislation; prepare the daily digest and periodic reports for the *Congressional Record;* furnish stationery supplies, electrical and mechanical equipment, and office furniture; record and print bills and reports; disburse the payroll; compile lobby registration information; and supervise, respectively, the House and Senate libraries, the recording studios, the document rooms, property supply and repair services, and switchboards.

The House and Senate sergeants at arms do not wear uniforms but they are the police officers of their respective chambers. They attend all House and Senate floor sessions and are responsible for enforcing rules and maintaining decorum, ensuring the security of buildings and visitors, and appointing the Capitol police chief. In addition, the House sergeant at arms is in charge of the mace, a traditional symbol of legislative power and authority. *(First female Senate sergeant at arms, box, p. 109)*

The House doorkeeper introduces the bearers of all messages, official guests, and members attending joint sessions. The doorkeeper is responsible for supervising doormen, pages, and barbers; issuing gallery passes; and performing a variety of custodial services. On the Senate side the sergeant at arms performs these functions.

The parliamentarians of the House and Senate sit in on all sessions to advise the presiding officers on parliamentary procedures. They help refer legislation to committees and they maintain compilations of the precedents of each chamber.

The House and Senate chaplains are officers of their respective chambers. The chaplains open each day's session with a prayer and provide other religious services to members, their families, and congressional staff.

The Office of the Senate Legal Counsel advises and represents senators, committees, officers, and staffers on legal matters relating to official Senate work and civil proceedings.

The House Office of the Law Revision Counsel develops and updates an official classification of U.S. laws. The office periodically prepares and publishes a new edition of the United States Code, including annual cumulative supplements of newly enacted laws.

documents, and other information and data, including memorandums on proposed legislation; and expanded its staff resources. The Congressional Research Service was expanded considerably to meet its wider responsibilities.

~ Required that no less than one-third of a House committee's investigative funds (for temporary staff) be used by the minority party. (The House voted in 1971 to disregard this provision. It was revived in 1974, killed in 1975, and taken up again in 1989.) *(Investigative funds, p. 110; Partisanship and minority staffing, p. 111)*

One more change in House staffing levels occurred in 1974. The House increased the number of permanent professional staff employees to eighteen and the number of clerical aides to twelve. This brought the total number of permanent committee aides to thirty, where it remains today.

In addition to permanent staff, House and Senate committees annually hire investigative aides. Investigative aides are considered to be temporary employees, but they often remain with a committee year after year.

The Senate in 1975 authorized an increase in committee staff in response to complaints of junior senators. They wanted to have, as Sen. Bob Packwood, R-Ore., stated, "the same access that the senior senators do to professional staff assistance." Senators were allowed to hire up to three staffers, called associate staff, depending on the type and number of committees a senator served on.

That change (S Res 60) was intended to prevent a senator who already had staff on a committee from getting more staff for that committee. Thus, it benefited primarily junior senators who had been excluded from separate staff on their committees because of their low-seniority status. The plan cut into the traditional power base that senior members enjoyed through their control of committee staff and was opposed by many of them for that reason.

The 1975 change also required senators to certify that their new aides worked only on committee business. But the funds to pay for the additional committee aides were merged with senators' general clerk-hire funds, thus allowing members to use the money as they wished. In addition, most associate staff work out of senators' personal offices and often are difficult to distinguish from the legislative assistants on senators' personal staffs.

Staff Explosion: Mixed Reviews

Congressional staffs expanded steadily following enactment of the 1946 Legislative Reorganization Act and they received another boost with the Legislative Reorganization Act of 1970. In 1947 there were 399 aides on House and Senate committees; by 1989 the number had jumped to 2,999—an increase of more than 650 percent. Similarly, in 1947 there were 2,030 House and Senate personal aides; in 1989 there were 11,406 personal staffers—an increase of more than 400 percent. *(Staff growth, table, p. 106)*

The post-World War II staff explosion came about for a variety of reasons: a desire for congressional independence from the executive branch, the increasing volume and complexity of legislative issues faced by Congress, competition among committees and their members, and an increase in mail and demands for services by constituents.

The continued growth of staff—especially committee

staff—after the 1970 Legislative Reorganization Act can be linked to the reformist movement that swept Congress in the early 1970s. This time period was marked by the election of more activist members, the decline of the congressional seniority system, greater demands exerted by special interests, and a growing sense that junior and minority party members should get fairer treatment. House committee staffs were two and three-quarters times as large in 1979 as they were in 1970, and Senate committee staffs doubled over the same time period.[14]

The congressional-executive relationship also was a factor in staff growth during the 1970s. Before the mid-1960s Congress still depended to a large extent on the executive branch for information and advice on existing programs and legislative proposals. But distrust of the executive branch, partially the result of the Vietnam War and the Watergate scandal, led Congress to hire more and better qualified committee staff to monitor and evaluate executive branch performance and recommendations and to initiate more of its own legislation.

Also during the 1970s there was an explosion in the size of White House and executive office staff, by which Congress felt threatened. As the executive branch grew, Congress felt compelled to create its own bureaucracy to keep up. Sen. Daniel Patrick Moynihan, D-N.Y., termed this process the "Iron Law of Emulation." According to Moynihan, "Whenever any branch of government acquires a new technique which enhances its power in relation to the other branches, that technique will soon be adopted by those other branches as well."[15]

Similarly, the growth of lobby groups in Washington led to an increase in staff on Capitol Hill. Members needed more help to deal with the volume of special interest issues confronting them. Sen. James Abourezk, D-S.D., once argued that "an active, if sometimes redundant, congressional staff is imperative" to protect the public interest in the face of the often powerful "private constituencies that influence Congress."

Staff growth leveled off during the 1980s and early 1990s. Both personal staff and committee staff numbers have remained fairly stable. This trend may be attributed to the mood of fiscal austerity created by the budget deficit and the Gramm-Rudman-Hollings deficit reduction law.

Another factor in the slowdown of staff expansion was the effort begun by the Reagan administration in 1981 to shrink the federal government. The president's staff in the White House and Executive Office of the President peaked at 5,721 in 1972; by 1988 the staff had dropped to 1,576. Although the number of White House staff had climbed to 1,760 in 1990 under President George Bush, it was still a far cry from the pre-1981 levels.[16]

Lawmakers—especially Republicans—echoed Reagan, calling for a reduction of the congressional bureaucracy. Both the House and Senate cut committee budgets 10 percent in 1981. The Republican-controlled Senate led the way, and the Democratic House felt pressured to follow suit.

Senate committee staffs underwent a one-shot 14 percent cut after the Republicans gained control in 1981 and promised to reverse the previous decade's trends. However, more than one-half of the cuts came from one committee, Judiciary. As significant as the cuts were, the Senate still had about 75 percent more committee staff overall in 1989 than in 1970.[17]

Political considerations forced the House Democratic leadership in 1981 to combine investigative funds for all committees in a single package. Until then the House took up each committee's budget one at a time on the House floor. Under the Republican move to trim congressional budgets, Democrats feared that funds for some committees might suffer further cuts if each committee's request was considered individually.

Impact

So many aides have been recruited in recent years that the House and Senate have been forced to construct new office buildings as well as to convert former hotels, apartments, and federal buildings into temporary offices.

As Congress has grown, it has changed as an institution. What is most apparent is that the legislative branch has become more bureaucratic. With staff growth has come waste and duplication of effort. Some observers charge that many of the newer congressional aides are interested in little more than self-aggrandizement and getting their bosses reelected. They maintain that the availability of larger staffs is drawing Congress into areas where it has no business legislating. On the other hand, some Congress watchers argue that thanks to the larger congressional staff, lawmakers are better equipped to deal with complex and sensitive legislative issues.

Today's staffers are more highly qualified than ever before, and they come increasingly from professional rather than political backgrounds. As a result, Congress receives better information on which to base its decisions.

At the same time, some employees on Capitol Hill, especially those who have been there for a number of years, believe staffers often see their jobs merely as way stations on the road to other prospects. Once, legislative work was a career, even a cause; today, the place is often compared to a corporation or a big government bureaucracy—better managed than before, with many competent people working hard, but impersonal. As one staffer put it: "It used to be a way of life. Now it's a job."

Sarah M. Martin, a staffer on Capitol Hill for forty years, explained the change: "When I first started work here, you got to know everybody on the Hill. We were almost one family, really. We helped each other out, no matter what the party affiliation."

Now, she said, "It's more time-consuming. The bigness—especially with the subcommittees—has broken up the closeness between members and their personal staffs and the committee staffs. People are out to advance themselves, to prove their worth, rather than to find a career. There's a lot of selfish motivation."

As recently as the early 1970s, administration of the congressional bureaucracy was more informal. Before the Senate payroll was computerized in 1972, Senate staff were paid by lining up in front of the Disbursing Office, where each employee was handed an envelope stuffed with his or her pay in cash. "You didn't even have to give them your name," recalled Chester Smith, a retired staff member of the Senate Rules Committee, who went to work on the Hill in 1946. "They knew who you were by your face. Now the pay-line would go all the way down to the Potomac [River] and back."

Committees and Subcommittees

The effect of committee staff expansion was predictable—personnel costs have ballooned. In fiscal year 1960,

Growth of Staff

	House		Senate	
Year	Personal	Committee	Personal	Committee
1891	n.a.	62	39	41
1914	n.a.	105	72	198
1930	870	112	280	163
1935	870	122	424	172
1947	1,440	193	590	290
1957	2,441	375	1,115	558
1967	4,055	589	1,749	621
1972	5,280	783	2,426	918
1976	6,939	1,548	3,251	1,534
1977	6,942	1,776	3,554	1,028
1978	6,944	1,844	3,268	1,151
1979	7,067	1,909	3,593	1,269
1980	7,371	1,917	3,746	1,191
1981	7,487	1,843	3,945	1,022
1982	7,511	1,839	4,041	1,047
1983	7,606	1,970	4,059	1,075
1984	7,385	1,944	3,949	1,095
1985	7,528	2,009	4,097	1,080
1986	7,920*	1,954	3,774*	1,075
1987	7,584	2,024	4,075	1,074
1988	7,564	1,976	3,977	970
1989	7,569	1,986	3,837	1,013

n.a. = not available

* Senate figures reflect the period immediately after Gramm-Rudman mandated staffing cuts. House figures are for the entire fiscal year, thus averaging post-Gramm-Rudman staffing levels with previous, higher levels.

Note: Figures for 1977-1989 committee staff are for the statutory and investigative staffs of standing committees. They do not include select committee staffs.

Sources: For 1891 through 1976, Harrison W. Fox, Jr., and Susan W. Hammond, *Congressional Staffs: The Invisible Force in American Lawmaking* (New York: The Free Press, 1977), 171. For 1977 through 1989, Norman J. Ornstein, Thomas E. Mann, and Michael J. Malbin, *Vital Statistics on Congress, 1991-1992* (Washington, D.C.: Congressional Quarterly), forthcoming.

approximately $12.3 million was appropriated for permanent committee staff and investigations staff in both the House and Senate. By fiscal 1984 the amount was more than $128.4 million.[18]

Another result was, not surprisingly, an increase in the volume of legislation considered by committees. While more employees were hired to deal with the increasing workload facing committee members, the additional staff created more work, necessitating still more staff. Many aides were policy initiators, pushing for certain reforms they personally favored. Others were encouraged by the members who hired them to dig up issues that the lawmakers could use to draw attention to themselves, in the media or back home in their own constituencies.

Although some indicators of the congressional workload—the number of bills introduced, reported, and passed; the number of votes taken; and the number of subcommittee and committee meetings—have decreased in the past decade, workload is still quite heavy. Congress now passes more omnibus bills, which contain many separate bills rolled into one big package. Confirmation hearings that intensely scrutinize a nominee, such as those for John Tower and Robert Bork, have been especially time-consuming in the past few years, as have congressional and executive ethics investigations. In addition, the budget deficit has curtailed members from introducing or considering legislation that will cost a lot of money; many members now concentrate their legislative efforts on low-cost, yet politically visible, issues, such as a constitutional amendment banning flag burning. However, the role of staff in all of these efforts is just as important as in the regular legislative work they do.

One of the most important changes that resulted from the growth of committee staff was the emphasis on subcommittee government—and the growth of subcommittee staff. This was especially true in the House, which diffused committee power in the 1970s reforms it passed.

In 1973 the House Democratic Caucus adopted a "subcommittee bill of rights" stating that a majority caucus within each committee would determine subcommittee chairmen, jurisdictions, and budgets. In a 1974 committee reorganization plan, the House required all committees with more than fifteen members to establish at least four subcommittees; the threshold committee size was changed to twenty members by the House Democratic Caucus in 1975. This move was significant because it institutionalized subcommittees in the House for the first time.

As the power of subcommittees grew so did their staffs. By the late 1970s the number of staffers working for subcommittees equaled the number assigned to full committees in the 1960s.

A further change in House practices adopted in 1975 affected subcommittee staff growth. The new rule allowed subcommittee chairmen and the highest ranking minority member on each panel to hire one staff person each to work directly for them on their subcommittee business.

Where House subcommittee staff grew by nearly 650 percent in the 1970s, Senate subcommittee staff grew by less than 50 percent. In 1979 just two committees, Judiciary and Governmental Affairs, employed nearly three-fourths of the Senate's subcommittee staff. Several committees do not even have subcommittees. Senate subcommittee staff did not grow so quickly because the Senate retained far more centralized staffing arrangements than the House. *(Details on committees and subcommittees, see Committee System chapter, p. 73)*

Political scientists Steven S. Smith and Christopher J. Deering explain the differences between the House and Senate in committee and subcommittee staffing:

> House committees, [which operate] under requirements that committee staff be shared with subcommittees and the minority, now have very similar distributions of staff between the full committee and subcommittees. But there are still a few cases where the full committee chair, through the senior full committee staff, exercises substantial control over at least the majority party staff of the committee and subcommittee. On the Science, Space, and Technology Committee, for example, the top full committee staff has traditionally scrutinized the hiring of subcommittee staff professionals to ensure technical competence and good coordination with the full committee staff. Ways and Means chair Dan Rostenkowski, [D-Ill.,] after becoming chair in 1981, reduced the number of staff appointments sub-

Laws, Rules Governing Hiring of Staff

Following is a brief description of the major laws and regulations Congress has approved since 1946 that affect the hiring and placement of congressional staff:

Legislative Reorganization Act of 1946

This act established a permanent complement of professional staff for all standing committees, and directed that staff be appointed on the basis of merit and not political affiliation. The latter directive is not always observed because committees prefer to hire their own Democratic or Republican "experts." Under the act, committees were allowed to hire four professional staff aides and six clerical aides. Although a provision recommending that each member hire an administrative assistant on his personal staff was dropped from the act, the Senate instituted the reform later that year.

Public Law 90-206

This 1967 postal rate-federal pay law included a ban on nepotism that prohibited public officials, including members of Congress, from hiring, appointing, promoting, or advancing relatives in the agency in which the official serves. The ban did not include relatives already employed, nor did it prevent an official in one agency or chamber of Congress from seeking to obtain employment for a relative in another agency or chamber.

Legislative Reorganization Act of 1970

This act increased from four to six the number of professional aides that could be employed by most standing committees of the House and Senate. The minority party was authorized to hire two of them and one of the six clerical aides. Committees were permitted to provide training for staff and to hire consultants. The act also required that one-third of House investigative staff funds be allocated to the minority (this provision was deleted in 1971 by the House Democratic Caucus).

House Committee Amendments of 1974

Changes adopted in 1974 tripled the staffs of most House standing committees. The number of professional aides went from six to eighteen and clerical employees from six to twelve, with the minority party allowed to appoint one-third of each category. (The latter provision was killed in 1975.)

House Democratic Caucus Action of 1975

The House Democratic Caucus overturned the 1974 House committee reorganization plan that gave Republicans one-third of investigative staff. Instead, it increased the number of statutory staff working on subcommittees by allowing subcommittee chairmen and ranking minority members each to hire one staff person to work on their subcommittees. The increase of up to twelve aides (since standing committees are permitted a total of six subcommittees) was considered to be an overall increase in committee staff to forty-two statutory aides. However, the actual number of committee aides permitted by statute remained at thirty.

House Resolution 359

In 1979 the House approved a rules change that permitted representatives to hire up to four additional employees if their jobs fit into one of the following five categories: a part-time employee; a "shared" employee; an intern; a temporary employee hired for three months or less; or a person who replaced an employee on leave without pay. This brought the total number of House personal staffers in a member's office to eighteen full-time and four part-time. (There are no limits on the number of Senate personal staff.)

Senate Resolution 60

The Senate in 1975 adopted S Res 60, which instituted the idea of associate committee staff—personal aides who would help senators with their committee work. The resolution authorized each senator to hire up to three committee assistants. S Res 60 subsequently was changed from a Senate rule to a statute.

Senate Committee Amendments of 1977

Legislation enacted in 1977 to reorganize Senate committees required committee staffs to be in proportion to the number of majority and minority members on each standing committee. The measure directed that a "majority of the minority members of any committee may, by resolution, request that at least one-third of the funds of the committee for statutory, investigative, and clerical personnel ... be allocated to the minority members."

Senate Resolution 281

Approved in 1980, S Res 281 directed each Senate committee, except the Select Committee on Ethics, to submit a single budget for all expenses anticipated for the fiscal year. (Money requested by the Ethics Committee comes from the Senate contingent fund.) The resolution eliminated the distinction between statutory and investigative committee staffs, which previously had separate budgets. The change made it much easier to get a true picture of actual Senate committee expenditures.

House Committee Funding for 1989

The House Administration Committee's report that accompanied the resolution funding committees in 1989 stated that the minority should have at least 20 percent of committee investigative staff positions, with an eventual goal of 33 percent. Some Republicans hailed this move as a step toward more equitable committee staffing.

committee chairs could make to those required by House rules. He makes it clear, through the senior full committee aides, that even subcommittee staff is responsible to the full committee chair and staff.

Senate committees, because they are not constrained by chamber or party rules requiring separate subcommittee staffs, continue to vary widely in the manner in which they staff subcommittee activities. Some Senate committees, such as Governmental Affairs, Judiciary, and Labor, are much like House committees in allowing subcommittee leaders to appoint their own staff. Others, such as Banking, do not appoint separate subcommittee staffs but assign certain subcommittee responsibilities to full committee staff assistants. In such cases, the staff assistant has two bosses, the full committee chair and the subcommittee chair. And in others, such as Agriculture, there is little meaningful differentiation among committee staff by subcommittee and usually little separate subcommittee activity, particularly with respect to drafting legislation. Three Senate committees with legislative jurisdiction—Rules and Administration, Select Intelligence, and [Veterans' Affairs]— do not have subcommittees or subcommittee staff.[19]

Personal Staff and Casework

The expansion of personal staffs has meant a tremendous increase in the amount of money it takes to run a member's office. In 1970 each representative was entitled to an annual clerk-hire allowance of $149,292 for a staff not to exceed fifteen employees for a district under five hundred thousand persons, or $157,092 for a staff not to exceed sixteen employees for a member representing a larger district. In 1979 the annual clerk-hire allowance for a staff of twenty-two employees was $288,156; by 1991 the allowance for the same number of staff rose to $475,000.[20]

Senators' staffing allowances have similarly increased. In 1970 the clerk-hire allowance ranged from $239,805 to $401,865 (the allowance varies according to state population). In 1979 the range was from $508,221 to

$1,021,167, and by this time most senators had an additional legislative assistance allowance of $157,626. By 1991 the clerk-hire allowance jumped to a range of $814,000 to $1,760,000; the legislative assistance allowance was $269,000.[21]

The modern congressional office more closely resembles a large company customer service department than the typical legislative office of an earlier period. Until World War I, a single clerk handled a member's entire correspondence. In those days, congressional mail usually involved awarding rural mail routes, arranging for Spanish-American War pensions, sending out free seeds and, occasionally, explaining legislation.[22]

House Postmaster Robert V. Rota has testified that the volume of incoming mail has skyrocketed over the past two decades. "Since I was elected as postmaster in 1972, the volume of incoming mail [in the House] has increased more than five-fold. . . . To process the mail received by the House of Representatives, we operate twenty-one hours a day. . . . Mail deliveries are received every hour on the hour."[23]

The demand for services—usually assistance with a constituent's problems with federal agencies—has increased as government has become more involved in the daily lives of Americans. But members also have helped to stimulate constituent demands. They have expanded use of mobile offices, radio programs, and newsletters to advertise the availability of their services and to garner political support.

The emphasis on constituent services is shown by the increase in personal staff working in a member's district or state office. In 1990 more than 41 percent of a representative's staff worked in a district office—up from 22.5 percent in 1972. More than 31 percent of a senator's staff worked in a state office in 1989, as opposed to only 12.5 percent in 1972.[24] Members contend that large staffs are necessary to serve constituents as well as to properly carry out government oversight, which, it is argued, often saves taxpayers' money in the long run through better surveillance of the administration of the laws.

R. Michael Jenkins

Shortly after becoming Speaker of the House in 1989, Thomas S. Foley, D-Wash., held this informal staff meeting to discuss the legislative schedule. Seated at Foley's left is Heather Foley, his wife and unpaid chief of staff.

Assistants or Policy Makers?

Congress's growing dependence on staff has enhanced the power of staff—the so-called unelected representatives. Some observers find this disturbing. As senators and representatives spend more and more time raising money for their reelection campaigns, they delegate more and more work to staff professionals, most of whom have advanced degrees and considerable experience and come to Capitol Hill ready to make substantive policy decisions. The extent of that influence is under continuing debate.

In his book *The Power Game,* journalist Hedrick Smith quotes several members of Congress who agreed they were highly dependent on their aides. Said House majority whip Tony Coelho, D-Calif., in 1986: "When I leave a meeting, I don't have time to do the follow up.... The staff controls that meeting, that issue. I don't have time to make phone calls, to listen to the lobbyists. What is power? Information. Follow-through. Drafting an op-ed article."

Smith quotes some senators as bemoaning the trend toward communication through aides. From Sen. William S. Cohen, R-Maine:

> More and more you are dependent on your staff. There is so much competition among staffs, fighting over issues, that sometimes you'll call a senator and ask, "Why are you opposing me on this?" and he'll say, "I didn't know I was." And you'll say, "Well, check with your staff and see."

From Sen. Ernest F. Hollings, D-S.C.:

> There are many senators who felt that all they were doing is running around and responding to the staff: my staff fighting with your staff, your staff competing with mine.... It is sad. I heard a senator the other day tell me another senator hadn't been in his office for three years; it is just staff. Everybody is working for the staff, staff, staff, driving you nutty, in fact. It has gotten to the point where the senators never actually sit down and exchange ideas and learn from the experience of others and listen. Now it is how many nutty whiz kids you get on the staff, to get you magazine articles and get you headlines and get all of these other things done.[25]

Others feel that the influence of congressional staff is exaggerated. After Senate Majority Leader Howard H. Baker, Jr., R-Tenn., retired from Congress and joined a Washington law firm, he said he was amazed that lobbyists paid so much attention to staff aides; he felt that much of the real work of the Senate was done by individual senators:

> I was struck by the fact that [lobbyists] had list after list of people on the staff they'd gone to see.... That's a side of Washington I hadn't clearly seen while I was in the Senate. I was surprised it was almost the total focus of this little group.... I think part of it is an illusion.... Because, you know, when I met with most committee chairmen every Tuesday morning around the conference table in my office, I saw how it worked. They would really go at it hammer and tongs on particular items within their jurisdiction. So I think the impact of staff is overrated. But God knows, there's enough of them, they generate enough memos, and I know they attract lobbyists and lawyers like flies.[26]

But some observers see positive results in the empowerment of staff. By initiating policy, the staffs help Congress retain its vitality and independence from the execu-

tive branch. According to political scientist Malbin: "Most other national legislatures do not give individual members similar staff resources; most legislatures depend on their cabinets for almost all policy initiatives. Congress is not so passive today, thanks largely to its staff." [27]

Committee Staff: Policy Experts

While congressional committees vary in their organization, most have dual staffs—one professional and one clerical. These generally are headed by a staff director and a chief clerk, respectively. Although the distinctions between the professional and clerical staffs are blurred on many committees, the duties of each can be separated roughly.

The clerical staff is responsible for the day-to-day running of the committee and assisting the members and professional staff. Some of its routine tasks include: keeping the committee calendar up to date, processing committee publications, referring bills that have been introduced to the appropriate departments and administration officials for comment, preparing the bill dockets, maintaining files, performing stenographic work, announcing hearings and contacting witnesses, and opening and sorting mail.

Professional staff members handle committee policy and legislative matters generally, including legal and other types of research, public relations, statistical and other technical work, and drafting and redrafting legislative language and amendments. *(Functions of committee staff, below)*

The clerical and professional aides just described are a committee's statutory, or permanent, staff. Their positions are established by rules of the House or Senate or by law and are funded annually in the legislative branch appropriations bill. Committees also hire additional personnel for investigative work. These employees are considered temporary, but they often remain with the committees for extended periods.

In the House, funds for investigative staff are approved separately from statutory staff funds. The Senate in 1981 eliminated the distinction between the two types for funding purposes. This was done to gain better financial control over soaring staff costs. Senate committees now submit all funding requests in one budget document to the Rules and Administration Committee for review.

Generally, House committees are entitled to thirty staffers paid out of statutory funds. Most of the committees put their highest-paid staff in this category and not under the investigative budget, which is reviewed by the House Administration Committee. Over the years, investigative employees have accounted for much of the increase in committee staff costs, as the budgets for these aides are flexible. In addition to staff salaries, House investigative budgets include money for office equipment, consultants, publications, and for travel within the United States.

House investigative budgets do not include the money the committees get for hiring statutory staff or for printing expenses, stenographic costs, foreign travel, stationery, and some communications expenses. The investigative total also does not include funding for the House Appropriations or Budget committees, both of which are included directly in the annual legislative appropriations bill and are not limited to thirty statutory staffers.

Committees seeking additional investigative help also may use the services of legislative or executive branch agencies. The congressional General Accounting Office, the Treasury Department, and the FBI, among others, frequently are called upon for assistance.

Functions

While staff responsibilities and influence vary from one committee to another, the following list includes the important functions performed by aides on almost all House and Senate committees:

Planning Agendas. Staffers work with chairmen to plan committee agendas, decide which issues to consider, schedule hearings and markups, and plan floor action.

Organizing Hearings. Staffers set up hearings on legislation and issues of interest to the committee leadership as well as on annual or periodic authorization measures on which the panel has jurisdiction. Aides select witnesses, prepare questions, inform the press, brief committee members, and occasionally substitute for members or the chairman if they cannot attend hearings. In many instances a member will prepare a list of questions for aides to ask witnesses if he or she cannot be present. Even when the chairman is present, senior aides with special knowledge sometimes are asked to question witnesses on technical subjects.

Oversight and Investigations. Much original research is conducted by staff members on issues that come before a committee. This usually involves a critique of existing legislation, court decisions, and current practices. Aides on the Armed Services and foreign policy committees, for example, often travel to areas under consideration by the committee. Sometimes staffers hold regional hearings to get opinions from citizens interested in a particular bill or subject.

Bill Markup and Amendment Drafting. Staff

aides assist in marking up bills by explaining technical provisions, outlining policy questions, analyzing proposed changes following committee decisions, and incorporating the decisions in successive revisions of the bill. Although staff members may assist in writing or rewriting proposed bills and amendments, they often serve as liaison between the Office of the Legislative Counsel (there is an office for each chamber), committee members, government agencies, and special interest groups during the drafting of legislation.

Preparing Reports. Committee reports that accompany bills sent to the full chamber are almost entirely staff products. Often, the reports are the only reference available to noncommittee members when a bill is considered by the House or Senate. Staff aides consult with the chairman or the majority party members to decide what should be emphasized in the report. Minority party members and opponents of the bill in question often may file "minority views," which as a rule are drafted by the committee's minority staff members. Then the staff writes the report, usually conforming to a standard format. Reports generally include three basic ingredients—the main body, which explains the bill and gives background and interpretation; the section-by-section analysis of the provisions of the bill; and a written comparison of the bill with existing law. *(Details, see Legislative Process chapter, p. 39)*

Preparing for Floor Action. The top committee aides, those most familiar with the legislation, often accompany the committee chairman, or the bill's sponsor or manager if not the chairman, when the bill is debated on the floor. They may be needed particularly to assist in formulating amendments to the bill or amendments to counter those introduced by other members in the chamber.

Conference Committee Work. The staffs of corresponding committees in each chamber work together on the preparation of conference reports and in resolving differences in legislation initially considered by those committees and subsequently passed by the House and Senate.

Liaison with Executive Branch, Special Interests. Staff aides communicate frequently with executive branch officials and lobbyists on legislative proposals before the committee. Some members regard this activity as the most consequential of all staff work. Rep. Bob Eckhardt, D-Texas, said in 1969: "The key point of contact is usually between a highly specialized lobbyist and the specialized staff people of a standing committee. Intimate friendships spring up there—it's the rivet point. Friendships that last terms. They probably have a greater influence on legislation, especially if it's technical." Lobbyists and representatives of special interest groups, particularly those that have Washington offices, often provide staff aides with detailed information and answers to questions.

Press Relations. Committee staff perform a number of press-related tasks. They alert reporters to upcoming hearings, markup sessions, and floor action on committee-reported measures. Aides answer questions from the press and public, provide background information on legislation before the committee and on recent committee decisions on legislation, and write press releases. In addition, they make committee members accessible to the media and generally work to obtain favorable publicity for the committee.

Recruitment and Tenure

Most committee employees are selected by the chairman, or the top-ranking minority party member, as a per-

Ken Heinen

Staff members stand by as Rep. John D. Dingell, D-Mich., chairman of the House Energy and Commerce Committee, con-fers with a committee member. Staffers cannot vote, but their imprint is on every other step in the legislative process.

quisite of office, subject only to nominal approval by the full committee.

From surveys and interviews with committee staff, one can make some generalizations about today's professional aides (as distinct from clerical aides). They are relatively young and most are male. Most committee professionals are residents of the District of Columbia metropolitan area, in contrast to members' personal office staff. The majority of the aides have advanced degrees, particularly law degrees, and many bring previous experience in the executive branch to their committee positions.[28] Susan Webb Hammond has observed a recent trend toward career development in committee staff positions, especially considering the level of experience and expertise required of most committee staffers.[29]

The tenure of committee employees is subject to the chairman or member who hired them, and aides can be fired with or without cause. Congressional aides do not need to be reminded about the precarious nature of committee employment. As one Capitol Hill observer pointed out, "Staff members all have friends whose chairman retired, switched committees, or was beaten, leaving them with a new chairman wanting to 'clean house.' They all know competent people who were fired without warning because the boss sensed a slight, or just felt it was time for a change."[30]

The power to fire congressional staff gives members significant control over individuals to whom they have delegated great responsibility. Members of Congress can instantly demote or dismiss a staffer they feel has exceeded their authority.

Salaries and Benefits

Salaries of committee employees increased dramatically in the decades after World War II. In 1945 House employees were listed under "clerk-hire" categories with annual base pay of $2,500. The 1970 Legislative Reorganization Act converted the "base pay" system of the House into a monthly salary system and raised the compensation levels of committee employees. The highest-paid committee aides in the House received an annual salary in 1991 of approximately $115,092; in the Senate, $99,215.

Both the House and the Senate are required by law to report on salaries, allowances, and expenses paid to members and members' personal and committee staffs. The "Report of the Clerk of the House" is issued quarterly; the "Report of the Secretary of the Senate," every six months. (Both reports are available to the public through the House and Senate Document rooms.)

Committee staff receive the same cost-of-living increases and insurance and retirement benefits as do other Capitol Hill employees. Vacation and sick leave policies vary according to committee.

Partisanship and Minority Staffing

Partisanship of committee employees has been and remains a controversial topic. For many years the chairman's prerogative prevailed in the selection of staff members. Thus, most of the employees were from the majority party.

The 1946 Legislative Reorganization Act omitted any provision for apportioning the professional staff of a committee between the chairman and the ranking minority member. The act simply stated that "staff members shall be assigned to the chairman and ranking minority member of such committee as the committee may deem advisable." Committees interpreted that provision in various ways, and the whim of the chairman often determined the number of minority aides hired.

In the 1960s Republicans began to press for formally recognized and permanently authorized minority staffing on all committees. Columnist Roscoe Drummond, writing in 1961, advanced the Republicans' arguments:

> If the Republican members of Congress are ever to be in a position to clarify, expound, and defend their stand on the major issues . . . and to advance constructive alternatives of their own, they must get a steady flow of adequate, reliable, competent research and information from an adequate, reliable, and competent professional staff. This staff must be in the service of the minority, selected by the minority, and working for it.[31]

Another problem facing minority staff is inequitable treatment. Sometimes minority staff are paid less than their counterparts working for the majority, and minority senators and representatives often must wait longer than majority members to appoint staff.[32]

Several changes were made in minority staffing in the 1970s. The 1970 Legislative Reorganization Act provided that at least three full-time minority staff aides were to be assigned to most committees of the House and Senate.

House

In January 1971 the House voted to delete the provisions of the 1970 Legislative Reorganization Act providing that one-third of committee investigative funds—used to hire part-time professionals and to assist members—be allocated to the minority side. The Democratic Caucus had voted to bind all House Democrats to vote for the deletion, a move that angered Republicans and revealed clearly the importance members attach to the issue of congressional staffing.

The minority staffing issue surfaced again in late 1974, as representatives debated a proposal to reorganize House committees. That plan called for giving Republicans ten of thirty staff members assigned to committees by statute and one-third of the investigative staff allotted to subcommittees by the House Administration Committee. But when the Democratic Caucus met in January 1975, a resolution was introduced to nullify the one-third minority investigative staff guarantee. The caucus agreed to a compromise that allowed subcommittee chairmen and top-ranking minority members to hire one staff person each to work on their subcommittees—up to a maximum of six subcommittees—but dropped the one-third minority investigative staff guarantee. House rules permitted standing committees a total of six subcommittees. Although the staff increase applied specifically to subcommittees, the revision was widely billed as an increase of twelve in the number of statutory committee employees. The actual number of committee employees permitted by statute remained at thirty.

The minority staffing compromise produced one of the most significant changes of the many revisions made in House rules during the 1970-75 period. Incorporated into the rules January 14, 1975, the compromise was seen as crucial to strengthening the subcommittees and giving House minority members a meaningful opportunity to influence legislation. In general, dispersing power among committee members and reducing the authority of House committee chairmen also meant a dispersal of control over committee staffs and budgets.

The idea of allocating one-third of investigative staff to the minority came up again in 1989. This time House Democrats agreed to let the minority have at least 20 percent of committee investigative staff positions, with an eventual goal of 33 percent. Although only 19 percent of the investigative staff positions were allocated to the minority in 1990, most Republicans agreed that progress was being made toward more equitable staffing and that the real problem was a shortage of funds for expansion.

Senate

As part of the Senate's 1975 change in committee staffing (S Res 60), all minority members were authorized to hire up to three personal committee aides.

In 1977 the Senate directed that committee staffs should be allocated in proportion to the number of majority and minority members on a standing committee. The measure further specified that a "majority of the minority members of any committee may, by resolution, request that at least one-third of the funds of the committee for statutory, investigative, and clerical personnel . . . be allocated to the minority members."

Majority-Minority Staff Cooperation

The degree of cooperation between the majority and minority staffs varies with each committee. It is difficult to be nonpartisan on Capitol Hill, and most staffers have party or philosophical preferences. Even more important, most staffers work for a single member or the majority or minority committee leadership and must act in accordance with their wishes. A few committees, however—Appropriations, ethics, and the Joint Committee on Taxation, among others—have traditions of professional nonpartisan staffing.

From the late 1940s to the late 1970s, the Senate Foreign Relations Committee had a bipartisan staff that served all committee members regardless of party or seniority. In 1979, however, a group of Republican senators led by Jesse Helms of North Carolina, S. I. Hayakawa of California, and Richard G. Lugar of Indiana, requested and received separate minority staff. In 1981, when Republicans took control of the Senate, the partisan staffing arrangement continued.

The benefits of a nonpartisan system are evident in the case of the Joint Tax Committee staff, maintains Michael Malbin, who studied the committee in the late 1970s. These aides serve as the principal staff on tax legislation for both the House Ways and Means and Senate Finance committees. On all major issues likely to be considered by the two committees on tax-related measures, the joint committee aides, according to Malbin, outline the political interests of both major parties. This information then is published before the committees meet so that all members of the House and Senate, the press, and the public can understand the issues and political implications before the committee begins its work.[33]

Jeffrey H. Birnbaum and Alan S. Murray, who followed the passage of the 1986 Tax Reform Act in their book, *Showdown at Gucci Gulch*, described the Joint Tax Committee in action, showing how important its nonpartisan staff are:

> [The staff of the joint committee] were not beholden to any single member. Their job was not political, and their bosses were many.... [They] served as a reservoir of in-house expertise for the entire Congress, especially the two tax-writing committees. Joint Tax aides shaped and analyzed every change in tax law proposed by their bosses and often came up with suggestions themselves. Their revenue estimates on the changes were gospel. In tax reform, an exercise driven by revenue estimates and income-distribution charts, Joint Tax pronouncements were crucial.[34]

Personal Staff: A Member's Right Arm

Personal staffs are set up differently in each congressional office. Whether a representative or senator chooses to emphasize constituent service or legislation probably makes the biggest difference in how the office is organized. A member's personality is another factor.

Most congressional offices have an administrative assistant (AA), legislative assistants (LA's), caseworkers, and at least one press secretary. Many also have an office manager, appointments secretary, legislative correspondent, and systems or computer manager.

The administrative assistant, sometimes called the executive assistant, often serves as the member's alter ego and directs and supervises the office. Frequently, the AA serves as the member's chief political adviser, keeping the member abreast of district and Capitol Hill politics. The AA usually is in charge of the staff, or shares these supervisory responsibilities with the staff who manage the legislative staff, clerical staff, and staff in the state or district offices.

Functions

In the modern Congress, no senator or representative tries to "go it alone." Some are more inclined than others to try to "micromanage" their affairs, but in general members depend on staff to handle the nuts-and-bolts work of a congressional office. Reliance on staff is underscored by this picture of a member's typical day:

> On a normal day, a senator or [representative] has two and sometimes three simultaneous committee hearings, floor votes, issues caucuses, meetings with other congressmen from his state or region, plus lobbyists, constituents, and press to handle. He will dart into one hearing, get a quick fill-in from his staffer, inject his ten minutes' worth and rush on to the next event, often told by an aide how to vote as he rushes onto the floor. Only the staff specialist has any continuity with substance. The member is constantly hopscotching.[35]

Constituent Service

A major responsibility of personal staffs, especially in the House, is service to the people back in the state or district. Staffers respond to a myriad of constituent requests—they untangle bureaucratic snarls in collecting Social Security or veterans' benefits; they answer questions about student loans and similar programs; they help home state or district organizations to navigate red tape for landing federal grants; they respond to constituent mail on legislative and national issues; and they produce newsletters and other mailings to keep constituents informed of their representative's or senator's activities.

Such services are important not only for the benefits they provide to constituents, but also for the relationship they help to foster between a member of Congress and a voter. Former congressional staffer Mark Bisnow says that

> [constituent service] is often considered one of the more beneficial things congressmen do, but the motivation goes beyond mere charity; personal touches typically matter to voters as much as larger issues of ideology, voting record, or even public reputation. As a result, constituents occupy almost deified status in the eyes of Hill offices, a flotilla of paid aides poised to handle their problems. Too bad for a challenger who can do nothing more than walk the district at his own expense.[36]

Junior members of Congress tend to focus more attention on constituent services than more senior members do, and House members spend more time on casework than do senators. In both chambers, however, senior legislators apparently receive proportionately more casework requests than do junior members, possibly because senior members are considered more powerful and better equipped to resolve constituents' problems.[37]

Caseworkers may be called research assistants or staff assistants. Their operations may be centered in either the member's Washington office, or the state/district office.

Legislation

The making of laws is the fundamental job of a member of Congress. To do the work, members need legislative assistants for substantive and political guidance through the daily congressional agenda of complex, interdependent issues. There are more committee meetings than a member can adequately prepare for. Other members, federal officials, special interest groups, and sometimes even the White House staff must be consulted before final decisions are made, and often there are lengthy floor debates going well into the evening. A member must rely heavily on staff at every major phase of the legislative process.

Congressional offices have one or more legislative assistants who work with the senator or representative on the member's committees and help to draft bills and amendments and recommend policy initiatives and alternatives. LA's also monitor committee sessions that the member cannot attend and they may write the lawmaker's speeches and prepare position papers. In many offices, LA's are supervised by a legislative director—normally the senior legislative assistant.

In Senate offices, where there are more staffers, a team of LA's in an office often will divide up and specialize in various issues. In the House, one or two LA's alone may handle legislation for the member, or, in some cases, the member delegates the handling of legislative correspondence and personally takes care of monitoring active legislation.

Other Duties

Personal staffers handle other chores besides casework and legislation. The press secretary serves as the member's

Teresa Zabala

Rep. Peter J. Visclosky, D-Ind., left, works with his executive assistant, Sarah Wells Duffy, in this 1985 picture. Duffy previously was a Washington lobbyist for the American Psychological Association.

chief spokesperson to the news media. Press aides compose news releases dealing with legislative issues as well as notable casework or grants efforts, write newsletters, and organize press conferences. Because they deal almost exclusively with hometown media outlets, some House press aides are based in the district offices rather than in Washington. Where there is no press secretary, press relations are handled by the AA or a legislative assistant. Senators, who receive more national publicity and represent larger areas, often have several deputy press secretaries or assistant press staff.

The office manager, who often is the second-level manager in a congressional office, is in charge of handling clerical and computer systems functions.

The appointments secretary, who also may be called an executive secretary or a scheduler, normally handles personal appointments and travel arrangements for the member. An executive secretary who has been in a member's office for some time often exercises indirect, if not direct, control over other staff members.

A legislative correspondent drafts responses to letters concerning pending legislation. In some offices, the LA may draft letters in a particular subject area; in others, the legislative correspondent drafts letters for the LA's regardless of the subject.

The systems manager coordinates the member's correspondence management system (CMS) operations, which produces form letters. With the enormous amount of mail members of Congress receive each year, CMS operations have become an important function.

Personal staff members also play an important role in the reelection campaigns of their member. They may com-

pile mailing lists, organize fundraisers, and, in the Senate, solicit campaign contributions. *(Details, see Legislative Work vs. Politics, p. 118)*

Relations with Committee Staff

Besides the help they get from personal aides, senior senators and representatives are assisted on legislative matters by staffs of the committees and subcommittees on which they serve. In addition, all senators since 1975 have been authorized up to three aides to help with their committee business. The chairman of a standing committee actually has two staffs. It is not unusual for an aide to do both committee work and personal casework for a member, no matter which payroll he or she is on. *(Committee staff structure, p. 109)*

Recruitment and Tenure

Personal aides are hired by the individual representative or senator. Although there are House and Senate employment offices, most hiring is based on informal contacts—who knows whom. Potential staffers may seek out members who are involved in particular issue areas, who are known to pay well, who are from a certain area of the country, or who have a particular ideological bent. Conversely, members may hire staffers for some of the same reasons.[38]

A major question for members is whether to hire from the state or district, or to go outside for persons with more experience. This is especially a problem for first-term representatives and senators who may not have many Washington contacts and who feel indebted to their campaign staff. As freshmen, these members may feel it is especially important to cultivate state and district contacts. A staffer who came to Washington with the then newly elected senator Pete Domenici, R-N.M., said he soon realized how important it is to strike a balance when hiring staff:

> We had a lot of people we felt we had to hire from the campaign. We brought a lot of them with us. . . . The big mistake we made was that we did not hire anyone who knew the Senate. . . . I had to check ten offices every time I wanted to find out how you did something. It was insane.[39]

The party loyalty of staff is a "secondary consideration" to most representatives and senators when making hiring decisions. "It may be [that members] consider their aides already self-screened: If someone wants to work for them, their politics must be compatible." [40]

Members are entitled to money from a clerk-hire allowance to run and staff their office. The clerk-hire money is divided equally among representatives. For senators, the money is divided according to the state's population. *(Details on clerk-hire allowance, see Salaries and Benefits section, below)*

The characteristics of personal staff vary greatly from those of committee staff. A vivid picture of personal aides was painted by a former House legislative assistant:

> House LA's tend to be young, commonly in their twenties; theirs can be an entry-level professional position requiring no previous Hill experience. (Committee staffers, in contrast, tend to be more specialized, and therefore older and of greater experience.) Their workaday world is informal and often frenetic. . . . Fifty-to-sixty hour work weeks are not unusual. Under constant time pressure and a multitude of urgent assignments, LA's typically switch among projects and topics by the half hour; they learn to write quickly, think politically, and argue combatively. In crowded offices, their desks nudged up against each other in ways that would affront a fire marshal, they do their own typing, photocopying, and phone-calling. They then suspend any calm reflections until things settle down again at six or seven or eight o'clock at night. . . .[41]

Like committee staff, personal staffers have little or no job security. Their tenure is up to the member who hired them. Neither personal nor committee staffers are protected under most labor laws that apply to other federal employees, a fact that earned Congress the nickname, "The Last Plantation." *(Details, see p. 121)*

Salaries and Benefits

There are few regulations to guide members in setting pay rates for their personal aides. Salaries for personal staff in both the House and the Senate are drawn from a clerk-hire allowance. The Senate also has a separate fund for legislative assistance. *(See House and Senate allowances, below)*

Each House member is limited to a certain number of employees: eighteen full-time and four part-time. There is no limit in the Senate.

There are ceilings on pay levels—in 1991 personal staff in the House could earn up to $101,331 annually; the Senate figure was $97,359. And there is a minimum pay level—1991 levels were $1,200 per year in the House and $1,530 in

the Senate—but these salaries are normally for interns. The House also is regulated by minimum wage laws; the minimum wage in 1991 was $4.25 per hour.

But setting salaries and benefits for personal staff is left to the discretion of each member of Congress. Similar jobs in different offices may command very different salaries. Formal policies on working hours, vacation time, sick leave, and maternity leave do not necessarily exist and vary from office to office. The House passed legislation in 1989 to bring its employees under the protections of the Fair Labor Standards Act, which means that House offices may have to provide overtime pay for certain employees and written job descriptions. However, as of early 1991 the House Administration Committee had yet to issue guidelines on how to implement the act. And once the guidelines were issued, it seemed likely that how the act was implemented would be left up to the discretion of each House office. *(Details, box, p. 116)*

Most House and Senate employees qualify for annual cost-of-living adjustments (COLAs), which also are given to federal employees. Beginning January 1, 1992, COLAs for members of Congress and staff were to be calculated by subtracting 0.5 percent from the previous year's Economic Cost Index, which measures inflation of private industry salaries. A ceiling on COLAs was set at 5 percent.

However, the additional cost-of-living funds are not automatically included in congressional staffers' paychecks. Instead, they are added to the members' committee and personal payroll funds. A member or committee chairman can choose to give his employees the increase, use the money to hire more staffers, or return the money to the Treasury at the end of the year.

The salaries of some congressional staff—such as the clerk of the House, secretary of the Senate, the parliamentarians, House counsel, and legislative counsel—are statutory. This means their salaries (and raises) are funded by legislative appropriations and, like members of Congress, their raises and cost-of-living increases are guaranteed.

House Allowance

In 1991 the clerk-hire allowance of each House member was $475,000 a year, which members could use to hire up to eighteen full-time and four temporary aides in their Washington and district offices. That allowance represented an increase of $236,420 since 1977. The increase in the staff allowance mainly has benefited junior members, who do not have the committee staff assistance enjoyed by their senior colleagues.

A maximum of $50,000 from a representative's clerk-hire allowance can be transferred to his official expenses allowance for use in other categories, such as computer and related services. In addition, a House member may allocate up to $50,000 from the official expenses allowance to supplement the clerk-hire allowance, provided that monthly clerk-hire disbursements do not exceed 10 percent of the total clerk-hire allowance.

Before 1979 the maximum number of personal aides a representative could hire was eighteen, with no exceptions. In July of that year the House approved a rules change permitting members to add up to four more staffers to their payrolls—without counting them toward the ceiling of eighteen—if their jobs fit into one of five categories:

~ A part-time employee, defined as one who does not work more than fifteen full working days a month or who is paid $1,270 a month or less.

New Rights for House Employees

Effective October 1, 1990, the Minimum Wage Act of 1989 brought employees of the House and the architect of the Capitol under the protections of the Fair Labor Standards Act (FLSA) of 1938. Senate employees were not included.

While nearly all congressional workers already were receiving at least the minimum wage, the FLSA introduced some new employee rights to Capitol Hill. It mandated the writing of job descriptions, the maintenance of accurate time sheets (which had never been required and possibly meant nightmarish new accounting concerns for office managers), and overtime pay for certain employees.

The FLSA also required "equal pay for equal work," which meant similarly qualified employees performing the same tasks had to receive comparable salaries. Some female staffers claimed that under the system that allowed House members to set pay entirely at their own discretion, women were paid markedly less than equally experienced men in the same jobs.

Equal pay requirements also meant intraoffice consistency might be required. If a representative paid a legislative assistant (LA) $25,000 to handle Education and Labor Committee issues and that LA left for another job, the representative would have to pay a new, similarly qualified Education and Labor LA at least $25,000.

Many on Capitol Hill feared that implementation of minimum wage provisions would wreak havoc on offices' accounting and compensation systems, not to mention their budgets. The House Administration Committee was supposed to issue guidelines to help House offices comply with the FLSA, but as of early 1991 no guidelines had been formulated. In the meantime, some House offices were requiring time sheets, for instance, while other offices simply exempted themselves from the act. Some of the issues that House Administration needed to address included the following:

Who was covered under overtime provisions? The FLSA exempted "executive," "professional," and "administrative" employees. But which congressional employees fit these descriptions?

Some cases were fairly clear: A staff attorney is a "professional"; an administrative assistant (AA) who hires and manages staffers is an "executive." But what about legislative assistants and legislative correspondents? Said one aide, "There's not a cookie-cutter de-scription of what an LA does—or an AA, or anybody else. That's the nature of the beast."

A possible resolution was that the House Administration Committee would set several job descriptions as templates for offices to follow in deciding which employees were due overtime pay.

What constituted an "employing authority?" Equal pay and job description provisions of the FLSA were applicable within individual "employing authorities." But was the House itself one big employing authority—requiring a midwestern Republican to give an LA the same duties and pay as a northeastern Democrat?

More likely, the definition would break an employing authority down to a more workable size—to the member, committee, and officer level. Even then, what about district offices? Under the FLSA, a caseworker in the district might have to be paid the same as another, similarly qualified caseworker with the same duties in Washington—despite any cost-of-living differences.

Where would overtime funds come from? Unless radical changes were made to the existing pay system—under which staffers were paid from the clerk-hire allowance (in the case of personal aides) or committee or officers' budgets—pay budgets would be strained when overtime was added. One possible solution would be to allow representatives to provide extra vacation time ("comp time") instead of overtime.

Enforcement of the law for House workers is the responsibility of the Office of Fair Employment Practices (OFEP). (There is no formal body for the architect's staff, but this office has an internal mechanism, according to an aide.) In the event of a serious complaint, an OFEP ruling would be the final arbiter of whether the office had conformed to the FLSA. *(OFEP, p. 124)*

But the role of the OFEP raised another set of highly sensitive questions about FLSA enforcement. Would the OFEP do spot checks on House members' offices to ensure compliance, or would it wait for complaints? And what remedies would be available to staffers whom the OFEP decided had been wronged?

Source: Adapted from Timothy J. Burger, "Minimum Wage Act, Which Goes Into Effect in Four Months, Will Change Life in House," *Roll Call*, June 11, 1990, 3.

~ A "shared" employee—an employee, such as a computer expert, who is on the payroll of two or more members simultaneously.

~ An intern in the member's Washington office, defined as an employee hired for up to 120 days and paid $1,160 a month or less.

~ A temporary employee, defined as a staff member hired for three months or less and assigned a specific task or function.

~ A person who temporarily replaces an employee on leave without pay.

In 1976 the House Administration Committee instituted a series of reforms governing staff allowances in the aftermath of the sex-payroll scandal that forced Rep. Wayne L. Hays, D-Ohio, to resign as chairman of the committee. At the same time, the House stripped the committee of its unilateral power to alter representatives' benefits and allowances.

The committee's reforms required all representatives, including chairmen of committees and subcommittees, to certify monthly the salaries and duties of their staff and to disclose any kinships between staff employees and any House member. Quarterly reports detailing how House allowances are spent were required for the first time. The reports of the clerk of the House are indexed by the name of the employee and by the member or House officer employing the person, showing the employee's title and salary.

The House allowed its Administration Committee, without further action by the full chamber, to adjust the clerk-hire allowance to reflect federal government cost-of-living raises.

Senate Allowance

The clerk-hire allowance of senators varies with the size of the member's state. For 1991 the annual allowance ranged from $814,000 for states with a population of fewer than one million residents to $1,760,000 for states with more than twenty-eight million.

Senators may hire as many aides as they wish within their allowance; typically, this ranges between twenty-five and sixty, depending on the size of the state and the salary level.

The Senate clerk-hire allowance has remained essentially unchanged since 1968, aside from annual cost-of-living adjustments and additional staff funds provided to some senators as a result of a 1975 Senate rules change authorizing junior members to hire committee aides.

Under the 1975 action, senators were allotted a separate allowance to appoint up to three additional staffers to do specialized work on a senator's committees. The fiscal 1978 appropriations bill for the legislative branch combined this additional committee assistance allowance with senators' administrative and clerical allowance, so the annual Senate clerk-hire allowance actually consisted of two separate allowances. In 1991 each senator was authorized $269,000 for legislative assistance in addition to the regular clerk-hire allowance.

The original intent of the 1975 change was to give junior senators assistance in meeting their committee responsibilities. But because there no longer is any limit on the number of staff that can be employed, a senator can use his legislative aides for either committee or personal staff work.

Questionable Hiring Practices

Nepotism has been a recurring problem in Congress. Some members have used their staff allowances to hire relatives and, in effect, supplement their own incomes.

On May 20, 1932, the House adopted a resolution providing that: "The Clerk of the House of Representatives is hereby authorized and directed to keep open for public inspection the payroll records of the disbursing officer of the House." The resolution was adopted without debate. Few members on the floor understood its import. The next day, however, newspapers published stories based upon examinations of the disbursing officer's records. They disclosed that ninety-seven members of the House devoted their clerk-hire allowance, in whole or in part, to paying persons having the same names as their own. Presumably these persons were relatives. The names were published, and "nepotism in Congress" became a subject of wide public discussion. At that time, however, nepotism was not illegal or even a violation of the standing rules.

Senate payroll information did not become open for public inspection until twenty-seven years later. On June 26, 1959, the Senate by voice vote adopted a resolution requiring the secretary of the Senate to make public the name, title, salary, and employer of all Senate employees. The resolution was the outgrowth of critical newspaper stories on the withholding of payroll information, coupled with additional disclosures of congressional nepotism.

A January 1959 news story by Scripps-Howard staff writer Vance Trimble contained a lengthy list of relatives he said were employed in 1958 by members of Congress. Trimble had obtained the names by checking out similar names in public House and Senate records. He filed a court suit to gain access to Senate payroll records.

On February 23, 1959, the Associated Press (AP) published a list of sixty-five representatives who had persons with "the same or similar family name" on their January payrolls. Three members who were on the AP list denied that their payroll namesakes were in any way related to them.

Nepotism also was a problem for Rep. Adam Clayton Powell, Jr., D-N.Y. Soon after his marriage in December 1960, Powell employed his Puerto Rican wife, Yvette Marjorie Flores, as a paid member of his congressional office staff. Mrs. Powell remained in Puerto Rico after the birth of a son in 1962, but she continued to draw a $20,578 annual salary as a clerk whose job was to answer mail from Spanish-speaking constituents.

The House in 1964 adopted a resolution aimed specifically at the Powell situation: it forbade members to hire employees who did not work either in the member's home district or in the representative's Washington, D.C., office. (That provision was made permanent in 1976.) Mrs. Powell, however, continued to live in Puerto Rico. Following a select committee investigation of that and other charges against Powell, the House on March 1, 1967, voted to exclude him from the 90th Congress. The Supreme Court ruled later, however, that the House action was unconstitutional, and Powell returned to Congress in 1969.

In 1967 Congress approved a measure to curb nepotism in federal employment. The measure, added to a postal rate-federal pay bill, prohibited public officials, including members of Congress, from appointing or trying to promote the appointment of relatives in the agency in which the officials served. The ban covered all officials, including the president, but it did not cover relatives already employed. And it did not prevent an official in one agency or chamber of Congress from seeking to obtain employment for a relative in another agency or chamber.

The *New Member Orientation Handbook*, prepared for all new members and updated periodically by the Senate Rules Committee and the House Administration Committee, lists twenty-seven classifications of relatives whose employment by representatives and senators is prohibited by law (5 U.S.C. 3110). Certification of an employee's relationship to a member of Congress must be made on payroll authorizations by the employing member or by the committee or subcommittee chairman.

In the late 1980s the hiring practices of Rep. Mary Rose Oakar, D-Ohio, and Del. Walter E. Fauntroy, D-D.C., came under scrutiny. In 1987 the House ethics committee found that Oakar broke House rules and federal laws when she paid a former staff member more than $45,000 in salary for nearly two years after the aide had moved to New York. Oakar was directed to repay the funds; the ethics commit-

Congressional Interns

Over many years members of Congress have been assisted by temporary employees known generally as congressional interns. The practice's origins are obscure, but it probably began with members hiring students of American government or the sons and daughters of constituents to work in their offices during the summer. The diverse and informal method of employment expanded greatly during the 1960s.

Congressional interns vary widely in their experience and their office responsibilities. Younger students may work at clerical tasks, help to answer mail, or conduct visitors around the Capitol. Those with more experience may be assigned to constituent casework, drafting speeches and reports, or helping committee staff. Some students receive college credit for working in Congress.

The ways they are paid vary as well (although many interns are not paid at all). Those under private internships are paid by their sponsors. The Congressional Fellows program of the American Political Science Association, for example, each year brings a few dozen experienced journalists, teachers, and government officials to Congress. Employees of federal agencies may be assigned to Congress for a time if necessary.

In the Senate interns may be paid from the annual staff allowance or other funds available to the office. The House has a more precise system. Under the Lyndon Baines Johnson congressional internship program, established in 1973 to employ students and teachers of government and social studies, each representative is allocated $2,320 a year to hire one intern for two months or two interns for one month each. The interns must work in the member's Washington office.

The House first established an internship program in 1965, with an annual allowance of $750 for each member's office. But the program was suspended from 1967 to 1971 when representatives objected to some interns' protests against the Vietnam War.

Source: Harrison W. Fox, Jr. and Susan Webb Hammond, *Congressional Staffs* (New York: The Free Press, 1977), 137-138. Pay figure updated for 1991.

John Savage, the son of Illinois Democratic representative Gus Savage, on his payroll around the time the younger Savage was living in Chicago and running for the Illinois legislature. The *Washington Post* reported that Savage was on Fauntroy's payroll from September 1987 until June 1988; that overlapped a two-year period during which Savage had sworn, in Illinois election documents, that he had lived continuously in the state. After the allegations became public, Fauntroy said Savage was the midwestern coordinator of Fauntroy's D.C. statehood campaign and that he reported daily to the Washington office. The Justice Department dropped its investigation of Fauntroy in April 1990, citing insufficient evidence.[42]

Election Year Dilemma: Legislative Work vs. Politics

In recent years the misuse of congressional staff for political gain has become a larger concern than nepotism. The issue invariably comes up at election time when incumbents are accused of using staffers to help in their reelection campaigns.

When members return home to campaign they take with them the customary entourage of staff aides, who must juggle their political work with their status as government employees paid with federal tax dollars. There is no specific federal law against performing political duties, although the practice is somewhat limited by rules in the House and, to a lesser extent, in the Senate.

A former congressional aide commented on the fine line between legislative work and politics:

> [Congress] by its nature is so intensely political that it becomes a practical impossibility to say in many instances where the discharge of official duties leaves off and aspirations to higher office (or reelection) begin. A [representative] and his staff, for example, are not supposed to use office typewriters, photocopy machines, and phone lines to solicit financial contributions for election campaigns, but who is to judge their ulterior motives in taking positions, proposing bills and amendments, writing speeches, or issuing press releases that happen to be of value in both legislative and campaign contexts?[43]

To avoid being criticized for using government-paid staff to work on their campaigns, incumbents use several approaches to make it legitimate or at least appear so.

"Because of what has gone under the bridge in the past, people are more aware and more careful," said one legislative aide who took a 50 percent pay cut in 1978 to help his boss, Sen. Robert P. Griffin, R-Mich., in his unsuccessful effort to win a third term. "My sense is that everybody is overly sensitive and overly paranoid about it."[44]

In some cases, House and Senate staffers go on vacation or temporarily take themselves off the government payroll. Others try to mix their congressional job with election campaign duties and agree to a cut in pay to reflect the reduction in their congressional work. Others remain on the payroll to avoid losing benefits but claim to put in a full day of constituent service at the member's district office before going to campaign headquarters to help their boss in his reelection bid. Nonetheless, staffers "simply doing their ordinary job is a large contribution in itself."[45]

tee concluded that further disciplinary action was not warranted. Oakar also was investigated for giving another aide a $10,000-a-year raise in October 1985, the same month she and the aide purchased a town house together. Although Oakar said the ethics committee had approved their living and working arrangement, she announced in March 1987 that she would sell the house. The aide had worked for Oakar for two years and received a second $10,000 raise in January 1987.

From 1989 to 1990 the Justice Department investigated allegations that Fauntroy improperly kept Thomas

Ethics Rules for Congressional Staff

Like members of Congress, House and Senate employees must abide by certain ethics rules. These restrictions deal with honoraria, outside income, gifts, travel, financial disclosure, and postemployment lobbying. Most of the rules were amended when Congress passed the Government Ethics Reform Act of 1989 (PL 101-194).

Honoraria

In the House, effective January 1, 1991, members and staff were prohibited from accepting honoraria. However, House employees could request that charitable contributions be made in their name in lieu of honoraria for speeches and appearances. Charitable contributions were limited to $2,000 per speech, appearance, or article, and they could not be made to any organization that benefited the person who spoke or any of his or her relatives. Those who had charitable contributions made on their behalf were barred from getting tax advantages.

Senators and their staff were not affected by the ban because the Senate chose to accept a lower salary than House members and continue accepting honoraria. Senate employees could accept honoraria of up to $2,000 per speech, appearance, or article.

Other Outside Income

Senior staff in the House—those employees who are compensated at or above the GS-16 salary level—were barred from keeping more than 15 percent of the Executive Level II salary ($96,600) in outside earned income; from being paid for working or affiliating with a law or other professional firm (they were allowed to teach for pay if the House Committee on Standards of Official Conduct approved); and from serving on boards of directors. Outside earned income included "wages, salary, fees, and other amounts paid for personal services, as opposed to items such as interest, rents, dividends, and capital gains, which represent a return on investments."

There were no limits on outside earnings for Senate employees.

Gifts

Under rules on acceptance of gifts, all House employees were forbidden to accept more than $200 in gifts from any one person (except relatives) in a calendar year. Exempted was the value of meals and drinks, unless they were part of overnight lodging. Gifts worth $75 or less were not counted toward the $200 total. Gifts to spouses and dependent children also had to be disclosed unless the gift was given "totally independent of" the recipients' relationship to the staffer.

Senate employees were prohibited from receiving more than $300 a year in gifts from any one source other than relatives. There also was a $100 limit on gifts from people with a direct interest in legislation. Gifts worth $75 or less were not counted toward the limit.

Travel

House staff could not receive more than thirty days of lodging a year from someone other than a relative. If the hospitality was extended more than four days, the employee had to ensure that it was in fact personal—not corporate-financed or being claimed as a business expense. Private sources could pay travel expenses for no more than four days of domestic travel and seven days for international trips (travel time was excluded for both categories). Travel expenses also could be paid for one accompanying relative. The House Committee on Standards of Official Conduct could waive gift and travel restrictions in "exceptional circumstances."

Private sources could pay travel expenses of Senate staff for no more than three days of domestic travel and seven days for international trips (both limits excluded travel time).

The travel expenses for an accompanying spouse also could be paid.

Financial Disclosure

The Government Ethics Act of 1989 for the first time brought all three branches of government under the same financial disclosure law, although each branch continued to be responsible for administering requirements for its own employees. The new rules on financial disclosure became effective beginning with reports due in 1991.

The income from any source worth more than $200 had to be reported. Gifts worth less than $75 did not need to be reported.

Employees who had charitable contributions made on their behalf in lieu of honoraria had to disclose the source and amount of the contributions. The charities receiving such contributions were to be disclosed in confidential reports to the House Committee on Standards of Official Conduct. In addition, the source and amount of any honoraria received by the spouse of a reporting individual had to be disclosed.

Also required was disclosure of travel reimbursements, including an itinerary and dates of travel.

Staffers were required to file a "termination report" within thirty days after they left office. The termination report was to contain complete financial disclosure information for the previous year up to the date of departure.

Postemployment Lobbying

Effective January 1, 1991, former House and Senate staff members (those at the GS-17 salary level or above) were barred for one year after leaving employment from lobbying the member, office, or committee for which they had worked.

Leadership staff members were barred from lobbying the members and employees of the leadership for the chamber in which they served.

Supreme Court Ruling

In March 1981 the Supreme Court let stand an appeals court ruling that it was up to Congress to determine whether and under what restraints congressional aides may double as campaign workers. The Court's decision appeared to clear the way for a senator or representative to keep staff aides on the government payroll even when they are working almost exclusively on the member's reelection campaign.

The 1981 appeals court ruling came in a suit brought by former Federal Election Commission attorney Joel D. Joseph in 1977 against Sen. Howard W. Cannon, D-Nev., and Chester B. Sobsey, Cannon's $40,000-a-year administrative assistant. Joseph charged that Sobsey had remained on the Senate payroll from March 1975 through November 1976 while working for Cannon's reelection.

The suit claimed that Cannon's approval of Sobsey's salary payments under those circumstances constituted a fraudulent claim against the government. But the appeals court held that to judge the legality of Cannon's actions would violate the Constitution's separation of powers doctrine. Only the House and Senate can judge such "political questions," the appeals court ruled.

The appeals court based much of its ruling on a conclusion that Congress itself has set no hard-and-fast standard that would have enabled Cannon to determine where to draw the line between Sobsey's official duties and his political chores. Existing rules governing staff campaign work are lenient and subject to differing interpretations. In the past both chambers have been extremely reluctant to police their members' use of staff in political campaigns. Congress never allowed its own staffers to be restricted by the Hatch Act—which prohibits federal government employees from participating in partisan political activities.

Under House regulations staff members, while not permitted to contribute cash to a campaign, may assist a member's reelection effort so long as their assigned congressional duties also are being fulfilled. Those duties are set by each member, as is the amount of vacation time granted. "If they are on their own time, they can do all the politicking they want," said a spokesman for the House Committee on Standards of Official Conduct.

Senate restrictions are even more lax. One House aide, who took himself off the payroll in 1978 to manage a Senate campaign, said: "The Senate rules have big wide holes in them large enough to let just about anybody work in the campaign from the federal staff."

The guiding document on the subject is a Senate Rules Committee report of October 17, 1977, which states that "other than actual handling of campaign funds, the Senate has not imposed any restrictions on the participation of a member of a senator's staff in that senator's reelection campaign." Several weeks after the 1981 appeals court decision in the Cannon case, the Senate Select Ethics Committee proposed incorporating into the Senate ethics code a 1977 ruling by the committee declaring that senators should remove from their congressional payrolls staffers who undertake political work to the detriment of their official Senate duties. But the proposal was never acted on by the full Senate.

Flexibility of Staff Use

Unlike the House, which does not allow personal staff aides to solicit and receive campaign contributions, the Senate provides that three members of each staff may be designated for that purpose. In fact, in the Cannon Supreme Court case, the senator argued that he had designated Sobsey as one of the staffers allowed to solicit and receive campaign funds.

The use of congressional staff on a campaign offers an enormous advantage to members over their challengers, who must use their own campaign funds to finance staff support. Critics of this practice have proposed that legislative aides' salaries for hours spent politicking be counted against the limits on campaign spending. But it is difficult to differentiate political activities from legislative work that is also usable in an election campaign. Some activities, such as managing a campaign, raising money, and dealing with poll results, are clearly political. But casework, speech writing, and preparation of responses on particular issues fall into a gray area.

Most of those engaged in campaign efforts at high levels are the administrative assistants—usually a member's top congressional aide and the one having the most political as well as legislative experience.

In 1978 Tom E. Coker served as campaign manager for Sen. Maryon P. Allen, D-Ala., in the Alabama Democratic primary—lost by Allen—while continuing to receive his $44,000 annual pay as her administrative assistant. Coker said he did not try to hide his political activity. "I didn't feel there was anything wrong with the amount of time I was putting in on the campaign," which he estimated at about 40 percent of his working day.

For four years Coker had been a chief political contact in the state for Sen. James B. Allen, D-Ala., working out of a third-floor office in the Capitol building. One source in the state Democratic party said the thirty-eight-year-old Coker was "one of the best political operatives the state has ever seen." When Allen died and his widow, Maryon, took his seat and sought the remaining two years of his term, it was considered natural for Coker to head her effort.

Asked if he had considered going off the government payroll, Coker said, "I didn't think too much about it. I felt the government had gotten more than their just due from me." He said he rarely had taken any time off, except for Sundays.

In Oregon, Republican Sen. Mark O. Hatfield's close friend and adviser, Gerald W. Frank, cut his staff salary from nearly $40,000 to $10,000 at the beginning of 1978 when he began to manage Hatfield's reelection campaign. His salary became the minimum that a Senate employee could earn and still be designated to receive campaign contributions in a Senate office. Because Frank said he spent more than half his time on official Senate business, he believed he should retain his ability to carry out campaign work.

In 1985 the Senate Ethics Committee issued an "interpretive ruling" (No. 402) stating that an unnamed senator's personal secretary could receive pay from the campaign committee for off-hours work she did for the senator's reelection. The secretary had been designated to receive campaign contributions for the senator.

Press secretaries often work on campaigns in the final weeks as media inquiries focus on politics. Joe Shafran, press aide to Rep. Marc L. Marks, R-Pa., was taken off the government payroll in 1978 because, Shafran said, Marks was exercising caution and did not want any criticism from his opponent. "Frankly, if I'd stayed on the payroll, I get the feeling nobody would have cared," Shafran remarked.

In close races, however, it is not unusual to find a massive shift of personnel from congressional work to the campaign. Because this offers an obvious target for an opponent, staff members in these contests almost always leave the government payroll.

Rep. Abner J. Mikva, an Illinois Democrat, won close elections in 1974 and 1976 and again in 1978. He had one of the most extensive House campaign operations in the country, one that included five campaign headquarters. Mikva began depleting his district office staff during the summer. Four staff persons working in his district, plus the campaign coordinator, were on the campaign payroll. And a legislative aide from his congressional office in Washington would leave Washington at the beginning of the year to work in Mikva's Skokie office and lay the groundwork for the campaign. After winning reelection, Mikva resigned in 1979 to become a federal judge.

In 1986 the House ethics committee investigated complaints that Rep. Mac Sweeney, R-Texas, was threatening to fire staff members who refused to perform campaign activities. The committee said it found no evidence of impropriety and it took no further action.

House Minority Whip Newt Gingrich, R-Ga., was investigated by the House ethics committee in 1989-90 for suggestions that he improperly used his congressional payroll for political purposes. The *Atlanta Business Chronicle* reported in its July 24, 1989, issue that Gingrich had given large, but temporary, year-end pay raises to staff members when they returned to his congressional office after taking leave without government pay to work on his campaign in the 1986 and 1988 elections.

Gingrich denied any wrongdoing and said he was being chastised for a legitimate practice that is widespread on Capitol Hill—members giving their staff year-end bonuses. He said the disclosures were part of a political vendetta against him for his actions in the ethics investigation of Speaker Jim Wright, D-Texas.

Gingrich said he commonly gave bonuses to his low-paid staffers when his office expense account had money left at the end of the year. House regulations stipulated that "year-end increases should be made only on a permanent basis." Nonetheless, Gingrich said, one-time bonuses

were common and at least half of the Georgia delegation provided year-end bonuses.

The most serious allegation was that the bonuses amounted to compensation for campaign work. Gingrich said that other congressional aides who did not work for the campaign also got bonuses. However, a review of 1988 payroll records in the House clerk's office showed that the largest bonuses went to two aides who did work on the campaign.

The investigation of Gingrich, which included other charges, was dropped in March 1990.

Capitol Hill: "The Last Plantation"

Although members of Congress have instituted voluntary rules to prohibit discrimination on Capitol Hill, they have exempted themselves from most civil rights laws and other worker-protection standards they have imposed on other employers. Noting congressional employees' lack of protection under federal employment laws, critics have dubbed Capitol Hill "the last plantation." *(Staff Exemption from Major Laws, box, p. 122)*

Members have argued that their employment practices should not be regulated like the private sector's because of Congress's political nature, which means that members must be free to choose staff who will be loyal to them. Many members also believe the principle of separation of powers would be violated if the executive branch had the power to enforce employment laws in the legislature.

For all the glamor of working in Congress, aides often face long hours, cramped quarters, and the sometimes whimsical demands of politicians at whose pleasure they serve. Women and blacks who work on the Hill are at a particular disadvantage: studies of congressional hiring patterns have found that they tend to be concentrated in low-paying jobs. A 1990 study of House personal staff

Rep. Henry A. Waxman, D-Calif., second from right, confers with aides during subcommittee markup of clean air legislation in 1989.

R. Michael Jenkins

Staff Exempted from Major Laws

In some ways congressional employees are privileged citizens. In other ways they lack rights enjoyed by all other Americans.

The Constitution immunizes members of Congress from intrusion by the other branches of government. Article I, Section 6 protects members against arrest for official acts or libel suits for statements uttered on the floor. Over the years Congress has extended the principle of immunity to its members and staffs, exempting them from many laws that regulate businesses and noncongressional government agencies.

Among the major laws that do not apply to Congress or that give congressional employees special status are the following:

Civil Rights Act of 1964

Title VII of this law (PL 88-352) and amendments to it contained in the Equal Employment Opportunity Act of 1972 (PL 92-261) barred discrimination in employment on the basis of race, color, religion, sex, or national origin. The law established the Equal Employment Opportunity Commission to hear complaints and seek compliance, and it authorized federal courts to order employers to remedy proven discrimination by a variety of means, including back pay and retirement benefits.

The House and Senate voluntarily comply with the act; rules in each chamber prohibit discrimination in employment on the basis of race, color, religion, sex, national origin, race, age, or handicap. Discrimination complaints in the House are heard and mediated by the Office of Fair Employment Practices, which was set up in 1988. Senate staffers may lodge discrimination complaints with the Senate Select Ethics Committee.

National Labor Relations Act

This 1935 law gave employees the right to form unions and required employers to bargain with them. The law proscribed unfair labor practices by both unions and employers, and gave both employers and employees the right to file charges with the National Labor Relations Board. That agency has the authority to investigate and provide relief where warranted.

Fair Labor Standards Act of 1938

This law established national minimum wage, overtime compensation, and child labor standards. In 1989 the Minimum Wage Act (PL 101-57) brought House employment practices under the Fair Labor Standards Act (FLSA). This might require House members to issue written job descriptions, provide "equal pay for equal work," and offer overtime pay.

Extending FLSA provisions to House employees indicated the pressures being exerted on members to impose comparable labor standards on Congress. However, as of early 1991, Senate employees were not covered under the act. (Details on FLSA provisions, see box, p. 116)

Equal Pay Act

This 1963 law (PL 88-38), which amended the Fair Labor Standards Act, guaranteed women the same pay as men for the same work.

Age Discrimination in Employment Act

Enacted in 1967 (PL 90-202) and amended in 1978 (PL 95-256), this law barred employers, employment agencies, and labor organizations from discriminating on the basis of age against any worker or job applicant aged forty to seventy.

Occupational Safety and Health Act

This 1970 law (PL 91-956) required employers to maintain certain health and safety standards for the protection of their employees. The law also authorized periodic government inspection of workplaces.

Privacy Act

In this 1974 law (PL 93-579), Congress required the executive branch to strictly limit access to information the government keeps on individuals, while permitting people to see their own files for correction or amendment.

Conflict of Interest, Disclosure

A 1962 law (PL 87-849) prohibited executive branch employees from participating in government dealings with companies in which they have a financial interest. Although the prohibition did not apply to members of Congress or staff, the Ethics in Government Act of 1978 (PL 95-521) required public disclosure of members' and staffs' financial interests.

Postemployment lobbying by members and staff was restricted by the 1989 Government Ethics Reform Act (PL 101-194). The law also barred acceptance of honoraria by House members and staff and limited outside earnings for them and other government personnel. (Details, box, p. 119)

Civil Service Reform

A 1978 law (PL 95-454) gave federal employees the right to join labor unions and bargain collectively on certain personnel matters. Previously, these rights had been granted only by executive order, subject to change by the president.

House and Senate employees have the right to organize into groups, but Congress has not given those groups the right to be bargaining agents for the workers.

found that even though there are three female employees for every two male employees, women are somewhat over-represented in lower-paying jobs and underrepresented in higher-paying jobs. The same study found that black House staff members receive 89 percent of the pay of their white counterparts and make up 9.4 percent of the total staff, while Hispanic staff earn 82 percent of the salaries of white staff. These differences in average salary are largely due to difference in positions held by minority staff as compared with white staff.[46]

Disabilities and Discrimination

In 1990 both the House and Senate attempted to bestow civil rights protections on their employees as part of a new civil rights act. The bill would have protected congressional employees under the 1964 Civil Rights Act, the 1967 Age Discrimination in Employment Act, and the 1973 Rehabilitation Act. Enforcement would have been carried out by the House Office of Fair Employment Practices and the Senate Ethics Committee. President Bush vetoed the bill, however, and the Senate sustained his veto.

Civil rights protections were extended to congressional employees with physical disabilities when Congress passed the 1990 Americans with Disabilities Act. The law prohibits discrimination on the basis of disability in employment and public accommodations and requires public transportation systems, other public services, and telecommunications systems to be accessible to the physically disabled. Unlike the general public, however, congressional employees alleging discrimination may not sue their employer in federal court. Claims of discrimination in the Senate are investigated and adjudicated exclusively by the Select Committee on Ethics or another entity the Senate desig-

nates. In the House, complaints are handled by the Office of Fair Employment Practices.

Aides and Ethics

Complaints about Congress's exemption from key employment laws gained new bite in 1988 when a spate of political scandals fueled the perception that Washington power brokers operated by their own set of ethical standards. One of the more bizarre cases involved the apparent suicide of a veteran House aide after he was accused in print of unorthodox personnel practices.

Tom Pappas, the top assistant to Rep. Roy Dyson, D-Md., leaped to his death May 1, 1988, the day that the *Washington Post* published allegations by former aides that Pappas had made extreme demands on their personal loyalty and time. The story, based on interviews with former Dyson aides, portrayed Pappas as an office power who overshadowed Dyson and who pressured the young men he hired to socialize with him. The charges included claims that Pappas had told one aide not to date for a year, fired another after he refused to stay at a party, and told another that he would have to perform a striptease at an office retreat.

A spokeswoman for Dyson said all of the former aides quoted in the story had been fired and had "a bone to pick." Although the story was laden with suggestions of homosexual activity on the staff, Dyson firmly denied that either he or Pappas was homosexual. Dyson said he thought some of the complaints against Pappas were reported out of context.

Despite the unusual nature of this particular case, it spotlighted the broad autonomy that members and senior staff exercise in personnel matters. Other unusual accusa-

Employees of the House "folding room," who stuff envelopes with members' newsletters to constituents, complained in 1988 that they were forced to work in "sweatshop" conditions.

Andrea Mohin/*Roll Call*

tions were directed at two California representatives by congressional aides.

In August 1987 the *San Jose Mercury-News* reported complaints against Rep. Ernie Konnyu, R-Calif., from two former aides and an E. F. Hutton lobbyist. One aide said Konnyu admonished her to move her name tag so that it did not draw attention to her small "boobs." She was dismissed in June 1987. The other woman said that in a job interview Konnyu told her to "stand up and turn around.... I want to see what you look like," and said she should wear frilly blouses and high heels. She was fired after declining his invitations to go out after work. Witnesses said the lobbyist scolded Konnyu in a restaurant when the representative touched her knee; Konnyu complained to the lobbyist's boss. Konnyu subsequently lost his seat in the 1988 primary election.

The House ethics committee sent a "letter of reproval," one of its lightest penalties, to Rep. Jim Bates, D-Calif., for sexually harassing women on his staff. The controversy surrounding Bates first surfaced in October 1988, when the Capitol Hill newspaper *Roll Call* published allegations by former aides that he had asked them for daily hugs, patted their behinds, and made other suggestive remarks and gestures. Two former aides filed a formal complaint with the ethics committee that same month. The panel said that Bates violated rules barring discrimination against employees on the basis of sex, and it directed Bates to write a formal apology to the two women who filed the complaint.

Poor physical working conditions on Capitol Hill also made the headlines in 1988. Employees of the House "folding room," who stuff envelopes with members' newsletters to constituents, were reported to work in "sweatshop" conditions. Workers complained of being forced to work seventy-hour weeks without overtime pay. A House committee investigating the complaints found that folding-room employees worked in a cramped basement room with poor air circulation and that they were exposed to noxious fumes.[47]

Complaint Procedures

Critics of congressional employment practices have argued that procedures for bringing complaints against members—through the ethics committees—were poorly understood and little used. According to critics, aggrieved staff members were more likely to go to the press with their complaints or quit their jobs.

After the rash of media reports in 1988 alleging mistreatment of staff, the House passed a resolution to provide new complaint procedures for its employees and job applicants who believed they had been discriminated against. The resolution is now embodied in House Rule 51. The resolution protects House employees and job applicants against employment discrimination on the basis of race, color, national origin, religion, sex, handicap, or age. However, members are allowed to consider political affiliation as a factor in hiring employees, and may hire solely applicants who come from their districts or states.

The resolution also set up a special in-house office, the Office of Fair Employment Practices (OFEP), to investigate discrimination complaints and decide what remedy an employee deserves. Employees of the office work under the supervision of the clerk of the House, but they are appointed by the chairman and ranking minority member of the House Administration Committee.

Under the resolution, employees have 180 days after an alleged violation to file a formal complaint, and the OFEP must first provide counseling to the employee and try to mediate the dispute before holding a formal hearing on the matter. OFEP decisions may be reviewed by an eight-member panel, composed of two Democratic and two Republican members of the House Administration Committee, two of the four elected officers of the House (who are appointed by the Speaker), and two House employees appointed by the minority leader.

Although similar resolutions have been introduced in the Senate, none had passed as of 1990. However, Senate Rule 42 bars discrimination in employment on the basis of "race, color, religion, sex, national origin, age, or state of physical handicap." Senate employees who believe they are being discriminated against may file their grievances with the Ethics Committee.

When the House passed the 1989 Minimum Wage Act increasing the minimum-wage level, it also extended to its employees (including folding-room employees) the rights and protections provided by the Fair Labor Standards Act of 1938—such as minimum wage, overtime compensation, and pay-equity measures. *(See box, p. 119)*

Another avenue for settling congressional employment grievances is the courts. A precedent-setting congressional job discrimination suit was settled out of court in 1979 for an undisclosed sum of money. The suit was filed in 1974 against former representative Otto E. Passman, D-La., by one-time aide Shirley Davis. The settlement was announced, but the amount of money paid Davis by Passman was never disclosed.

The suit established the constitutional right of a congressional employee who claims to be a victim of sex discrimination to sue a member of Congress for damages. However, the out-of-court settlement left undecided the question of whether the Constitution's "speech or debate" clause provides a member of Congress with immunity from job discrimination suits in at least some circumstances. The "speech or debate" clause protects members from court suits for actions taken in Congress as part of their official duties.

The suit filed by Davis against Passman initially was thrown out of court by a federal district judge, who ruled that no law existed to provide Davis with protection from job discrimination by a member of Congress. On appeal, however, the Supreme Court ruled that the Constitution itself gives individuals the right to sue members of Congress, regardless of the provisions of any particular statute, for alleged constitutional violations.

In its decision, the Court dealt only with Davis's right to sue Passman, not the merits of her complaint. The case was then sent back to the lower federal courts to be decided on the merits, but the out-of-court settlement was announced before the courts acted.

Notes

1. Paul S. Rundquist, "Congress and Parliaments," *CRS Review*, March 1989, 32.
2. Michael J. Malbin, *Unelected Representatives: Congressional Staff and the Future of Representative Government* (New York: Basic Books, 1980), 28.
3. William L. Morrow, *Congressional Committees*, (New York: Charles Scribner's Sons, 1969), 52.
4. Harrison W. Fox, Jr., and Susan Webb Hammond, *Congres-*

sional Staffs: The Invisible Force in American Lawmaking (New York: The Free Press, 1977), 15.

5. Ibid.

6. Ibid., 20.

7. Richard A. Baker, *The Senate of the United States: A Bicentennial History* (Malabar, Fla.: Robert E. Krieger, 1988), 89-90.

8. Robert C. Byrd, *The Senate, 1789-1989: Addresses on the History of the United States Senate* (Washington, D.C.: Government Printing Office, 1988), 538.

9. Baker, *The Senate of the United States*, 89-90.

10. Michael J. Malbin, "Delegation, Deliberation, and the New Role of Congressional Staff," in *The New Congress*, ed. Thomas E. Mann and Norman J. Ornstein (Washington, D.C.: American Enterprise Institute for Public Policy Research, 1981), 138.

11. Byrd, *The Senate, 1789-1989*, 550.

12. Ibid., 549.

13. Fox and Hammond, *Congressional Staffs*, 22.

14. Norman J. Ornstein, Thomas E. Mann, and Michael J. Malbin, *Vital Statistics on Congress, 1991-1992* (Washington, D.C.: Congressional Quarterly), forthcoming.

15. Hedrick Smith, *The Power Game: How Washington Works* (New York: Random House, 1988), 282.

16. Harold W. Stanley and Richard G. Niemi, *Vital Statistics on American Politics*, 3rd ed. (Washington, D.C.: CQ Press), forthcoming.

17. Ornstein, Mann, and Malbin, *Vital Statistics on Congress, 1991-1992*, forthcoming.

18. Paul Dwyer, "Legislative Branch Appropriations for Committee and Personal Staff and Agency Contributions: FY 1960-FY 1984," Congressional Research Service report, Feb. 14, 1984.

19. Steven S. Smith and Christopher J. Deering, *Committees in Congress*, 2nd ed. (Washington, D.C.: CQ Press, 1990), 153.

20. Norman J. Ornstein, Thomas E. Mann, Michael J. Malbin, Allen Schick, and John F. Bibby, *Vital Statistics on Congress, 1984-1985* (Washington, D.C.: American Enterprise Institute for Public Policy Research, 1984), 132; and Ornstein, Mann, and Malbin, *Vital Statistics on Congress, 1991-1992*, forthcoming.

21. Ornstein, Mann, Malbin, Schick, and Bibby, *Vital Statistics on Congress, 1984-1985*, 135; and Ornstein, Mann, and Malbin, *Vital Statistics on Congress, 1991-1992*, forthcoming.

22. Stephen Isaacs, "The Capitol Game," *Washington Post*, Feb. 16, 17, 18, 19, 20, 22, 23, 24, 1975.

23. House Subcommittee on Legislative Branch Appropriations, *House Legislative Branch Appropriations Hearings for Fiscal 1991*, 101st Congress, 2nd sess., 1990, 90, 92.

24. Ornstein, Mann, and Malbin, *Vital Statistics on Congress, 1991-1992*, forthcoming.

25. Smith, *The Power Game*, 284, 289-290.

26. Ibid., 285.

27. Malbin, "Delegation, Deliberation, and the New Role of Congressional Staff," 170.

28. Fox and Hammond, *Congressional Staffs*, 43-46.

29. Richard E. Cohen, "The Hill People," *National Journal*, May 16, 1987, 1172.

30. Malbin, "Delegation, Deliberation, and the New Role of Congressional Staff," 151.

31. Kenneth Kofmehl, *Professional Staffs of Congress* (West Lafayette, Ind.: Purdue Research Foundation, 1962), 212.

32. Fox and Hammond, *Congressional Staffs*, 27.

33. Malbin, *Unelected Representatives*, 170-187.

34. Jeffrey H. Birnbaum and Alan S. Murray, *Showdown at Gucci Gulch: Lawmakers, Lobbyists, and the Unlikely Triumph of Tax Reform* (New York: Vintage Books, 1987), 217, 214.

35. Smith, *The Power Game*, 282.

36. Mark Bisnow, *In the Shadow of the Dome: Chronicles of a Capitol Hill Aide* (New York: William Morrow, 1990), 76.

37. Roger H. Davidson and Walter J. Oleszek, *Congress and Its Members*, 3rd ed. (Washington, D.C.: CQ Press, 1990), 138.

38. Fox and Hammond, *Congressional Staffs*, 49.

39. Richard F. Fenno, Jr., *The Emergence of a Senate Leader:*

Pete Domenici and the Reagan Budget (Washington, D.C.: CQ Press, 1991), 4-5.

40. Bisnow, *In the Shadow of the Dome*, 131.

41. Ibid., 91.

42. Saundra Tory, "Fauntroy Won't Be Prosecuted: Justice Department Closes Investigation into Hiring of Aide," *Washington Post*, April 25, 1990, A1.

43. Bisnow, *In the Shadow of the Dome*, 192.

44. Christopher Buchanan, "Campaigning by Staff Aides Is Still a Common Practice," *Congressional Quarterly Weekly Report*, Oct. 28, 1978, 3116.

45. Bisnow, *In the Shadow of the Dome*, 192.

46. Richard Shapiro and Maria Touya, "1990 House of Representatives Employment Practices: A Study of Staff Salary, Tenure, and Demographics" (Washington, D.C.: Congressional Management Foundation, 1990), 19-20.

47. Peter Osterlund, "Changing Capitol's Simon Legree Image," *Christian Science Monitor*, May 20, 1988, 4.

Selected Readings

Baker, Richard A. *The Senate of the United States: A Bicentennial History*. Malabar, Fla.: Robert E. Krieger, 1988.

Birnbaum, Jeffrey H., and Alan S. Murray. *Showdown at Gucci Gulch: Lawmakers, Lobbyists, and the Unlikely Triumph of Tax Reform*. New York: Vintage Books, 1987.

Bisnow, Mark. *In the Shadow of the Dome: Chronicles of a Capitol Hill Aide*. New York: William Morrow, 1990.

Byrd, Robert C. *The Senate, 1789-1989: Addresses on the History of the United States Senate*. Washington, D.C.: Government Printing Office, 1988.

Chaleff, Ira, Burdett A. Loomis, Gary D. Serota, and James A. Thurber. *Setting Course: A Congressional Management Guide*. 3rd ed. Washington, D.C.: American University, 1988.

Cooper, Joseph, and G. Calvin Mackenzie. *The House at Work*. Austin: University of Texas Press, 1981.

Cummings, Frank. *Capitol Hill Manual*. 2nd ed. Washington, D.C.: Bureau of National Affairs, 1984.

Davidson, Roger H., and Walter J. Oleszek. *Congress and Its Members*. 3rd ed. Washington, D.C.: CQ Press, 1990.

Fenno, Richard F., Jr. *The Emergence of a Senate Leader: Pete Domenici and the Reagan Budget*. Washington, D.C.: CQ Press, 1991.

____. *The Making of a Senator: Dan Quayle*. Washington, D.C.: CQ Press, 1989.

____. *The Presidential Odyssey of John Glenn*. Washington, D.C.: CQ Press, 1990.

Fox, Harrison W., Jr., and Susan Webb Hammond. *Congressional Staffs: The Invisible Force in American Lawmaking*. New York: The Free Press, 1977.

Francis, Charles C., and Jeffrey B. Trammell, eds. *The Almanac of the Unelected: Staff of the U.S. Congress*. 2nd ed. Washington, D.C.: The Almanac of the Unelected, 1989.

Jones, Rochelle, and Peter Woll. *The Private World of Congress*. New York: The Free Press, 1979.

Kofmehl, Kenneth. *Professional Staffs of Congress*. West Lafayette, Ind.: Purdue Research Foundation, 1962.

Malbin, Michael J. "Delegation, Deliberation, and the New Role of Congressional Staff." In *The New Congress*, edited by Thomas E. Mann and Norman J. Ornstein. Washington, D.C.: American Enterprise Institute for Public Policy Research, 1981.

____. *Unelected Representatives: Congressional Staff and the Future of Representative Government*. New York: Basic Books, 1980.

Miller, James A. *Running in Place: Inside the Senate*. New York: Simon and Schuster, 1986.

Morrow, William L. *Congressional Committees*. New York: Charles Scribner's Sons, 1969.

Redman, Eric. *The Dance of Legislation*. New York: Simon and Schuster, 1973.

Reid, T. R. *Congressional Odyssey: The Saga of a Senate Bill*.

New York: W. H. Freeman, 1980.

Smith, Hedrick. *The Power Game: How Washington Works.* New York: Random House, 1988.

Smith, Steven S., and Christopher J. Deering. *Committees in Congress.* 2nd ed. Washington, D.C.: CQ Press, 1990.

U.S. Congress. House. Committee on House Administration. *New Member Orientation Handbook.* Washington, D.C.: Government Printing Office, 1988.

Wolpe, Bruce C. *Lobbying Congress: How the System Works.* Washington, D.C.: Congressional Quarterly, 1990.

Pressures on Congress

It is said that a member of Congress has a dance card that is always full. The frantic pace of members' schedules is the result not only of the demands of time, but also the tugs from divergent interests, the no-win decision-making dilemmas into which members are continually thrust. In the course of deciding just who to offend and how least to offend them, members are subjected to relentless pressures from their constituents, the news media, their colleagues and leaders, the president, the judicial branch, and the omnipresent Washington lobbyists. An understanding of these multiple forces can help to explain why a member's vote or noncommittal public position may seem contrary to his or her personal philosophy.

Constituency

Under representative government it is the duty of members of the national legislature to respond to constituent demands. This derives inevitably from the Constitution's requirement that the House of Representatives be elected directly by the people every two years—as well as from the 1913 amendment that substituted direct election of senators for selection by state legislatures. The relationship between a member of Congress and constituents is the crux of self-government in the United States.

The extent to which a member of Congress seeks to follow the wishes of his constituents is determined to a considerable extent by the issue at stake. Probably no member would wish to actively oppose construction in his district of a dam or post office wanted by his constituents—although the cost might give him pause in a period of budgetary constraint. Few members, if any, would follow locally popular policies if convinced that they would seriously endanger the nation. Between these extremes lies a spectrum of different blends of pressure from constituents and conscience. It is in this area that members must make most of their decisions.

Frequently, of course, a senator or representative experiences no conflict between his own views and what he believes are the views of his constituents. But members would be less than human if they did not sometimes compromise their convictions to fit the demands of voters, or filter their perception of voters' demands to fit their convictions. Agreement between the member and his constituents is more normal than disagreement, especially in homogeneous districts and states.

Large and diverse constituencies make it difficult for members to gauge constituent opinion on each issue. In some still-homogeneous House districts, primarily rural or urban ones, voters may care deeply about only a few issues. Members may satisfy constituents by following their views on those matters while their votes on other legislation escape notice. More and more House districts contain a cross-section of urban, suburban, and rural interests, and virtually all states, even the smallest, are divided by economic, cultural, or other differences. Such heterogeneous constituencies force senators and most representatives to build coalitions among groups, heed a wide range of problems, and take risky stands on issues about which many voters feel strongly.

Election Pressures

The most recent election margin and potential reelection challenges weigh heavily on a senator or representative who is calculating how far to stray from opinion back home in the state or district. Members with safe seats are most likely to concentrate on national concerns. But members who won narrow election victories—and those whose margins declined from previous levels—feel bound to court constituent support in order to stay in Congress. Attention to constituent concerns usually accelerates as elections approach, and the tendency to emphasize local rather than national concerns increases with the competitiveness of the district. Representatives, because they face reelection every two years, are almost constantly campaigning. Senators, even though they serve six-year terms, are more vulnerable than House members to serious reelection challenges from governors, ambitious House members, or other seasoned politicians. And the extent to which a legislator feels obliged to follow his constituents' views depends in large part on his vulnerability.

Because election returns are perhaps the most impressive indicators of constituent opinion, a member of Congress is highly conscious of the margins by which he and his predecessors have been elected. Ward-by-ward, precinct-by-precinct analyses of voting statistics assume major significance when state legislatures redistrict House seats. A representative whose constituency is significantly altered through redistricting may assess the views of the new constituency through consideration of past voting records as well as ethnic, occupational, and other characteristics. Elections for other offices, when held between congressional races, also serve as indicators of trends within the constituency.

Keeping in Touch

Serving in Congress has not always been a full-time profession. Well into the twentieth century members traveled to Washington for relatively brief sessions, then returned home to their regular occupations, allowing them to maintain personal relationships with their constituents. After World War II congressional sessions lengthened and district populations grew. Serving in Congress became a full-time occupation, and senators and representatives have been forced to work harder to stay in touch with their constituencies.

Members in recent years have been spending more time traveling to maintain ties with voters. Senators and representatives must balance their increased workload with necessary fence-mending trips home if they expect to be reelected. Reimbursement for home travel is one of many benefits of incumbency that contribute to a member's ability to win reelection.

Casework

The contribution made by good casework—helping individual constituents in dealing with government agencies—toward reelection is well known on Capitol Hill. Many consider it more important in garnering votes than the stands the member takes on legislative matters. A member's staff may perform investigative, advocacy, or referral functions on up to several thousand cases a year, and over the years a representative or senator may build up a substantial personal following that would not readily abandon the incumbent in favor of a challenger. This loy-

alty can cut across party lines.

In more homogeneous districts, where rival candidates are likely to agree on basic legislative matters, the member's effectiveness in serving the interests of constituents may be the principal election issue. As long as he or she does not outrage the people of the district or state by consistently or blatantly ignoring their opinions on controversial issues, the representative or senator who carefully tends to constituents' requests is considered very hard to beat.

Constituent Pressure

Constituent pressure manifests itself in the form of millions of letters and postcards sent to members of Congress each year, either asking assistance or urging support or opposition on issues before the House and Senate.

Pressure groups inspire much legislative mail—along with telegrams and telephone calls—through highly organized lobbying campaigns. Mail in the form of printed or mimeographed postcards, identical letters, or letters with the recurrence of phrases and arguments reveals that the writers have been supplied with the message. Such mail may be given less weight than spontaneous communications that reflect individual constituent thought.

However, interest-group-inspired mail may contain an implied threat: If an organization can prompt people to write, it may be able to deliver their votes. While mail is an inexact gauge of constituent sentiment, in general members of Congress treat constituent mail with great respect and attempt to use it as an indicator of what the most popular course of action might be.

Constituents may come to Washington to contact their representatives or senators about legislation or to seek their assistance on individual matters, but the largest num-

Wide World Photos

Touching base with the voters on the courthouse steps: Sen. Howard H. Baker, Jr., R-Tenn., shares a joke with **constituents in 1973.**

ber of visitors from the home state or district are tourists who stop by the member's office. They may take advantage of the opportunity to make known their views or needs, but they are more likely to seek information and aid as tourists in the nation's capital.

The staff welcomes constituents, knowing the importance of the direct impression they will take back to the district or state. Passes to House and Senate visitors' galleries are handed out and special tours of the White House and some executive agencies may be arranged.

Though most visitors can be handled by the staff, some are anxious to see the member personally. He or she may be reluctant to interrupt other work, yet even more reluctant to turn down such a request. Despite their enormous workload, most representatives make some effort to greet office visitors.

Pork-Barrel Politics

Pork-barrel politics is the term used to describe the way in which all members try to protect their electoral bases through the distribution of funds for federal dams, military bases, grants, and other government benefits in their home state or district. The member with a reputation for "bringing home the bacon" is very hard to beat. But since the 1980s many federal spending programs have suffered sharp cuts—or disappeared altogether—as lawmakers wrestle to control mounting budget deficits.

Federal spending programs give members opportunities to channel projects and programs to their states and districts. By securing the construction of a dam or preventing the closing of a military base, a representative or senator contributes directly to the livelihood of both business and labor.

In federal public works programs where spending is concentrated in local areas, Congress itself still designates the precise location of projects through legislation. In particular, Congress has kept a firm hold on the distribution of federal water projects that dredge harbors and build dams to control floods or store water. Typically, local officials and business owners conceive a water project, then congressional delegations champion the plan in Congress. Even if a project's costs far outweigh its benefits, House and Senate "logrolling" usually ensures support from other members who later will have their own projects to push.

While these projects constitute only a small portion of the total federal budget, their usefulness as aids to reelection campaigns makes them important factors in the internal politics of Capitol Hill. Chairmen of committees controlling authorizations and appropriations for such projects are in a position to exert pressure on colleagues eager to obtain similar favors for their own constituents. Votes on questions that have no intrinsic connection with public works may thus be determined by pork-barrel considerations.

Government contracts and installations are other examples of federal "goodies" that members of Congress strive to provide for the folks back home. The government employs nearly five million civilian and military personnel, and its multibillion dollar payroll contributes heavily to those local economies where federal facilities are situated.

Federal research and development programs disburse billions of dollars a year to U.S. universities, federal laboratories, private companies, and other facilities. The government buys goods and equipment from private suppliers, and major government contractors routinely spread sub-

R. Michael Jenkins

During his fourteen years in Congress, Rep. Wes Watkins, D-Okla., steered home millions of dollars in water projects, roads, investment capital, recreation and tourism projects, and funding for research programs. Watkins used a wall map to keep track of federal assistance to his district.

contracts for federal work around the country, ensuring that senators and representatives from several states will take interest.

Officials in most federal agencies have the authority to award contracts and place new government installations, but even in those programs, senators and representatives often have influence on where federal money is spent.

Because Congress appropriates funds for most agencies, officials feel obliged to respect the wishes of Congress, particularly committee chairmen and other powerful leaders with jurisdiction over their programs. Therefore, members of Congress are not averse to claiming credit for allocation of projects whose location was in fact decided within an executive department.

State and local grants are also objects of pursuit. Beginning in the 1960s, the composition of the federal budget shifted as Congress created new programs channeling funds to state and local governments to spend for specific or general purposes. Federal grants address what are considered to be national problems, but congressional debates often revolve around their local benefits.

In voting on funding for such federal grant programs, most members focus on benefits to their states or districts. To win House and Senate support, proponents carefully put together plans for allocating the funds that spread benefits to all possible states and districts.

Congress often influences decisions on where grants are to be distributed when setting criteria or adjusting funding levels. Bureaucrats who are eager to solidify congressional support for their programs are responsive to members' pressure to allocate grants to their states and districts.

The Media

One of the greatest pressures on members of Congress is the media. Since the House and Senate conduct most of the nation's business in sessions open to the public, the news media cover Capitol Hill more thoroughly than any other branch of government. More than four thousand reporters hold credentials to the House and Senate press galleries, and about four hundred cover Congress exclusively.

The relationship between Congress and the press is a two-way proposition. Senators and representatives, while coping with constant press scrutiny, use news organizations to keep the public informed about their legislative accomplishments. Most members know that favorable coverage in local media makes them hard to defeat. Journalists, on the other hand, rely on members to supply them with news.

Coverage by the local and national media can produce different consequences for senators and representatives. Many House members retain close ties to their constituents, including newspaper publishers and broadcast station owners in their districts. They deal regularly with a handful of Capitol Hill reporters, developing close working relationships that help them influence media coverage. These advantages contribute to the high reelection success rate in the House.

For senators, controlling media coverage can be more difficult. They are more likely to draw national coverage, sometimes in unflattering ways. And senators, because their constituencies make up entire states, usually deal with newspapers and broadcast stations from the larger cities. Close attention by national media has made it more difficult for senators to take stands on national issues that differ from their constituents' views. Senate Foreign Relations Committee Chairman Frank Church, D-Idaho, for instance, was defeated for reelection in 1980 in part because national media coverage highlighted his foreign policy views that were out of step with his state's conservative politics.

Finally, the congressional hand may be strengthened when reporters rely on Capitol Hill sources for news about the executive branch. White House and agency officials tend to be tight-lipped about some government developments, for political as well as policy reasons. But members of Congress and their staffs, often political opponents of the administration, are usually more willing to talk.

Though press coverage heightens pressure on senators and representatives constantly to justify their performances, many members relish the attention that reporters pay them. Most learn ways to cope with media pressures, and many turn coverage to their own advantage. They can do this by the following means:

They distribute weekly news columns, appear on radio or television talk shows, grant personal interviews to reporters, give floor speeches on major issues, and hold press conferences and briefings.

Most members employ press secretaries, often former journalists themselves, to handle relations with reporters, steer journalists to knowledgeable staff members, and set up interviews with the members. Press staffers crank out reams of press releases, directed at both national and local media, and often timed to meet daily press deadlines or make the early evening television news.

Investigations

By far the most effective method of achieving national publicity for members is to conduct congressional investigations, particularly ones that lend themselves to sensational headlines.

Sen. Harry S. Truman, D-Mo., was propelled into the national spotlight—and the Democratic vice presidential nomination—by his investigation of the national defense program during World War II. In the postwar period investigations of communism provided a fast ticket to fame for Sen. Joseph R. McCarthy, R-Wis., and a place on the national Republican ticket for Rep. Richard Nixon, Calif.

Televised hearings on organized crime in the early 1950s transformed Sen. Estes Kefauver, D-Tenn., from a little-known senator to a leading competitor for his party's presidential nomination. More recently, televised hearings brought national prominence in the 1970s to members of the Senate Watergate Committee, who investigated wrongdoing in the Nixon White House, and in the 1980s to those who conducted the Iran-contra arms sale inquiry.

Local Media

Local media also have an impact since members are eager to provide interviews and information to reach constituents.

Members and journalists generally agree that local press coverage of Congress tends to be much more favorable to members than national coverage, and that reporter-member relationships are usually friendly.

Local newspapers and broadcast stations, with fewer resources at their disposal, are less likely than the national media to pursue time-consuming investigations. Pressures to use restraint are strong on the small Washington bureau, which usually centers its coverage on a handful of congressional offices and relies on legislators to keep it informed of executive or regulatory agency action concerning its city or state.

The growing number of radio reporters who cover Capitol Hill for local outlets has made congressional coverage more regional. Even more than local print reporters, regional radio and television journalists need access to members for taped interviews for broadcast by their stations.

News leaks from members or staff provide key information to reporters, while the resulting stories provide members with ammunition for use in reelection campaigns and legislative battles within Congress, the White House, and federal agencies.

Many veteran Washington politicians in both the executive and legislative branches are adept at selectively leaking confidential information to the press. But Congress, historically more open than the executive in its dealings with reporters, may contribute more than its share of leaks.

Leaks can serve many purposes: to raise an alarm about proposed government action, to set the stage for further maneuvering, to take first credit for significant developments, or simply to embarrass the political opposition. As the media began covering Congress and the executive branch more intensively—and as more members of Congress gained access to secret or classified briefings and documents—Capitol Hill became fertile ground for journalists seeking inside information.

While representatives and senators frequently attempt to use leaks to their own advantage, Congress has long been plagued by improper or injudicious release of information received in confidence. For example, the Senate Watergate Committee was plagued by leaks during its highly publicized investigation into the wrongdoing in the Nixon White House. And Speaker Jim Wright, D-Texas, was accused of improperly disclosing to reporters classified information about CIA activities in Nicaragua.

Ever since the Intelligence committees were established in the mid-1970s, presidents and other administration officials have complained about leaks of classified information from Capitol Hill. Committee members acknowledge that leaks occur from Congress, but they generally insist that the administration is the major source.

Reporters who rely on congressional sources come under real, if unspoken, pressure to steer away from stories that would anger members who provide them information. Reporters who ruffle the feathers of too many congressional sources are likely to find themselves consistently "beaten" on stories by competing journalists.

Spotlight on Members

Media investigations have revealed misconduct by members of Congress—and prodded the House and Senate to tighten congressional codes of ethics. In the past the press customarily overlooked personal problems of members. Reporters drew a fine line between public officials' private lives and activities that abused the public trust or brought personal financial gain. Since the 1970s, however, media coverage has contributed to the downfall of several powerful senators and representatives involved in congressional scandals.

House Ways and Means Committee Chairman Wilbur D. Mills, D-Ark., once the unquestioned master of congressional tax legislation, lost that post and eventually retired from Congress after a series of highly publicized incidents involving an Argentine striptease dancer.

Rep. Wayne L. Hays, D-Ohio, powerful chairman of the House Administration Committee and Democratic Congressional Campaign Committee, resigned after the *Washington Post* reported that he had kept a mistress on the House payroll.

Media attention to congressional ethics continued in the late 1970s and 1980s. The press and television gave heavy coverage to several disclosures, notably the Korean lobbying and Abscam scandals, that cast doubt on congressional integrity. Those revelations, particularly because they were covered on network news broadcasts that reached every member's constituency, damaged the reputation of Congress.

The first session of the 101st Congress was a particularly scandal-ridden year. It was capped by the resignation of House Speaker Wright, amid questions about the ethics of his financial dealings. House Majority Whip Tony Coelho, D-Calif., also resigned after a questionable "junk bond" deal disclosed by the *Washington Post* prompted intense scrutiny of Coelho's personal finances and a call for an investigation by the House ethics committee.

Some other ethics cases in 1989 included an investigation of five senators, including Majority Whip Alan Cranston, D-Calif., who faced questions about the propriety of their intervention with federal regulators on behalf of a failing savings and loan; an inquiry into a book-promotion deal by House GOP Whip Newt Gingrich of Georgia; the conviction of Rep. Robert Garcia, D-N.Y., of extortion and conspiracy charges; the conviction of Rep. Donald E. "Buz" Lukens, R-Ohio, of a misdemeanor for having sex with a sixteen-year-old girl; and allegations of sexual misconduct by three House members.

Members of Congress sometimes have tried to intimidate reporters and editors while seeking to discredit their papers' editorial policies. A major confrontation between Congress and the news media occurred in 1971, after CBS broadcast a controversial and award-winning television documentary, "The Selling of the Pentagon."

The program, which attacked the public relations efforts of the Defense Department, led to a clash between television and Congress that was similar in many respects to the clash that same year between the print media (the *New York Times*) and the executive branch over publication of the Pentagon Papers, the Defense Department's secret history of the Vietnam War.

Reporters besiege Speaker Thomas S. Foley, D-Wash., and Majority Leader Richard A. Gephardt, D-Mo., following a meeting of the House Democratic Caucus on the federal budget for fiscal 1991.

R. Michael Jenkins

The House Interstate and Foreign Commerce Committee at one point voted 25-13 to cite CBS and Frank Stanton, the network's president, for contempt of Congress. Stanton had refused to supply the panel's Investigations Subcommittee with film clips from the production that had not been used on the telecast. But the full House refused to go along, voting 226-181 to kill the panel's contempt resolution.

Televised Floor Coverage

Television coverage of floor proceedings is permitted in both the House and the Senate. Gavel-to-gavel coverage is provided by the Cable Satellite Public Affairs Network (C-SPAN).

After a two-month test period, the Senate on July 29, 1986, voted overwhelmingly to allow permanent television coverage of floor proceedings. The Senate's struggle to allow the broadcasting of proceedings was a long one: broadcasting floor proceedings was first proposed in 1944 by then-senator Claude Pepper, D-Fla. Foes of live broadcasts bemoaned what they foresaw as the demise of their body's historic role as the slower, more deliberative chamber of Congress.

However, just as opponents had worried that the coming of television would change the fundamental character of the Senate—leisurely debate, deference to the rights of the individual, lengthy quorum calls, and unpredictable schedules—proponents had hoped that televised sessions might make the Senate more efficient. Neither came to pass.

The Senate long has consented to live TV and radio coverage of committee proceedings, but the House banned such coverage from 1952 until 1970, when the Legislative Reorganization Act authorized coverage at the discretion of a majority of each House committee. TV has played an important part in some proceedings such as the 1974 Nixon impeachment action and the 1987 Iran-contra affair investigation.

Regular televised sessions of House floor proceedings began in 1979, and members soon became extremely conscious of how their speeches were received by viewers at home.

A controversy erupted in 1984 when a group of Republican members, disgruntled over the scheduling priorities of the Democratic leadership, began criticizing opposition leaders during "special orders"—the time granted at the end of a legislative day for speeches on whatever topics members select. As is often the case during special orders, the House chamber was largely empty. This would not ordinarily be apparent since, as stipulated by the rules, the television cameras focused only on the member speaking. The protesting Republicans, for the benefit of the television audience, on this day spoke provocatively and gestured dramatically, as if the absence of any rebuttal to their arguments was a sign of weakness in the Democrats. Speaker Thomas P. O'Neill, Jr., D-Mass., retaliated when, without warning, he ordered the TV cameras to pan the empty chamber.

The fact that both sides lost their composure in an angry exchange on the incident during the next day's regular session was indicative of how seriously members take media coverage.

Since 1960 the growing role of television in U.S. election campaigns undoubtedly has changed the political habits of members. A media-conscious membership—coupled with failing party discipline and weakening congressional leadership—could damage the ability of Congress to conduct its legislative business. On one hand, media visibility for younger and maverick members can open Congress to new ideas and spur the House and Senate to action. On the other hand, the result can be a Congress that is internally divided, with more members likely to focus on attaining higher office, which renders them less likely to behave as a part of a group and institution.

Internal Pressures

Though Congress is composed of 535 forceful, politically minded individuals, internal pressures on members, both formal and unspoken, contribute greatly to Congress's output. They come into play among colleagues, usually out of public view, at institutional, professional, and social levels. House Speaker Sam Rayburn, D-Texas, summed up their significance when he advised House members that "to get along, you have to go along."

Party Pressures

Party pressures in Congress were not anticipated by the nation's founders. The Constitution, in setting up the legislative branch, made no provision for partisan leaders to organize the House and Senate and discipline their members. Yet party affiliations through two centuries have been the most important determinants of how members acquire power and use it. A member's party identification—as a Republican or a Democrat—still is the single most reliable factor for predicting how a member votes and performs.

Arm-twisting powers of House and Senate leaders have eroded since Rayburn's day, as Congress has become a more democratic institution. The growing role of television in congressional campaigns—along with the rise of special-interest groups armed with political action funds for favored candidates—hastened the decline of party allegiances. By the early 1980s members found they could campaign for reelection more effectively by becoming independent-minded powers in their own right.

However, even with a restless new breed of member, congressional leaders can call on institutional loyalties and personal debts as they work to forge majorities on legislation. Other colleagues—committee and subcommittee chairmen, members of state delegations, regional and special interest caucuses, and even personal friends—influence members' votes by offering specialized knowledge or personal advice on issues.

Rules and customs in both chambers place forceful weapons in the hands of the power structure to help it work its will. Members who cooperate are often rewarded with a choice committee assignment, a coveted public works project, or a display of personal approval from the leadership—an act that enhances members' prestige among their colleagues and hence their effectiveness as legislators. By the same token, members who have not supported party leaders on important issues have been relegated to minor committees, denied the benefits of pork-barrel appropriations, and shunned by the leadership and even rank-and-file party colleagues. Their refusal to go along may make them so ineffective at serving their constituents' interests that their chances for reelection are endangered.

The penalties for acting independently of party leaders and committee chairmen were reduced in the 1970s by structural and procedural reforms that weakened the arbitrary power of senior party members, broadened the influence of subcommittees, and made the committee assignment and chairmen selection processes more democratic. Nonetheless, today's members still must contend with many formidable internal pressures when deciding how to cast their votes.

Changing Leadership Styles

Congressional leadership styles have changed with the times. Nowadays, as congressional reforms and mass-media politics have continued to weaken their influence, House and Senate leaders rarely even pretend that they have power to reward or punish members to ensure loyalty. Congressional party leaders more and more have been forced to follow their members instead of the other way around. In both the House and Senate, leaders nurture control by sensing what most members are thinking and by taking care of their political needs.

In the House the Speaker still can apply relatively forceful pressure on members to toe his party's line, though he is hardly the all-powerful leader that often dominated the House in other eras. Majority and minority leaders as well as party whips, in the course of canvassing party members on pending issues, still may apply pressure to ensure that the leadership line is followed. Party caucuses for both Democrats and Republicans periodically have pressured members to adopt party positions on legislation, sometimes even binding party members to support those positions.

Most congressional leaders in recent years have preferred to use tact and persuasion rather than overt pressure to win support for party measures. Speaker Rayburn once said, "My experience with the speakership has been that you can't lead people by driving them. Persuasion and reason are the only ways to lead them. In that way, the Speaker has influence and power in the House."

Some congressional leaders have enhanced their influence over rank-and-file members by withholding pressure in cases where the member's vote would be against his constituents' interests. Joseph W. Martin, Jr., R-Mass., a contemporary of Rayburn's who served two terms as Speaker and eight more as House minority leader, wrote in his memoirs:

> Unless it was absolutely necessary, I never asked a man to side with me if his vote would hurt him in his district. Whenever I could spare a man this kind of embarrassment, I did so and saved him for another time when I might need him more urgently. In fact, I often counseled members against taking positions on legislation that could cost them the next election.

Expressions of personal friendship toward fellow members also help congressional leaders stack up IOUs.

Committee assignments are a key reward used by congressional leaders, as part of a "carrot-and-stick" approach involving the promise of prestigious committee assignments for members who cooperate and undesirable ones for those who don't. Banishment to a series of unprestigious committees can spell doom for a member's prospects.

House and Senate committee chairmen can exert strong pressure, both on members of their panels and on the full membership on the floor. Though reforms in the mid-1970s reduced their arbitrary powers and spread some

authority among subcommittee chairmen while concentrating others in the leadership, full committee chairmen nonetheless hold considerable sway over legislation within their purview.

Distribution of public works is another effective pressure method. This can be a powerful lever in the hands of a congressional leader or committee chairman because the political success or failure of members is based at least partly on how much "boodle" the member can win for his district.

Distribution of campaign funds is yet another means through which congressional leaders exert pressure on members. Both the Democratic and Republican parties have Senate and House campaign committees that parcel out funds to party members for help in their campaigns.

The committees usually do not participate in party primaries, only in the general elections. Their effectiveness as a pressure tool is limited, because party leaders rarely will threaten to cut off funds to a recalcitrant member if it might mean the election of a candidate of the opposition party. Thus, while party leaders can offer the "carrot" of additional campaign money as an inducement to follow the party line, they can scarcely afford to employ the "stick" of cutting off funds altogether. *(Campaign aid, box, p. 35)*

In particular, changes in federal campaign financing laws in the mid-1970s spawned the rapid spread of political action committees (PACs) armed with campaign funds to contribute to friendly legislators. Representing corporations, labor unions, professional, trade, and innumerable other interest groups, PACs by the 1980s were contributing millions of dollars to members of Congress.

The growth of PACs paralleled the spread of single interest groups involved in political campaigns on behalf of their own particular views. They contributed to the splintering of national party authority and gave members of Congress more freedom from internal party pressures.

Regional and Philosophical Alliances

Regional and philosophic alliances also contribute to the pressure on members. Congress, as a representative institution, gives full play to the myriad regional, cultural, economic, and ethnic differences that divide the American people. As party discipline declined, special interest groups took active political roles, and senators and representatives began forming more coalitions and caucuses, both informal and highly organized, to pursue shared goals.

Some state delegations in the House and Senate have traditionally worked closely together to protect their state's most important needs. Since the 1970s members increasingly have organized themselves into formal caucuses—defined along ethnic, sex, regional, or economic lines—to form united fronts on behalf of blacks, women, Spanish Americans, the steel and textile industries, the Sun Belt and Frost Belt states, and many other interests that make up larger parts of their constituencies.

For much of this century, a "conservative coalition" of Republicans and southern Democrats has been Congress's most visible alliance. The coalition has never had a staff or formal organization, but it is discernible in voting patterns in both the House and Senate. The coalition did not function on every House and Senate roll-call vote but only on the major economic or social issues.

Bolstered by Republican election gains in 1980, the coalition in 1981 provided the backbone of congressional support for President Ronald Reagan's conservative economic, defense, and social policies.

State delegations in Congress always have worked together informally for common purposes. Some delegations meet regularly, perhaps for a weekly breakfast or luncheon discussion, to talk over state and national issues. They may collaborate to capture their share of federal grants and projects, to back colleagues for key committee positions, and to support party leadership candidates.

In addition, informal caucuses have proliferated on Capitol Hill. By the 1990s senators and representatives had formed more than a hundred organizations representing a variety of interests. Some were established as formal links among political allies who often disagree with their party leaders. Others emerged, as regional rivalries intensified within the nation over energy and economic policy, to advance the cause of industrial states, energy-producing regions, the steel, coal, and textile industries, and many other economic and social interests.

Caucus alliances have thrived especially in the House, where many members may feel isolated and anonymous, even within their own parties. Such groups operate outside official House and Senate procedures, and their impact on legislation is mixed. Some members complain that caucuses further disperse power in Congress, but others maintain that such groups provide a focus for issues that congressional leaders and committees might otherwise ignore. Some groups, particularly in the Senate, are little more than a circle of lunch companions. Other groups have scores of members, assess regular dues, hire large staffs, and use congressional telephones and office space.

A major political caucus is the Democratic Study Group (DSG), founded in 1959. Formed to counter the informal conservative coalition's power to block liberal legislation, the DSG set up a formal research and coordinating organization for House Democrats with moderate and liberal leanings. DSG members supplied crucial votes for passage of major education, civil rights, and other social welfare legislation. The DSG staff produces weekly reports on bills about to come to the House floor, longer fact sheets and special reports on major legislative issues, and campaign ammunition for members to use against Republican opponents. The group also has had an elaborate whip call system to give members advance warning about caucuses and unexpected votes on the floor.

The DSG was the prototype for other intraparty alliances in the House, among Republicans as well as Democrats. Republican moderates, for instance, set up the House Wednesday Group in 1963 to develop constructive opposition at a time when Democrats controlled the White House as well as the House and Senate. House Republican conservatives organized the Republican Study Committee.

House debates on President Reagan's economic program in 1981-82 focused attention on informal groups of House members who sometimes split from their party majorities. Conservative southern Democrats, known as the "Boll Weevils," formed an informal caucus, the Conservative Democratic Forum, and, against the entreaties of party leaders, provided important support for Reagan's budget and tax-cutting measures. At the same time, about twenty Republican moderates from northern states organized informally as the "Gypsy Moths" to counter the impact of the administration's economic policies on their urban and industrial districts.

During the 1970s minority groups gained more members in the House. During the same period, women began playing more active political roles and winning seats in both the House and Senate. As their numbers grew, members of Congress from minority groups joined together to form special caucuses to share information and interests: the Congressional Black Caucus, the Congresswomen's Caucus, and the Hispanic Caucus representing members with Spanish-American ethnic backgrounds.

The emergence of special caucus groups, especially in the House, has partly filled a void left by Congress's weakening party leadership. They give members forums for voicing concerns and marshaling support behind common positions. But special groups also may contribute to the splintering of legislative authority and hamper efforts to shape compromise legislation. Rep. John N. Erlenborn, R-Ill., in 1978 complained that the proliferating caucus organizations "lead to nothing but increased expenses, increased staff, decreased available working space, and a further growth of purely provincial points of view."

Other members, however, maintain that caucuses play a coordinating role in Congress, keeping members informed on floor proceedings, and making sure that their point of view is heard in debates. In addition, a caucus may offer the White House and other executive branch officials a focal point for exchanging information and building congressional support for administration proposals.

The President

The president is the strongest source of pressure on Congress. No one else can influence the legislative branch in the way the president and his staff can. No one else can orchestrate the pressure as thoroughly or sustain it as long. How does he do it? The Constitution is silent. Presidents have had to find their own ways. Strong presidents have done so by lobbying, in person or through staff; they have worked to stir public opinion; they have used government jobs, contracts, and other forms of patronage; they have threatened to veto bills; and—when all else failed—they have gone ahead and vetoed them.

The president's rapport with Congress begins with his constitutional duty to "from time to time give to the Congress Information of the State of the Union, and recommend to their Consideration such Measures as he shall judge necessary and expedient." The president also sends Congress an annual budget message setting forth his views on the economy and his plans for taxes and spending. But the Constitution only hints at how a president is supposed to go about persuading Congress to pass his programs. A strong president's success at pressuring Congress depends on Congress's own internal cohesiveness; the popularity of the president and his program; whether the issue is foreign or domestic; and whether the White House and Congress are in the hands of different political parties.

No president has ever come to office more schooled in the ways of Congress than Lyndon B. Johnson. He had worked at the Capitol thirty-two years—as a secretary, member of the House, senator, Senate minority leader, majority leader, and vice president. With President Johnson cracking the whip in 1965, Congress passed the most sweeping domestic programs since Franklin Roosevelt: aid to schools, voting rights, health care for the aged, rent supplements for the poor, and freer immigration.

Many presidents enjoy a honeymoon with Congress early in their first term, only to watch their success rate gradually decline. President Reagan came to office in 1981 promising to reduce the scope of the federal government.

Congress swiftly answered his call for deep cuts in spending and taxes, but lawmakers later had second thoughts about his program. Although President George Bush had served two terms in the House (1967-71), he made a poor showing in Congress until his success in the Persian Gulf war in 1991.

Congressional Lobbying

Early presidents kept their congressional lobbying discreet and their helpers few, careful to respect the separation of powers. In recent years presidential lobbying has become open and elaborate.

Beginning with Dwight D. Eisenhower, presidents appointed full-time legislative liaison officers to their White House staff. In addition, all federal departments now have their own congressional liaison forces.

Phone calls, luncheon meetings, summonses to the Oval Office, even cloakroom buttonholing by the liaison staff remain important sources of pressure on members and how they vote. If a president tolerates a congressional liaison who maintains poor working relations with Congress—a charge that was leveled at Jimmy Carter during the early years of his term—his effectiveness can suffer drastically. President Bush's efforts to transform presidential relations with Congress from Ronald Reagan's Hill-bashing to his own chummy camaraderie were reflected in his congressional liaison team.

Going to the People

Going to the people is another way in which the president can move Congress when direct pressure fails. Going over congressional heads to the public has always required cultivation of the news media. Today radio and television permit a president to go over the heads of reporters too, in order to marshal public opinion.

The all-time master of this was Franklin Roosevelt, whose Sunday radio talks known as "fireside chats" became a popular hallmark of his presidency. The effect of these broadcasts on Congress was nothing short of phenomenal. In the spring of 1933 Congress approved a spate of Roosevelt proposals, pausing to change scarcely so much as a comma. At the time the president's program was known as the "Roosevelt Revolution," but he said he preferred "New Deal." In Roosevelt's first hundred days, Congress approved an emergency banking bill, a 25 percent cut in government spending, farm relief, public works, relief for the states, the Civilian Conservation Corps, and other important measures. Although the going got much tougher later on, Roosevelt still won passage of the Trade Agreements Act, Social Security, and the Public Utilities Holding Company Act.

Patronage

Patronage is a "carrot" the president can use as part of a carrot-and-stick approach to influencing Congress. In return for voting with the president, a member can hope for favorable treatment for his associates in appointments to federal jobs and judgeships.

The veto threat is the most concrete form of pressure the president can apply on Congress. Even the threat of a veto can appear as a sword of Damocles hanging over a member's head, both because of the risk involved in directly challenging the chief executive and because the two-

Lyndon Baines Johnson Library

One of the most forceful presidential lobbyists was Lyndon B. Johnson, shown here with Senate Majority Leader Mike Mansfield, D-Mont., (left) and Minority Leader Everett McKinley Dirksen, R-Ill.

thirds majority required to override a veto is more difficult to muster than a mere majority of each chamber originally needed to pass the bill.

The Veto Threat

In the postwar era the veto has been used most frequently by Republican presidents working to block the programs of a Democratic-controlled Congress. Nixon vetoed a social services appropriations bill on national television, but the veto was subsequently overridden. President Gerald R. Ford vetoed sixty-six bills during his two years in office; he vetoed seventeen major bills in 1975 alone. Reagan vetoed seventy-eight bills from 1981 to 1988; nine vetoes were overridden. President Bush vetoed twenty public bills and one private bill during his first two years in office; none of the vetoes was overridden.

Jimmy Carter in 1980 became the first president since Harry S. Truman to have vetoes overridden by a Congress controlled by his own party. This happened on a debt-limit bill that killed an import fee he had imposed on foreign oil and again later in the year on a bill increasing salaries of doctors at veterans' hospitals.

The Federal Courts

The federal courts can nullify an act of Congress. If the courts find that the law is in conflict with the Constitution, the law is wiped off the books as if it had never been enacted. Most scholars agree that the primary significance of this power is the awareness of every senator and representative that the laws they pass can be vetoed by the courts if they are seen as running afoul of the Constitution.

The power of judicial review, as it is called, was articulated in 1803 when the Supreme Court decisively claimed for itself the power to review acts of Congress in the famous case of *Marbury v. Madison.* By virtue of this authority, the Court can assure the country that Congress will not be able to dominate the government or to put into effect laws violating the basic guarantees of the Constitution.

It was half a century after this case before the Court struck down another act of Congress. Although the power of judicial review has been exercised more frequently in the twentieth century, overall the Court has found relatively few acts of Congress to be unconstitutional: slightly more than one hundred over two centuries of history, only a few of which were of major importance.

In general the Court has interpreted the power of Congress to enact legislation as broadly as it has its own authority to review those laws. The Court has basically adhered to the view set out by one of its members in 1827, that "it is but a decent respect due to the wisdom, the integrity, and the patriotism of the legislative body, by which any law is passed, to presume in favor of its validity until its violation of the Constitution is proved beyond all reasonable doubt."

In the 1970s and early 1980s the Supreme Court used its power of judicial review to nullify acts of Congress on a range of issues. The Court ruled that Congress unconstitutionally had allowed federal power to intrude on such principles as states' rights, individual rights, and the rights of private enterprise.

Congress does not lack ways of influencing the Court—or responding to what it finds to be ill-advised judicial decisions. Congress can restrict courts' jurisdictions on certain matters, it can move to impeach a judge, it can alter the salary structure for judges, and the Senate can refuse to confirm judicial nominees. Congress actually can reverse some court decisions either by statute—or by approving a constitutional amendment, which is then ratified by the states. This has happened four times, resulting in the Eleventh, Fourteenth, Sixteenth, and Twenty-sixth Amendments.

In recent years congressional discontent has centered on the Supreme Court's rulings allowing abortions, permitting the use of busing for school desegregation, and forbidding prayer in public schools. Congress considered a number of bills in the 1970s and 1980s that would withdraw these subjects from the jurisdiction of the federal courts.

Critics of the abortion and busing rulings tried unsuccessfully—as had school prayer proponents earlier—to win approval of constitutional amendments overturning the Court's decisions permitting abortion and busing.

Late in the 1970s critics of these rulings tried a different tack, proposing legislation that simply would take away the Court's authority to rule in these matters. Scholars disagreed over the scope of congressional power to impose such limits on the Court's jurisdiction, but there was no denying that the Constitution does permit Congress to make "exceptions" to the appellate jurisdiction of the Supreme Court.

Rejection of court nominees is another tool available to Congress when it wants to wield its power over the judicial branch. The Senate must "advise and consent" in the president's selection of candidates for judicial offices, including Supreme Court justices and other federal court judges.

In recent decades the Senate has rejected a number of Supreme Court nominations. In 1968 it rejected President Lyndon Johnson's attempt to elevate Associate Justice Abe Fortas to chief justice. Two of President Richard Nixon's nominees to the Court—Clement F. Haynsworth, Jr., and G. Harrold Carswell—were rejected, in 1969 and 1970, respectively. President Ronald Reagan's third nominee for the Supreme Court, Robert H. Bork, was rejected in 1987. Reagan then nominated Douglas H. Ginsburg, who withdrew from consideration under Senate scrutiny.

Lobbying

From abortion to zero population growth, every imaginable issue before Congress has attracted the attention of competing interest groups. Across the country they and their lobbyists have become a potent force in the political process. Their ranks include both traditional rich and powerful Capitol Hill lobbies and many "grass-roots" coalitions that derive power from their numbers and persistence.

Lobbying is sanctioned by the Constitution. The First Amendment protects the right of the people to "petition the government for redress of grievances." Central to a democratic society is the freedom to ask questions, make suggestions, and debate results. Lobbying is an element of such widespread political participation. It allows competing points of view to be heard and provides information to those who make decisions. There is no guarantee that all of the many voices will be heard, let alone heeded. Lobbyists are not equal; some are more powerful than others.

The most visible lobbyists are those who work full time in Washington. Their employers include trade or public relations firms, large corporations, organizations with particular interests, and other groups. Political insiders populate the field; many lobbyists once held jobs on congressional staffs or in federal agencies. Former members of Congress frequently find jobs as lobbyists or as "rainmakers," valued by law firms because they attract clients eager for inside contacts and lobbying.

Because of the weaknesses of existing lobby registration laws, it is impossible to come up with an exact number of lobbyists in Washington. Estimates range from ten thousand to twenty thousand—variously described as political consultants, lawyers, foreign representatives, legislative specialists, consumer advocates, trade association representatives, or government affairs specialists.

Some lobbyists focus on arcane details of specific laws; others concentrate on broader policy changes. Many handle a wide range of issues and a variety of clients; others tackle only one area. Whatever their approach, lobbyists are important players in the legislative process.

A century ago lobbyists were widely portrayed as unscrupulous characters, hanging out in the halls and lobbies of the Capitol. As the lobbying profession grew in size and sophistication, it lost much of the stigma attached to it from past scandals.

Lobbying Techniques

Among the most famous lobbyists of the past was the self-described "King of the Lobby," Samuel Ward, whose legislative successes in the mid-1800s were so dazzling that Congress decided to investigate him. When the investigating committee asked Ward about his well-known, elegant dinners for politicians, he replied: "At good dinners people do not talk shop, but they give people a right, perhaps, to ask a gentleman a civil question and get a civil answer."

At dinners and cocktail parties, at plush resorts where legislators combine speech-making and vacationing, well-heeled lobbyists continue to use Ward's methods. Other, less prosperous groups emphasize letter-writing and telephone calls.

Often a lobbyist's best technique is simply to provide accurate information, either directly to a legislator or at a subcommittee hearing. The credibility gained then gives the lobbyist more influence in arguing his or her point of view. A record of reliability can also win a quick hearing should a lobbyist find a minor clause damaging to his client. Information packets, drafts of bills, and scenarios of how a bill would affect an industry are among the ways lobbyists approach legislators and their staffs.

An interest group may urge its members to write directly to their legislators. This grass-roots lobbying can be extremely effective, especially in the case of large organizations, such as the American Association of Retired Persons, with twenty-four million members. The National Rifle Association, with three million members, has almost legendary lobbying influence.

The credibility provided by a huge membership also accrues to groups with economic power. The Business Roundtable, consisting of the chief executive officers of major corporations, always gets a respectful hearing on Capitol Hill.

Other groups, without such ready access, have resorted to dramatic demonstrations to get attention from Congress. Civil rights activists, environmentalists, war protesters, farmers, and others have adopted this tactic. One antiabortion group has made an annual demonstration the heart of its lobbying effort.

Campaign Contributions

In addition to direct lobbying contacts, organizations can influence legislators by giving money to their political campaigns. Although campaign financing laws restrict donations, powerful lobbies make certain that responsive legislators get sizable contributions.

Campaign contributions to members of Congress serve two important functions for lobbying organizations. Political support not only can induce a member to back a group's legislative interests, but it also can help ensure that members who are sympathetic to the group's goals remain in office.

Corporations and labor unions are not allowed to make direct campaign contributions, but their employees and members can form political action committees, or PACs, which then channel their donations to particular candidates. Trade associations and membership groups also steer money to candidates through PACs. House and Senate candidates in 1990 received $150.6 million from PACs. PAC donations accounted for 38 percent of campaign funding for House candidates and 22 percent for Senate candidates.

Regulation of Lobbying

Abuses of lobbying have led to periodic efforts by Congress to regulate it. But only one comprehensive lobbying law—the Federal Regulation of Lobbying Act of 1946—

Lobbyists crowd the corridor as a House subcommittee marks up banking legislation in 1989.

R. Michael Jenkins

and a handful of more specialized measures have been enacted.

The principle behind the 1946 law was disclosure, not regulation. The law simply requires lobbyists to register their names and subjects of interest, along with what they spend. But loopholes mean that not all groups are listed and that financial reports do not accurately reflect expenditures. The Supreme Court in 1954 upheld the constitutionality of the 1946 law, but its narrow interpretation of the statute made enforcement almost impossible.

An uproar over the activities of former White House aide Michael K. Deaver led Congress in 1989 to rewrite restrictions on lobbying by former executive branch officials—and on its own members. The Deaver episode came to symbolize the "revolving-door" problem—officials trading their top government positions for high-paying jobs lobbying former colleagues on issues they previously oversaw.

The 1989 law bars cabinet secretaries and other top White House officials from lobbying any other senior executive branch officials for a year after leaving office. And, for the first time, members of Congress are prohibited from lobbying in the legislative branch for a year after leaving office.

A separate lobbying measure was passed in 1989 after Sen. Robert C. Byrd, D-W.Va., angered at a Washington lobbying firm's effort to steer appropriations, used his clout as Appropriations Committee chairman to push into law a measure forcing the disclosure of lobbyists hired to pursue federal monies from Congress or the executive branch. The legislation requires recipients of federal grants, loans, or contracts to file information on the names of, and fees paid to, lobbyists hired in pursuit of those funds. It also prohibits recipients of such funds from using federal money to lobby for them.

Selected Readings

Birnbaum, Jeffrey H., and Alan S. Murray. *Showdown at Gucci Gulch: Lawmakers, Lobbyists, and the Unlikely Triumph of Tax Reform.* New York: Vintage Books, 1987.

Cheney, Richard B., and Lynne V. Cheney. *Kings of the Hill: Power and Personality in the House of Representatives.* New York: Cross Road Publishing, 1983.

Cigler, Allan J., and Burdett A. Loomis. *Interest Group Politics.* 3rd ed. Washington, D.C.: CQ Press, 1991.

Cook, Timothy E. *Making Laws and Making News: Media Strategies in the U.S. House of Representatives.* Washington, D.C.: Brookings Institution, 1989.

Davidson, Roger H., and Walter J. Oleszek. *Congress and Its Members.* 3rd ed. Washington, D.C.: CQ Press, 1990.

Dodd, Lawrence C., and Bruce I. Oppenheimer, eds. *Congress Reconsidered.* 4th ed. Washington, D.C.: CQ Press, 1989.

Fenno, Richard F., Jr., *Home Style: House Members in Their Districts.* Boston: Little, Brown, 1978.

Fisher, Louis. *The Politics of Shared Power: Congress and the Executive.* 2nd ed. Washington, D.C.: CQ Press, 1987.

Frantzich, Stephen E. *Write Your Congressman: Constituent Communications and Representation.* New York: Praeger, 1986.

Graber, Doris A. *Mass Media and American Politics.* 3rd ed. Washington, D.C.: CQ Press, 1989.

———. *Media Power in Politics.* 2nd ed. Washington, D.C.: CQ Press, 1990.

Hess, Stephen. *The Ultimate Insiders: U.S. Senators in the National Media.* Washington, D.C.: Brookings Institution, 1986.

Kingdon, John W. *Congressmen's Voting Decisions.* 2nd ed. New York: Harper and Row, 1980.

Kornacki, John J., ed. *Leading Congress: New Styles, New Strategies.* Washington, D.C.: Congressional Quarterly, 1990.

Magleby, David B., and Candice J. Nelson. *The Money Chase: Congressional Campaign Finance Reform.* Washington, D.C.: Brookings Institution, 1990.

Pedersen, Wesley, ed. *Winning at the Grassroots: How to Succeed in the Legislative Arena by Mobilizing Employees and Other Allies.* Washington, D.C.: Public Affairs Council, 1989.

Peterson, Mark A. *Legislating Together: The White House and Capitol Hill from Eisenhower to Reagan.* Cambridge, Mass.: Harvard University Press, 1990.

Thurber, James A. *Divided Democracy: Cooperation and Conflict between the President and Congress.* Washington, D.C.: CQ Press, 1991.

The Washington Lobby. 5th ed. Washington, D.C.: Congressional Quarterly, 1987.

Wolpe, Bruce C. *Lobbying Congress: How the System Works.* Washington, D.C.: Congressional Quarterly, 1990.

Wright, Jim. *You and Your Congressman.* New York: Capricorn Books, 1976.

Zorack, John L. *The Lobbying Handbook.* Washington, D.C.: Professional Lobbying and Consulting Center, 1990.

Appendix

⚈

How a Bill Becomes Law

This graphic shows the most typical way in which proposed legislation is enacted into law. There are more complicated, as well as simpler, routes, and most bills never become law. The process is illustrated with two hypothetical bills, House bill No. 1 (HR 1) and Senate bill No. 2 (S 2). Bills must be passed by both houses in identical form before they can be sent to the president. The path of HR 1 is traced by a solid line, that of S 2 by a broken line. In practice, most bills begin as similar proposals in both houses.

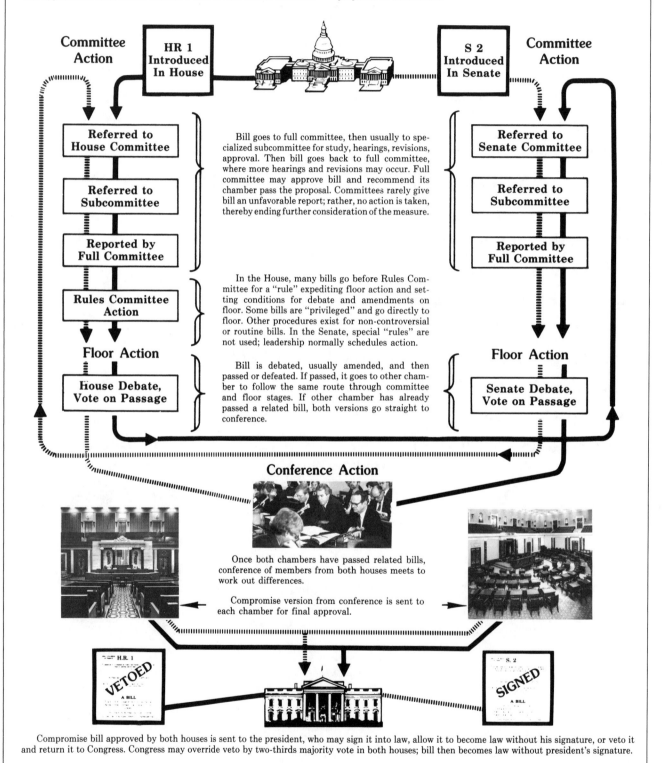

Committee Action

HR 1 Introduced In House

S 2 Introduced In Senate

Committee Action

Referred to House Committee

Referred to Senate Committee

Bill goes to full committee, then usually to specialized subcommittee for study, hearings, revisions, approval. Then bill goes back to full committee, where more hearings and revisions may occur. Full committee may approve bill and recommend its chamber pass the proposal. Committees rarely give bill an unfavorable report; rather, no action is taken, thereby ending further consideration of the measure.

Referred to Subcommittee

Referred to Subcommittee

Reported by Full Committee

Reported by Full Committee

Rules Committee Action

In the House, many bills go before Rules Committee for a "rule" expediting floor action and setting conditions for debate and amendments on floor. Some bills are "privileged" and go directly to floor. Other procedures exist for non-controversial or routine bills. In the Senate, special "rules" are not used; leadership normally schedules action.

Floor Action

Floor Action

Bill is debated, usually amended, and then passed or defeated. If passed, it goes to other chamber to follow the same route through committee and floor stages. If other chamber has already passed a related bill, both versions go straight to conference.

House Debate, Vote on Passage

Senate Debate, Vote on Passage

Conference Action

Once both chambers have passed related bills, conference of members from both houses meets to work out differences.

Compromise version from conference is sent to each chamber for final approval.

H.R. 1 VETOED A BILL

S. 2 SIGNED A BILL

Compromise bill approved by both houses is sent to the president, who may sign it into law, allow it to become law without his signature, or veto it and return it to Congress. Congress may override veto by two-thirds majority vote in both houses; bill then becomes law without president's signature.

Political Party Affiliations in Congress and the Presidency, 1789-1991

Year	Congress	House			Senate			President
		Majority party	Principal minority party	Other (except vacancies)	Majority party	Principal minority party	Other (except vacancies)	
1991-1993	102nd	D-267	R-167	1	D-56	R-44	-	R (Bush)
1989-1991	101st	D-259	R-174	-	D-55	R-45	-	R (Bush)
1987-1989	100th	D-258	R-177	-	D-55	R-45	-	R (Reagan)
1985-1987	99th	D-252	R-182	-	R-53	D-47	-	R (Reagan)
1983-1985	98th	D-268	R-166	-	R-55	D-45	-	R (Reagan)
1981-1983	97th	D-243	R-192	-	R-53	D-46	1	R (Reagan)
1979-1981	96th	D-276	R-157	-	D-58	R-41	1	D (Carter)
1977-1979	95th	D-292	R-143	-	D-61	R-38	1	D (Carter
1975-1977	94th	D-291	R-144	-	D-60	R-37	2	R (Ford)
1973-1975	93rd	D-239	R-192	1	D-56	R-42	2	R (Nixon-Ford)
1971-1973	92nd	D-254	R-180	-	D-54	R-44	2	R (Nixon)
1969-1971	91st	D-243	R-192	-	D-57	R-43	-	R (Nixon)
1967-1969	90th	D-247	R-187	-	D-64	R-36	-	D (L. Johnson)
1965-1967	89th	D-295	R-140	-	D-68	R-32	-	D (L. Johnson)
1963-1965	88th	D-258	R-177	-	D-67	R-33	-	D (L. Johnson)
								D (Kennedy)
1961-1963	87th	D-263	R-174	-	D-65	R-35	-	D (Kennedy)
1959-1961	86th	D-283	R-153	-	D-64	R-34	-	R (Eisenhower)
1957-1959	85th	D-233	R-200	-	D-49	R-47	-	R (Eisenhower)
1955-1957	84th	D-232	R-203	-	D-48	R-47	1	R (Eisenhower)
1953-1955	83rd	R-221	D-211	1	R-48	D-47	1	R (Eisenhower)
1951-1953	82nd	D-234	R-199	1	D-49	R-47	-	D (Truman)
1949-1951	81st	D-263	R-171	1	D-54	R-42	-	D (Truman)
1947-1949	80th	R-245	D-188	1	R-51	D-45	-	D (Truman)
1945-1947	79th	D-242	R-190	2	D-56	R-38	1	D (Truman)
1943-1945	78th	D-218	R-208	4	D-58	R-37	1	D (F. Roosevelt)
1941-1943	77th	D-268	R-162	5	D-66	R-28	2	D (F. Roosevelt)
1939-1941	76th	D-261	R-164	4	D-69	R-23	4	D (F. Roosevelt)
1937-1939	75th	D-331	R-89	13	D-76	R-16	4	D (F. Roosevelt)
1935-1937	74th	D-319	R-103	10	D-69	R-25	2	D (F. Roosevelt)
1933-1935	73rd	D-310	R-117	5	D-60	R-35	1	D (F. Roosevelt)
1931-1933	72nd	D-220	R-214	1	R-48	D-47	1	R (Hoover)
1929-1931	71st	R-267	D-167	1	R-56	D-39	1	R (Hoover)
1927-1929	70th	R-237	D-195	3	R-49	D-46	1	R (Coolidge)
1925-1927	69th	R-247	D-183	4	R-56	D-39	1	R (Coolidge)
1923-1925	68th	R-225	D-205	5	R-51	D-43	2	R (Coolidge)
1921-1923	67th	R-301	D-131	1	R-59	D-37	-	R (Harding)
1919-1921	66th	R-240	D-190	3	R-49	D-47	-	D (Wilson)
1917-1919	65th	D-216	R-210	6	D-53	R-42	-	D (Wilson)
1915-1917	64th	D-230	R-196	9	D-56	R-40	-	D (Wilson)
1913-1915	63rd	D-291	R-127	17	D-51	R-44	1	D (Wilson)
1911-1913	62nd	D-228	R-161	1	R-51	D-41	-	R (Taft)
1909-1911	61st	R-219	D-172	-	R-61	D-32	-	R (Taft)
1907-1909	60th	R-222	D-164	-	R-61	D-31	-	R (T. Roosevelt)
1905-1907	59th	R-250	D-136	-	R-57	D-33	-	R (T. Roosevelt)
1903-1905	58th	R-208	D-178	-	R-57	D-33	-	R (T. Roosevelt)
1901-1903	57th	R-197	D-151	9	R-55	D-31	4	R (T. Roosevelt)
								R (McKinley)
1899-1901	56th	R-185	D-163	9	R-53	D-26	8	R (McKinley)
1897-1899	55th	R-204	D-113	40	R-47	D-34	7	R (McKinley)
1895-1897	54th	R-244	D-105	7	R-43	D-39	6	D (Cleveland)
1893-1895	53rd	D-218	R-127	11	D-44	R-38	3	D (Cleveland)
1891-1893	52nd	D-235	R-88	9	R-47	D-39	2	R (B. Harrison)
1889-1891	51st	R-166	D-159	-	R-39	D-37	-	R (B. Harrison)
1887-1889	50th	D-169	R-152	4	R-39	D-37	-	D (Cleveland)
1885-1887	49th	D-183	R-140	2	R-43	D-34	-	D (Cleveland)

		House			Senate			
Year	Congress	Majority party	Principal minority party	Other (except vacancies)	Majority party	Principal minority party	Other (except vacancies)	President
1883-1885	48th	D-197	R-118	10	R-38	D-36	2	R (Arthur)
1881-1883	47th	R-147	D-135	11	R-37	D-37	1	R (Arthur)
								R (Garfield)
1879-1881	46th	D-149	R-130	14	D-42	R-33	1	R (Hayes)
1877-1879	45th	D-153	R-140	-	R-39	D-36	1	R (Hayes)
1875-1877	44th	D-169	R-109	14	R-45	D-29	2	R (Grant)
1873-1875	43rd	R-194	D-92	14	R-49	D-19	5	R (Grant)
1871-1873	42nd	R-134	D-104	5	R-52	D-17	5	R (Grant)
1869-1871	41st	R-149	D-63	-	R-56	D-11	-	R (Grant)
1867-1869	40th	R-143	D-49	-	R-42	D-11	-	R (A. Johnson)
1865-1867	39th	U-149	D-42	-	U-42	D-10	-	R (A. Johnson)
								R (Lincoln)
1863-1865	38th	R-102	D-75	9	R-36	D-9	5	R (Lincoln)
1861-1863	37th	R-105	D-43	30	R-31	D-10	8	R (Lincoln)
1859-1861	36th	R-114	D-92	31	D-36	R-26	4	D (Buchanan)
1857-1859	35th	D-118	R-92	26	D-36	R-20	8	D (Buchanan)
1855-1857	34th	R-108	D-83	43	D-40	R-15	5	D (Pierce)
1853-1855	33rd	D-159	W-71	4	D-38	W-22	2	D (Pierce)
1851-1853	32nd	D-140	W-88	5	D-35	W-24	3	W (Fillmore)
1849-1851	31st	D-112	W-109	9	D-35	W-25	2	W (Fillmore)
								W (Taylor)
1847-1849	30th	W-115	D-108	4	D-36	W-21	1	D (Polk)
1845-1847	29th	D-143	W-77	6	D-31	W-25	-	D (Polk)
1843-1845	28th	D-142	W-79	1	W-28	D-25	1	W (Tyler)
1841-1843	27th	W-133	D-102	6	W-28	D-22	2	W (Tyler)
								W (W. Harrison)
1839-1841	26th	D-124	W-118	-	D-28	W-22	-	D (Van Buren)
1837-1839	25th	D-108	W-107	24	D-30	W-18	4	D (Van Buren)
1835-1837	24th	D-145	W-98	-	D-27	W-25	-	D (Jackson)
1833-1835	23rd	D-147	AM-53	60	D-20	NR-20	8	D (Jackson)
1831-1833	22nd	D-141	NR-58	14	D-25	NR-21	2	D (Jackson)
1829-1831	21st	D-139	NR-74	-	D-26	NR-22	-	D (Jackson)
1827-1829	20th	J-119	Ad-94	-	J-28	Ad-20	-	DR (John Q. Adams)
1825-1827	19th	Ad-105	J-97	-	Ad-26	J-20	-	DR (John Q. Adams)
1823-1825	18th	DR-187	F-26	-	DR-44	F-4	-	DR (Monroe)
1821-1823	17th	DR-158	F-25	-	DR-44	F-4	-	DR (Monroe)
1819-1821	16th	DR-156	F-27	-	DR-35	F-7	-	DR (Monroe)
1817-1819	15th	DR-141	F-42	-	DR-34	F-10	-	DR (Monroe)
1815-1817	14th	DR-117	F-65	-	DR-25	F-11	-	DR (Madison)
1813-1815	13th	DR-112	F-68	-	DR-27	F-9	-	DR (Madison)
1811-1813	12th	DR-108	F-36	-	DR-30	F-6	-	DR (Madison)
1809-1811	11th	DR-94	F-48	-	DR-28	F-6	-	DR (Madison)
1807-1809	10th	DR-118	F-24	-	DR-28	F-6	-	DR (Jefferson)
1805-1807	9th	DR-116	F-25	-	DR-27	F-7	-	DR (Jefferson)
1803-1805	8th	DR-102	F-39	-	DR-25	F-9	-	DR (Jefferson)
1801-1803	7th	DR-69	F-36	-	DR-18	F-13	-	DR (Jefferson)
1799-1801	6th	F-64	DR-42	-	F-19	DR-13	-	F (John Adams)
1797-1799	5th	F-58	DR-48	-	F-20	DR-12	-	F (John Adams)
1795-1797	4th	F-54	DR-52	-	F-19	DR-13	-	F (Washington)
1793-1795	3rd	DR-57	F-48	-	F-17	DR-13	-	F (Washington)
1791-1793	2nd	F-37	DR-33	-	F-16	DR-13	-	F (Washington)
1789-1791	1st	Ad-38	Op-26	-	Ad-17	Op-9	-	F (Washington)

Note: Figures are for the first session of each Congress.

Abbreviations: Ad—Administration; AM—Anti Masonic; D—Democratic; DR—Democratic Republican; F—Federalist; J—Jeffersonian; NR—National Republican; Op—Opposition; R—Republican; U—Unionist; W—Whig.

Sources: U.S. Bureau of the Census, *Historical Statistics of the United States, Colonial Times to 1970* (Washington, D.C.: Government Printing Office), 1975; *Congressional Quarterly Weekly Report.*

Speakers of the House of Representatives, 1789-1991

Congress		Speaker	Congress		Speaker
1st	(1789-1791)	Frederick A. C. Muhlenberg, -Pa.	52nd	(1891-1893)	Charles F. Crisp, D-Ga.
2nd	(1791-1793)	Jonathan Trumbull, F-Conn.	53rd	(1893-1895)	Crisp
3rd	(1793-1795)	Muhlenberg	54th	(1895-1897)	Reed
4th	(1795-1797)	Jonathan Dayton, F-N.J.	55th	(1897-1899)	Reed
5th	(1797-1799)	Dayton	56th	(1899-1901)	David B. Henderson, R-Iowa
6th	(1799-1801)	Theodore Sedgwick, F-Mass.	57th	(1901-1903)	Henderson
7th	(1801-1803)	Nathaniel Macon, D-N.C.	58th	(1903-1905)	Joseph G. Cannon, R-Ill.
8th	(1803-1805)	Macon	59th	(1905-1907)	Cannon
9th	(1805-1807)	Macon	60th	(1907-1909)	Cannon
10th	(1807-1809)	Joseph B. Varnum, -Mass.	61st	(1909-1911)	Cannon
11th	(1809-1811)	Varnum	62nd	(1911-1913)	James B. "Champ" Clark, D-Mo.
12th	(1811-1813)	Henry Clay, -Ky.	63rd	(1913-1915)	Clark
13th	(1813-1814)	Clay	64th	(1915-1917)	Clark
	(1814-1815)	Langdon Cheves, D-S.C.	65th	(1917-1919)	Clark
14th	(1815-1817)	Clay	66th	(1919-1921)	Frederick H. Gillett, R-Mass.
15th	(1817-1819)	Clay	67th	(1921-1923)	Gillett
16th	(1819-1820)	Clay	68th	(1923-1925)	Gillett
	(1820-1821)	John W. Taylor, D-N.Y.	69th	(1925-1927)	Nicholas Longworth, R-Ohio
17th	(1821-1823)	Philip P. Barbour, D-Va.	70th	(1927-1929)	Longworth
18th	(1823-1825)	Clay	71st	(1929-1931)	Longworth
19th	(1825-1827)	Taylor	72nd	(1931-1933)	John Nance Garner, D-Texas
20th	(1827-1829)	Andrew Stevenson, D-Va.	73rd	(1933-1934)	Henry T. Rainey, D-Ill.[1]
21st	(1829-1831)	Stevenson	74th	(1935-1936)	Joseph W. Byrns, D-Tenn.
22nd	(1831-1833)	Stevenson		(1936-1937)	William B. Bankhead, D-Ala.
23rd	(1833-1834)	Stevenson	75th	(1937-1939)	Bankhead
	(1834-1835)	John Bell, W-Tenn.	76th	(1939-1940)	Bankhead
24th	(1835-1837)	James K. Polk, D-Tenn.		(1940-1941)	Sam Rayburn, D-Texas
25th	(1837-1839)	Polk	77th	(1941-1943)	Rayburn
26th	(1839-1841)	Robert M. T. Hunter, D-Va.	78th	(1943-1945)	Rayburn
27th	(1841-1843)	John White, W-Ky.	79th	(1945-1947)	Rayburn
28th	(1843-1845)	John W. Jones, D-Va.	80th	(1947-1949)	Joseph W. Martin, Jr., R-Mass.
29th	(1845-1847)	John W. Davis, D-Ind.	81st	(1949-1951)	Rayburn
30th	(1847-1849)	Robert C. Winthrop, W-Mass.	82nd	(1951-1953)	Rayburn
31st	(1849-1851)	Howell Cobb, D-Ga.	83rd	(1953-1955)	Martin
32nd	(1851-1853)	Linn Boyd, D-Ky.	84th	(1955-1957)	Rayburn
33rd	(1853-1855)	Boyd	85th	(1957-1959)	Martin
34th	(1855-1857)	Nathaniel P. Banks, R-Mass.	86th	(1959-1961)	Rayburn
35th	(1857-1859)	James L. Orr, D-S.C.	87th	(1961)	Rayburn
36th	(1859-1861)	William Pennington, R-N.J.		(1962-1963)	John W. McCormack, D-Mass.
37th	(1861-1863)	Galusha A. Grow, R-Pa.	88th	(1963-1965)	McCormack
38th	(1863-1865)	Schuyler Colfax, R-Ind.	89th	(1965-1967)	McCormack
39th	(1865-1867)	Colfax	90th	(1967-1969)	McCormack
40th	(1867-1868)	Colfax	91st	(1969-1971)	McCormack
	(1868-1869)	Theodore M. Pomeroy, R-N.Y.	92nd	(1971-1973)	Carl Albert, D-Okla.
41st	(1869-1871)	James G. Blaine, R-Maine	93rd	(1973-1975)	Albert
42nd	(1871-1873)	Blaine	94th	(1975-1977)	Albert
43rd	(1873-1875)	Blaine	95th	(1977-1979)	Thomas P. O'Neill, Jr., D-Mass.
44th	(1875-1876)	Michael C. Kerr, D-Ind.	96th	(1979-1981)	O'Neill
	(1876-1877)	Samuel J. Randall, D-Pa.	97th	(1981-1983)	O'Neill
45th	(1877-1879)	Randall	98th	(1983-1985)	O'Neill
46th	(1879-1881)	Randall	99th	(1985-1987)	O'Neill
47th	(1881-1883)	Joseph Warren Keifer, R-Ohio	100th	(1987-1989)	Jim Wright, D-Texas
48th	(1883-1885)	John G. Carlisle, D-Ky.	101st	(1989)	Wright[2]
49th	(1885-1887)	Carlisle		(1989-1991)	Thomas S. Foley, D-Wash.
50th	(1887-1889)	Carlisle	102nd	(1991-1993)	Foley
51st	(1889-1891)	Thomas Brackett Reed, R-Maine			

Abbreviations: (D) Democrat; (F) Federalist; (R) Republican; (W) Whig.

Source: 1989-1990 Congressional Directory: 101st Congress (Washington, D.C.: Government Printing Office, 1989), 520-529.

[1]Rainey died in 1834, but was not replaced until the next Congress.

[2]Wright resigned and was succeeded by Foley on June 6, 1989.

Leaders of the House since 1899

Congress		House Floor Leaders		House Whips	
		Majority	Minority	Majority	Minority
56th	(1899-1901)	Sereno E. Payne (R N.Y.)	James D. Richardson (D Tenn.)	James A. Tawney (R Minn.)	Oscar W. Underwood (D Ala.)[6]
57th	(1901-1903)	Payne	Richardson	Tawney	James T. Lloyd (D Mo.)
58th	(1903-1905)	Payne	John Sharp Williams (D Miss.)	Tawney	Lloyd
59th	(1905-1907)	Payne	Williams	James E. Watson (R Ind.)	Lloyd
60th	(1907-1909)	Payne	Williams/Champ Clark (D Mo.)[1]	Watson	Lloyd[7]
61st	(1909-1911)	Payne	Clark	John W. Dwight (R N.Y.)	None
62nd	(1911-1913)	Oscar W. Underwood (D Ala.)	James R. Mann (R Ill.)	None	John W. Dwight (R N.Y.)
63rd	(1913-1915)	Underwood	Mann	Thomas M. Bell (D Ga.)	Charles H. Burke (R S.D.)
64th	(1915-1917)	Claude Kitchin (D N.C.)	Mann	None	Charles M. Hamilton (R N.Y.)
65th	(1917-1919)	Kitchin	Mann	None	Hamilton
66th	(1919-1921)	Franklin W. Mondell (R Wyo.)	Clark	Harold Knutson (R Minn.)	None
67th	(1921-1923)	Mondell	Claude Kitchin (D N.C.)	Knutson	William A. Oldfield (D Ark.)
68th	(1923-1925)	Nicholas Longworth (R Ohio)	Finis J. Garrett (D Tenn.)	Albert H. Vestal (R Ind.)	Oldfield
69th	(1925-1927)	John Q. Tilson (R Conn.)	Garrett	Vestal	Oldfield
70th	(1927-1929)	Tilson	Garrett	Vestal	Oldfield/John McDuffie (D Ala.)[8]
71st	(1929-1931)	Tilson	John N. Garner (D Texas)	Vestal	McDuffie
72nd	(1931-1933)	Henry T. Rainey (D Ill.)	Bertrand H. Snell (R N.Y.)	John McDuffie (D Ala.)	Carl G. Bachmann (R W.Va.)
73rd	(1933-1935)	Joseph W. Byrns (D Tenn.)	Snell	Arthur H. Greenwood (D Ind.)	Harry L. Englebright (R Calif.)
74th	(1935-1937)	William B. Bankhead (D Ala.)[2]	Snell	Patrick J. Boland (D Pa.)	Englebright
75th	(1937-1939)	Sam Rayburn (D Texas)	Snell	Boland	Englebright
76th	(1939-1941)	Rayburn/John W. McCormack (D Mass.)[3]	Joseph W. Martin Jr. (R Mass.)	Boland	Englebright
77th	(1941-1943)	McCormack	Martin	Boland/Robert Ramspeck (D Ga.)[9]	Englebright
78th	(1943-1945)	McCormack	Martin	Ramspeck	Leslie C. Arends (R Ill.)
79th	(1945-1947)	McCormack	Martin	Ramspeck/John J. Sparkman (D Ala.)[10]	Arends
80th	(1947-1949)	Charles A. Halleck (R Ind.)	Sam Rayburn (D Texas)	Leslie C. Arends (R Ill.)	John W. McCormack (D Mass.)
81st	(1949-1951)	McCormack	Martin	J. Percy Priest (D Tenn.)	Arends
82nd	(1951-1953)	McCormack	Martin	Priest	Arends
83rd	(1953-1955)	Halleck	Rayburn	Arends	McCormack
84th	(1955-1957)	McCormack	Martin	Carl Albert (D Okla.)	Arends
85th	(1957-1959)	McCormack	Martin	Albert	Arends
86th	(1959-1961)	McCormack	Charles A. Halleck (R Ind.)	Albert	Arends
87th	(1961-1963)	McCormack/Carl Albert (D Okla.)[4]	Halleck	Albert/Hale Boggs (D La.)[11]	Arends
88th	(1963-1965)	Albert	Halleck	Boggs	Arends
89th	(1965-1967)	Albert	Gerald R. Ford (R Mich.)	Boggs	Arends
90th	(1967-1969)	Albert	Ford	Boggs	Arends
91st	(1969-1971)	Albert	Ford	Boggs	Arends
92nd	(1971-1973)	Hale Boggs (D La.)	Ford	Thomas P. O'Neill Jr. (D Mass.)	Arends
93rd	(1973-1975)	Thomas P. O'Neill Jr. (D Mass.)	Ford/John J. Rhodes (R Ariz.)[5]	John J. McFall (D Calif.)	Arends
94th	(1975-1977)	O'Neill	Rhodes	McFall	Robert H. Michel (R Ill.)
95th	(1977-1979)	Jim Wright (D Texas)	Rhodes	John Brademas (D Ind.)	Michel
96th	(1979-1981)	Wright	Rhodes	Brademas	Michel
97th	(1981-1983)	Wright	Robert H. Michel (R Ill.)	Thomas S. Foley (D Wash.)	Trent Lott (R Miss.)
98th	(1983-1985)	Wright	Michel	Foley	Lott
99th	(1985-1987)	Wright	Michel	Foley	Lott
100th	(1987-1989)	Thomas S. Foley (D Wash.)	Michel	Tony Coelho (D Calif.)	Lott
101st	(1989-1991)	Foley/Richard A. Gephardt (D Mo.)[12]	Michel	Coelho/William H. Gray III (D Pa.)[13]	Dick Cheney (R Wyo.)/Newt Gingrich (R Ga.)[14]
102nd	(1991-1993)	Gephardt	Michel	Gray	Gingrich

Sources: Randall B. Ripley, *Party Leaders in the House of Representatives* (Washington, D.C.: Brookings Institution), 1967; *Congressional Directory* (Washington, D.C.: Government Printing Office), various years; *Biographical Directory of the American Congress, 1774-1971*, comp. Lawrence F. Kennedy, 92nd Cong., 1st sess., 1971, S. Doc. 8; *Congressional Quarterly Weekly Report.*

1. Clark became minority leader in 1908.
2. Bankhead became Speaker of the House on June 4, 1936. The post of majority leader remained vacant until the next Congress.
3. McCormack became majority leader on Sept. 26, 1940, filling the vacancy caused by the elevation of Rayburn to the post of Speaker of the House on Sept. 16, 1940.
4. Albert became majority leader on Jan. 10, 1962, filling the vacancy caused by the elevation of McCormack to the post of Speaker of the House on Jan. 10, 1962.
5. Rhodes became minority leader on Dec. 7, 1973, filling the vacancy caused by the resignation of Ford on Dec. 6, 1973, to

become vice president.

6. Underwood did not become minority whip until 1901.

7. Lloyd resigned to become chairman of the Democratic Congressional Campaign Committee in 1908. The post of minority whip remained vacant until the beginning of the 62nd Congress.

8. McDuffie became minority whip after the death of Oldfield on Nov. 19, 1928.

9. Ramspeck became majority whip on June 8, 1942, filling the vacancy caused by the death of Boland on May 18, 1942.

10. Sparkman became majority whip on Jan. 14, 1946, filling the vacancy caused by the resignation of Ramspeck on Dec. 31, 1945.

11. Boggs became majority whip on Jan. 10, 1962, filling the vacancy caused by the elevation of Albert to the post of majority leader on Jan. 10, 1962.

12. Gephardt became majority leader on June 14, 1989, filling the vacancy created when Foley succeeded Wright as Speaker of the House on June 6, 1989.

13. Gray became majority whip on June 14, 1989, filling the vacancy caused by the resignation of Coelho on June 15, 1989.

14. Gingrich became minority whip on March 23, 1989, filling the vacancy caused by the resignation of Cheney on March 17, 1989, to become secretary of defense.

U.S. House of Representatives

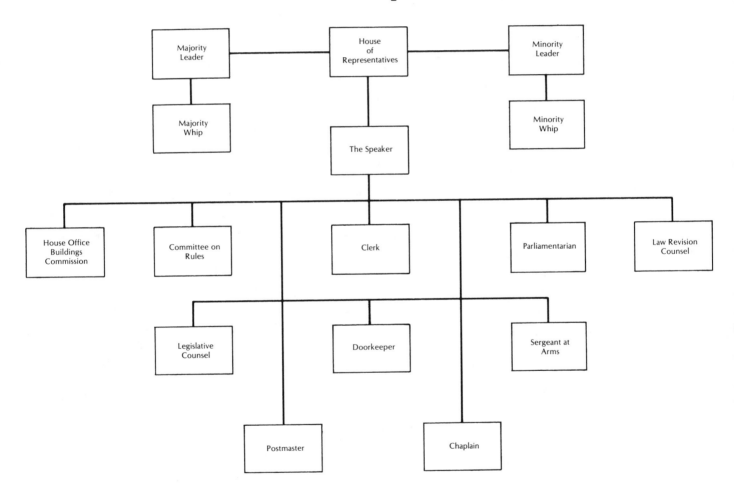

Leaders of the Senate since 1911

Congress		Senate Floor Leaders		Senate Whips	
		Majority	Minority	Majority	Minority
62nd	(1911-1913)	Shelby M. Cullom (R Ill.)	Thomas S. Martin (D Va.)	None	None
63rd	(1913-1915)	John W. Kern (D Ind.)	Jacob H. Gallinger (R N.H.)	J. Hamilton Lewis (D Ill.)	None
64th	(1915-1917)	Kern	Gallinger	Lewis	James W. Wadsworth Jr. (R N.Y.)/Charles Curtis (R Kan.)[8]
65th	(1917-1919)	Thomas S. Martin (D Va.)	Gallinger/Henry Cabot Lodge (R Mass.)[1]	Lewis	Curtis
66th	(1919-1921)	Henry Cabot Lodge (R Mass.)	Martin/Oscar W. Underwood (D Ala.)[2]	Charles Curtis (R Kan.)	Peter G. Gerry (D R.I.)
67th	(1921-1923)	Lodge	Underwood	Curtis	Gerry
68th	(1923-1925)	Lodge/Charles Curtis (R Kan.)[3]	Joseph T. Robinson (D Ark.)	Curtis/Wesley L. Jones (R Wash.)[9]	Gerry
69th	(1925-1927)	Curtis	Robinson	Jones	Gerry
70th	(1927-1929)	Curtis	Robinson	Jones	Gerry
71st	(1929-1931)	James E. Watson (R Ind.)	Robinson	Simeon D. Fess (R Ohio)	Morris Sheppard (D Texas)
72nd	(1931-1933)	Watson	Robinson	Fess	Sheppard
73rd	(1933-1935)	Joseph T. Robinson (D Ark.)	Charles L. McNary (R Ore.)	Lewis	Felix Hebert (R R.I.)
74th	(1935-1937)	Robinson	McNary	Lewis	None.
75th	(1937-1939)	Robinson/Alben W. Barkley (D Ky.)[4]	McNary	Lewis	None
76th	(1939-1941)	Barkley	McNary	Sherman Minton (D Ind.)	None
77th	(1941-1943)	Barkley	McNary	Lister Hill (D Ala.)	None
78th	(1943-1945)	Barkley	McNary	Hill	Kenneth Wherry (R Neb.)
79th	(1945-1947)	Barkley	Wallace H. White Jr. (R Maine)	Hill	Wherry
80th	(1947-1949)	Wallace H. White Jr. (R Maine)	Alben W. Barkley (D Ky.)	Kenneth Wherry (R Neb.)	Scott Lucas (D Ill.)
81st	(1949-1951)	Scott W. Lucas (D Ill.)	Kenneth S. Wherry (R Neb.)	Francis Myers (D Pa.)	Leverett Saltonstall (R Mass.)
82nd	(1951-1953)	Ernest W. McFarland (D Ariz.)	Wherry/Styles Bridges (R N.H.)[5]	Lyndon B. Johnson (D Texas)	Saltonstall
83rd	(1953-1955)	Robert A. Taft (R Ohio)/William F. Knowland (R Calif.)[6]	Lyndon B. Johnson (D Texas)	Leverett Saltonstall (R Mass.)	Earle Clements (D Ky.)
84th	(1955-1957)	Lyndon B. Johnson (D Texas)	William F. Knowland (R Calif.)	Earle Clements (D Ky.)	Saltonstall
85th	(1957-1959)	Johnson	Knowland	Mike Mansfield (D Mont.)	Everett McKinley Dirksen (R Ill.)
86th	(1959-1961)	Johnson	Everett McKinley Dirksen (R Ill.)	Mansfield	Thomas H. Kuchel (R Calif.)
87th	(1961-1963)	Mike Mansfield (D Mont.)	Dirksen	Hubert H. Humphrey (D Minn.)	Kuchel
88th	(1963-1965)	Mansfield	Dirksen	Humphrey	Kuchel
89th	(1965-1967)	Mansfield	Dirksen	Russell Long (D La.)	Kuchel
90th	(1967-1969)	Mansfield	Dirksen	Long	Kuchel
91st	(1969-1971)	Mansfield	Dirksen/Hugh Scott (R Pa.)[7]	Edward M. Kennedy (D Mass.)	Hugh Scott (R Pa.)/Robert P. Griffin (R Mich.)[10]
92nd	(1971-1973)	Mansfield	Scott	Robert C. Byrd (D W.Va.)	Griffin
93rd	(1973-1975)	Mansfield	Scott	Byrd	Griffin
94th	(1975-1977)	Mansfield	Scott	Byrd	Griffin
95th	(1977-1979)	Robert C. Byrd (D W.Va.)	Howard H. Baker Jr. (R Tenn.)	Alan Cranston (D Calif.)	Ted Stevens (R Alaska)
96th	(1979-1981)	Byrd	Baker	Cranston	Stevens
97th	(1981-1983)	Howard H. Baker Jr. (R Tenn.)	Robert C. Byrd (D W.Va.)	Ted Stevens (R Alaska)	Alan Cranston (D Calif.)
98th	(1983-1985)	Baker	Byrd	Stevens	Cranston
99th	(1985-1987)	Bob Dole (R Kan.)	Byrd	Alan K. Simpson (R Wyo.)	Cranston
100th	(1987-1989)	Byrd	Bob Dole (R Kan.)	Cranston	Alan K. Simpson (R Wyo.)
101st	(1989-1991)	George J. Mitchell (D Maine)	Dole	Cranston	Simpson
102nd	(1991-1993)	Mitchell	Dole	Wendell H. Ford (D Ky.)	Simpson

Sources: Walter J. Oleszek, "Party Whips in the United States Senate," *Journal of Politics* 33 (November 1971): 955-979; *Congressional Directory* (Washington, D.C.: Government Printing Office), various years; *Biographical Directory of the American Congress, 1774-1971*, comp. Lawrence F. Kennedy, 92nd Cong., 1st sess., 1971, S. Doc. 8; *Majority and Minority Leaders of the Senate,* comp. Floyd M. Riddick, 94th Cong., 1st ses., 1975, S. Doc. 66; *Congressional Quarterly Weekly Report.*

1. Lodge became minority leader on Aug. 24, 1918, filling the vacancy caused by the death of Gallinger on Aug. 17, 1918.
2. Underwood became minority leader on April 27, 1920, filling the vacancy caused by the death of Martin on Nov. 12, 1919. Gilbert M. Hitchcock (D Neb.) served as acting minority leader in the interim.
3. Curtis became majority leader on Nov. 28, 1924, filling the vacancy caused by the death of Lodge on Nov. 9, 1924.

4. Barkley became majority leader on July 22, 1937, filling the vacancy caused by the death of Robinson on July 14, 1937.
5. Bridges became minority leader on Jan. 8, 1952, filling the vacancy caused by the death of Wherry on Nov. 29, 1951.
6. Knowland became majority leader on Aug. 4, 1953, filling the vacancy caused by the death of Taft on July 31, 1953. Taft's vacant seat was filled by a Democrat, Thomas Burke, on Nov. 10, 1953. The division of the Senate changed to 48 Democrats,

47 Republicans, and 1 Independent, thus giving control of the Senate to the Democrats. However, Knowland remained as majority leader until the end of the 83rd Congress.
7. Scott became minority leader on Sept. 24, 1969, filling the vacancy caused by the death of Dirksen on Sept. 7, 1969.
8. Wadsworth served as minority whip for only one week, from

Dec. 6 to Dec. 13, 1915.
9. Jones became majority whip filling the vacancy caused by the elevation of Curtis to the post of majority leader.
10. Griffin became minority whip on Sept. 24, 1969, filling the vacancy caused by the elevation of Scott to the post of minority leader.

U.S. Senate

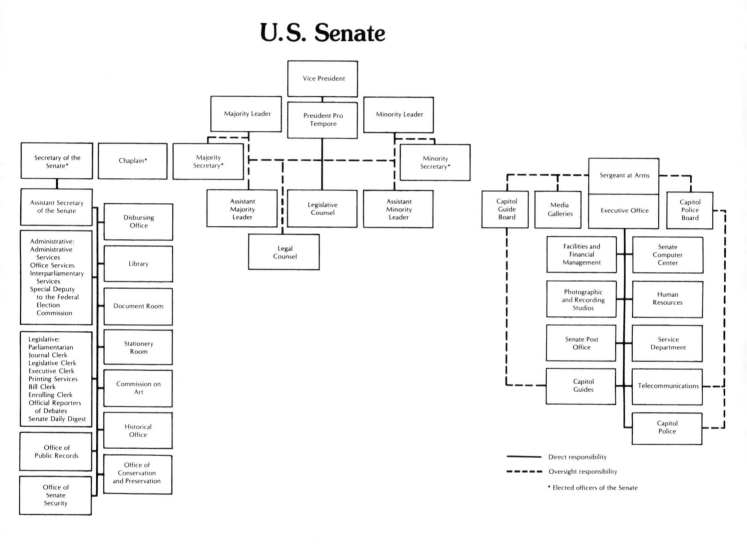

Recorded Votes in the House and the Senate, 1947-1990

Year	House	Senate	Year	House	Senate
1947	84	138	1969	177	245
1948	75	110	1970	266	422
1949	121	226	1971	320	423
1950	154	229	1972	329	532
1951	109	202	1973	541	594
1952	72	129	1974	537	544
1953	71	89	1975	612	602
1954	76	181	1976	661	688
1955	73	88	1977	706	635
1956	74	136	1978	834	516
1957	100	111	1979	672	497
1958	93	202	1980	604	531
1959	87	215	1981	353	483
1960	93	207	1982	459	465
1961	116	207	1983	498	381
1962	124	227	1984	408	292
1963	119	229	1985	439	381
1964	113	312	1986	451	359
1965	201	259	1987	488	420
1966	193	238	1988	451	379
1967	245	315	1989	379	312
1968	233	280[a]	1990	536	326

Note: House figures reflect the total number of quorum calls, yea-and-nay votes, and recorded votes, while Senate figures include only yea-and-nay votes.

Source: Norman J. Ornstein, Thomas E. Mann, and Michael J. Malbin, *Vital Statistics on Congress, 1991-1992* (Washington, D.C.: CQ Press), forthcoming.

[a] This figure does not include one yea-and-nay vote that was ruled invalid for lack of a quorum.

Attempted and Successful Cloture Votes, 1919-1991

Congress		First Session		Second Session		Total	
		Attempted	Successful	Attempted	Successful	Attempted	Successful
66th	(1919-1921)	1	1	0	0	1	1
67th	(1921-1923)	1	0	1	0	2	0
68th	(1923-1925)	0	0	0	0	0	0
69th	(1925-1927)	0	0	2	1	2	1
70th	(1927-1929)	5	2	0	0	5	2
71st	(1929-1931)	0	0	0	0	0	0
72nd	(1931-1933)	0	0	0	0	0	0
73rd	(1933-1935)	1	0	0	0	1	0
74th	(1935-1937)	0	0	0	0	0	0
75th	(1937-1939)	0	0	2	0	2	0
76th	(1939-1941)	0	0	0	0	0	0
77th	(1941-1943)	0	0	1	1	1	1
78th	(1943-1945)	0	0	1	1	1	1
79th	(1945-1947)	0	0	4	0	4	0
80th	(1947-1949)	0	0	0	0	0	0
81st	(1949-1951)	0	0	2	0	2	0
82nd	(1951-1953)	0	0	0	0	0	0
83rd	(1953-1955)	0	0	1	0	1	0
84th	(1955-1957)	0	0	0	0	0	0
85th	(1957-1959)	0	0	0	0	0	0
86th	(1959-1961)	0	0	1	0	1	0
87th	(1961-1963)	1	0	3	1	4	1
88th	(1963-1965)	1	0	2	1	3	1
89th	(1965-1967)	2	1	5	0	7	1
90th	(1967-1969)	1	0	5	1	6	1
91st	(1969-1971)	2	0	4	0	6	0
92nd	(1971-1973)	10	2	10	2	20	4
93rd	(1973-1975)	10	2	21	6	31	8
94th	(1975-1977)	22	12	4	4	26	16
95th	(1977-1979)	5	1	8	2	13	3
96th	(1979-1981)	4	1	17	9	21	10
97th	(1981-1983)	7	2	19	6	26	8
98th	(1983-1985)	7	2	12	9	19	11
99th	(1985-1987)	9	1	14	9	23	10
100th	(1987-1989)	23	5	20	6	43	11
101st	(1989-1991)	9	6	14	5	23	11

Note: The number of votes required to invoke cloture was changed March 7, 1975, from two-thirds of those present and voting, to three-fifths of the total Senate membership, as Rule 22 of the standing rules of the Senate was amended.

Source: Norman J. Ornstein, Thomas E. Mann, and Michael J. Malbin, *Vital Statistics on Congress, 1991-1992* (Washington, D.C.: CQ Press), forthcoming.

Vetoes and Overrides, 1947-1991

Congress		Total no. of presiden- tial vetoes	No. of regular vetoes	No. of pocket vetoes	Vetoes overridden		House attempts to over- ride vetoes	Senate attempts to over- ride vetoes
					Total	Percentage of regular vetoes		
80th	(1947-1949)	75	42	33	6	14.3	8	8
81st	(1949-1951)	79	70	9	3	4.3	5	5
82nd	(1951-1953)	22	14	8	3	21.4	4	4
83rd	(1953-1955)	52	21	31	0	—	0	0
84th	(1955-1957)	34	12	22	0	—	1	1
85th	(1957-1959)	51	18	33	0	—	1	1
86th	(1959-1961)	44	22	22	2	9.1	5	6
87th	(1961-1963)	20	11	9	0	—	0	0
88th	(1963-1965)	9	5	4	0	—	0	0
89th	(1965-1967)	14	10	4	0	—	0	0
90th	(1967-1969)	8	2	6	0	—	0	0
91st	(1969-1971)	11	7	4	2	28.6	4	4
92nd	(1971-1973)	20	6	14	2	33.3	3	4
93rd	(1973-1975)	39	27	12	5	18.5	12	10
94th	(1975-1977)	37	32	5	8	25.0	17	15
95th	(1977-1979)	19	6	13	0	—	2	0
96th	(1979-1981)	12	7	5	2	28.6	2	2
97th	(1981-1983)	15	9	6	2	22.2	4	3
98th	(1983-1985)	24	9	15	2	22.2	2	2
99th	(1985-1987)	20	13	7	2	15.4	3	3
100th	(1987-1989)	18	8	10	4	50.0	5	4
101st	(1989-1991)	21	15	6	4	26.7	4	0

Source: Norman J. Ornstein, Thomas E. Mann, and Michael J. Malbin, *Vital Statistics on Congress, 1991-1992* (Washington, D.C.: CQ Press), forthcoming.

Longest Sessions of Congress

Rank	Congress	Session	Dates	Length in days*	Recesses Senate	Recesses House
1	76th	3rd	Jan. 3, 1940-Jan. 3, 1941	366	July 11-July 22, 1940	July 11-July 22, 1940
2	77th	1st	Jan. 3, 1941-Jan. 2, 1942	365		
	81st	2nd	Jan. 3, 1950-Jan. 2, 1951	365	Sept. 23-Nov. 27, 1950	Apr. 6-Apr. 18, 1950 Sept. 23-Nov. 27, 1950
4	80th	2nd	Jan. 6, 1948-Dec. 31, 1948	361	June 20-July 26, 1948 Aug. 7-Dec. 31, 1948	June 20-July 26, 1948 Aug. 7-Dec. 31, 1948
5	88th	1st	Jan. 9, 1963-Dec. 30, 1963	356		Apr. 11-Apr. 22, 1963
6	91st	1st	Jan. 3, 1969-Dec. 23, 1969	355	Feb. 7-Feb. 19, 1969 Apr. 3-Apr. 14, 1969 July 2-July 7, 1969 Aug. 13-Sept. 3, 1969 Nov. 26-Dec. 1, 1969	Feb. 7-Feb. 17, 1969 Apr. 3-Apr. 14, 1969 May 28-June 2, 1969 July 2-July 7, 1969 Aug. 13-Sept. 3, 1969 Nov. 6-Nov. 12, 1969 Nov. 26-Dec. 1, 1969
7	65th	2nd	Dec. 3, 1917-Nov. 21, 1918	354	Dec. 18, 1917-Jan. 3, 1918	Dec. 18, 1917-Jan. 3, 1918
	93rd	1st	Jan. 3, 1973-Dec. 22, 1973	354	Feb. 8-Feb. 15, 1973 Apr. 18-Apr. 30, 1973 May 23-May 29, 1973 June 30-July 9, 1973 Aug. 3-Sept. 5, 1973 Oct. 18-Oct. 23, 1973 Nov. 21-Nov. 26, 1973	Feb. 8-Feb. 19, 1973 Apr. 19-Apr. 30, 1973 May 24-May 29, 1973 June 30-July 10, 1973 Aug. 3-Sept. 5, 1973 Oct. 4-Oct. 9, 1973 Oct. 18-Oct. 23, 1973 Nov. 15-Nov. 26, 1973
	96th	1st	Jan. 15, 1979-Jan. 3, 1980	354	Feb. 9-Feb. 19, 1979 Apr. 10-Apr. 23, 1979 May 24-June 4, 1979 June 27-July 9, 1979 Aug. 3-Sept. 5, 1979 Nov. 20-Nov. 26, 1979 Adjourned *sine die* Dec. 20, 1979	Feb. 8-Feb. 13, 1979 Apr. 10-Apr. 23, 1979 May 24-May 30, 1979 June 29-July 9, 1979 Aug. 2-Sept. 5, 1979 Nov. 20-Nov. 26, 1979 Adjourned *sine die* Jan. 3, 1980
10	79th	1st	Jan. 3, 1945-Dec. 21, 1945	353	Aug. 1-Sept. 5, 1945	July 21-Sept. 5, 1945
11	99th	1st	Jan. 3, 1985-Dec. 20, 1985	352	Jan. 7-Jan. 21, 1985 Feb. 7-Feb. 18, 1985 Apr. 4-Apr. 15, 1985 May 9-May 14, 1985 May 24-June 3, 1985 June 27-July 8, 1985 Aug. 1-Sept. 9, 1985 Nov. 23-Dec. 2, 1985	Jan. 3-Jan. 21, 1985 Feb. 7-Feb. 19, 1985 Mar. 7-Mar. 19, 1985 Apr. 4-Apr. 15, 1985 May 23-June 3, 1985 June 27-July 8, 1985 Aug. 1-Sept. 4, 1985 Nov. 21-Dec. 2, 1985
12	80th	1st	Jan. 3, 1947-Dec. 19, 1947	351	July 27-Nov. 17, 1947	July 27-Nov. 17, 1947
	100th	1st	Jan. 6, 1987-Dec. 22, 1987	351	Jan. 6-Jan. 12, 1987 Feb. 5-Feb. 16, 1987 Apr. 10-Apr. 21, 1987 May 21-May 27, 1987 July 1-July 7, 1987 Aug. 7-Sept. 9, 1987 Nov. 20-Nov. 30, 1987	Jan. 8-Jan. 20, 1987 Feb. 11-Feb. 18, 1987 Apr. 9-Apr. 21, 1987 May 21-May 27, 1987 July 1-July 7, 1987 July 15-July 20, 1987 Aug. 7-Sept. 9, 1987 Nov. 10-Nov. 16, 1987 Nov. 20-Nov. 30, 1987
14	78th	1st	Jan. 6, 1943-Dec. 21, 1943	350	July 8-Sept. 14, 1943	July 8-Sept. 14, 1943

Rank	Congress	Session	Dates	Length in days*	Recesses	
					Senate	House
15	91st	2nd	Jan. 19, 1970-Jan. 2, 1971	349	Feb. 10-Feb. 16, 1970 Mar. 26-Mar. 31, 1970 Sept. 2-Sept. 8, 1970 Oct. 14-Nov. 16, 1970 Nov. 25-Nov. 30, 1970 Dec. 22-Dec. 28, 1970	Feb. 10-Feb. 16, 1970 Mar. 26-Mar. 31, 1970 May 27-June 1, 1970 July 1-July 6, 1970 Aug. 14-Sept. 9, 1970 Oct. 14-Nov. 16, 1970 Nov. 25-Nov. 30, 1970 Dec. 22-Dec. 29, 1970
	96th	2nd	Jan. 3, 1980-Dec. 16, 1980	349	Apr. 3-Apr. 15, 1980 May 22-May 28, 1980 July 2-July 21, 1980 Aug. 6-Aug. 18, 1980 Aug. 27-Sept. 3, 1980 Oct. 1-Nov. 12, 1980 Nov. 25-Dec. 1, 1980	Feb. 13-Feb. 19, 1980 Apr. 2-Apr. 15, 1980 May 22-May 28, 1980 July 2-July 21, 1980 Aug. 1-Aug. 18, 1980 Aug. 28-Sept. 3, 1980 Oct. 2-Nov. 12, 1980 Nov. 21-Dec. 1, 1980

Source: 1989-1990 Congressional Directory: 101st Congress (Washington, D.C.: Government Printing Office, 1989), 520-529.

* Includes days in recess.

Index

17.95